Advanced Topology Optimization: Methods and Applications

Advanced Topology Optimization: Methods and Applications

Guest Editor

Yun-Fei Fu

MDPI

Basel • Beijing • Wuhan • Barcelona • Belgrade • Novi Sad • Cluj • Manchester

Guest Editor
Yun-Fei Fu
College of Mechanical and
Electronic Engineering
Shandong University of
Science and Technology
Qingdao
China

Editorial Office
MDPI AG
Grosspeteranlage 5
4052 Basel, Switzerland

This is a reprint of the Special Issue, published open access by the journal *Computation* (ISSN 2079-3197), freely accessible at: https://www.mdpi.com/journal/computation/special_issues/M12E68ZGVN.

For citation purposes, cite each article independently as indicated on the article page online and as indicated below:

Lastname, A.A.; Lastname, B.B. Article Title. *Journal Name* **Year**, *Volume Number*, Page Range.

ISBN 978-3-7258-7104-9 (Hbk)
ISBN 978-3-7258-7105-6 (PDF)
https://doi.org/10.3390/books978-3-7258-7105-6

Contents

About the Editor

Yun-Fei Fu

Yun-Fei Fu is a Professor in the College of Mechanical and Electronic Engineering at Shandong University of Science and Technology, China, and Director of the Qingdao Key Laboratory of Lightweight Design and Additive Manufacturing for Aerospace Propulsion. His research interests include lightweight structural design, topology optimization, computational modeling of composite materials, and additive manufacturing. He completed full-time postdoctoral research at the University of Alberta, Canada, and earlier held a part-time appointment as an Associate Research Fellow and served as a Casual Academic at Deakin University, Australia. He received his PhD from Deakin University, where he developed the Smooth-Edged Material Distribution for Optimizing Topology (SEMDOT) algorithm. He has been recognized with several academic honors, including the Taishan Scholars Youth Expert title, and is a Fellow of the National Institute of Professional Engineers and Scientists (FNIPES). He actively contributes to the academic community through editorial and professional service roles.

Preface

Topology optimization has evolved from a primarily academic research topic into a transformative engineering design technology. By enabling the systematic distribution of material within a prescribed domain to achieve optimal performance, it has reshaped the way engineers conceive lightweight structures, high-efficiency components, and multifunctional systems. Today, topology optimization is no longer confined to theoretical formulations; it plays an increasingly central role in real-world applications spanning aerospace, automotive, civil infrastructure, energy systems, and modern manufacturing.

Despite decades of progress, the field continues to face important challenges. Engineering practice demands optimization frameworks that can account for realistic manufacturing constraints, handle large-scale and high-dimensional design spaces, couple multiple physical phenomena, and produce geometries that are interpretable and ready for downstream CAD and fabrication workflows. At the same time, emerging technologies, advanced composites, and smart materials are opening new possibilities while also introducing new design requirements. These developments call for both deeper theoretical insights and more application-driven computational strategies.

This reprint brings together a collection of peer-reviewed contributions originally published in the Special Issue "Advanced Topology Optimization: Methods and Applications" in the journal *Computation*, published by MDPI. The aim of this reprint is to present a comprehensive overview of current advances in topology optimization, highlighting both methodological innovations and practical implementations across diverse engineering domains.

The chapters in this reprint cover diverse topics across the interdisciplinary field of topology optimization, including manufacturing-oriented design with practical constraints and CAD-ready representations, as well as studies involving multi-physics and dynamic problems. Overall, the reprint highlights a clear shift from purely theoretical formulations toward design methodologies that are manufacturable and well integrated with real engineering workflows, helping bridge the gap between optimization theory and practical engineering realization.

As an Editor of the journal *Computation*, Guest Editor of this Special Issue, and Editor of this reprint, I am particularly encouraged by the openness and diversity of the research community reflected in these chapters. The field of topology optimization benefits greatly from collaboration among experts in mechanics, applied mathematics, computer science, and manufacturing. Continued dialogue across these disciplines is essential for advancing both the theoretical foundations and the practical impact of optimization-based design.

I would like to express my sincere gratitude to all authors for their high-quality contributions, to the reviewers for their careful and constructive evaluations, and to the editorial team at MDPI and *Computation* for their professional support throughout the publication process. It is my hope that this reprint will serve as a valuable reference for researchers, graduate students, and practicing engineers, and that it will inspire further innovation in the rapidly evolving field of topology optimization.

Yun-Fei Fu
Guest Editor

computation

Editorial

Advanced Topology Optimization: Methods and Applications

Yun-Fei Fu [1,2]

1 College of Mechanical and Electronic Engineering, Shandong University of Science and Technology, Qingdao 266590, China; yunfei.fu@sdust.edu.cn

2 Qingdao Key Laboratory of Ligh tweight Design and Additive Manufacturing for Aerospace Propulsion, Qingdao 266590, China

1. Introduction

Structural topology optimization is a powerful computational design paradigm that seeks the most efficient material distribution within a prescribed design domain to satisfy given performance requirements. Over the past decades, a variety of mature and widely adopted algorithms have been developed, including the Solid Isotropic Material with Penalization (SIMP) method [1], Bi-directional Evolutionary Structural Optimization (BESO) method [2], the level-set method [3], Moving Morphable Components (MMCs) method [4], Floating Projection Topology Optimization (FPTO) method [5], and Smooth-Edged Material Distribution for Optimizing Topology (SEMDOT) approach [6,7]. As a core technique in lightweight structural design, topology optimization has been extensively applied across aerospace, automotive, civil engineering, and defense industries [8–12].

Although topology optimization has made major progress in theory and computation, several challenges still prevent its widespread adoption in complex engineering practice. These challenges include the incorporation of realistic manufacturing constraints, the efficient solution of large-scale and high-dimensional optimization problems, robust coupling with multi-physics phenomena, and the generation of interpretable, CAD-ready geometries suitable for direct downstream manufacturing. Moreover, emerging application scenarios—such as additive manufacturing, structural dynamics, and thermal–fluid devices—place increasing demands on topology optimization frameworks, requiring them to move beyond traditional static and single-physics formulations. Addressing these issues requires not only methodological and algorithmic innovations, but also improvements in numerical efficiency, modeling fidelity, and application-oriented optimization strategies.

Driven by recent advances in theory and computational methods, this Special Issue, "Advanced Topology Optimization: Methods and Applications", aims to showcase state-of-the-art research and practical developments in the field. The collected papers cover a wide range of topics, including advanced optimization methodologies, improvements in computational efficiency, manufacturing-oriented design, and multi-physics coupling, highlighting the expanding influence of topology optimization across diverse engineering disciplines. A total of twelve peer-reviewed papers were selected, covering both methodological advances and application-oriented studies. These contributions address topics ranging from algorithmic development and numerical strategies to engineering applications in additive manufacturing, structural dynamics, CAD-ready design, and thermal–fluid device design. The following section provides concise summaries of each contribution, outlining their main ideas and key findings within the context of recent advances in topology optimization.

2. Contributions

Huang et al. (Contribution 1) addressed the long-standing challenge of unclear structural boundary identification in meshless topology optimization via the SEMDOT method. The study introduced non-overlapping cell-based density variables within a meshless framework to explicitly describe material presence and absence and further developed a non-penalized SEMDOT formulation using an interpolation-based heuristic sensitivity scheme. The effectiveness of the proposed approach was demonstrated through two- and three-dimensional compliance minimization examples, showing its capability to generate optimized structures with continuous and smooth edges or surfaces without manual post-processing.

Cao et al. (Contribution 2) highlighted that while topology optimization has strong potential to improve the lightweight design, strength, and fatigue performance of rock-cutting tools, its practical application remains constrained by complex dynamic loading conditions, material–structure coupling in severe wear environments, data scarcity for adaptive design, and insufficient validation of manufacturing compatibility and long-term reliability.

Pehnec et al. (Contribution 3) presented a topology optimization approach that combines a parameterized level-set formulation with genetic algorithm-based global optimization. By employing B-spline interpolation to reduce the number of design variables, the method enables the effective use of evolutionary optimization and overcomes the strong dependence of traditional level-set methods on initial solutions. A novel genetic algorithm penalty operator was introduced to improve convergence behavior by penalizing similar individuals within the population. The proposed approach demonstrated robustness against local minima and was shown to be effective for typical two-dimensional benchmark problems.

Miler et al. (Contribution 4) proposed a multi-objective optimization framework with embedded topology optimization for multi-body systems, enabling the simultaneous optimization of component topology and spatial arrangement. To alleviate the high computational cost caused by repeated topology optimization calls within the genetic algorithm, two acceleration strategies were introduced, involving mesh coarsening and iteration reduction during early generations. The results showed that both strategies significantly reduced computational time while maintaining comparable optimization performance, demonstrating their effectiveness in improving the efficiency of multi-objective topology optimization.

Zhang et al. (Contribution 5) proposed a multi-constraint topology optimization strategy for flight control rudder structures by simultaneously incorporating additive manufacturing overhang constraints and flutter-related mass center control within a unified density-based framework. By introducing a build-direction-aware projection filter and a smooth Heaviside mass center constraint, the approach enables the concurrent satisfaction of lightweight design, structural stiffness, aeroelastic stability, and AM manufacturability requirements during the optimization process. Numerical results demonstrated that the proposed method significantly reduces support material usage and residual deformation while improving flutter velocity, highlighting its effectiveness in achieving manufacturable, dynamically stable, and high-performance AM-ready rudder designs without post-processing.

Zhang et al. (Contribution 6) proposed an integrated optimization strategy combining discrete element method simulation and topology optimization to reduce the excessive mass of chain drive systems in long-distance scraper conveyors. The study showed that a non-equally spaced scraper arrangement can maintain conveying capacity while reducing the number of scrapers in chains of equal length, and that further topology optimization of the scraper structure leads to additional mass reduction. The proposed approach achieved a significant overall weight reduction of the chain drive system, resulting in lower no-load energy consumption and improved operational efficiency.

Kyriakidis et al. (Contribution 7) investigated the mechanical performance of topology-optimized shin pad structures incorporating advanced lattice geometries and materials using finite element analysis under impact scenarios representative of real contact sports. By replicating median and extreme stud kick impact conditions, the study evaluated the energy absorption and injury prevention capabilities of the proposed designs. The results showed that lattice geometries, particularly gyroid structures, promote more uniform stress distribution and significantly reduce transmitted forces, while the use of a matrix reinforced with reused ground tire rubber further enhances strength, damping, and absorption performance.

Huang et al. (Contribution 8) addressed the computational inefficiency of filtering operations in variable-density topology optimization by introducing a novel filter implementation based on the k-d tree data structure. By transforming conventional neighborhood searches into highly efficient spatial searches, the proposed method significantly accelerates the optimization process while preserving solution accuracy. The approach supports a wide range of manufacturability constraints, including symmetry, local volume control, periodic patterns, and stamping-oriented overhang constraints, without increasing computational cost. Numerical examples demonstrated that the method is particularly effective for large-scale optimization problems, complex geometric constraints, and unstructured meshes, highlighting its strong potential for scalable and efficient engineering design applications.

Sardone et al. (Contribution 9) introduced a CAD-embedded, time-dependent structural topology optimization framework that integrates an adjoint-based optimization core within a visual programming environment. The framework integrates a parametric CAD interface with a dynamic finite element solver to support topology optimization under harmonic and seismic loading. Case studies on tall building facades subjected to earthquake excitation demonstrated the framework's ability to reduce displacement at targeted degrees of freedom and dynamically adapt material distributions.

Sun et al. (Contribution 10) presented a multifidelity topology optimization framework for thermal–fluid devices that combines a computationally efficient Darcy–convection model with high-fidelity Navier–Stokes–convection analysis to balance temperature reduction and pressure-loss control. The approach employs SEMDOT to decouple geometric smoothness, enabling the generation of CAD-ready boundaries during low-fidelity optimization. Candidate designs are evaluated using high-fidelity simulations under consistent operating conditions, demonstrating that the optimized layouts achieve simultaneous reductions in peak temperature and pressure drop compared with conventional channel designs. The results further showed that the proposed multifidelity strategy provides a more favorable Pareto distribution than conventional RAMP-based pipelines.

Christensen and Alexandersen (Contribution 11) proposed a gradient-based topology optimization framework for heat sinks incorporating phase-change materials (PCMs) to attenuate temperature oscillations induced by cyclic thermal loading. The method integrates transient thermal analysis with adjoint sensitivity evaluation and the Globally Convergent Method of Moving Asymptotes (GCMMA) optimizer, enabling the optimized distribution of PCM and conductive material through a homogenized material representation. Numerical investigations showed that exploiting latent heat effects can significantly reduce temperature variability, while manufacturability-oriented penalization produces near-discrete designs with only limited loss in performance. The study demonstrates that adjoint-driven PCM topology optimization provides an effective and systematic strategy for thermal oscillation control.

Liu et al. (Contribution 12) provided a comprehensive perspective on the development of the SEMDOT framework, positioning it as an effective solution to the long-standing boundary fuzziness and jagged-edge issues inherent in element-based topology optimization methods. The review systematically traces the theoretical evolution of SEMDOT, covering both penalty-based and non-penalty-based formulations. Open-access implementations have further accelerated its adoption and reproducibility across the research community.

https://doi.org/10.3390/computation14020029

As the Guest Editor and SEMDOT developer, whose primary expertise is in mechanical engineering rather than in mathematics or computational mechanics, I (Yun-Fei Fu) acknowledge that certain aspects of the SEMDOT algorithm have not yet been developed with full mathematical rigor. As discussed in this review, SEMDOT is still evolving, and its theoretical foundations would benefit from deeper mathematical analysis and critical examination. We therefore sincerely encourage more researchers—particularly those with strong expertise in applied mathematics and computational mechanics—to engage with SEMDOT, whether by improving its theoretical formulation, extending its numerical framework, or offering constructive criticism. Such open discussion and collaboration are essential for refining the method and advancing it toward a more rigorous and comprehensive optimization platform.

3. List of Contributions

Contribution 1: Huang, J.; Long, K.; Chen, Y.; Geng, R.; Saeed, A.; Zhang, H.; Tao, T. A Framework of the Meshless Method for Topology Optimization Using the Smooth-Edged Material Distribution for Optimizing Topology Method. Computation 2025, 13, 6. https://doi.org/10.3390/computation13010006

Contribution 2: Cao, Y.; Zhang, Q.; Zhang, S.; Tian, Y.; Dong, X.; Song, X.; Wang, D. Optimization of Rock-Cutting Tools: Improvements in Structural Design and Process Efficiency. Computation 2025, 13, 152. https://doi.org/10.3390/computation13070152

Contribution 3: Pehnec, I.; Sedlar, D.; Marinic-Kragic, I.; Vučina, D. A New Approach to Topology Optimization with Genetic Algorithm and Parameterization Level Set Function. Computation 2025, 13, 153. https://doi.org/10.3390/computation13070153

Contribution 4: Miler, D.; Hoić, M.; Tomić, R.; Jokić, A.; Mašović, R. Simultaneous Multi-Objective and Topology Optimization: Effect of Mesh Refinement and Number of Iterations on Computational Cost. Computation 2025, 13, 168. https://doi.org/10.3390/computation13070168

Contribution 5: Zhang, H.; Shi, S.; Ding, X.; Yang, J.; Xiong, M. Topology Optimization for Rudder Structures Considering Additive Manufacturing and Flutter Effects. Computation 2025, 13, 208. https://doi.org/10.3390/computation13090208

Contribution 6: Zhang, Q.; Liu, W.; Jia, A.; Sun, S.; Li, X.; Song, X. Mining Scraper Conveyors Chain Drive System Lightweight Design: Based on DEM and Topology Optimization. Computation 2025, 13, 225. https://doi.org/10.3390/computation13090225

Contribution 7: Kyriakidis, I.F.; Kladovasilakis, N.; Pechlivani, E.M.; Tsongas, K. Mechanical Evaluation of Topologically Optimized Shin Pads with Advanced Composite Materials: Assessment of the Impact Properties Utilizing Finite Element Analysis. Computation 2025, 13, 236. https://doi.org/10.3390/computation13100236

Contribution 8: Huang, J.; Saeed, A.; Long, K.; Chen, Y.; Geng, R.; Jia, J.; Tao, T. An Efficient Filter Implementation Method and Its Applications in Topology Optimization Utilizing k-d Tree Data Structure. Computation 2025, 13, 262. https://doi.org/10.3390/computation13110262

Contribution 9: Sardone, L.; Sotiropoulos, S.; Fiore, A. A CAD-Integrated Framework for Dynamic Structural Topology Optimisation via Visual Programming. Computation 2025, 13, 267. https://doi.org/10.3390/computation13110267

Contribution 10: Sun, Y.; Fu, Y.-F.; Xu, S.; Guo, Y. Multifidelity Topology Design for Thermal–Fluid Devices via SEMDOT Algorithm. Computation 2026, 14, 19. https://doi.org/10.3390/computation14010019

Contribution 11: Christensen, M.B.M.; Alexandersen, J. Topology Optimisation of Heat Sinks Embedded with Phase-Change Material for Minimising Temperature Oscillations. Computation 2026, 14, 23. https://doi.org/10.3390/computation14010023

https://doi.org/10.3390/computation14020029

Contribution 12: Liu, M.; Hu, W.; Gong, X.; Zhou, H.; Zhao, B. State-of-the-Art Overview of Smooth-Edged Material Distribution for Optimizing Topology (SEMDOT) Algorithm. Computation 2026, 14, 27. https://doi.org/10.3390/computation14010027

Funding: This work was supported by the Taishan Scholar Youth Expert Program (No. tsqnz20250732).

Acknowledgments: This Special Issue was made possible through the valuable contributions of the authors and reviewers. The Guest Editor sincerely thanks all those involved for their efforts and support.

Conflicts of Interest: The author declares no conflicts of interest.

References

1. Bendsøe, M.P.; Sigmund, O. *Topology Optimization: Theory, Methods, and Applications*; Springer: Berlin/Heidelberg, Germany, 2004.
2. Huang, X.; Xie, M. *Evolutionary Topology Optimization of Continuum Structures: Methods and Applications*; John Wiley & Sons: Chichester, UK, 2010.
3. Wang, M.Y.; Wang, X.; Guo, D. A level set method for structural topology optimization. *Comput. Methods Appl. Mech. Eng.* **2003**, *192*, 227–246. [CrossRef]
4. Zhang, W.; Li, D.; Yuan, J.; Song, J.; Guo, X. A new three-dimensional topology optimization method based on moving morphable components (MMCs). *Comput. Mech.* **2017**, *59*, 647–665. [CrossRef]
5. Huang, X. On smooth or 0/1 designs of the fixed-mesh element-based topology optimization. *Adv. Eng. Softw.* **2021**, *151*, 102942. [CrossRef]
6. Fu, Y.F. Smooth Topological Design of Continuum Structures for Additive Manufacturing. Ph.D. Thesis, Deakin University, Geelong, Australia, 2021.
7. Fu, Y.F.; Rolfe, B. *Smooth Topological Design of Continuum Structures*; CRC Press: Boca Raton, FL, USA, 2025.
8. Zhu, J.H.; Zhang, W.H.; Xia, L. Topology optimization in aircraft and aerospace structures design. *Arch. Comput. Methods Eng.* **2016**, *23*, 595–622. [CrossRef]
9. Li, C.; Kim, I.Y. Multi-material topology optimization for automotive design problems. *Proc. Inst. Mech. Eng. Part D J. Automob. Eng.* **2018**, *232*, 1950–1969. [CrossRef]
10. Manguri, A.; Hassan, H.; Saeed, N.; Jankowski, R. Topology, size, and shape optimization in civil engineering structures: A review. *CMES-Comput. Model. Eng. Sci.* **2025**, *142*, 933–971.
11. Xue, H.; Wang, T.; Cui, X.; Wang, Y.; Huang, G. Ballistic performance of additive manufacturing 316l stainless steel projectiles based on topology optimization method. *Defence Technol.* **2024**, *35*, 1–17. [CrossRef]
12. Meng, L.; Zhang, W.; Quan, D.; Shi, G.; Tang, L.; Hou, Y.; Breitkopf, P.; Zhu, J.; Gao, T. From topology optimization design to additive manufacturing: Today's success and tomorrow's roadmap. *Arch. Comput. Methods Eng.* **2020**, *27*, 805–830. [CrossRef]

https://doi.org/10.3390/computation14020029

computation

MDPI

Review

State-of-the-Art Overview of Smooth-Edged Material Distribution for Optimizing Topology (SEMDOT) Algorithm

Minyan Liu, Wanghua Hu, Xuhui Gong *, Hao Zhou and Baolin Zhao

Institute of Electronic Engineering, China Academy of Engineering Physics, Mianyang 621900, China; liumynwpu@163.com (M.L.)
* Correspondence: casa0627@163.com

Abstract

Topology optimization is a powerful and efficient design tool, but the structures obtained by element-based topology optimization methods are often limited by fuzzy or jagged boundaries. The smooth-edged material distribution for optimizing topology algorithm (SEMDOT) can effectively deal with this problem and promote the practical application of topology optimization structures. This review outlines the theoretical evolution of SEMDOT, including both penalty-based and non-penalty-based formulations, while also providing access to open access codes. SEMDOT's applications cover diverse areas, including self-supporting structures, energy-efficient manufacturing, bone tissue scaffolds, heat transfer systems, and building parts, demonstrating the versatility of SEMDOT. While SEMDOT addresses boundary issues in topology optimization structures, further theoretical refinement is needed to develop it into a comprehensive platform. This work consolidates the advances in SEMDOT, highlights its interdisciplinary impact, and identifies future research and implementation directions.

Keywords: topology optimization; smooth boundary; SEMDOT

1. Introduction

Topology optimization is a computational design method that allocates a certain amount of material within a given design domain to obtain the best structure that meets the design requirements [1,2]. Topology optimization does not rely on experience and trial and error, is highly efficient, and has been widely used in aerospace, automotive, construction, and medical fields [3–7].

Topology optimization methods can be divided into material description models (MDM) and boundary description models (BDM) according to the expression of the model. MDM discretizes the design domain into a series of density units, and the density in each design unit determines the presence or absence of material at the position in the design domain. The main topology optimization methods included in this classification are the homogenization method, solid isotropic microstructures with penalization (SIMP) [8], evolutionary structural optimization (ESO) [9], and bi-directional evolutionary structural optimization (BESO) [10].

The SIMP method has become one of the most widely used topology optimization methods due to its advantages such as clear concept, stable iteration, and easy combination with various filtering methods [11–13]. However, due to the definition of pseudo-density, the optimization results of this method usually retain the jagged boundaries between elements and there are gray elements with intermediate density, which may be detrimental to the subsequent simulation analysis and manufacturing research of the structure [14].

In order to avoid the influence of undesirable boundaries on the structure and promote the practical application of topology optimization methods based on element density, Fu et al. [15] proposed the SEMDOT algorithm in 2020. SEMDOT allows the generation of smooth and clear structural boundaries during the topology optimization process without the need for post-processing, such as shape optimization and iso-surface extraction, which effectively improves the design efficiency. Figure 1 illustrates the comparison of optimized structure boundaries using the SIMP method and the SEMDOT method. The SIMP method produces jagged and grayscale boundaries, while the SEMDOT method avoids this issue. The SEMDOT algorithm has released a theoretical framework and related codes for 2D and 3D optimization.

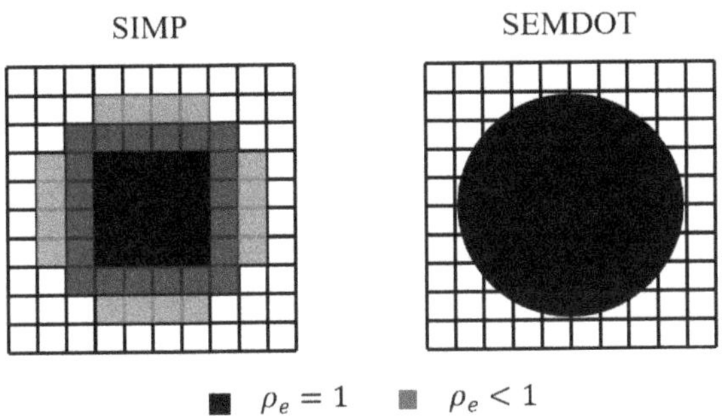

Figure 1. Comparison of boundaries between optimization results of SIMP and SEMDOT methods.

Therefore, this review mainly discusses the theoretical development of SEMDOT, shares the acquisition of open access codes, and investigates the applications of this method in different fields to further promote the development and application of this method.

2. Theoretical Development of SEMDOT

Currently, SEMDOT has developed two methods: one based on penalty and the other based on non-penalty. The concept of the penalty method originates from the SIMP method proposed by Sigmund [8]. In the topology optimization problem based on elements, the 0 or 1 distribution of element density is a discrete problem. By assuming the element density as a variable that can continuously vary between 0 and 1 and introducing a penalty factor to make the density value converge to 0 and 1, the discrete problem is transformed into a continuous optimization problem. The penalty method in SEMDOT is the same as SIMP. However, the penalty method changes the physical meaning of element density and increases the complexity of parameters. In the optimization results, the penalty factor cannot fully make the element density values converge to 0 and 1. Therefore, SEMDOT has been further improved and the non-penalty-based SEMDOT method has been developed, which will be introduced separately below.

2.1. Penalty-Based SEMDOT

In the SEMDOT algorithm, the smooth boundary of the structure is realized based on the grid points. As shown in Figure 2, the grid points are introduced into the element, and the sum of the grid point density $\rho_{e,g}$ is the density of the element; finite element

https://doi.org/10.3390/computation14010027

calculations are performed based on the assembled density of elements [16]. The grid point density is the actual design variable, and its material interpolation can be expressed as

$$E_e(\rho_{e,g}) = \rho_{e,g}^p E_1 \quad (1)$$

where $E_e(\rho_{e,g})$ is the Young's modulus function of the grid point density, E_1 is the Young's modulus of the base material, and p is the penalty factor.

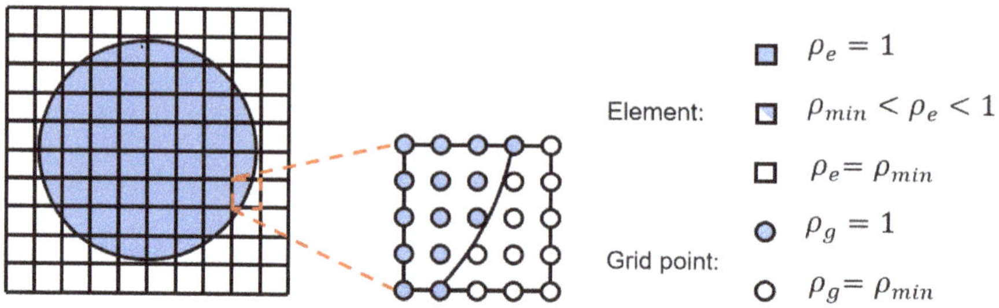

Figure 2. Illustration of smooth-edged material distribution.

In the SEMDOT method, the boundary elements are usually a heterogeneous combination of solid and void materials, and the properties of the boundary elements are calculated using the linear difference between these two phases. The element stiffness matrix can be expressed as Equation (2). The detailed calculation method can be found in reference [15].

$$\begin{aligned} \mathbf{K}_e(X_e) &= (1 - X_e)\mathbf{K}_e^0 + X_e\mathbf{K}_e^1 \\ &= (1 - X_e)\rho_{min}^p\mathbf{K}_e^1 + X_e\mathbf{K}_e^1 \end{aligned} \quad (2)$$

where $\mathbf{K}_e(X_e)$ is the stiffness matrix function, $\mathbf{K}_e^0$ is the stiffness matrix of the void element, $\mathbf{K}_e^1$ is the stiffness matrix of the solid element, and ρ_{min} is the minimum density given to avoid calculation singularities.

Taking the minimum compliance problem as an example, the penalty-based sensitivity of boundary elements is shown in Equation (3). For more detailed derivation and calculation, please refer to reference [17].

$$\begin{aligned} \frac{\partial C(X_e)}{\partial X_e} &\approx (1 - X_e)\left.\frac{\partial C(X_e)}{\partial X_e}\right|_{X_e=\rho_{min}} + X_e\left.\frac{\partial C(X_e)}{\partial X_e}\right|_{X_e=1} \\ &= -p\left[(1 - X_e)\rho_{min}^{p-1} + X_e\right]\boldsymbol{u}_e^T\mathbf{K}_e^1\boldsymbol{u}_e \end{aligned} \quad (3)$$

where $\boldsymbol{u}_e$ is the load displacement vector of the eth element.

2.2. Non-Penalty-Based SEMDOT

Considering that the material penalty scheme changes the relationship between material properties and element values, Long et al. [17] further improved the SEMDOT algorithm using discrete variable sensitivity calculation and proposed a non-penalty scheme. Specifically, the calculation of the element stiffness also adopted linear interpolation of solid and void materials, as shown in Equation (4), but did not include the penalty factor p. Long et al. [17] have given a detailed theoretical derivation of this method. The non-penalty-based SEMDOT exhibits a more robust mathematical foundation compared to the penalty-based SEMDOT.

$$\begin{aligned} \mathbf{K}_e(X_e) &= (1 - X_e)\mathbf{K}_e^0 + X_e\mathbf{K}_e^1 \\ &= (1 - X_e)\rho_{min}\mathbf{K}_e^1 + X_e\mathbf{K}_e^1 \end{aligned} \quad (4)$$

https://doi.org/10.3390/computation14010027

The non-penalty scheme calculates the discrete sensitivity of the optimization objective. Taking the minimum compliance problem as an example, the approximate calculation of the discrete sensitivity is shown in Equation (5). For more detailed derivation and calculation, please refer to reference [17].

$$\begin{aligned}\frac{\partial C(X_e)}{\partial X_e} &\approx (1 - X_e)\left.\frac{\partial C(X_e)}{\partial X_e}\right|_{X_e=\rho_{min}} + X_e \left.\frac{\partial C(X_e)}{\partial X_e}\right|_{X_e=1} \\ &= -[(1 - X_e)\rho_{min} + X_e]\boldsymbol{u}_e^T\mathbf{K}_e^1\boldsymbol{u}_e\end{aligned} \tag{5}$$

Taking the non-penalty-based SEMDOT method as an example, the flowchart for topology optimization is shown in Figure 3 and Table 1.

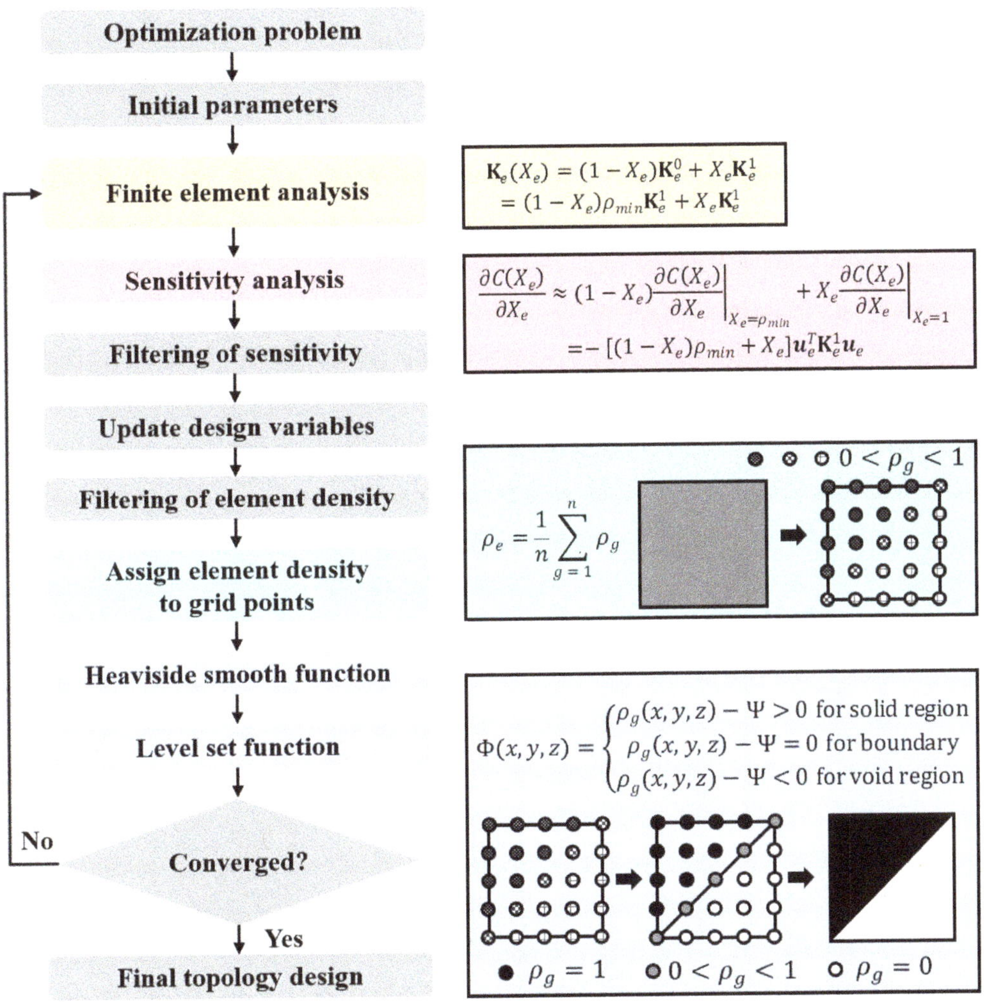

Figure 3. Flowchart for topology optimization using the SEMDOT algorithm.

Table 1. The focus of key steps in the optimization process.

	Step	Highlight
1	Optimization problem	Define the objective function and constraint function
2	Initial parameters	Set material properties and initial element density distribution
3	Finite element analysis	Assemble stiffness matrix based on element density
4	Sensitivity analysis	Calculate the gradients of the objective function and constraint function with respect to the design variables
5	Filtering of sensitivity	Reduce numerical instability
6	Update design variables	through MMA algorithm
7	Filtering of element density	Reduce numerical instability
8	Assign element density to grid points	Calculate node density and grid point density based on element density
9	Heaviside smooth function	Project the grid point density to 0 or 1
10	Level set function	Characterize smooth boundaries

3. Open Access Code for SEMDOT

The penalty-based SEMDOT was open-sourced in 2020; please refer to [15] for details. The algorithm uses the method of moving asymptotes (MMA) proposed by Svanberg [18] to update the design variables. The objective function of the code is to minimize structural compliance while also investigating the influence of the projection function on convergence stability.

For 3D topology optimization, Ibhadode and Fu et al. [19] open-sourced the Freeform 3D topology optimization (FreeTO) code in 2024. As shown in Figure 4, FreeTO supports free-form initialization, and SEMDOT is used here to achieve smooth structure boundaries. The code is demonstrated through six practical design cases, showing its effectiveness in compliance minimization, compliant mechanisms, and self-supporting problems. For the self-support problem, which is a combination of topology optimization and additive manufacturing (AM), the code uses the AM filter proposed by Langelaar [20].

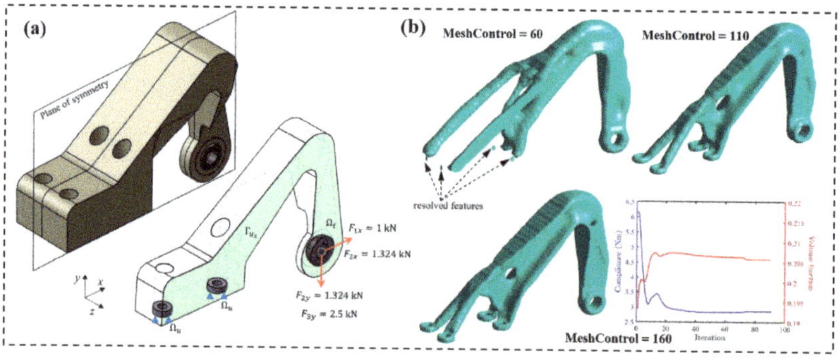

Figure 4. Optimize an airplane bearing bracket using FreeTO (**a**) initial design of airplane bearing bracket with bolt connections and external load; (**b**) optimization results with different numbers of mesh and iteration history. Reprinted from [19], under the terms of the CC BY 4.0 license.

In addition to the two codes mentioned above, Fu and Rolfe [21] also open-sourced several codes in their book published in 2024, such as the computational framework combining SEMDOT with homogenization theory and the maximum stress minimization.

4. Applications of SEMDOT

Recently, the SEMDOT method has been combined with different optimization frameworks and applied in different research fields, as shown in Table 2. Zhou et al. [22] validated the effectiveness of the SEMDOT algorithm by optimizing the Zhou–Rozvold (ZR) problem. Huang et al. [23] combined the non-penalization SEMDOT method with a meshless

https://doi.org/10.3390/computation14010027

framework. In meshless analysis, non-overlapping cell variables are used instead of nodal or Gaussian-based variables to characterize the existence or absence of subregions. The optimization efficiency and applicability of this method are verified by 2D and 3D compliance minimization problems. As shown in Figure 5, the optimization results of the 3D cantilever beam are smooth and continuous enough without additional post-processing. Fu et al. [24] applied SEMDOT to optimize cellular structures. Moreover, Zhou et al. [25] established a multi-scale parallel computing method based on the non-penalized SEMDOT algorithm, as shown in Figure 5, introducing linear interpolation grid points for optimization at both scales to achieve a multi-scale system with smooth and clear boundaries.

Table 2. Applications of SEMDOT in different fields.

Application of SEMDOT	References
Zhou–Rozvany problem	[22]
Meshless framework	[23]
Cellular structures	[24]
Multi-scale optimization	[25,26]
Multilevel topology optimization	[27]
Self-support of AM	[19,28–30]
Energy performance of AM	[31,32]
Bone tissue engineering	[33]
Heat transfer	[34]
Construction industry	[35,36]
Natural frequency	[37]

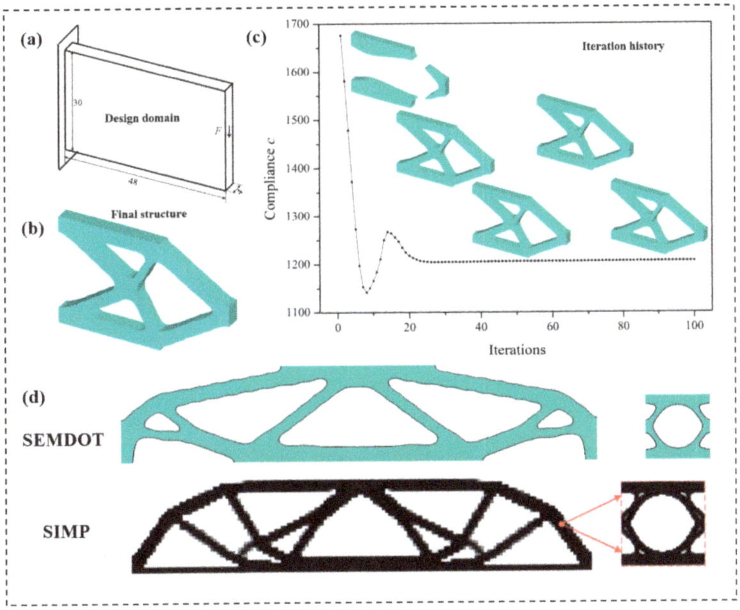

Figure 5. Optimization example using meshless framework: (**a**) design domain of 3D cantilever beam, where F is the external force along the negative Z-axis direction. Reprinted from [23], under the terms of the CC BY 4.0 license; (**b**) final optimization result. Reprinted from [23], under the terms of the CC BY 4.0 license; (**c**) iteration history and multi-scale method. Reprinted from [23], under the terms of the CC BY 4.0 license; (**d**) comparison of SEMODT and SIMP multi-scale optimization results. Reprinted from [25], under the terms of the CC BY 4.0 license.

https://doi.org/10.3390/computation14010027

Regarding the combination of SEDMOT and AM, the industrial frame is optimized in the open source code paper mentioned above [19]. As shown in Figure 6, compared with the optimization results without considering self-support, the AM filter effectively ensures the self-support topology, with only a few unresolved features generated near the load position. Mohseni et al. [28] combined deep learning and transfer learning with SEMDOT to improve the design efficiency of complex parts and the manufacturability using additive manufacturing. Fu et al. [29] used SEMDOT and the AM filter to investigate the effects of different printing directions and critical overhang angles on the self-supporting topology. Numerical experiments demonstrate that the SEMDOT algorithm can be satisfactorily integrated with Langelaar's AM filter, enabling the generation of highly printable structures across various printing orientations or critical overhang angles. Moreover, Fu et al. [38] also verified the manufacturability of the designed structure through 3D printing experiments, the structures without and with self-supporting constraints were manufactured by fused deposition modeling (FDM). This method is also applicable to selective laser melting (SLM) technology; please refer to [30] for details.In addition to focusing on manufacturability, Yi et al. [31,32] also considered the energy performance of AM in the design stage, taking tool path length as an equivalent indicator and establishing a design for AM (DfAM) framework. DfAM reduced energy consumption by about 6% in 2D optimization and by about 2% in 3D optimization.

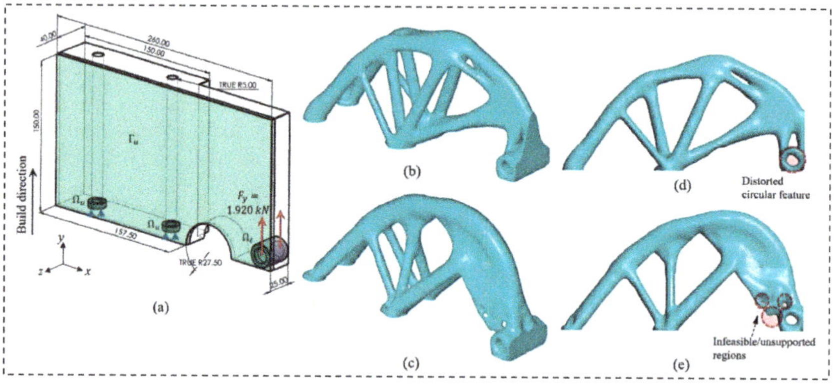

Figure 6. The effect of self-supporting constraints on structures [19]: (**a**) The design domain of an industrial frame; (**b**) optimized structure without self-supporting constraints; (**c**) optimized structure with self-supporting design; (**d**) front-view of (**b**) showing a distorted circular feature; (**e**) front-view of (**c**) showing a few infeasible/unsupported features. Reprinted from [19], under the terms of the CC BY 4.0 license.

Topology optimization also has great application potential in the biomedical field. For example, the design of bone tissue engineering scaffolds needs to consider factors such as mechanics, diffusion, porosity, and connectivity. Liu et al. [33] designed a porous bone scaffold with anisotropic mechanical characteristics that can reduce stress shielding based on the SEMDOT method and homogenization theory. The smoothing effect of the SEMDOT algorithm on structural boundaries avoids grayscale elements without practical physical significance and troublesome jagged boundaries in subsequent finite element simulations. In terms of heat transfer, Zhang et al. [34] studied the topology optimization problem of natural convection heat transfer and used the SEMDOT method to generate accurate boundaries, providing guidance for practical manufacturing. As shown in Figure 7, Sun et al. [36] achieved topology design of thermal fluid devices through SEMDOT algorithm, and smooth and clear structural boundaries promoted robust CAD reconstruction and high

https://doi.org/10.3390/computation14010027

fidelity verification. In the construction field, Ribeiro et al. [35] used the non-penalized SEMDOT algorithm to optimize the Sheikh-Ibrahim steel girder joint's tension cover plate, which significantly improved the manufacturability through standard cutting techniques.

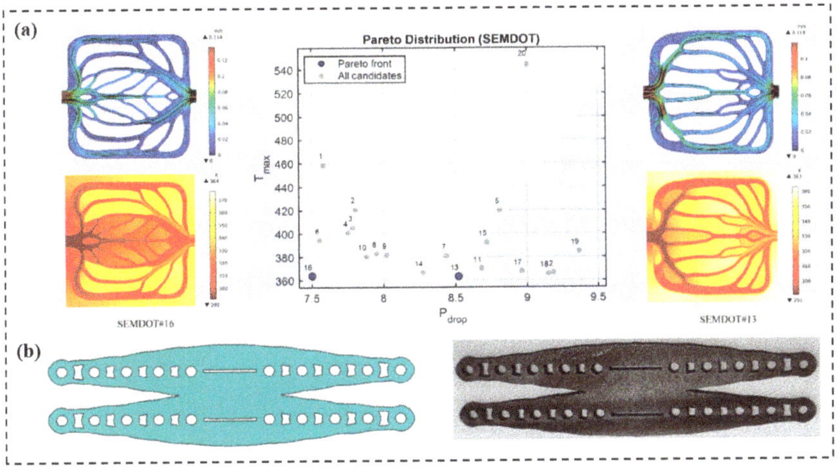

Figure 7. Application of SEMDOT in different fields: (**a**) thermal fluid devices. Reprinted from [36], under the terms of the CC BY 4.0 license; (**b**) Sheikh-Ibrahim steel girder joint's tension cover plate. Reprinted from [35], under the terms of the CC BY 4.0 license.

It is noteworthy that Ifediorah et al. [39] developed the Optiworks software based on the SEMDOT algorithm, which constitutes a human-centric framework for high-resolut ion topology optimization. The user interface is shown in Figure 8. Compared to commercial software tools, the lightweight architecture and faster computation time of Optiworks significantly reduce the computational effort required to solve complex optimization problems, further promoting the application of the SEMDOT algorithm.

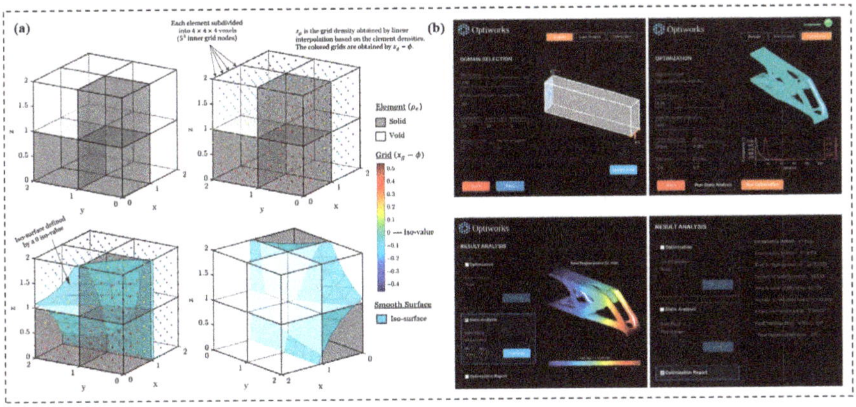

Figure 8. The Optiworks software [39]: (**a**) smooth boundary algorithm; (**b**) the user interface of Optiworks. Reprinted from [39], under the terms of the CC BY 4.0 license.

5. Discussion

Currently, SEMDOT has two iterative versions. Compared with the penalty-based SEMDOT, the non-penalty-based SEMDOT algorithm uses discrete sensitivity and the impact of the penalty coefficient on the topological structure does not need to be discussed.

https://doi.org/10.3390/computation14010027

In some applications, the non-penalty-based SEMDOT method can produce better solutions, better convergence, and more reasonable topological structures. It should be noted that, since the developers have a mechanical engineering background rather than a mathematical one, the SEMDOT algorithm may exhibit limitations in mathematical rigor.

In the related research on smoothing the boundaries of topological structures, Huang et al. [40,41] and Xu et al. [42] proposed floating projection topology optimization (FPTO) with a complete mathematical derivation, and Gao et al. [43,44] established isogeometric analysis (IGA). Da et al. [9] proposed an implicit smooth boundary representation based on nodal sensitivities for the ESO method. Li et al. [45] developed the boundary density evolution (BDE) method based on the SIMP method. These methods have also achieved satisfactory optimization results in different optimization cases. Compared with the above algorithms, the framework of SEMDOT is closer to the SIMP method, so the filtering or solving methods currently developed for SIMP can also be easily applied to SEMDOT, which can further enhance the applicability of SEMDOT in different optimization problems.

Regarding the comparison of different algorithms, it has been demonstrated in compliance minimization, compliant mechanism design, and heat conduction problems that using the non-penalty-based SEMDOT method can yield better solutions, stronger convergence, and a more reasonable topological structure compared to the penalty-based SEMDOT method [17]. Compared to the SIMP method, Liu et al.'s research on porous bone scaffolds indicates that the optimized results of SIMP using density filtering and Heaviside projection still exhibit certain differences from the target values in terms of the anisotropic elastic tensor when reaching the maximum iteration step. However, using the SEMDOT method can satisfy the convergence conditions at the maximum iteration step [33]. Fu et al.'s numerical experiments also demonstrate that SEMDOT converges faster than SIMP due to its distribution of intermediate elements exclusively along boundaries and the introduction of new termination criteria [15]. In terms of computational cost, although the SEMDOT method introduces the concept of grid point density within the element, the actual variables involved in finite element calculations are the element densities assembled from grid point densities, rather than the grid point densities themselves. Therefore, it does not significantly increase computational costs.

The application of topology optimization is becoming increasingly widespread. For instance, it has been used to optimize dynamic processes that change over time [46], or it has been applied in the engineering field by combining with additive manufacturing processes [47]. In addition to focusing on the structural boundary features, the current topology optimization methods also have the problem of high computational cost in practical applications. For optimization problems with high mesh resolution, it may take several hours or days of time cost [48]. Some scholars have proposed various acceleration and optimization strategies for this issue [49–51]. SEMDOT also needs to consider the computational cost issue in its application promotion. SEMDOT has been successfully combined with deep learning and transfer learning and applied in automated design for additive manufacturing (DfAM) [28]. It is worth emphasizing that manufacturing serves as a bridge connecting topology optimization design and application, but the manufacturing constraints and optimization problems considered in current research are still relatively simple [52,53]. The SEMDOT algorithm can generate smooth boundaries that are beneficial to manufacturing, but further consideration of more complex manufacturing constraints is needed in the future.

https://doi.org/10.3390/computation14010027

6. Conclusions

In conclusion, while topology optimization has matured into a powerful design paradigm, a significant amount of work remains to be conducted. SEMDOT is still some distance away from becoming a good platform; the authors hope that more researchers can contribute to the improvement and iterative of the algorithm. In the future, further research is needed for more complex manufacturing constraint optimization problems to promote the engineering application of topology optimization methods.

Author Contributions: Conceptualization, W.H. and X.G.; investigation, H.Z.; writing—original draft preparation, M.L.; writing—review and editing, M.L.; supervision, B.Z. All authors have read and agreed to the published version of the manuscript.

Funding: This research received no external funding.

Data Availability Statement: No new data were created or analyzed in this study. Data sharing is not applicable to this article.

Acknowledgments: The authors would like to thank Yun-Fei Fu from Shandong University of Science and Technology for his generous support throughout the writing, figure preparation, and publication of this manuscript.

Conflicts of Interest: The authors declare no conflicts of interest.

References

1. Fu, Y.; Rolfe, B.; Chiu, L.N.S.; Huang, X. Topology Optimization of Continuum Structures Using Smooth Boundary Representation. In Proceedings of the 13th World Congress of Structural and Multidisciplinary Optimization, Beijing, China, 20–24 May 2019.
2. Habashneh, M.; Cucuzza, R.; Aela, P.; Movahedi Rad, M. Reliability-Based Topology Optimization of Imperfect Structures Considering Uncertainty of Load Position. *Structures* **2024**, *69*, 107533. [CrossRef]
3. Li, Z.; Xu, H.; Zhang, S. A Comprehensive Review of Explicit Topology Optimization Based on Moving Morphable Components (MMC) Method. *Arch. Comput. Methods Eng.* **2024**, *31*, 2507–2536. [CrossRef]
4. Ma, C.; Li, M.; Liu, J.; Li, M.; He, J.; Totis, G.; Hua, C.; Wang, L.; Cui, G.; Xue, R.; et al. High-Efficiency Topology Optimization Method for Thermal-Fluid Problems in Cooling Jacket of High-Speed Motorized Spindle. *Int. Commun. Heat Mass Transf.* **2025**, *169*, 109533. [CrossRef]
5. Li, Y.; Wu, H.; Xie, X.; Zhang, L.; Yuan, P.F.; Xie, Y.M. FloatArch: A Cable-Supported, Unreinforced, and Re-Assemblable 3D-Printed Concrete Structure Designed Using Multi-Material Topology Optimization. *Addit. Manuf.* **2024**, *81*, 104012. [CrossRef]
6. Zeng, Q.; Duan, S.; Zhao, Z.; Wang, P.; Lei, H. Inverse Design of Energy-Absorbing Metamaterials by Topology Optimization. *Adv. Sci.* **2023**, *10*, 2204977. [CrossRef]
7. Liu, Y.; Wang, Y.; Ren, H.; Meng, Z.; Chen, X.; Li, Z.; Wang, L.; Chen, W.; Wang, Y.; Du, J. Ultrastiff Metamaterials Generated through a Multilayer Strategy and Topology Optimization. *Nat. Commun.* **2024**, *15*, 2984. [CrossRef]
8. Sigmund, O. A 99 Line Topology Optimization Code Written in Matlab. *Struct. Multidiscip. Optim.* **2001**, *21*, 120–127. [CrossRef]
9. Da, D.; Xia, L.; Li, G.; Huang, X. Evolutionary Topology Optimization of Continuum Structures with Smooth Boundary Representation. *Struct. Multidiscip. Optim.* **2018**, *57*, 2143–2159. [CrossRef]
10. Zhou, S.; Cadman, J.; Chen, Y.; Li, W.; Xie, Y.M.; Huang, X.; Appleyard, R.; Sun, G.; Li, Q. Design and Fabrication of Biphasic Cellular Materials with Transport Properties—A Modified Bidirectional Evolutionary Structural Optimization Procedure and MATLAB Program. *Int. J. Heat Mass Transf.* **2012**, *55*, 8149–8162. [CrossRef]
11. Wang, Q.; Han, H.; Wang, C.; Liu, Z. Topological Control for 2D Minimum Compliance Topology Optimization Using SIMP Method. *Struct. Multidiscip. Optim.* **2022**, *65*, 38. [CrossRef]
12. Costa, G.; Montemurro, M.; Pailhès, J. NURBS Hyper-Surfaces for 3D Topology Optimization Problems. *Mech. Adv. Mater. Struct.* **2021**, *28*, 665–684. [CrossRef]
13. Xu, S.; Liu, J.; Zou, B.; Li, Q.; Ma, Y. Stress Constrained Multi-Material Topology Optimization with the Ordered SIMP Method. *Comput. Methods Appl. Mech. Eng.* **2021**, *373*, 113453. [CrossRef]
14. Fu, Y.F. Recent Advances and Future Trends in Exploring Pareto-Optimal Topologies and Additive Manufacturing Oriented Topology Optimization. *Math. Biosci. Eng.* **2020**, *17*, 4631–4656. [CrossRef] [PubMed]
15. Fu, Y.F.; Rolfe, B.; Chiu, L.N.S.; Wang, Y.; Huang, X.; Ghabraie, K. SEMDOT: Smooth-Edged Material Distribution for Optimizing Topology Algorithm. *Adv. Eng. Softw.* **2020**, *150*, 102921. [CrossRef]

https://doi.org/10.3390/computation14010027

16. Zhou, J.; Wang, Y.; Chiu, L.N.S.; Ghabraie, K. On the Suitability of Simplified Sensitivity Estimation for Partial Elements in Topology Optimization. *Eng. Optim.* **2025**, 1–23. [CrossRef]
17. Long, K. On Non-Penalization SEMDOT Using Discrete Variable Sensitivities. *J. Optim. Theory Appl.* **2022**, *198*, 644–677. [CrossRef]
18. Svanberg, K. The Method of Moving Asymptotes (MMA) with Some Extensions. *Optim. Large Struct. Syst.* **1993**, 555–566. [CrossRef]
19. Ibhadode, O.; Fu, Y.F.; Qureshi, A. FreeTO-Freeform 3D Topology Optimization Using a Structured Mesh with Smooth Boundaries in Matlab. *Adv. Eng. Softw.* **2024**, *198*, 103790. [CrossRef]
20. Langelaar, M. An Additive Manufacturing Filter for Topology Optimization of Print-Ready Designs. *Struct. Multidiscip. Optim.* **2017**, *55*, 871–883. [CrossRef]
21. Fu, Y.; Rolfe, B.N. *Smooth Topological Design of Continuum Structures Yun-Fei Fu and Bernard Rolfe*; CRC Press: Boca Raton, FL, USA, 2025.
22. Zhou, J.; Fu, Y.F.; Ghabraie, K. Systematic Benchmarking of Topology Optimization Methods Using Both Binary and Relaxed Forms of the Zhou-Rozvany Problem. *CMES-Comput. Model. Eng. Sci.* **2025**, *143*, 3233–3251. [CrossRef]
23. Huang, J.; Long, K.; Chen, Y.; Geng, R.; Saeed, A.; Zhang, H.; Tao, T. A Framework of the Meshless Method for Topology Optimization Using the Smooth-Edged Material Distribution for Optimizing Topology Method. *Computation* **2024**, *13*, 6. [CrossRef]
24. Fu, Y.F.; Long, K.; Zolfagharian, A.; Bodaghi, M.; Rolfe, B. Topological Design of Cellular Structures for Maximum Shear Modulus Using Homogenization SEMDOT. *Mater. Today Proc.* **2023**, *101*, 38–42. [CrossRef]
25. Zhou, J.; Wang, Y.; Chiu, L.N.S.; Ghabraie, K. Multiscale Design Based on Non-Penalization Smooth-Edged Material Distribution for Optimizing Topology (SEMDOT). *IOP Conf. Ser. Mater. Sci. Eng.* **2024**, *1307*, 012022. [CrossRef]
26. Zhou, J.; Fu, Y.F.; Ghabraie, K. Multiscale Topology Design Based on Non-Penalisation Smooth-Edged Material Distribution for Optimising Topology (SEMDOT). *Materials* **2025**, *18*, 2394. [CrossRef]
27. Gonçalves, M.; Andrade-Campos, A.; Barroqueiro, B. On the Design of Mechanical Heterogeneous Specimens Using Multilevel Topology Optimization. *Adv. Eng. Softw.* **2023**, *175*, 103314. [CrossRef]
28. Mohseni, M.; Khodaygan, S. Design for Additive Manufacturing of Topology-Optimized Structures Based on Deep Learning and Transfer Learning. *Rapid Prototyp. J.* **2024**, *30*, 1411–1433. [CrossRef]
29. Fu, Y.F.; Ghabraie, K.; Rolfe, B.; Wang, Y.; Chiu, L.N.S. Smooth Design of 3d Self-Supporting Topologies Using Additive Manufacturing Filter and Semdot. *Appl. Sci.* **2021**, *11*, 238. [CrossRef]
30. Fu, Y.F.; Rolfe, B.; Chiu, L.N.S.; Wang, Y.; Huang, X.; Ghabraie, K. Parametric Studies and Manufacturability Experiments on Smooth Self-Supporting Topologies. *Virtual Phys. Prototyp.* **2020**, *15*, 22–34. [CrossRef]
31. Yi, L.; Wu, X.; Glatt, M.; Ravani, B.; Aurich, J.C. Framework to Improve the Energy Performance During Design for Additive Manufacturing. In Proceedings of the 3rd Conference on Physical Modeling for Virtual Manufacturing Systems and Processes, Pacific Grove, CA, USA, 19–23 June 2023; pp. 213–232. [CrossRef]
32. Yi, L.; Wu, X.; Nawaz, A.; Glatt, M.; Aurich, J.C. Improving Energy Performance in the Product Design for Additive Manufacturing Using a Multi-Player Competition Algorithm. *J. Clean. Prod.* **2023**, *391*, 136173. [CrossRef]
33. Liu, M.; Wang, Y.; Wei, Q.; Ma, X.; Zhang, K.; Li, X.; Bao, C.; Du, B. Topology Optimization for Reducing Stress Shielding in Cancellous Bone Scaffold. *Comput. Struct.* **2023**, *288*, 107132. [CrossRef]
34. Zhang, K.; Li, B.; Du, F.; Liu, H.; Hong, J. Topology Optimization of Natural Convection Heat Transfer Using SEMDOT Algorithm Based on the Reduced-Order Model. *Int. Commun. Heat Mass Transf.* **2021**, *129*, 105676. [CrossRef]
35. Ribeiro, T.; Fu, Y.F.; Bernardo, L.; Rolfe, B. Topology Optimisation of Structural Steel with Non-Penalisation SEMDOT: Optimisation, Physical Nonlinear Analysis, and Benchmarking. *Appl. Sci.* **2023**, *13*, 11370. [CrossRef]
36. Sun, Y.; Fu, Y.-F.; Xu, S.; Guo, Y. Multifidelity Topology Design for Thermal–Fluid Devices via SEMDOT Algorithm. *Computation* **2026**, *14*, 19. [CrossRef]
37. Fu, Y.; Rolfe, B. Non-Penalization Topology Optimization for Maximizing Natural Frequency Using SEMDOT. 2023. Available online: https://www.ingentaconnect.com/contentone/iass/piass/2023/00002023/00000001/art00001 (accessed on 1 October 2023).
38. Fu, Y.F.; Rolfe, B.; Chiu, L.N.S.; Wang, Y.; Huang, X.; Ghabraie, K. Design and Experimental Validation of Self-Supporting Topologies for Additive Manufacturing. *Virtual Phys. Prototyp.* **2019**, *14*, 382–394. [CrossRef]
39. Ifediorah, C.; Ibhadode, O. Optiworks: A Human-Centric Framework for High-Resolution Topology Optimization. *Digit. Eng.* **2025**, *4*, 100041. [CrossRef]
40. Huang, X. Smooth Topological Design of Structures Using the Floating Projection. *Eng. Struct.* **2020**, *208*, 110330. [CrossRef]
41. Huang, X.; Li, W. Three-Field Floating Projection Topology Optimization of Continuum Structures. *Comput. Methods Appl. Mech. Eng.* **2022**, *399*, 115444. [CrossRef]
42. Xu, T.; Huang, X.; Lin, X.; Xie, Y.M. Topology Optimization of Continuum Structures for Buckling Resistance Using a Floating Projection Method. *Comput. Methods Appl. Mech. Eng.* **2024**, *429*, 117204. [CrossRef]

https://doi.org/10.3390/computation14010027

43. Gao, J.; Xue, H.; Gao, L.; Luo, Z. Topology Optimization for Auxetic Metamaterials Based on Isogeometric Analysis. *Comput. Methods Appl. Mech. Eng.* **2019**, *352*, 211–236. [CrossRef]
44. Gao, J.; Gao, L.; Luo, Z.; Li, P. Isogeometric Topology Optimization for Continuum Structures Using Density Distribution Function. *Int. J. Numer. Methods Eng.* **2019**, *119*, 991–1017. [CrossRef]
45. Li, X.; Qin, C.; Wei, P.; Su, C. A Boundary Density Evolutionary Topology Optimization of Continuum Structures with Smooth Boundaries. *Int. J. Numer. Methods Eng.* **2022**, *123*, 158–179. [CrossRef]
46. Sardone, L.; Sotiropoulos, S.; Fiore, A. A CAD-Integrated Framework for Dynamic Structural Topology Optimisation via Visual Programming. *Computation* **2025**, *13*, 267. [CrossRef]
47. Yap, Y.L.; Toh, W.; Giam, A.; Yong, F.R.; Chan, K.I.; Tay, J.W.S.; Teong, S.S.; Lin, R.; Ng, T.Y. Topology Optimization and 3D Printing of Micro-Drone: Numerical Design with Experimental Testing. *Int. J. Mech. Sci.* **2023**, *237*, 107771. [CrossRef]
48. Shin, S.; Shin, D.; Kang, N. Topology Optimization via Machine Learning and Deep Learning: A Review. *J. Comput. Des. Eng.* **2023**, *10*, 1736–1766. [CrossRef]
49. Limkilde, A.; Evgrafov, A.; Gravesen, J. On Reducing Computational Effort in Topology Optimization: We Can Go at Least This Far! *Struct. Multidiscip. Optim.* **2018**, *58*, 2481–2492. [CrossRef]
50. Martínez-Frutos, J.; Martínez-Castejón, P.J.; Herrero-Pérez, D. Efficient Topology Optimization Using GPU Computing with Multilevel Granularity. *Adv. Eng. Softw.* **2017**, *106*, 47–62. [CrossRef]
51. Li, H.; Knapik, S.; Li, Y.; Park, C.; Guo, J.; Mojumder, S.; Lu, Y.; Chen, W.; Apley, D.W.; Liu, W.K. Convolution Hierarchical Deep-Learning Neural Network Tensor Decomposition (C-HiDeNN-TD) for High-Resolution Topology Optimization. *Comput. Mech.* **2023**, *72*, 363–382. [CrossRef]
52. Liu, S.; Li, Q.; Liu, J.; Chen, W.; Zhang, Y. A Realization Method for Transforming a Topology Optimization Design into Additive Manufacturing Structures. *Engineering* **2018**, *4*, 277–285. [CrossRef]
53. Ranjan, R.; Samant, R.; Anand, S. Integration of Design for Manufacturing Methods with Topology Optimization in Additive Manufacturing. *J. Manuf. Sci. Eng. Trans. ASME* **2017**, *139*, 061007. [CrossRef]

https://doi.org/10.3390/computation14010027

computation

MDPI

Article

Topology Optimisation of Heat Sinks Embedded with Phase-Change Material for Minimising Temperature Oscillations

Mark Bjerre Müller Christensen and Joe Alexandersen *

Institute of Mechanical and Electrical Engineering, University of Southern Denmark, 5230 Odense M, Denmark
* Correspondence: joal@sdu.dk

Abstract

This study presents a gradient-based topology optimisation framework for heat sinks embedded with phase-change material (PCM) that targets the mitigation of temperature oscillations under cyclic thermal loads. The approach couples transient thermal diffusion modelling in FEniCS with automatic adjoint sensitivities and GCMMA, and uses a simple analytical homogenisation to parametrise a composite of PCM and conductive material. With latent-heat buffering using PCM, the optimised layouts reduce the temperature variance by 41% when the full time history is used and by 32% when only the quasi-steady-state cycle is used. To improve physical manufacturability, explicit penalisation yields near-discrete designs with only ∼10% performance loss, preserving most oscillation reduction benefits. The results demonstrate that adjoint-driven PCM topology optimisation can systematically suppress thermal oscillations.

Keywords: topology optimisation; phase-change material; temperature oscillation; heat sink; FEniCS; dolfin-adjoint

1. Introduction

1.1. Motivation

As electronics become a larger part of our everyday lives, the importance of the reliability, cost, and life-time of electronic components increases. A major cause for failure in electronic components is the mechanical stresses induced by the mismatch in thermal coefficient of expansion (TCE) across materials in an electronic component and an increase in temperature. In cases where the electronic component has a transient cyclic heat production, these mechanical stresses can further lead to fatigue failures [1] if not managed correctly through adequate cooling. In practice, the temperature of electronic components with high heat production are kept cool with heat sinks, which are placed on top of the component and dissipate the heat produced by the component to the surrounding air; an "example" can be seen in Figure 1.

This paper focuses on heat sinks with embedded phase-change material (PCM) (henceforth referred to as "PCM heat sink") for controlling the amplitude of the temperature oscillations caused by a transient thermal load. PCMs are materials that change phase over a certain temperature interval. During this phase change, energy is stored or released through the latent heat of fusion. The idea is to use the thermal storage potential in the latent heat of fusion as a thermal buffer to smoothen the temperature oscillations caused by cyclic thermal loading.

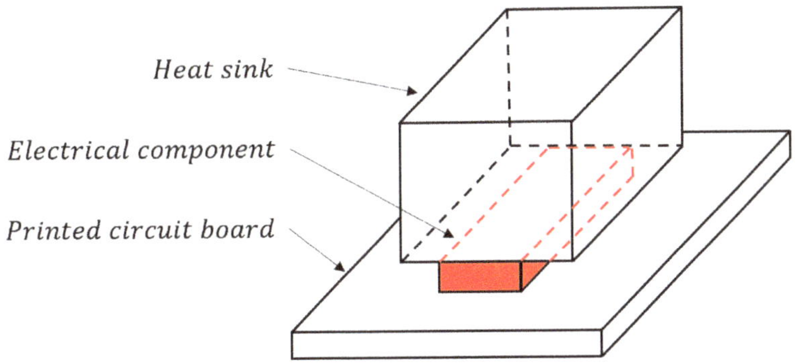

Figure 1. Three-dimensional sketch of generic electronics cooling problem.

A major issue with PCM from a thermal design aspect is that most common PCMs have low thermal conductivity, making it hard to transfer the heat from the electronic component into the PCM. Therefore, PCM is usually paired with a highly thermally conductive material (HCM) in the form of fins or foams which ensure the distribution of heat to the PCM [2]. In the literature, numerous simple fin designs in just as many operational modes have been investigated through extensive parametric investigations in order to determine the best-performing design [2,3]. Most of these studies are based on a steady thermal loading, which makes the physical problem easier to compute. This approach results in a poor understanding of the best use of PCM in an PCM heat sink under transient thermal loading. This paper aims to deepen the understanding of the optimal design of PCM heat sinks with respect to reducing the amplitudes in thermal oscillation induced by cyclic thermal loading. However, instead of continuing the tradition of parametric investigations, which are costly to perform, limited by the parametrisation of the HCM design, and specific in their applications, this paper seeks to deepen understanding with the help of gradient-based topology optimisation (TO). Unlike prior steady or parametric PCM studies, this work formulates a transient, adjoint-based topology optimisation for PCM heat sinks that directly targets oscillation suppression under cyclic loads.

There is no commercially available software capable of performing TO with respect to reducing the amplitudes in thermal oscillation induced by cyclic thermal loading. Therefore, a Python implementation was developed. The Python code uses the FEniCS package in conjunction with the dolfin-adjoint module to perform the TO. Following the preprint and code release, it has already been used by others to further extend it to a level-set method [4] and further applied to the design of electric aircraft battery packs [5].

1.2. Literature

Several numerical and experimental studies have been conducted to improve the performance of two-dimensional plate fin-based PCM heat sinks investigating the effects of the number of fins, heat sink height, and fin thickness [2,3,6]. However, these studies have focused on optimising the performance with regard to the temperature or time until a critical temperature is reached. These studies also suffer from a restriction to simple designs, as this makes the construction of parametric studies possible. As an alternative to this restrictive approach, this paper seeks to employ TO to optimise the two-dimensional plate fin-based PCM heat sinks.

For a general overview of TO for heat transfer applications, we recommend that the reader look at the available review papers [7–9] on the subject. The usage of TO for optimising the layout of PCM and HCM for heat sinks is sparsely represented in the literature, whereas the use of PCM and HCM for thermal energy storage is more

https://doi.org/10.3390/computation14010023

common. Varanasi and Ananthasuresh [10] presented the first use of TO for PCMs, using a density-based TO to minimise the difference between the initial and final temperature over a selected part of the heat sink boundary. They modelled the PCM heat sink as a transient thermal diffusion problem involving phase change using COMSOL Multiphysics and MATLAB. They used an enthalpy method for modelling the phase change, a solid isotropic material with penalisation (SIMP) method for interpolating the conductivity, and an optimality criterion method to update the design. The results showed a 35% reduction in the objective functional when the optimised design was compared to a conventional design. However, the designs suffer from poor resolution due to the limited computational power available at the time. Ho et al. [11] optimised PCM heat sinks for maximum cooling in lieu of convective cooling, thus storing the energy from the heat source in the PCM. They applied a transient thermal diffusion problem with the modified heat capacity method, comparing performance between designs optimised using steady and unsteady models both numerically and experimentally. Subsequently, they added the effect of natural convection in the melted PCM [12]. Iradukunda et al. [13] does indeed treat the subject of PCM-integrated heat sinks using TO, but uses a very simple steady-state heat transfer model for the actual optimisation. Thus, it cannot be classified as true TO of PCM heat sinks. However, they did show improved thermal buffering from topology-optimised designs, which is the objective pursued in the present work. Similarly, Bianco et al. [14] optimised using a steady-state model with heat generation in place of an actual phase change model, but investigated the application of density-based TO to minimise the thermal resistance under constant wall temperature. Despite using a simplified model, the optimised design showed an up to two times improvement of the heat flux compared to a conventional design. Recently, Guibert et al. [4] presented a level-set method for heat sinks with PCMs, heavily based on the preprint of the present manuscript [15] and the associated freely available code [16]. They subsequently extended and applied their method to the design of electric aircraft battery packs [5].

As mentioned, the use of TO for thermal energy storage systems is more common and still relevant to summarise, since all of the work actually makes use of transient heat transfer analysis using models that include the latent heat of fusion. Pizzolato et al. [17] was the first to use TO to improve heat transfer performance in a latent heat thermal energy storage system (LHTES). In the initial study, only thermal diffusion was considered, but this was later extended to include the effects of natural convection [18,19]. They found that optimised designs based on pure thermal diffusion had higher heat transfer rates during the initial melting phase compared to optimised designs based on models including convective heat transfer in the liquid PCM. Meanwhile, designs based on models including convection had a higher charge rate if the storage unit had stored more than 80.2% of its energy storage capacity. There exist several further examples on TO for the PCM and HCM of LHTES [20–25], the details of which will not be discussed herein.

FEniCS [26,27] is a widely used collection of open-source components for automating the process of solving partial differential equations using the finite element method. In the context of TO, it has been used by a number of authors, and the following only presents a brief selection. Laurain [28] presented a compact educational structural TO code written using FEniCS to perform compliance minimisation using a level-set method. Qian [29] used FEniCS to perform TO to improve the printability of the optimised design on a three-dimensional printer by adding undercut and overhang angle control. Mezzadri et al. [30] used FEniCS to perform TO of self-supporting support structures for additive manufacturing. Yan et al. [31] presented a general-purpose TO platform for multidisciplinary problems with FEniCS as the multiphysics solver. Jauregui et al. [32] presented a reusable modu-

https://doi.org/10.3390/computation14010023

lar TO software, capable of using FEniCS as the simulation tool. Recently, Jia et al. [33] presented a TO software built upon the newer FEniCSx library.

1.3. Contributions

This paper aims to build upon the current understanding of PCM heat sinks with help of gradient-based TO with a specific focus on reducing the temperature oscillation in the electronic components resulting from a transient cyclic thermal load from the electronic components. Based on a simplified model of a PCM heat sink, a TO code using FEniCS version 2019 is applied to optimise the layout of the PCM and HCM in order to reduce the amplitude of temperature oscillations. The novelty in this research lies in the application of density-based TO to a complex time-dependent objective functional; providing insight into the complex problem that is reducing the amplitude of the temperature oscillations; and the use of a simple homogenisation-based design parametrisation for TO of PCMs and HCMs. For latent-heat buffering using PCM, the framework reduces the temperature variance objective by 41% (full transient) and 32% (quasi-steady-state), and delivers near-discrete layouts with only ∼10% loss.

This paper presents the major methods and assumptions used for the simulation and optimisation of the heat sink, and the resulting designs from the optimisation under different conditions. The optimised designs are investigated, and based on these investigations it is expected that some patterns will emerge that can help further the understanding of PCM heat sinks.

1.4. Paper Layout

The rest of the paper is organised as follows: Section 2 presents the methods and assumptions used to set up a physical model of the PCM heat sink; Section 3 presents the optimisation problem and methods used to perform TO; Section 4 describes how the methods are implemented to produce the results and presents the verification of the implementation of the methods; Section 5 presents the optimised designs of PCM heat sinks for different use cases; Section 6 discusses the results and assumptions behind the physical model and TO and their implications; and Section 7 presents the main conclusions of the paper.

2. Physical Model

As this paper aims to optimise PCM heat sinks with respect to the temperature of electronic components, the thermal problem is the most important to solve. The presence of PCM adds a lot of complexity to the thermal problem; the melting and solidification requires a transient model, the latent heat of fusion introduces non-linearities, and the liquid PCM causes natural convection heat transfer due to buoyancy effects, which requires a fluid simulation to model fully.

TO requires many subsequent evaluations of the physics. Therefore, it is desired to keep the physical model as simple as possible to keep the computational time to a manageable level. Therefore, the effects of natural convection will be neglected in this study. This choice is expected to result in some errors in the physical model, as a review of modelling PCMs in LHTES [34] found that natural convection had a major effect on the melting of PCMs. Pizzolato et al. [18] showed that optimised designs for LHTES differ significantly when only melting is considered, but that the designs look similar when treating only solidification. Nonetheless, herein it is assumed that the PCM heat sinks can be modelled as a transient thermal diffusion problem with two materials and phase change. The effect of these errors will need to be investigated in future works.

https://doi.org/10.3390/computation14010023

For this paper, the PCM heat sink is modelled as a simplified two-dimensional model consisting of a unit square with a heat flux applied at the boundary $\partial\Omega_{HS}$ simulating the heat produced in the electronic component and a cooling flux applied at the boundary $\partial\Omega_C$. The remaining boundaries are considered adiabatic. A sketch of the simplified two-dimensional model of the PCM heat sink can be seen in Figure 2.

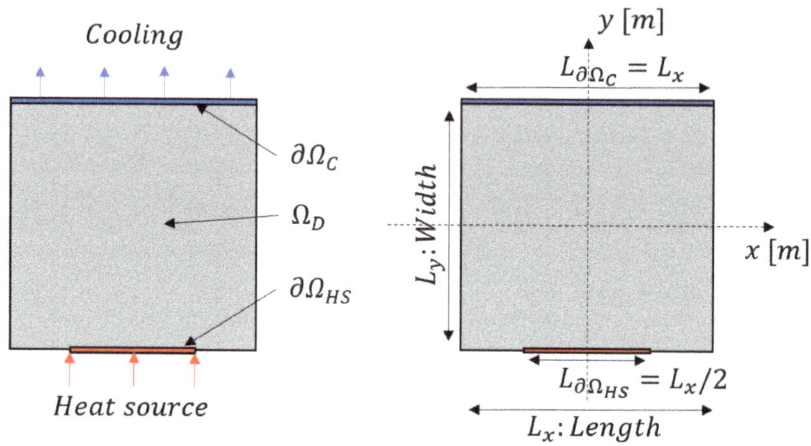

Figure 2. Two-dimensional sketch of the simplified PCM heat sink used to define the design domain for the TO.

2.1. The Transient Thermal Diffusion Problem

The PCM heat sink is modelled using the following thermal diffusion problem:

$$\rho_m c_p \frac{\partial T}{\partial t} - k_T \frac{\partial^2 T}{\partial x_i \partial x_i} = 0 \tag{1}$$

where $\rho_m c_p \frac{\partial T}{\partial t}$ is the thermal storage term; $-k_T \frac{\partial^2 T}{\partial x_i \partial x_i}$ is the diffusion term; T is the continuous temperature field; x_i is a vector containing all the spatial dimensions; k_T is the thermal conductivity; ρ_m is the mass density; c_p is the specific heat; and t is time.

In order for FEniCS to solve the thermal diffusion problem, the weak form has to be derived. Using a backward difference scheme to handle the time derivative, the weak form is derived to the following after integration-by-parts:

$$R = \int_\Omega \rho_m c_p v \frac{T^{(n)} - T^{(n-1)}}{\Delta t} dA + \int_\Omega k_T \frac{\partial v}{\partial x_i} \frac{\partial T^{(n)}}{\partial x_i} dA + \int_{\partial\Omega} v \left(-k_T \frac{\partial T^{(n)}}{\partial n} \right) ds = 0 \tag{2}$$

where Δt is the size of the time step used for the backward difference scheme; $T^{(n)}$ is the continuous temperature field at the current time step n; $T^{(n-1)}$ is the continuous temperature field at the previous time step; v is test function; $\partial\Omega$ is the boundary of the design domain; and $-k_T \frac{\partial T}{\partial n}$ is the normal flux over the boundary. Note that the weak form is provided in the semi-discrete form, being continuous in the spatial dimension and discrete over time, in order to be consistent with the notation used in the code.

2.2. Material Interpolation

As the PCM heat sink consists of both PCM and HCM, the physical model has to be able to handle two materials. To make the subsequent implementation of TO easier, the two materials were implemented with an interpolation scheme depending on the material density variable field, ρ, representing the percentage of HCM, such that $\rho = 0$ is PCM,

https://doi.org/10.3390/computation14010023

$\rho = 1$ is HCM, and $\rho \in]0;1[$ is a mixture. The material properties important for the physical model are $\rho_m c_p$ and k_T.

As seen in Section 1.2, the SIMP method is a common method for material interpolation when performing TO. It introduces a power-law interpolation that artificially decreases the material properties per volume for intermediate densities, which usually incentivises TO to create optimised designs without intermediate material (henceforth referred to as "discrete designs") to make the best use of the material. However, during the initial testing it was found that the optimised designs based on the SIMP and other interpolation methods had a tendency to contain significant amounts of intermediate material, making them unphysical. Therefore, it was deemed necessary to implement an interpolation scheme that has a physical meaning for intermediate density variables. To do this, a simple analytical homogenisation was chosen.

Homogenisation is a method that computes effective macroscopic material properties of a microstructure consisting of a locally, periodically repeating pattern of a base cell; see Figure 3.

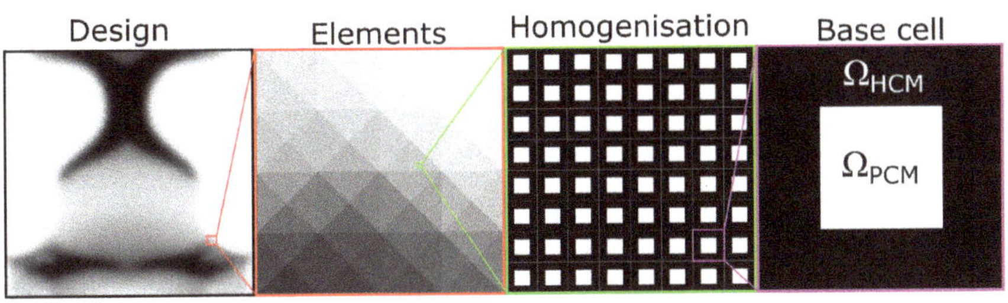

Figure 3. Homogenisation is based on the assumption that intermediate material can be seen as a local, regular, periodical repetition of a base cell.

A microstructural design variable is then connected to the macroscopic effective properties to allow for optimisation. The chosen microstructure is a square base cell with a square of PCM in the centre with a frame of HCM around it. The macroscopic design variable is defined as the relative material density of HCM, $\rho = \frac{|\Omega_{HCM}|}{|\Omega_{HCM} \cup \Omega_{PCM}|}$, which in turn is coupled to the microscopic design variable, defined as the width of the HCM frame dictated by the volume of HCM. This definition is further described in Appendix A, where the simple analytical homogenisation is derived and verified with acceptable accuracy.

The thermal conductivity k_T is computed as the total thermal conductivity based on an one-dimensional steady-state heat conduction analysis of the base cell:

$$k_T(\rho) = \frac{1}{\frac{1-\sqrt{1-\rho}}{k_{THCM}} + \frac{\sqrt{1-\rho}}{(1-\sqrt{1-\rho})k_{THCM} + (\sqrt{1-\rho})k_{TPCM}}} \tag{3}$$

The volumetric heat capacity, defined as the mass density multiplied by the specific heat capacity, $\rho_m c_p$, is computed as a volumetric average:

$$\rho_m c_p(\rho) = (\rho)\rho_{mHCM} c_{pHCM} + (1-\rho)\rho_{mPCM} c_{pPCM} \tag{4}$$

2.3. Latent Heat of Fusion

To model the latent heat of fusion, the apparent heat capacity method is used. The method introduces a temperature-dependent apparent heat capacity, $c_{pPCM} \Rightarrow c_{pPCM}\left(T^{(n)}\right)$, where the value of the heat capacity is increased in the phase change temperature range to incorporate the latent heat of fusion into the thermal storage term. Assuming

https://doi.org/10.3390/computation14010023

the change in heat capacity between the liquid and solid state of the PCM is negligible, $c_{pPCM}\left(T^{(n)}\right)$ can be modelled as the following piece-wise function:

$$c_{pPCM}(T^{(n)}) = \begin{cases} c_{pPCM} & \text{if } T^{(n)} < T_{melt} - \frac{\Delta T_{melt}}{2} \\ c_{pPCM} + \frac{L_{heat}}{\Delta T_{melt}} & \text{if } T_{melt} - \frac{\Delta T_{melt}}{2} \leq T^{(n)} \leq T_{melt} + \frac{\Delta T_{melt}}{2} \\ c_{pPCM} & \text{if } T^{(n)} < T_{melt} + \frac{\Delta T_{melt}}{2} \end{cases} \tag{5}$$

where T_{melt} is the melting temperature; ΔT_{melt} is the phase change temperature range; and L_{heat} is the latent heat of fusion. Deriving the sensitivities in later steps requires a continuous function; therefore, the piece-wise function is approximated with smooth Heaviside step functions:

$$c_{pPCM}(T^{(n)}) = c_{pPCM} + \frac{L_{heat}}{\Delta T_{melt}} \left(\frac{1}{1 + e^{-2k_H\left(T^{(n)} - \frac{\Delta T_{melt}}{2}\right)}} - \frac{1}{1 + e^{-2k_H\left(T^{(n)} + \frac{\Delta T_{melt}}{2}\right)}} \right) \tag{6}$$

where k_H is a factor that corresponds to the sharpness of the transition.

For clarity of what the Heaviside function does, the temperature-dependent apparent heat capacity, $c_{pPCM}(T^{(n)})$ is plotted using the piece-wise function and the smooth Heaviside step function; see Figure 4.

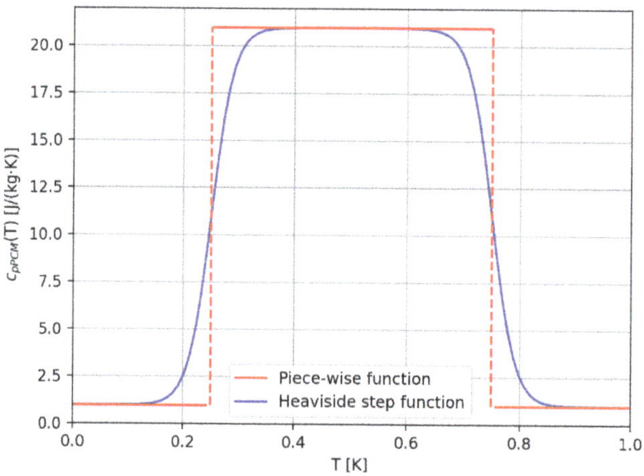

Figure 4. The temperature-dependent apparent heat capacity, $c_{pPCM}(T^{(n)})$ plotted at different temperatures with the piece-wise function and the smooth Heaviside step function.

2.4. Boundary Conditions

The fluxes used to model the heat source and cooling are modelled as Neumann boundary conditions. For the heat source, a uniformly distributed time-dependent heat rate is used to simulate the transient thermal loading from the electrical component:

$$-k_T \frac{\partial T}{\partial n}\bigg|_{\partial \Omega_{HS}} = -q_{HS}(t) = -\frac{P_{elec}}{A}(1 + sin(2\pi\omega t)) \tag{7}$$

where $-k_T \frac{\partial T}{\partial n}\big|_{\partial \Omega_{HS}}$ is the heat flux normal to the boundary $\partial\Omega_{HS}$; P_{elec} is the average heat transfer rate produced by the electronic component; A is the area of the electronic component; ω is the oscillation frequency of the heat rate produced by the electronic component.

https://doi.org/10.3390/computation14010023

The cooling is modelled as a convection cooling rate using Newton's law of cooling:

$$-k_T\frac{\partial T}{\partial n}\bigg|_{\partial\Omega_C} = q_C(T_s) = h_{conv}(T_s - T_\infty) \tag{8}$$

where $-k_T\frac{\partial T}{\partial n}\big|_{\partial\Omega_C}$ is the heat flux normal to the boundary $\partial\Omega_C$; h_{conv} is the convection heat transfer coefficient; T_s is the surface temperature; and T_∞ is the temperature of the surroundings. Note that the term for the heat source is negative, while the term for the cooling is positive. This is due to the fact that FEniCS considers the normal to be positive in the direction away from the body.

2.5. Weak Form and Approximations

Inserting Equations (3), (4) and (6)–(8) into (2) results in the following weak form, which can be used to model the physics behind the PCM heat sink:

$$\begin{aligned} R = \int_\Omega \rho_m c_p(\rho, T^{(n)}) v \frac{T^{(n)} - T^{(n-1)}}{\Delta t} dA + \int_\Omega k_T(\rho) \frac{\partial v}{\partial x_i}\frac{\partial T^{(n)}}{\partial x_i} dA \\ - \int_{\partial\Omega_{HS}} v q_{HS}(t) ds + \int_{\partial\Omega_C} v h_{conv}(T^{(n)} - T_\infty) ds = 0 \end{aligned} \tag{9}$$

This weak form is a non-linear function due to the implementation of the latent heat of fusion, where the heat capacity is dependent on the current temperature $T^{(n)}$, which means it requires a non-linear solver to solve the model. A non-linear solver takes extra iterative solver steps to deal with the non-linearity, which increases the computational cost and time of solving the model.

To keep the computational time as short as possible, the non-linear model is approximated by a time-lagging model by making the $\rho_m c_p$ dependent on the temperature from the previous time step $T^{(n-1)}$ rather than the current time step $T^{(n)}$. This removes the need for the extra iterative solver steps from the non-linear solver at the cost of introducing an error into the model. The final weak form used to model the PCM heat sink in this paper thereby becomes

$$\begin{aligned} R = \int_\Omega \rho_m c_p(\rho, T^{(n-1)}) v \frac{T^{(n)} - T^{(n-1)}}{\Delta t} dA + \int_\Omega k_T(\rho) \frac{\partial v}{\partial x_i}\frac{\partial T^{(n)}}{\partial x_i} dA \\ - \int_{\partial\Omega_{HS}} v q_{HS}(t) ds + \int_{\partial\Omega_C} v h_{conv}(T^{(n)} - T_\infty) ds = 0 \end{aligned} \tag{10}$$

3. Optimisation Problem

3.1. Topology Optimisation

TO aims to find the most optimal distribution of two materials to minimise a chosen objective functional. In density-based TO, the material distribution is described with a spatially varying material density variable field, ρ. To avoid simple solutions and keep different cases comparable, a volume constraint is added to the optimisation problem, restricting the use of HCM. A constraint on the HCM is used for the simple fact that it is the best material from a heat transfer performance point of view. This is also common in the literature and, thus, this is a sensible option. The optimisation problem used in this paper can be seen in the following equation:

$$\begin{aligned} \min_{\rho} \quad & f_0(T(\rho), \rho) \\ \text{s.t.} \quad & h_0(\rho) = \frac{\int_\Omega \rho(x_i) dA}{\int_\Omega \Phi dA} - 1 \leq 0 \\ & 0 \leq \rho(x_i) \leq 1 \end{aligned} \tag{11}$$

https://doi.org/10.3390/computation14010023

where f_0 is the objective functional; ρ is the continuous material density variable field; $T(\rho)$ is the temperature field that satisfies the physical model; $h_0(\rho)$ is the volume constraint; Ω is the continuous design domain; and Φ is the maximum allowable volume fraction of HCM.

3.2. Objective Functional

The objective of the optimisation is to minimise the amplitude of the temperature oscillation at the electronic component that is introduced by the cyclic transient heat rate from the electronic component. This is quantified with the ϕ, which is the temporal average variance of the spatial average temperature at $\partial\Omega_{HS}$, as this is where the PCM heat sink is connected to the electronic component (henceforth referred to as "the variance"). In order for the TO to reduce the amplitude of the temperature oscillation, the variance, ϕ, is chosen as the objective functional f_0 for the TO. Thereby, the objective function is defined as

$$f_0 = \phi = \frac{1}{N_t} \sum_{n=1}^{N_t} \left(T_{elec}^{(n)} - \overline{T}_{elec} \right)^2 \tag{12}$$

where N_t is the final number of time steps; n is the time step; $T_{elec}^{(n)}$ is the spatial average temperature over the heat source boundary, $\partial\Omega_{HS}$, at each time step (henceforth referred to as "the temperature at the heat source"); and $\overline{T}_{elec}$ is the temporal mean of $T_{elec}^{(n)}$. The temperature at the heat source $T_{elec}^{(n)}$ is defined as

$$T_{elec}^{(n)} = \frac{\int_{\partial\Omega_{HS}} L_z T^{(n)} ds}{\int_{\partial\Omega_{HS}} L_z ds} \tag{13}$$

where L_z is the out-of-plane length of the heat sink; and $T^{(n)}$ is the temperature field at time step n. The temporal mean of $T_{elec}^{(n)}$ is computed with

$$\overline{T}_{elec} = \frac{1}{N_t} \sum_{n=1}^{N_t} T_{elec}^{(n)} \tag{14}$$

The chosen objective function exclusively focuses on minimising the temperature variation over time. However, in practical electronics thermal management, the maximum temperature level is an important metric and is usually constrained from above. This is not included in the present work, but a constraint on the maximum heat source temperature could be added to Equation (11) for practical use cases.

3.3. Filtering

A direct implementation of the density-based TO method to a heat transfer problem can result in designs that are mesh-dependent and may contain unphysical chequerboard patterns [35]. To alleviate these problems, different filtering strategies have been proposed [36]. For this paper, a filtering method based on a partial differential equation (PDE) [37] is used, as it takes advantage of the ease of implementing and solving PDEs in FEniCS. The filtered density field $\tilde{\rho}$ is found by solving the following PDE [37]:

$$-r^2 \frac{\partial^2 \tilde{\rho}}{\partial x_i x_i} + \tilde{\rho} = \rho \tag{15}$$

where r is a filter parameter linked to the amount of smoothing applied by the filter. The PDE is combined with a homogeneous Neumann boundary condition, to ensure that

https://doi.org/10.3390/computation14010023

volume is conserved throughout the filtering process. For the optimisation, the filtered density variable $\tilde{\rho}$ is used as the design input for the physical model of the PCM heat sink.

3.4. The Adjoint Method

In order to perform gradient-based TO, the sensitivities of the constraint and objective functionals with respect to the material density variable field, ρ, have to be computed. As the TO is characterised by having a large number of design variables and a small number of constraints, the adjoint method is particularly efficient for computing the sensitivities, as it only requires one additional problem per functional to compute it.

In short, the adjoint method computes the sensitivities using the following Equation:

$$\frac{df_j}{d\rho} = \frac{\partial f_j}{\partial \rho} - \lambda^T \frac{\partial \boldsymbol{R}}{\partial \rho} \tag{16}$$

where f_j are functionals of interest; $\boldsymbol{\rho}$ is a vector containing the density variables; $\boldsymbol{R}$ is a vector containing the residuals; and $\boldsymbol{\lambda}$ is a vector containing the adjoint variables. The adjoint variables are computed by solving the adjoint system of Equations:

$$\left(\frac{\partial \boldsymbol{R}}{\partial u}\right)^T \boldsymbol{\lambda} = \left(\frac{\partial f_j}{\partial u}\right)^T \tag{17}$$

where $\boldsymbol{u}$ is a vector containing the state variables.

For time-dependent systems, the adjoint system also becomes time-dependent and, thus, another full time series solution must be solved. Furthermore, the full time history of the state variables and the system Jacobian must be saved (or recomputed) for the adjoint system. Although this is "just" a doubling of the computational cost, this is much more significant for time-dependent problems, since their computational cost is so high already from the time stepping procedure. For further details on adjoint sensitivity analysis of time-dependent systems, please see the literature on the subject [38,39]. To circumvent the cumbersome work of deriving and implementing the full time-dependent adjoint system, the automatic adjoint capabilities of the dolfin-adjoint module [40] are used in combination with FEniCS.

4. Implementation

4.1. Packages

In order to implement the methods described in the previous section, a Python code was created, for which a minimal working example is available on GitHub—see the "Data Availability Statement" at the end of the paper. Python (version 3.10) was chosen due to its open source nature and vast number of modules that can automate many of the computational steps required for TO. For this paper, the FEniCS (legacy FEniCS version 2019.1.0) module is used for solving the physical model, and the dolfin-adjoint (dolfin-adjoint version 2019.1) module is used to compute the adjoint sensitivities. The optimisation problem is solved using the Globally Convergent Method of Moving Asymptotes (GCMMA) [41] and was implemented into the Python code through the code provided by Deetman [42].

4.2. The Code

In order to perform TO, the process is broken down into the following computational steps:

1. Defining the initial design as a uniform distribution of material.
2. Solve the physical problem with FEniCS.
3. Compute the objective and constraint sensitivities using the adjoint method.
4. Update the design using GCMMA.

https://doi.org/10.3390/computation14010023

5. Check for convergence. If the convergence criteria are not satisfied, update the geometry and go back to step 2; otherwise, stop the optimisation loop.
6. Save the final optimised design.

First, the physical model is defined. The material properties, model parameters, geometry, discretisation schemes, and boundary conditions are defined using FEniCS. The geometry is meshed with a mapped mesh using triangular elements in a cross pattern; see Figure 5. The mesh uses triangular elements as these are the only ones compatible with the FEniCS version used for this paper. The temperature fields, $T^{(n)}$ and $T^{(n-1)}$ are approximated with continuous first-order elements, while the material density variable field, ρ, is approximated using piece-wise constant discontinuous elements.

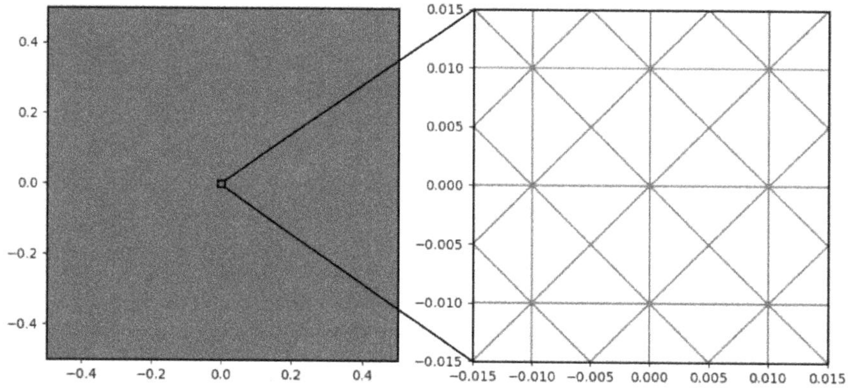

Figure 5. Plot of the mapped mesh using triangular element used for this paper.

The solver for the physical problem is set up as a custom function, forward(), that takes in the filtered material design variable field, $\tilde{\rho}$, as an input. In order to solve the physical model, an iterative time loop is set up, solving the physical model for each time step until the final time step is reached, $n = N_t$. The temperature at the heat source $T_{elec}^{(n)}$ is stored for each time step and used to compute the variance ϕ.

The computation of the sensitivities is automated with dolfin-adjoint. For this, the objective and constraint functionals have to be defined in a ReducedFunctional class, which stores all the operations performed with FEniCS and defines the control parameter. With this, the dependencies are stored, and both the functionals and the sensitivities of the functionals can be computed based on the current material design variable field, ρ.

In order to update the design, GCMMA requires the current material design variable field, ρ, and the resulting objective and constraint functionals, together with the sensitivities of the functionals, which pair up nicely with the capabilities of the ReducedFunctional class from dolfin-adjoint. The GCMMA is set to run a maximum of two inner iterations to keep the computational time to a reasonable level, since transient simulations are very costly. To check whether the optimisation has converged, the code uses the change in the objective functional, f_0, and the measure of non-discreteness, M_{nd} (described in detail in Section 5.4.1), over the optimisation iteration. The optimisation is considered converged if the absolute changes in both f_0 and M_{nd} are below 10^{-3} for three consecutive optimisation iterations. If the convergence criterion is not met, the optimisation is allowed to run a maximum of 300 optimisation iterations.

The TO is set up as a custom function, optimisation(), which takes in the initial material density variable field, ρ, the initial filtered material density variable field $\tilde{\rho}$, Reduced functionals of the objective and constraint functionals, lists of historical values for convergence plots, and the α value. The operations of optimisation() are enveloped in with a "with pyadjoint.stop_annotating() as _:" command which stops the dolfin-adjoint from storing the operations, which can otherwise lead to a large memory consumption. A minimal working example of the code is available on GitHub—see the "Data Availability Statement" at the end of this paper.

Verification of the implementation is presented in Appendix B.

4.3. Data

This section presents the data used for the production of the results, unless stated otherwise. The dimensions used for the model are presented in Table 1, the material properties are presented in Table 2, and the model parameters are presented in Table 3.

Table 1. Geometry and discretisation.

Description	Symbol	Value	Units
Domain size	$L_x \times L_y \times L_z$	$1 \times 1 \times 1$	[m]
Mesh size	$n_{epsq} \times n_x \times n_y$	$4 \times 100 \times 100$	[-]
Final time	t_{fin}	20	[s]
Number of time steps	N_t	500	[-]
Time step size	Δt	0.04	[s]

Table 2. Material properties.

Description	Symbol	Value	Units
Thermal conductivity HCM	k_{THCM}	10	$\left[\frac{W}{m \cdot K}\right]$
Density HCM	ρ_{mHCM}	1	$\left[\frac{kg}{m^3}\right]$
Heat capacity HCM	c_{pHCM}	1	$\left[\frac{J}{kg \cdot K}\right]$
Thermal conductivity PCM	k_{TPCM}	0.01	$\left[\frac{W}{m \cdot K}\right]$
Density PCM	ρ_{mPCM}	1	$\left[\frac{kg}{m^3}\right]$
Heat capacity PCM	c_{pPCM}	1	$\left[\frac{J}{kg \cdot K}\right]$
Melting temperature	T_{melt}	0.5	[K]
Melting temperature range	ΔT_{melt}	0.5	[K]
Latent heat of fusion	L_{heat}	10	$\left[\frac{J}{kg}\right]$

Table 3. Model parameters.

Description	Symbol	Value	Units
Heat transfer coefficient	h_{conv}	5	$\left[\frac{W}{m^2 \cdot K}\right]$
Initial temperature	T_{ini}	0	[K]
Surrounding temperature	T_∞	0	[K]
Average heat rate from electronic component	P_{elec}	1	[W]
Heat rate oscillation frequency	ω	1	[Hz]
Maximum volume fraction of HCM	Φ	0.3	[-]
Steepness factor for smooth Heaviside step function	k_H	25	[-]
Filter parameter	r	0.01	[-]

The material properties are chosen arbitrarily but represent physically relevant contrasts in material properties. The ratio in thermal conductivity is 1000:1, which is common for metals as the HCM. The contrast in effective heat capacity between solid/fluid and

https://doi.org/10.3390/computation14010023

melting PCM can be computed based on Equation (5) from the latent heat of fusion. For the values in Table 2, the effective heat capacity is 21 during melting/solidification, which yields a contrast of 21:1. There are many commercially available PCMs on the market, with a wide range of properties [43,44], and our values lie within that range.

5. Results

This section presents and discusses the results obtained from running the TO under different conditions. All designs are visualised with grey-scale plots of the filtered material density variable field, $\tilde{\rho}$, where white indicates the PCM, black indicates the HCM, and grey indicates a mix of the two materials. The colourbar for all the designs can be seen in Figure 6.

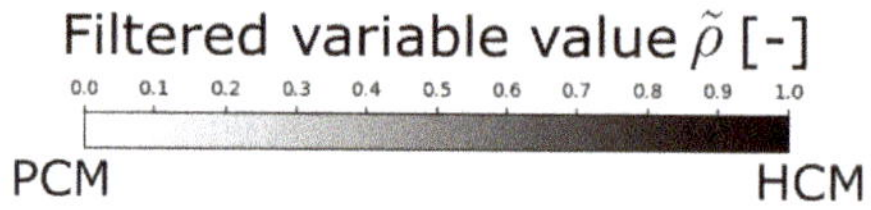

Figure 6. Colourbar for all the designs presented in this paper.

To test the effect of including phase change, three different cases are considered for the TO. The three cases considered are Case 1—Without phase change and with $c_{pPCM} = 1$; Case 2—Without phase change and with $c_{pPCM} = 21$; and Case 3—With phase change and with $c_{pPCM} = 1$. Note that the two materials are still referred to as HCM and PCM, even though no phase change occurs to keep the descriptions consistent. The phase change is designed so that the effective heat capacity of the PCM is equal to the high c_{pPCM} when phase change is occurring and low c_{pPCM} otherwise. The c_{pPCM} used for the cases are shown in Figure 7. These cases are chosen to see how effectively the TO can make use of the phase-change process itself and to determine what favourable design features can be attributed to the inclusion of phase change and what is due to the increase in thermal storage.

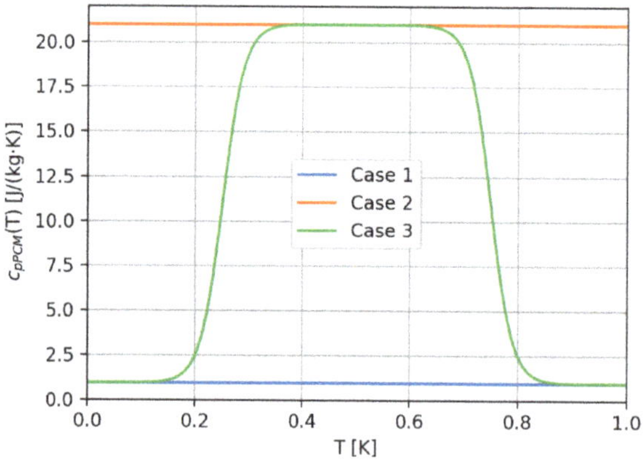

Figure 7. Effect heat capacity for the three cases investigated: Case 1—No phase change with low c_{pPCM}; Case 2—No phase change with high c_{pPCM}; Case 3—With phase change.

5.1. Considering the Full Time History

The results presented in this section are based on a 20 s simulation of the PCM heat sink, and ϕ is computed using all time steps. The TO takes 39 h for Case 1, 37 h for Case 2, and 37 h for Case 3 to produce the optimised results on a single core of an Intel Xeon Gold 6130 @ 2.776 GHz. For the TO of all cases, it is found that ϕ decreases as the number of optimisation iterations increases, and all cases reach the defined convergence criteria.

https://doi.org/10.3390/computation14010023

The resulting optimised designs and their performances compared to the initial design are presented in Figure 8. The initial design consists of a uniform distribution of material, equivalent to a foam consisting of 30% HCM and 70% PCM.

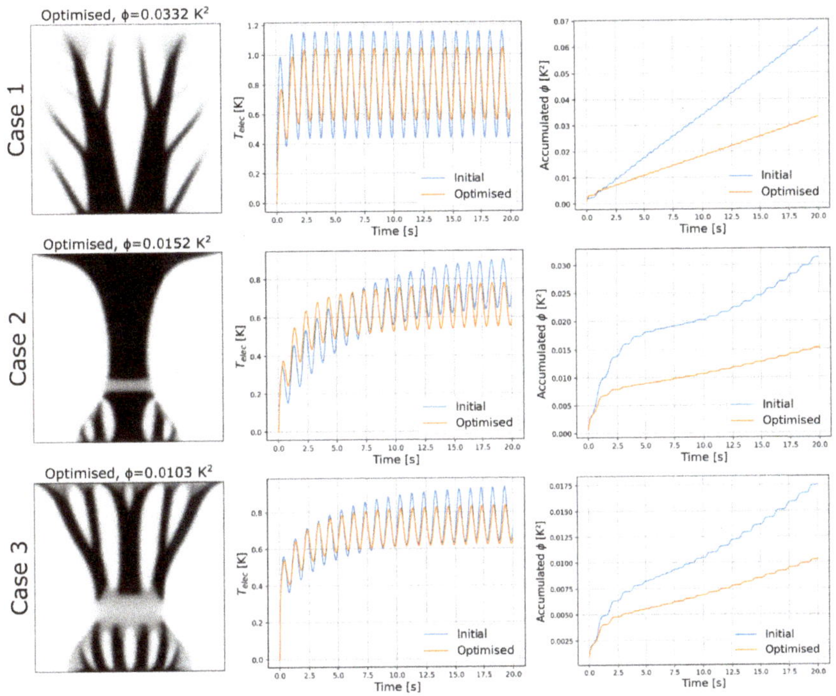

Figure 8. Optimised designs, T_{elec} over time and accumulated ϕ over time for the three cases. The T_{elec} over time, and accumulated ϕ over time are plotted against the values from the initial design. Top: Optimised design based on Case 1, Middle: Optimised design based on Case 2, Bottom: Optimised design based on Case 3.

It can be seen that the optimised design for Case 1 consists of two major narrowing fins of HCM reaching from the heat source to the cooling side, with smaller branches reaching into the PCM. The major fins are not connected directly to the cooling side, but are separated by smaller sections of intermediate material located at the ends of the major fins. The optimised designs for Case 2 and Case 3 consist of shorter fins close to the heat source reaching towards the cooling side, followed by a section of intermediate material, and then an expanding structure connecting the section of intermediate material to the cooling side. The designs generally have fewer fins reaching into the PCM than when compared to the design based on Case 1. The optimised design for Case 3 has more PCM layered in-between the HCM when compared to the optimised design for Case 2.

From the plots of T_{elec} over time in Figure 8, it can be seen that all optimised designs result in a reduced amplitude in the temperature oscillation. For Case 2 and Case 3, the optimised designs also reduce the time until a quasi-steady-state is reached. This makes sense as both the amplitude and the initial transient have an effect on the variance ϕ, as the TO considers the entire 20 s simulated as input.

It can also be seen that all three optimised designs improved the performance of the heat sink by reducing the variance, ϕ. Comparing the ϕ values to those of the initial design, the optimised design based on Case 1 shows a 50% reduction, the optimised design based

https://doi.org/10.3390/computation14010023

on Case 2 shows a 52% reduction, and the optimised design based on Case 3 shows a 41% reduction. Overall, Case 3 has the best performance of the three cases, which is because all of the PCM phases have a large heat capacity for all temperatures.The plots of the accumulated ϕ over time in Figure 8, show that the improvements in ϕ occur at different points of the time history. It can be seen that the optimised design based on Case 1 reduces ϕ gradually over time, while the designs based on Case 2 and Case 3 reduce the variance ϕ drastically in the first 5 s of the simulated time, after which it is further reduced gradually over time. This further supports that reducing the time until quasi-steady-state is reached has an effect on the performance for Case 2 and Case 3.

To verify the optimised designs from the TO, a cross-check is performed, where the variance ϕ of the designs based on the three cases is tested. If the TO is set up correctly, the designs should perform best in the cases they were optimised for and worse in other cases, compared to the designs that were optimised for that case. The results from the cross-check are shown in Table 4.

Table 4. Results from cross-check designs based on full time history, showing normalised ϕ for each design tried in three different cases: Case 1—No phase change and low c_{pPCM}; Case 2—No phase change and high c_{pPCM}; Case 3—With phase change.

Tested at	Optimised for		
	Case 1	**Case 2**	**Case 3**
Case 1	1	2.96	2.63
Case 2	2.06	1	1.29
Case 3	1.59	0.99	1

It can be seen that the majority of the optimised designs perform best in the cases they were optimised for, indicating that the TO is generally effective at optimising the design in most cases. However, when testing at Case 3, the optimised design for Case 2 performs ever so slightly better than the optimised design for Case 3. This is likely a result of the complicated objective functional or the severe non-linearity introduced with the apparent heat capacity method, which makes it difficult for the TO to optimise the designs without becoming stuck in a local minimum.

Thermal Energy and Heat Flux Fields

To further understand the optimised designs, the time history of the thermal energy field and heat flux in the y-direction are investigated. The thermal energy field is defined as

$$E_{term}^{(n)} = \rho_m c_p(\tilde{\rho}) T^{(n)} + (1-\tilde{\rho}) L_{heat} f_{melt}^{(n)} \tag{18}$$

where $f_{melt}^{(n)}$ is the melt fraction. The melt fraction is a piece-wise function that varies linearly from zero, when no material has changed phase, to one, when all material has changed phase, over the phase change temperature range ΔT_{melt}. For this paper it is approximated with smooth Heaviside step functions:

$$\begin{aligned} f_{melt}^{(n)} = & \frac{T^{(n)} - \left(T_{melt} - \frac{\Delta T_{melt}}{2}\right)}{\Delta T_{melt}} \left(\frac{1}{1 + e^{-2k_H\left(T^{(n)} - \frac{\Delta T_{melt}}{2}\right)}} \right) \\ & - \frac{T^{(n)} - \left(T_{melt} + \frac{\Delta T_{melt}}{2}\right)}{\Delta T_{melt}} \left(\frac{1}{1 + e^{-2k_H\left(T^{(n)} + \frac{\Delta T_{melt}}{2}\right)}} \right) \end{aligned} \tag{19}$$

The results of all the simulations are presented as animated GIFs in the Supplementary Materials. In order to illustrate the transient process in this paper, plots of the thermal energy field and heat flux are presented at $t = 19.24$ s, $t = 19.48$ s, and $t = 19.76$ s. The chosen times correspond to the time steps closest to the highest, medium, and lowest values of the oscillating heat input rate $q_{HS}(t)$ for the last oscillation period simulated.

First, the fields for the initial design are investigated. The overall characteristics of the physics are very similar for all three cases, so only Case 1 is shown in Figure 9. It can be seen that both the thermal energy and the heat flux in the y-direction are smooth. The stored thermal energy is highest when $q_{HS}(t)$ is at its medium level and most of the stored energy is located close to the heat source. The thermal energy is relatively low when $q_{HS}(t)$ is at its lowest level. From the flux in the y-direction, it can be seen that the heat is transferred from the heat source to the cooling side when $q_{HS}(t)$ is at its high and medium levels. When $q_{HS}(t)$ is at its lowest level, only very limited heat transfer occurs. This indicates that the initial design of the heat sink transports most of the thermal energy from the heat source to the cooling side, which leads to the large variance seen in Figure 8.

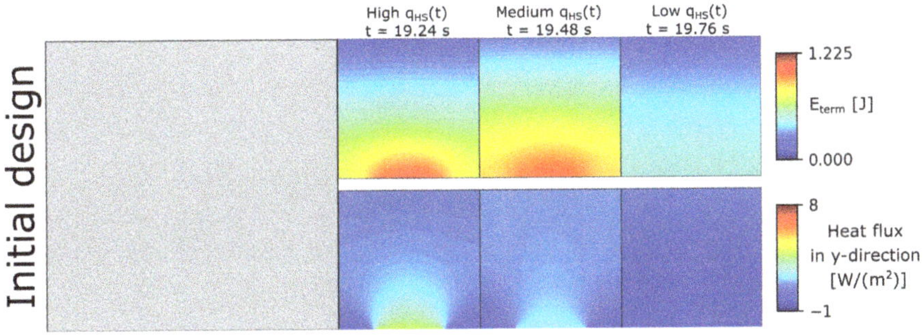

Figure 9. The thermal energy field and heat flux in the y direction at $t = 19.24$ s, $t = 19.48$ s, and $t = 19.76$ s. Based on the initial design under the conditions of Case 1.

For the optimised design based on Case 1, the thermal energy and the heat flux in the y-direction can be seen in Figure 10. It can be seen that most of the thermal energy is stored in the PCM in the bottom half of the PCM heat sink when $q_{HS}(t)$ is at its high and medium levels. When $q_{HS}(t)$ is at its low level, there is a lot less thermal energy in the heat sink. It can be seen that the thermal energy is led out into all the corners of the heat sink, resulting in a fairly even energy distribution, which is probably a result of the PCM and HCM having the same heat capacity. By looking at the heat flux in the y-direction, the heat transfer into the PCM in the corners of the heat sink can be observed in the high positive heat flux in the smaller fins reaching into the PCM when $q_{HS}(t)$ is at its high and medium levels. When $q_{HS}(t)$ is at its low level, a negative heat flux can be seen in the smaller fins, indicating that the thermal energy is drawn out of the PCM.

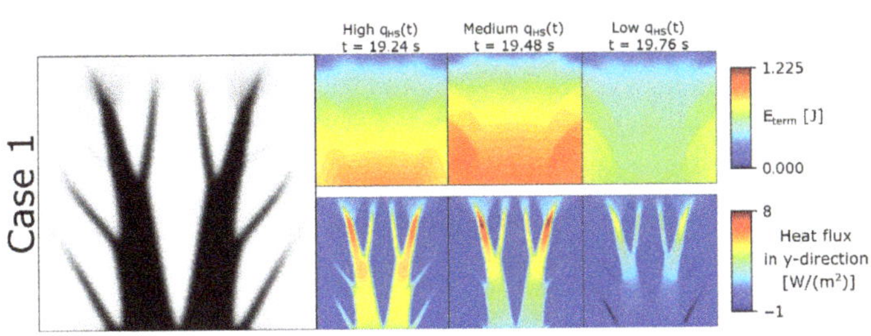

Figure 10. The thermal energy field and heat flux in the y direction at high $q_{HS}(t)$, medium $q_{HS}(t)$, and low $q_{HS}(t)$, for the optimised design based on Case 1.

https://doi.org/10.3390/computation14010023

For the optimised design based on Case 2, the thermal energy and the heat flux in the y-direction can be seen in Figure 11. The design looks very different from the design based on Case 1. From the thermal energy, it can be seen that energy is stored very locally in the PCM closest to the heat source when $q_{HS}(t)$ is at its high and medium levels and is expended when $q_{HS}(t)$ is at its low level. The design seems to isolate the main bulk of the PCM at the sides behind a thin region of intermediate material, resulting in a relatively low amount of energy being stored in it throughout the presented time frames. The section with intermediate material also seems to limit heat transfer away from the lower half of the PCM heat sink, as the thermal energy in the upper half of the heat sink is a lot lower than that in the area close to the heat sink. Looking at the heat flux in the y-direction, it can be seen that the highest heat flux, when $q_{HS}(t)$ is high, is located close to the heat source. When $q_{HS}(t)$ is medium and low, it is located just above the section with intermediate material. Furthermore, when $q_{HS}(t)$ is low, a negative heat flux can be seen close to the heat source, indicating heat transfer back to the heat source. It is the interpretation of the authors that the optimised design is aimed at reducing the transient time as much as possible. As the shorter fins close to the heat source are surrounded by the low thermally conductive PCM, the optimised design keeps the heat from being stored in the PCM further away, which reduces the thermal storage capacity available to the heat sink, leading to a shorter transient period.

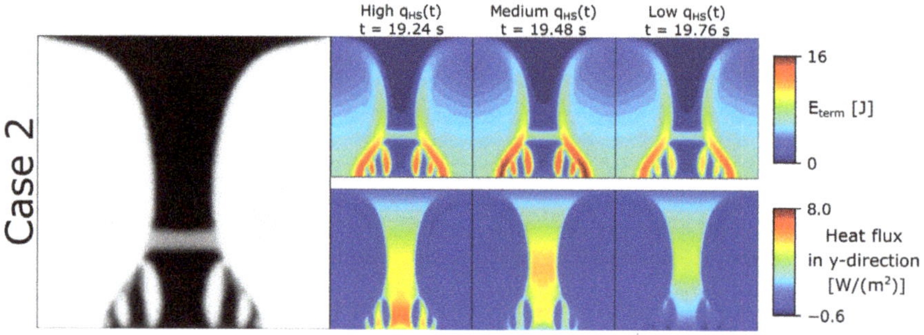

Figure 11. The thermal energy field and heat flux in the y direction at high $q_{HS}(t)$, medium $q_{HS}(t)$, and low $q_{HS}(t)$ for the optimised design based on Case 2.

For the optimised design based on Case 3, the thermal energy and the heat flux in the y-direction can be seen in Figure 12. In general, the thermal energy looks very similar to the Case 2. Thermal energy is stored very locally in the PCM closest to the heat source when $q_{HS}(t)$ is at its high and medium levels, and is expended when $q_{HS}(t)$ is low. Like the design for Case 2, this design also seems to isolate the main bulk of the PCM at the sides behind a thin region of intermediate material, resulting in a relatively low amount of energy being stored in the bulk. The section with intermediate material also seems to limit heat transfer away from the lower half of the PCM heat sink, as the thermal energy in the upper half of the heat sink is a lot lower than that in the area close to the heat sink. When looking at the heat flux in the y-direction, it can be seen that the flux is lot lower when $q_{HS}(t)$ is low, when compared to the Case 2 design, and that there is no negative heat flux close to the heat source.

https://doi.org/10.3390/computation14010023

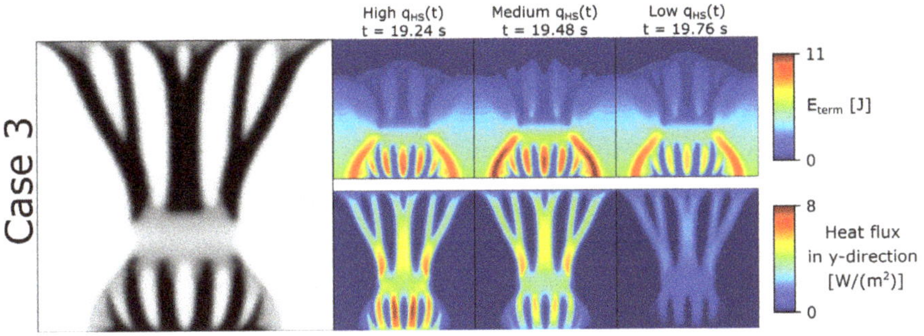

Figure 12. The thermal energy field and heat flux in the y direction at high $q_{HS}(t)$, medium $q_{HS}(t)$, and low $q_{HS}(t)$, for the optimised design based on Case 3.

In general, it can be seen that the TO is able to produce optimised designs that reduce the variance in T_{elec} compared to the initial designs. It was found that apart from the amplitude of the temperature oscillation, the transient time until the quasi-steady-state is reached also has an effect on the variance, and that the optimised designs exploit this. Especially for the designs based on Case 2 and Case 3, we can see a reduction in contributions to ϕ in the first 5 s of the simulated time.

The investigation of thermal energy and heat flux in the y-direction shows that the optimised designs based on Case 1 tend to spread out the thermal energy into the PCM when the $q_{HS}(t)$ is at its high and medium levels, while the designs based on Case 2 and Case 3 keep the thermal energy very close to the heat source. For Case 2 and Case 3, the heat transfer to the cooling side is further restricted with a section consisting of intermediate material, which limits the heat flux in the y-direction.

5.2. Considering Only the Quasi-Steady-State

There are three ways the TO can reduce the variance ϕ: by reducing the amplitude in the temperature oscillation; by reducing the transient period to move the mean closer to the centre of the oscillation; or by reducing the mean, which also reduces the effect of the initial transient period. In terms of preventing thermal fatigue, the amplitude of the temperature oscillation is the most important factor. Therefore, the transient part is removed by only considering the physics once the quasi-steady-state is reached—a point which will depend on the current design. It would be a cumbersome exercise to derive and implement the adjoint problem by hand, since this introduces design-dependent simulation times and initial conditions for the integration. However, this process is fully automated with dolfin-adjoint, and thus relatively easy to implement. This is expected to result in optimised designs that are better at reducing the amplitude of the temperature oscillation compared to the optimised designs based on the entire 20 s temperature history.

For this TO, the simulation is run until the maximum relative change in the temperature oscillation period is below 1%. The T_{elec} signal from the last period is then used to calculate the mean and variance. In order to make comparisons, the TO was performed on all the three cases. The TO takes 10 h for Case 1, 40 h for Case 2, and 34 h for Case 3 to produce the optimised results on one core of Intel Xeon Gold 6130 @ 2.776 GHz. This is a big reduction for Case 1, as the simulation reaches the quasi-steady state a lot earlier than 20 s, due to its low thermal storage. The computational times for Case 2 and Case 3 are more comparable to the 20 s simulations, as their simulations reach steady state around the 20 s mark.

https://doi.org/10.3390/computation14010023

5.2.1. Optimised Designs and Performance

The resulting optimised designs and their performances compared to the initial design and 20 s designs are presented in Figure 13. The temperature at the heat source, T_{elec}, is plotted for the last two periods after the quasi-steady state is reached. The variance, ϕ, is computed based on the last period for all cases, in order to make the results comparable. It can be seen that the optimised design based on Case 1 and its T_{elec} over time look very similar to those based on the 20 s simulation, which makes sense as Case 1 only has a short transient period. The optimised designs based on Case 2 and Case 3, however, differ significantly from the 20 s designs. The design based on Case 2 consists of one major fin and two less prominent fins of intermediate material connecting the heat source to the cooling side, shorter fins that reach from the heat source to the PCM in the lower half of the heat sink, and intermediate material that is located close to the heat source. The optimised design based on Case 3 consists of three major fin structures reaching from the heat source towards the side with cooling, smaller fins reaching from the heat source into the PCM in the lower half of the heat sink, and intermediate material at the ends of the fins, leaving more PCM close to the heat source when compared to the Case 2 design.

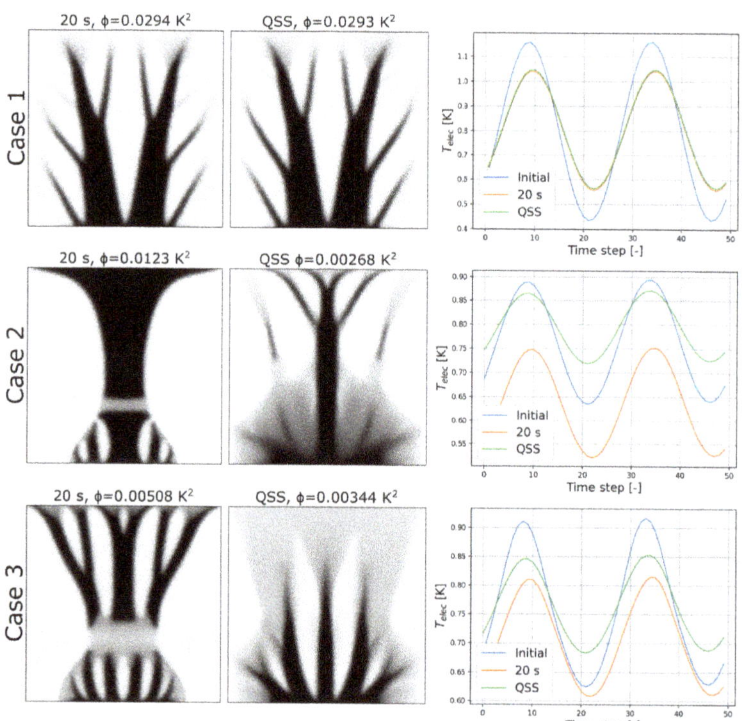

Figure 13. Optimised designs based on the quasi-steady-state compared to the 20 s designs and the initial designs for the three cases. The ϕ values are computed using T_{elec} from the last period only. The plots shows T_{elec} over time at the last two periods of the simulated time for the three cases.

The optimised designs based on Case 2 and 3 show a reduction in the amplitude of the oscillation of T_{elec} and an increase in the average T_{elec} when compared to the 20 s designs. Comparing the variance, ϕ, to the 20 s designs, the optimised design based on Case 2 shows a 78% reduction and the optimised design based on Case 3 shows a 32% reduction. This is

https://doi.org/10.3390/computation14010023

expected, as the TO can only reduce the ϕ by reducing the amplitude of the oscillation of T_{elec} when considering the quasi-steady-state.

It can be seen that when considering only the quasi-steady-state, the temperature variance, ϕ, is lower in Case 2 than Case 3. This is contrary to what was found when looking at the 20 s designs, but makes sense from a physics perspective. When reducing the transient part has a big impact on the variance, then Case 3 must be better, as it has a lower thermal storage capacity and can therefore reach the quasi-steady-state earlier. Meanwhile, in this case, where the transient part is neglected, the higher thermal storage capacity of Case 2 allows it to store more heat to smoothen out the temperature oscillations.

To verify the optimised designs from the TO, a cross-check is performed, where the variance ϕ of the designs based on the three cases is tested. The result from the cross-check are shown in Table 5.

Table 5. Results from cross-check designs based on the quasi-steady-state, showing normalised ϕ for each design tried in three different cases: Case 1—No phase change and low c_{pPCM}; Case 2—No phase change and high c_{pPCM}; Case 3—With phase change.

Tested at	Optimised for		
	Case 1	**Case 2**	**Case 3**
Case 1	1	1.39	1.26
Case 2	1.44	1	1.01
Case 3	1.32	1.36	1

It can be seen that all the optimised designs are performing best in the cases they were optimised for, indicating that the TO is effective at optimising the design for this problem. However, it can be seen that Case 2 has a very similar performance to Case 3 when tested on Case 2. As it is Case 2 that is close to performing worse than the other designs in this case, it is postulated that the complicated objective function has a larger effect on the TO reaching a local minimum than the non-linearity on the apparent heat capacity method.

5.2.2. Thermal Energy and Heat Flux Fields

The optimised designs are further investigated by looking at the thermal energy and flux in the y-direction. The results of this investigation are shown in Figures 14–16.

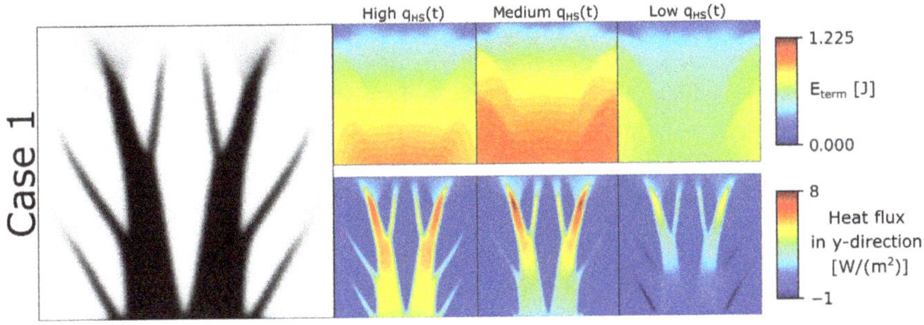

Figure 14. The thermal energy field and heat flux in the y direction at high $q_HS(t)$, medium $q_HS(t)$, and low $q_HS(t)$ for the optimised design based on the quasi-steady-state under Case 1.

https://doi.org/10.3390/computation14010023

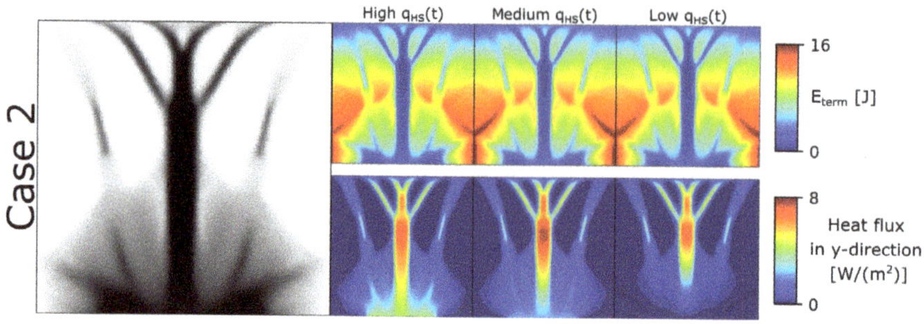

Figure 15. The thermal energy field and heat flux in the y direction at high $q_HS(t)$, average $q_HS(t)$, and low $q_HS(t)$ for the optimised design based on the quasi-steady-state under Case 2.

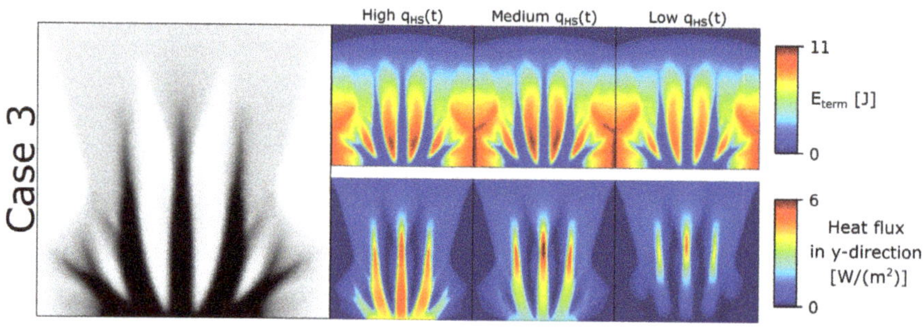

Figure 16. The thermal energy field and heat flux in the y direction at high $q_HS(t)$, average $q_HS(t)$, and low $q_HS(t)$ for the optimised design based on the quasi-steady-state under Case 3.

For the optimised design based on Case 1, the thermal energy and the heat flux in the y-direction can be seen in Figure 14. It can be seen that the thermal energy and the heat flux in the y-direction are very similar to what was seen in Figure 10 for the 20 s design. This makes sense as the designs are very similar.

For the optimised design based on Case 2, the thermal energy and the heat flux in the y-direction can be seen in Figure 15. Looking at the thermal energy, it can be seen that the thermal energy is stored in much more evenly in the PCM when compared to the 20 s design. Most of the thermal energy is stored in the PCM in the sides. The differences in the thermal energy over the presented time steps are fairly small compared to the general level of thermal energy in the heat sink, making the hard to detect in the presented times frames. However, a higher thermal energy can be seen in the PCM just outside the intermediate material close to the heat sink when $q_HS(t)$ is at its medium level and low level than when $q_HS(t)$ is at its high level. The small change in thermal energy indicates a smaller temperature oscillation, and the reason for seeing the high thermal energy when $q_HS(t)$ is at its medium and low levels can be explained by the slow thermal response due to the high thermal storage and low heat conductivity in the intermediate material around the heat source. From the flux in the y-direction, it can be seen that the flux in the upper half of the heat sink stays approximately the same over time, indicating that the heat transferred when $q_{HS}(t)$ is low must come from stored energy in the bottom half of the PCM heat sink.

For the optimised design based on Case 3, the thermal energy and the heat flux in the y-direction can be seen in Figure 16. Looking at the thermal energy, it can be seen that the thermal energy is stored much more evenly in the PCM when compared to the 20 s design. The majority of the stored thermal energy is located in the PCM at the sides and between the major fins close to the heat source. The fact that the PCM is placed closer to the heat source than in the Case 2 design makes sense, as the PCM needs to enter the

https://doi.org/10.3390/computation14010023

phase change temperature range before it obtains its increased thermal storage—whereas for Case 2, the full thermal storage potential is achieved at any temperature. From the flux in the y-direction, it can be seen that the flux in the upper half of the heat sink stays approximately the same over time, again indicating that the heat transferred when $q_{HS}(t)$ is low must come from stored energy in the bottom half of the PCM heat sink.

From the investigation of the optimised designs based on the quasi-steady-state, it is found that the amplitude of the temperature oscillation can be better reduced by only considering the quasi-steady-state as input to TO. This has the greatest impact on designs based on Case 2 and Case 3, which utilise a lot more of the PCM for storing thermal energy compared to the 20 s designs, resulting in a more even distribution of thermal energy and a lower final variance, ϕ. It is found that reaching the quasi-steady-state is computationally faster for Case 1 and Case 3, but took longer time for Case 2, when comparing the computation times from the TO of the 20 s designs.

5.3. Varying Time Step Sizes

Reaching the quasi-steady-state can take a very long simulation time, especially if the thermal storage is high, which increases the computational time. Therefore, the possibility of using varying time step sizes is investigated.

For this investigation, the simulation initially uses large time steps, scaled by the thermal diffusivity of the PCM, until the heat transfer rate over the cooling side has surpassed 95% of the average heat transfer from the heat source. At that point, the time step is reduced to the time steps size used in the other simulations and the simulation is run until the maximum relative change in the temperature oscillation period is below 1%. The initial large time step size is computed by the following expression:

$$\Delta t_{large} = L_y{}^2 \frac{\rho_{PCM} c_{pPCM}}{k_{TPCM}} \tag{20}$$

which characterises the diffusion time scale. As for the previous quasi-steady-state designs, T_{elec} from the last period is then used to calculate the variance, ϕ. In order to make comparisons, the TO is performed on the same three cases from earlier sections. The TO using the varying time step size takes 6 h for Case 1, 10 h for Case 2, and 13 h for Case 3 to produce the optimised results on a single core of an Intel Xeon Gold 6130 @ 2.776 GHz. This is equivalent to a 40% to 75% reduction in computational time compared to using a constant time step size. However, this speed-up comes at the cost of accuracy, as will be seen below.

Figure 17 shows the resulting optimised designs and their performances, compared to the optimised designs based on the quasi-steady-state from Section 5.2, which use a constant time step size. It can be seen that the topologies of the optimised designs are somewhat similar to their constant time step counterparts. However, there are significant differences in the amount of fins, placement of major fins, and the amount of intermediate material. Especially for the non-linear PCM case (Case 3), the degree of greyscale is significant for the constant time step case, whereas the adaptive time step case is significantly more discrete.

From the temperature signal over time, it can be seen that for Case 1 and Case 2 there is a good agreement in T_{elec} between the two methods for time stepping. However, for Case 3 there is a rather large difference, where the design based on varying time step sizes results in a higher average and a larger amplitude of the oscillation. This indicates that the more discrete design is actually a poorer-performing local minimum. This discrepancy is probably caused by the initial large time step size introducing a substantial error due to ignoring the full non-linearity introduced into the model with the apparent heat capacity method, as described in Section 2.5. This size of the discrepancy could be reduced by decreasing the large time step size, but this increases the computational time again and makes the varying time step size approach less effective. Overall, the simple adaptive scheme introduced herein cannot be recommended for the non-linear problem with PCM. More theoretically rigorous adaptivity should be considered in the future.

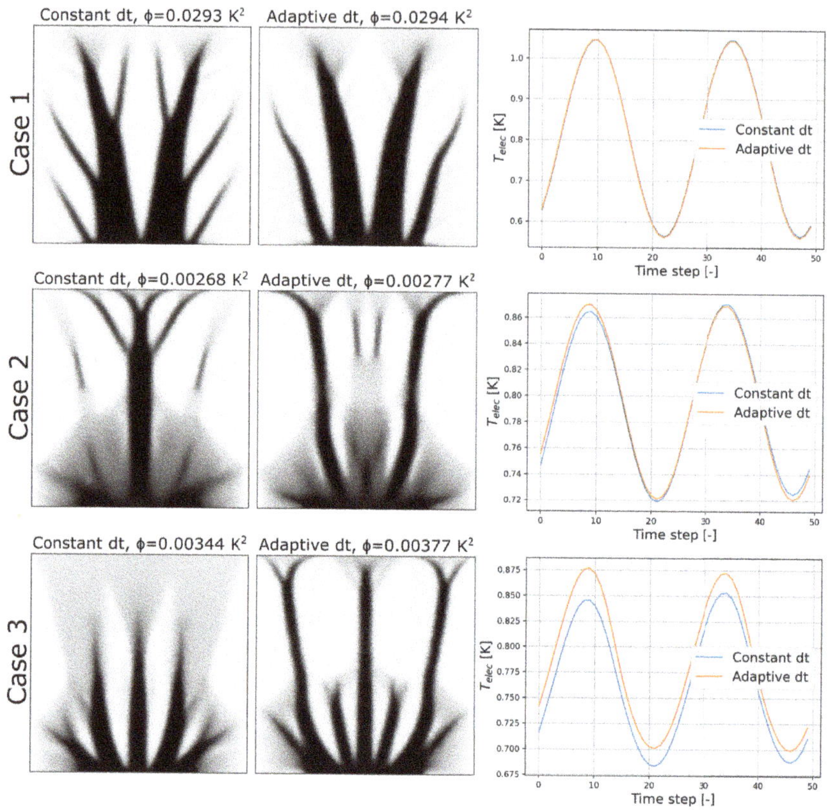

Figure 17. Optimised designs based on the quasi-steady-state with adaptive time step sizes compared to optimised designs based on the quasi-steady-state with a constant time step size for the three cases. The plots shows T_{elec} over time at the last two periods of the simulated time for the three cases.

5.4. *Effect of Forcing Discrete Designs*

Thus far, a composite material has been considered, where intermediate material density variables represent a porous HCM skeleton embedded with PCM. This causes the manufacturing to be more expensive, as it requires precise control of the density of an HCM foam to create such a composite material. Therefore, the effects of forcing discrete designs were investigated to see whether creating a more manufacturable design would be possible, without losing too much performance.

5.4.1. Explicit Penalisation

As briefly discussed in Section 2.2, classical material penalisation approaches, such as SIMP, cannot be applied successfully to the presented design problem. Thus, to push the optimised designs towards being discrete, the objective functional was modified using the following explicit penalty on the design variables:

$$f_0 = \phi + \alpha \int_{\Omega} \rho(1-\rho)dA \tag{21}$$

https://doi.org/10.3390/computation14010023

where α is the explicit penalisation factor, used to control the level of explicit penalisation. The integral $\int_\Omega \rho(1-\rho)dA$ has a minimum when ρ is equal to zero or one, whereby the non-discrete designs are penalised. It should be noted that the explicit penalty is applied on the mathematical design field, ρ, not the physical density field, $\tilde{\rho}$. This approach is prone to converge to poor local minima if the α value is set to high. Therefore, a continuation approach is used, where the optimisation is allowed to converge before the explicit penalisation factor, α, is gradually increased.

The non-discreteness of a design is quantified with the measure of non-discreteness, M_{nd}, defined by Sigmund [45] as the following functional:

$$M_{nd} = 100\frac{4\int_\Omega \rho(1-\rho)dA}{\int_\Omega 1dA} \tag{22}$$

This normalises the integral from (21) to be zero for an entirely discrete design and 100 for an entirely non-discrete design with $\rho = 0.5$.

5.4.2. Optimised Designs and Performance

In order to investigate the effect of removing the intermediate material, explicit penalisation is added to optimised designs based on the quasi-steady-state for all three cases, presented in Section 5.2. All optimisations reach the defined convergence criteria.

The resulting optimised designs can be seen in Figure 18. In general, it can be seen that the optimised designs become more discrete and simpler as the explicit penalisation factor α is increased. From the optimised designs, it can be seen that the smaller fins reaching into the PCM disappear and the HCM is moved to the major fin structures as explicit penalisation is increased. This makes sense, as the filter, in combination with a high penalisation of intermediate material, effectively penalises the boundary between the PCM and the HCM. It is found that for higher explicit penalisation factors, $\alpha > 10^0$, further penalisation does not cause any major design changes. Essentially, the explicit penalisation has a two-fold contribution towards manufacturability. Firstly, it reduces the amount of intermediate composite material, and secondly, it reduces the complexity of the design.

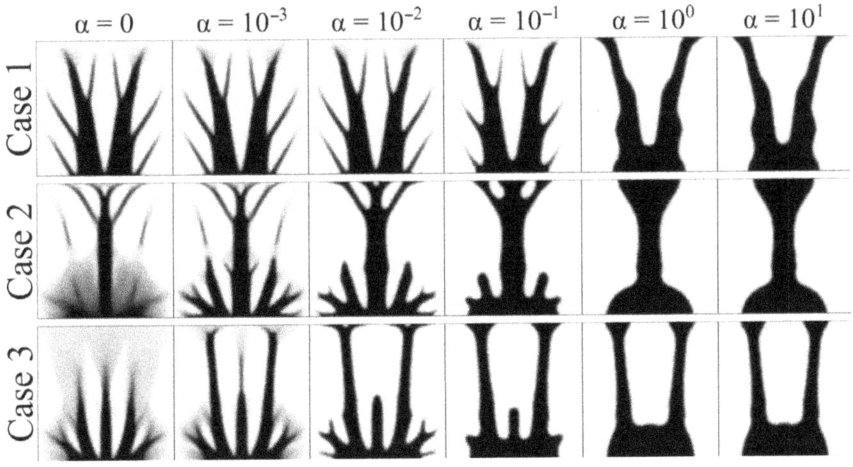

Figure 18. Overview of optimised designs for $t_{fin} = 20$ s of three different cases with varying amount of explicit penalisation.

To investigate the relation between the performance and explicit penalty, the variance, ϕ, was plotted against the measure of non-discreteness, M_{nd}, for the three cases, with different levels of explicit penalisation. The results can be seen in Figure 19 and show that ϕ generally increases as M_{nd} decreases towards the lower end. This is primarily because the complexity of the design is reduced significantly when the explicit penalty is high. It can be seen that the optimised designs can generally become more discrete without worsening the performance too much—and significantly so for Cases 2 and 3. By allowing a 10% increase in the variance, ϕ, from the optimised design without penalisation, the measure of non-discreteness, M_{nd}, can be reduced to $M_{nd} = 22$ with $\alpha = 10^{-1}$ for Case 1, $M_{nd} = 20$ with $\alpha = 10^{-2}$ for Case 2, and $M_{nd} = 22$ with $\alpha = 10^{-2}$ for Case 3.

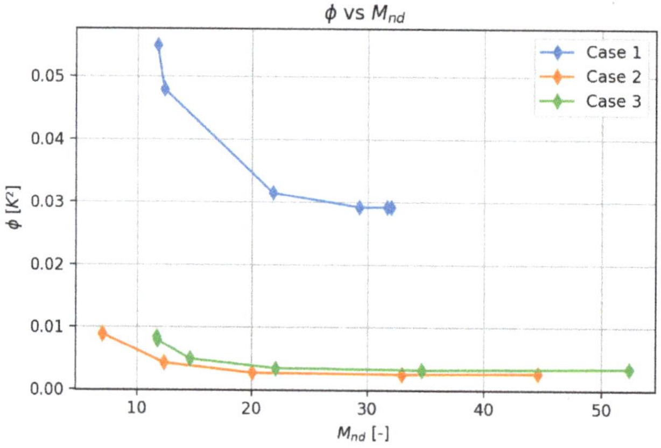

Figure 19. Variance in T_{elec}, ϕ, plotted against the measure of non-discreteness M_{nd} for the three cases.

To verify the optimised designs, a cross-check is performed, where the performance of the designs with varying explicit penalisation factors are tested. To attribute significance to design characteristics, the designs should perform best in the cases they were optimised for and worse in other cases, compared to the design that was optimised for that case. For the cross-check, $\alpha = [0, 10^{-1}, 10^{1}]$ were considered.

Table 6 shows that the majority of the optimised designs perform best in the cases that they were optimised for, indicating that the TO is effectively optimising the design in most cases. However, the optimised designs for Case 2 when $\alpha = 10^{-1}$ and $\alpha = 10^{1}$ are not the best performing designs when tested on Case 2. When $\alpha = 10^{-1}$, the design optimised for Case 3 performs slightly better than that for Case 2, and when $\alpha = 10^{1}$, both the designs optimised for Case 1 and Case 3 perform significantly better than that for Case 2. This indicates that the explicit penalisation results in the optimised design based on Case 2 being stuck at a local minimum. A cause for this could be that the initial design based on Case 2 only contains one major fin instead of two major fins found in the optimised designs based on Case 1 and Case 3. As the explicit penalisation removes the smaller fins close to the heat source, the contact boundary between the HCM and PCM is reduced, resulting in a reduction in the thermal storage capacity. As the two major fin designs have a larger contact boundary between the HCM and the PCM than a single major fin, it makes sense that the optimised designs based on Case 1 and Case 3 perform better than the optimised design based on Case 2, as the penalisation is increased. This local minimum may be avoided by using another continuation strategy.

https://doi.org/10.3390/computation14010023

Table 6. Results from cross-check, showing normalised ϕ for each design tried in three different cases: Case 1—No phase change and low c_{pPCM}; Case 2—No phase change and high c_{pPCM}; Case 3—With phase change. The designs are optimised using the quasi-steady-state.

Tested at	**Optimised for**								
	$\alpha = 0$			$\alpha = 10^{-1}$			$\alpha = 10^{1}$		
	Case 1	**Case 2**	**Case 3**	**Case 1**	**Case 2**	**Case 3**	**Case 1**	**Case 2**	**Case 3**
Case 1	1	1.39	1.26	1	2.02	1.61	1	1.48	1.05
Case 2	1.44	1	1.01	1.01	1	0.93	0.70	1	0.71
Case 3	1.32	1.36	1	1.02	1.35	1	1.12	1.52	1

6. Discussion

From the presented results, it can clearly be seen that it is possible to generate designs that reduce the temperature oscillation by applying TO to the layout of the PCM and the HCM. The results show that a PCM heat sink has the best performance in Case 2, indicating that actual PCM with phase change is not as effective at storing heat as a material with a constant higher heat capacity. However, in practice, not many materials have a heat capacity to match the thermal storage capacity equivalent to a material in phase change. So, the quest for the most optimal layout of PCM is still relevant. Furthermore, the effects of natural convection in the melted PCM are neglected in this paper, which results in a lower effective heat transfer through the PCM compared to the real world. This could further affect the ranking of PCM versus solid material with high heat capacity.

The physical model and material properties used to model the heat sink in this paper are purely academic, and the designs produced are therefore not directly applicable to any real-world problems. The reason for this was to investigate the effect of certain parameters in a systematic way. For real-world application, the PCM will most likely have a smaller phase change temperature range compared to the general temperature ranges and have a significantly higher latent heat of fusion, making the problem even more non-linear. For a real-world problem, the transient model is therefore expected to require significantly smaller time steps or solve the full non-linear system every time step. Both will increase the computational time significantly.

The computational times reported in this paper are relatively high (up to 40 h) for the relatively small models with only 40,000 nodes. Moving forwards, this can be sped up by running the TO code in parallel, but the limited size of the spatial discretisation limits the scalability. Furthermore, since the physical model requires a transient solver to model the phase change, the time stepping part of the code will inherently be serial, and, thus, the speed up from parallel computing will be limited to the scalability of the solver for each time step. The approach of using varying time step size shows some promise in reducing the computational time, but also shows an increase in error for the case of the phase change. This error could probably be reduced with a more sophisticated method of adapting the time step size.

7. Conclusions

This paper presented a framework for topology optimisation of the layout of PCM and HCM in heat sinks to reduce temperature oscillations in electronic components under cyclic thermal loads. Leveraging the thermal-buffering effect of PCM, optimised layouts achieved a 41% reduction in temperature variance over the full transient history and 32% in the quasi-steady regime.

The Python implementation combined FEniCS for transient thermal analysis, dolfin-adjoint for automatic sensitivity computation, and an open-source GCMMA solver for optimisation. The physical model treated the PCM heat sink as a transient thermal dif-

https://doi.org/10.3390/computation14010023

fusion problem, neglecting natural convection in the melted PCM. This is a significant simplification that introduces physical errors, but allows for efficient computations using a simplified model. Phase change was modelled using the apparent heat capacity method, and material interpolation employed an analytical homogenisation approach. The objective functional was defined as the temporal variance of the spatially averaged temperature at the electronic component.

Three cases were considered: Case 1 (no phase change, low c_{pPCM}), Case 2 (no phase change, high c_{pPCM}), and Case 3 (with phase change). Using the full 20 s time history, all optimised designs outperformed the initial layout. For Cases 2 and 3, improvements were achieved by reducing both oscillation amplitude and transient duration, making it difficult to isolate the effect of oscillation suppression alone. To address this, a second batch of optimisations focused on the quasi-steady-state cycle. Here, Case 2 showed a 78% reduction in variance, while Case 3 achieved 32%, confirming the importance of thermal storage capacity in minimising oscillations.

To reduce computational cost, a varying time-step approach was tested, cutting run-time by 40% for Case 2 and 75% for Case 3. However, this came at a significant expense of accuracy for Case 3. More advanced adaptive schemes could improve this trade-off in the future.

Finally, manufacturability was explored by introducing explicit penalisation to remove intermediate material. This produced near-discrete designs with only ∼10% performance loss, though smaller fin structures were eliminated as penalisation increased.

In summary, gradient-based topology optimisation can effectively tailor PCM-HCM layouts to mitigate temperature oscillations under cyclic loads. The greatest improvements were obtained when optimisation targeted the quasi-steady-state regime. The results highlight the critical role of thermal storage capacity and demonstrate practical strategies for balancing performance, manufacturability, and computational efficiency.

Future work should validate these findings experimentally, incorporate de-homogenised designs, and extend the framework to realistic material properties and boundary conditions for industrial applications.

Supplementary Materials: The following supporting information can be downloaded at https://www.mdpi.com/article/10.3390/computation14010023/s1, Figure S1: initialDesigns_energy, Figure S2: initialDesigns_fluxy, Figure S3: case1_20s_energy, Figure S4: case1_20s_fluxy, Figure S5: case2_20s_energy, Figure S6: case2_20s_fluxy, Figure S7: case3_20s_energy, Figure S8: case3_20s_fluxy, Figure S9: case1_qss_energy, Figure S10: case1_qss_fluxy, Figure S11: case2_qss_energy, Figure S12: case2_qss_fluxy, Figure S13: case3_qss_energy, Figure S14: case3_qss_fluxy.

Author Contributions: Conceptualisation, J.A.; methodology, M.B.M.C. and J.A.; software, M.B.M.C.; validation, M.B.M.C.; formal analysis, M.B.M.C. and J.A.; investigation, M.B.M.C. and J.A.; resources, J.A.; data curation, M.B.M.C.; writing—original draft preparation, M.B.M.C.; writing—review and editing, J.A. and M.B.M.C.; visualisation, M.B.M.C.; supervision, J.A.; project administration, J.A. All authors have read and agreed to the published version of the manuscript.

Funding: This research received no external funding.

Data Availability Statement: A minimal working example is available on GitHub: https://github.com/sdu-multiphysics/heatSinkPCM/ (accessed on 13 December 2025).

Acknowledgments: Part of the computations were performed on the UCloud interactive HPC system, which is managed by the eScience Center at the University of Southern Denmark.

Conflicts of Interest: The authors declare no conflicts of interest.

https://doi.org/10.3390/computation14010023

Appendix A. Simple Homogenisation-Based Parametrisation

Appendix A.1. Derivation of $k_T(\rho)$

The base cell can be viewed as a composite wall with one-dimensional heat transfer, based on the assumption that dominant heat transfer is along the fin direction. While two-dimensional effects exist in practise, the approach is intended as a computationally efficient surrogate.

Assuming one-directional heat transfer, the thermal conductivity k_T of the base cell can be derived as the total thermal resistance of the composite wall:

$$k_{Total} = \frac{L_{total}}{R_{total} A_{total}} \tag{A1}$$

where k_{Total} is the total thermal conductivity through the composite wall; R_{total} is the total thermal resistance; L_{total} is the total length of the composite wall in the direction of the heat transfer; and A_{total} is the total cross-sectional area of the wall.

In order to compute the total thermal resistance, the base cell is broken down into three distinct sections and their thermal resistances are computed; see Figure A1.

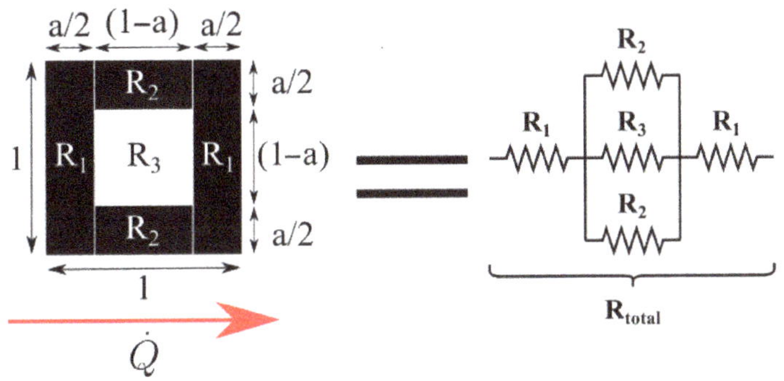

Figure A1. By assuming one-dimensional heat transfer, the base cell can be broken down into sections with their own thermal resistance. The red arrow shows the heat flux direction.

The thermal resistance depends on the material properties and dimensions of the section:

$$R = \frac{L}{kA} \tag{A2}$$

where L is the length in the direction of the heat transfer; k is the thermal conductivity; A is the cross-sectional area through which the heat transfer occurs. With this, the thermal resistances of the three sections are derived:

$$R_1 = \frac{\frac{a}{2}}{k_{THCM} 1 t_{bc}} \tag{A3}$$

$$R_2 = \frac{1-a}{k_{THCM}(\frac{a}{2}) t_{bc}} \tag{A4}$$

$$R_3 = \frac{1}{k_{TPCM} t_{bc}} \tag{A5}$$

where t_{bc} is the thickness of the base cell (out of plane dimension); and a is a parameter describing the amount of HCM.

https://doi.org/10.3390/computation14010023

The middle section of the composite wall consists of three sections in parallel; the equivalent resistance is expressed as

$$\frac{1}{R_{mid}} = \frac{1}{R_2} + \frac{1}{R_3} + \frac{1}{R_2} \quad \text{(A6)}$$

leading to:

$$R_{mid} = \frac{R_2 R_3}{2R_3 + R_2} \quad \text{(A7)}$$

Now the total thermal resistance can be considered as sections in series:

$$R_{total} = R_1 + R_{mid} + R_1 \quad \text{(A8)}$$

The total thermal conductivity becomes

$$k_{Total} = \frac{1}{(2R_1 + R_{mid})t_{bc}} \quad \text{(A9)}$$

which can be reduced to the following term where k_{Total} is dependent on a:

$$k_{Total}(a) = \frac{1}{\frac{a}{k_{THCM}} + \frac{1-a}{ak_{THCM}+(1-a)k_{TPCM}}} \quad \text{(A10)}$$

The relation between a and the ρ can be expressed by the following function:

$$\rho = 1 - (1-a)^2 \quad \text{(A11)}$$

from which it follows that

$$a = 1 - \sqrt{1-\rho} \quad \text{(A12)}$$

Combining (A12) into (A10), k_T can be expressed in terms of ρ:

$$k_T(\rho) = \frac{1}{\frac{1-\sqrt{1-\rho}}{k_{THCM}} + \frac{\sqrt{1-\rho}}{(1-\sqrt{1-\rho})k_{THCM}+(\sqrt{1-\rho})k_{TPCM}}} \quad \text{(A13)}$$

Appendix A.2. Verification of Homogenisation

To verify the accuracy of the above simple homogenisation approach, a test problem is computed using both full-scale and homogenised models. The problem is a 1×1 square with a heat flux along the lower half of the left-hand side and a fixed zero temperature along the right half of the top side. The size of the PCM inclusion, a, is set in both to be constant value of 0.5, as well as linearly increasing from the outer edge to the middle. The simulations are carried out in COMSOL Multiphysics [46].

Figure A2 shows the temperature fields, as well as flux arrows and temperature contours, for the two different designs. It can clearly be seen that the overall distributions are very similar for the full-scale and homogenised models. The homogenised model does predict lower temperatures at the heat source, meaning that it over-predicts the heat transfer abilities of the composite microstructure. However, the contour lines are incredibly similar in shape, with small variations in the full scale solution due to fully resolving the discontinuous material properties. Lastly, the flux vectors are also very similar in an average sense, but the homogenised model obviously does not capture small-scale variations in direction due to the homogenisation model—completely as expected.

Figure A3 shows the volume-averaged relative error between the full-scale and homogenised models for an increasing number of unit cells for various sizes of the PCM

https://doi.org/10.3390/computation14010023

inclusion. It can be seen that generally the error is below 14% when 20 × 20 unit cells are used. This is an acceptable accuracy given the high degree of qualitative agreement in the fields, as shown in Figure A2. The values of the temperatures do not matter too much, as long as the correct distributions and tendencies are observed. For the varying field, shown in Figure A2c,d, the volumetric-averaged relative error is only 4.9%. This lends credibility to the accuracy of the homogenised model even for varying fields, such as those resulting from TO.

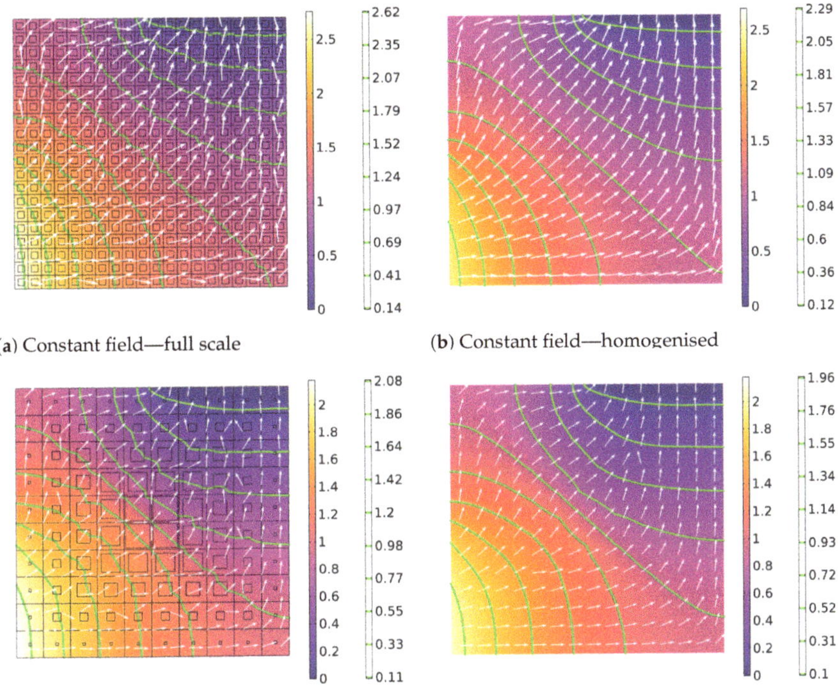

(**a**) Constant field—full scale

(**b**) Constant field—homogenised

(**c**) Varying field—full scale

(**d**) Varying field—homogenised

Figure A2. Temperature fields using full-scale and homogenised analysis for a design field with both constant and varying sizes of PCM inclusion. Fluxes are illustrated using white arrows and contour lines are shown in green.

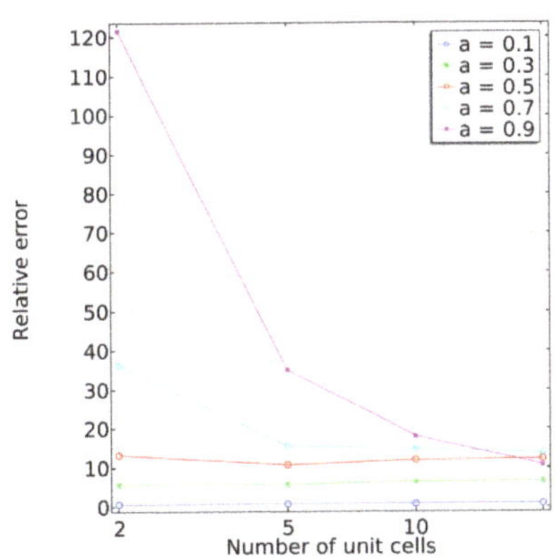

Figure A3. Volume-averaged relative error between full-scale and homogenised models for an increasing number of unit cells for various sizes of PCM inclusion.

https://doi.org/10.3390/computation14010023

Appendix B. Verification of Implementation

Appendix B.1. Comparison with COMSOL

To verify the implementation of the physical model in FEniCS, a 20 s simulation of a benchmark design was conducted and compared to results from the same model simulated with the commercial finite element programme COMSOL Multiphysics [46] using a non-linear solver. Figure A4 shows the design and results from the comparison. It was found that there is a good agreement between the results, with a maximum relative error of 1.451%, whereby the implementation of the physical model in FEniCS is considered verified.

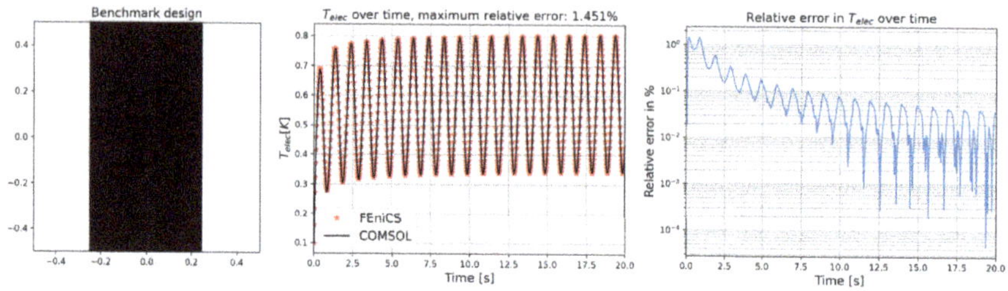

Figure A4. Verification of the implementation of the physical problem with FEniCS by comparison with COMSOL Multiphysics. The results are based on a $4 \times 100 \times 100$ mesh using a time step size of 0.02 s. Left: Design used as benchmark for the comparison. Middle: The temperature at the heat source, T_{elec}, over time. Right: The relative error of the temperature at the heat source, T_{elec}, over time.

The accuracy of the physical model largely depends on the choice of time step size, due to the highly non-linear smooth Heaviside step function used for the apparent heat capacity method and by the approximation of the non-linear physical model with a time-lagging one. However, the time step size also has a great impact on the computational time. Therefore, the effects of time step size on the error and computational time are investigated by comparing the results from FEniCS with varying time step sizes with the results from COMSOL using a much smaller time step size and a non-linear solver. For the FEniCS simulation, both the time-lagging and non-linear solver are also used to show the effects of using a time-lagging physical model. The result of this comparison is the maximum relative error in T_{elec} plotted against the time step size and computational time; see Figure A5.

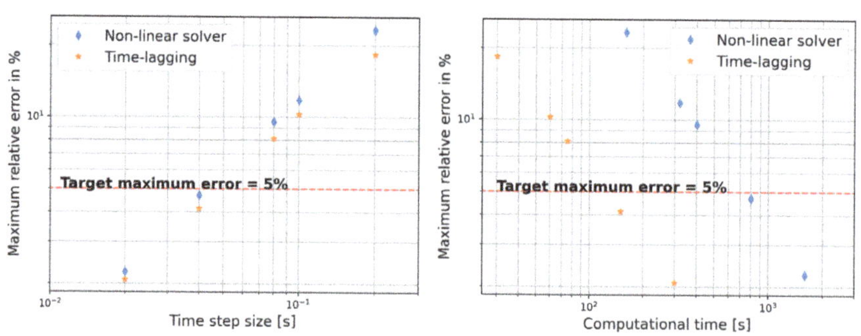

Figure A5. Investigation of maximum relative error in the temperature at the heat source T_{elec} for different time step sizes when comparing FEniCS simulations with a COMSOL simulation using a non-linear solver. The results are based on a COMSOL simulation using a time step size of 2×10^{-3}. Left: The error plotted against time step size. Right: The error plotted against computational time. The computational time is based on the average simulation time when the physical model is run on i7-1165G7 @ 2.80 GHz with 4 GB.

https://doi.org/10.3390/computation14010023

From Figure A5 it can be seen that the maximum relative error converges with a decrease in time step size, as there is a linear relationship between the time step size and maximum relative error in the log–log plot. It can be seen that the maximum relative error is similar when using a time-lagging and non-linear physical model when using the same time step size. Looking at the computational time for solving the physical model, the non-linear model is much more computationally expensive compared to the time-lagging model. In order to limit the computational time, a maximum relative error of 5% is deemed acceptable, whereby the time-lagging physical model with a time step size of 0.04 s is chosen for the simulation of the physical model when evaluating the designs for the TO.

Appendix B.2. Finite Difference Check

To verify the accuracy of the adjoint sensitivities, a finite difference check is performed using a central difference scheme. Figure A6 shows the relative error between the finite difference approximation and the adjoint sensitivity of the objective functional at element number 2400, $\frac{\partial f_0}{\partial \rho_{2400}}$, at different perturbation sizes. From Figure A6, it can be seen that the convergence rate for $\varepsilon \geq 10^{-3}$ agrees with the expected convergence rate of a central difference scheme of $\approx O(\varepsilon^2)$ [47]. For perturbation size $\varepsilon < 10^{-3}$, the rounding errors become significant, which increases the relative error. This relation between perturbation size and error is well known in finite difference approximations and is called "step-size dilemma" [47]. Conducting finite difference checks for additional element numbers showed that the tendencies seen in $\frac{\partial f_0}{\partial \rho_{2400}}$ are representative of all elements. As the convergence rate for $\varepsilon \geq 10^{-3}$ matches the expected convergence rate for the central difference scheme and the relative error is small, the implementation of the adjoint method is considered verified.

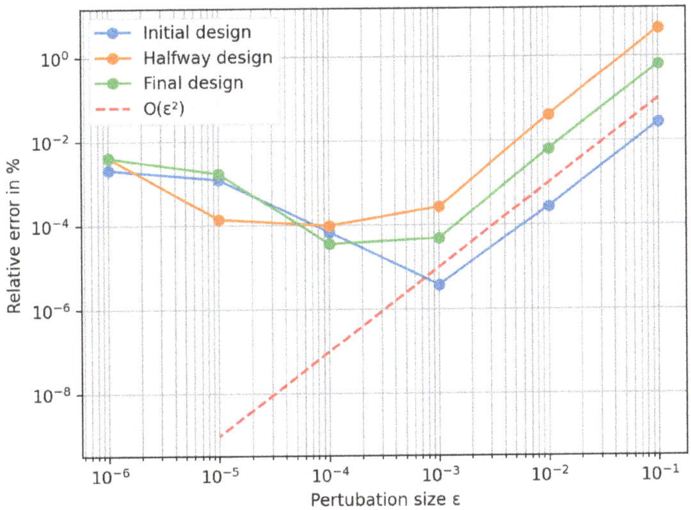

Figure A6. Finite difference check, showing the relative error between the adjoint sensitivity computed with dolfin-adjoint and central difference scheme at different perturbation sizes at different stages of the optimisation. The expected convergence rate of a central difference scheme $O(\varepsilon^2)$ is plotted for reference. The optimisation is based on a $4 \times 40 \times 40$ mesh.

References

1. Depiver, J.a.; Mallik, S.; Harmanto, D. Solder joint failures under thermo-mechanical loading conditions—A review. *Adv. Mater. Process. Technol.* **2021**, *7*, 1–26. [CrossRef]
2. Sahoo, S.K.; Das, M.K.; Rath, P. Application of TCE-PCM based heat sinks for cooling of electronic components: A review. *Renew. Sustain. Energy Rev.* **2016**, *59*, 550–582. [CrossRef]

https://doi.org/10.3390/computation14010023

3. Kalbasi, R.; Afrand, M.; Alsarraf, J.; Tran, M.D. Studies on optimum fins number in PCM-based heat sinks. *Energy* **2019**, *171*, 1088–1099. [CrossRef]
4. Guibert, A.T.R.; Bookwala, M.; Kim, H.A. Level-set topology optimization of heat sinks with phase-change material. *Int. J. Heat Mass Transf.* **2024**, *231*, 125818. [CrossRef]
5. Guibert, A.T.; Bookwala, M.; Kim, A.A., Design of Electric Aircraft Battery Packs Embedded With Phase-Change Material via Level-Set Topology Optimization. In Proceedings of the AIAA SCITECH 2025 Forum, Orlando, FL, USA, 6–10 January 2025. [CrossRef]
6. Hosseinizadeh, S.; Tan, F.; Moosania, S. Experimental and numerical studies on performance of PCM-based heat sink with different configurations of internal fins. *Appl. Therm. Eng.* **2011**, *31*, 3827–3838. [CrossRef]
7. Dbouk, T. A review about the engineering design of optimal heat transfer systems using topology optimization. *Appl. Therm. Eng.* **2017**, *112*, 841–854. [CrossRef]
8. Alexandersen, J.; Andreasen, C.S. A Review of Topology Optimisation for Fluid-Based Problems. *Fluids* **2020**, *5*, 29. [CrossRef]
9. Fawaz, A.; Hua, Y.; Le Corre, S.; Fan, Y.; Luo, L. Topology optimization of heat exchangers: A review. *Energy* **2022**, *252*, 124053. [CrossRef]
10. Varanasi, S.; Ananthasuresh, G.K. Analysis and Topology Optimization of Heat Sinks with a Phase- Change Material on COMSOL Multiphysics^{TM} Platform. In Proceedings of the COMSOL Users Conference 2006, Bangalore, India, 7 November 2006.
11. Ho, J.; See, Y.; Leong, K.; Wong, T. An experimental investigation of a PCM-based heat sink enhanced with a topology-optimized tree-like structure. *Energy Convers. Manag.* **2021**, *245*, 114608. [CrossRef]
12. See, Y.; Ho, J.; Leong, K.; Wong, T. Experimental investigation of a topology-optimized phase change heat sink optimized for natural convection. *Appl. Energy* **2022**, *314*, 118984. [CrossRef]
13. Iradukunda, A.C.; Vargas, A.; Huitink, D.; Lohan, D. Transient thermal performance using phase change material integrated topology optimized heat sinks. *Appl. Therm. Eng.* **2020**, *179*, 115723. [CrossRef]
14. Bianco, N.; Fragnito, A.; Iasiello, M.; Mauro, G.M. Design of PCM-based heat sinks through topology optimization. *J. Phys. Conf. Ser.* **2023**, *2509*, 012001. [CrossRef]
15. Christensen, M.B.M.; Alexandersen, J. Topology optimisation of heat sinks embedded with phase-change material for minimising temperature oscillations. *HAL* **2023**, hal-04185641. Available online: https://hal.science/hal-04185641v1/ (accessed on 13 December 2025).
16. Christensen, M.B.M.; Alexandersen, J. Online Resource, heatSinkPCM Code at GitHub. 2023. Available online: https://github.com/sdu-multiphysics/heatSinkPCM/ (accessed on 12 January 2026).
17. Pizzolato, A.; Sharma, A.; Maute, K.; Sciacovelli, A.; Verda, V. Topology optimization for heat transfer enhancement in Latent Heat Thermal Energy Storage. *Int. J. Heat Mass Transf.* **2017**, *113*, 875–888. [CrossRef]
18. Pizzolato, A.; Sharma, A.; Maute, K.; Sciacovelli, A.; Verda, V. Design of effective fins for fast PCM melting and solidification in shell-and-tube latent heat thermal energy storage through topology optimization. *Appl. Energy* **2017**, *208*, 210–227. [CrossRef]
19. Pizzolato, A.; Sharma, A.; Ge, R.; Maute, K.; Verda, V.; Sciacovelli, A. Maximization of performance in multi-tube latent heat storage—Optimization of fins topology, effect of materials selection and flow arrangements. *Energy* **2020**, *203*, 114797. [CrossRef]
20. Zhao, M.; Tian, Y.; Hu, M.; Zhang, F.; Yang, M. Topology optimization of fins for energy storage tank with phase change material. *Numer. Heat Transf. Part A Appl.* **2020**, *77*, 284–301. [CrossRef]
21. Yao, Q.; Zhao, C.; Zhao, Y.; Wang, H.; Li, W. Topology optimization for heat transfer enhancement in latent heat storage. *Int. J. Therm. Sci.* **2021**, *159*, 106578. [CrossRef]
22. Tian, Y.; Liu, X.; Xu, Q.; Luo, Q.; Zheng, H.; Song, C.; Zhu, Z.; Gao, K.; Dang, C.; Wang, H.; et al. Bionic topology optimization of fins for rapid latent heat thermal energy storage. *Appl. Therm. Eng.* **2021**, *194*, 117104. [CrossRef]
23. Laasri, I.A.; Elmaazouzi, Z.; Outzourhit, A.; Mghazli, M.O. Investigation of different topology-optimized fin structures in a cylindrical latent heat thermal energy storage unit. *Therm. Sci. Eng. Prog.* **2022**, *33*, 101372. [CrossRef]
24. Peremans, B.; Blommaert, M.; Baelmans, M. Topology optimization of a rectangular phase change material module. *J. Energy Storage* **2023**, *70*, 107891. [CrossRef]
25. Zhang, X.; Yang, X.; Zhang, Y.; Xu, J.; Guo, X. Phase change heat transfer enhancement based on topology optimization of fin structure. *Int. J. Heat Mass Transf.* **2023**, *214*, 124402. [CrossRef]
26. Alnæs, M.; Blechta, J.; Hake, J.; Johansson, A.; Kehlet, B.; Logg, A.; Richardson, C.; Ring, J.; Rognes, M.E.; Wells, G.N. The FEniCS Project Version 1.5. *Arch. Numer. Softw.* **2015**, *3*, 9–23. [CrossRef]
27. Logg, A.; Mardal, K.A.; Wells, G. (Eds.) *Automated Solution of Differential Equations by the Finite Element Method: The FEniCS Book*; Lecture Notes in Computational Science and Engineering; Springer: Berlin/Heidelberg, Germany, 2012; Volume 84. [CrossRef]
28. Laurain, A. A level set-based structural optimization code using FEniCS. *Struct. Multidiscip. Optim.* **2018**, *58*, 1311–1334. [CrossRef]
29. Qian, X. Undercut and overhang angle control in topology optimization: A density gradient based integral approach. *Int. J. Numer. Methods Eng.* **2017**, *111*, 247–272. [CrossRef]

https://doi.org/10.3390/computation14010023

30. Mezzadri, F.; Bouriakov, V.; Qian, X. Topology optimization of self-supporting support structures for additive manufacturing. *Addit. Manuf.* **2018**, *21*, 666–682. [CrossRef]
31. Yan, J.; Xiang, R.; Kamensky, D.; Tolley, M.T.; Hwang, J.T. Topology optimization with automated derivative computation for multidisciplinary design problems. *Struct. Multidiscip. Optim.* **2022**, *65*, 151. [CrossRef]
32. Jauregui, C.M.; Hyun, J.; Neofytou, A.; Gray, J.S.; Kim, H.A. Avoiding reinventing the wheel: reusable open-source topology optimization software. *Struct. Multidiscip. Optim.* **2023**, *66*, 145. [CrossRef]
33. Jia, Y.; Wang, C.; Zhang, X.S. FEniTop: A simple FEniCSx implementation for 2D and 3D topology optimization supporting parallel computing. *Struct. Multidiscip. Optim.* **2024**, *67*, 140. [CrossRef]
34. Jegadheeswaran, S.; Pohekar, S.D. Performance enhancement in latent heat thermal storage system: A review. *Renew. Sustain. Energy Rev.* **2009**, *13*, 2225–2244. [CrossRef]
35. Sigmund, O.; Petersson, J. Numerical instabilities in topology optimization: A survey on procedures dealing with checkerboards, mesh-dependencies and local minima. *Struct. Optim.* **1998**, *16*, 68–75. [CrossRef]
36. Lazarov, B.S.; Wang, F.; Sigmund, O. Length scale and manufacturability in density-based topology optimization. *Arch. Appl. Mech.* **2016**, *86*, 189–218. [CrossRef]
37. Lazarov, B.S.; Sigmund, O. Filters in topology optimization based on Helmholtz-type differential equations. *Int. J. Numer. Methods Eng.* **2011**, *86*, 765–781. [CrossRef]
38. Michaleris, P.; Tortorelli, D.A.; Vidal, C.A. Tangent operators and design sensitivity formulations for transient non-linear coupled problems with applications to elastoplasticity. *Int. J. Numer. Methods Eng.* **1994**, *37*, 2471–2499. [CrossRef]
39. Choi, K.K.; Kim, N.H. *Structural Sensitivity Analysis and Optimization 1*; Mechanical Engineering Series; Springer: New York, NY, USA, 2005. [CrossRef]
40. Mitusch, S.; Funke, S.; Dokken, J. dolfin-adjoint 2018.1: Automated adjoints for FEniCS and Firedrake. *J. Open Source Softw.* **2019**, *4*, 1292. [CrossRef]
41. Svanberg, K. A Class of Globally Convergent Optimization Methods Based on Conservative Convex Separable Approximations. *SIAM J. Optim.* **2002**, *12*, 555–573. [CrossRef]
42. Deetman, A. GCMMA-MMA-Python. 2020. Available online: https://github.com/arjendeetman/GCMMA-MMA-Python (accessed on 3 October 2022).
43. Hirschey, J.; Gluesenkamp, K.R.; Mallow, A.; Graham, S. Review of Inorganic Salt Hydrates with Phase Change Temperature in Range of 5°C to 60°C and Material Cost Comparison with Common Waxes. In Proceedings of the 5th International High Performance Buildings Conference at Purdue, West Lafayette, IN, USA, 9–12 July 2018.
44. Kraiem, M.; Karkri, M.; Fois, M.; Sobolciak, P. Thermophysical Characterization of Paraffins versus Temperature for Thermal Energy Storage. *Buildings* **2023**, *13*, 877. [CrossRef]
45. Sigmund, O. Morphology-based black and white filters for topology optimization. *Struct. Multidiscip. Optim.* **2007**, *33*, 401–424. [CrossRef]
46. *COMSOL Multiphysics*, version 6; Software for Multiphysics Simulation; COMSOL AB: Stockholm, Sweden, 2023.
47. Haftka, R.T.; Gürdal, Z. *Elements of Structural Optimization*, 3rd rev. and expanded ed.; Number v. 11 in Solid Mechanics and Its Applications; Kluwer Academic Publishers: Dordrecht, The Netherlands; Boston, MA, USA, 1992.

https://doi.org/10.3390/computation14010023

computation

MDPI

Article

Multifidelity Topology Design for Thermal–Fluid Devices via SEMDOT Algorithm

Yiding Sun [1], Yun-Fei Fu [2], Shuzhi Xu [3,*] and Yifan Guo [1,*]

[1] Department of Mechanical Engineering, University of Alberta, Edmonton, AB T6G 1H9, Canada; yiding1@ualberta.ca
[2] College of Mechanical and Electronic Engineering, Shandong University of Science and Technology, Qingdao 266590, China; yunfei.fu@sdust.edu.cn
[3] Department of Mechanical Engineering, Graduate School of Engineering, The University of Osaka, 2-1, Yamadaoka, Suita 565-0871, Osaka, Japan
* Correspondence: xu@syd.mech.eng.osaka-u.ac.jp (S.X.); guo15@ualberta.ca (Y.G.)

Abstract

Designing thermal–fluid devices that reduce peak temperature while limiting pressure loss is challenging because high-fidelity (HF) Navier–Stokes–convection simulations make direct HF-driven topology optimization computationally expensive. This study presents a two-dimensional, steady, laminar multifidelity topology design framework for thermal–fluid devices operating in a low-to-moderate Reynolds number regime. A computationally efficient low-fidelity (LF) Darcy–convection model is used for topology optimization, where SEMDOT decouples geometric smoothness from the analysis field to produce CAD-ready boundaries. The LF optimization minimizes a P-norm aggregated temperature subject to a prescribed volume fraction constraint; the inlet–outlet pressure difference and the P-norm parameter are varied to generate a diverse candidate set. All candidates are then evaluated using a steady incompressible HF Navier–Stokes–convection model in COMSOL 6.3 under a consistent operating condition (fixed flow; pressure drop reported as an output). In representative single- and multi-channel case studies, SEMDOT designs reduce the HF peak temperature (e.g., ~337 K to ~323 K) while also reducing the pressure drop (e.g., ~18.7 Pa to ~12.6 Pa) relative to conventional straight-channel layouts under the same operating point. Compared with a conventional RAMP-based pipeline under the tested settings, the proposed approach yields a more favorable Pareto distribution (normalized hypervolume 1.000 vs. 0.923).

Keywords: topology optimization; multifidelity design; heat transfer; pressure drop; CAD reconstruction; SEMDOT

1. Introduction

Heat transfer devices such as cooling channels and heat sinks are crucial to thermal management across electronics, power systems, and advanced manufacturing. As heat fluxes rise with device miniaturization and performance demands, there is growing pressure to design flow–thermal architectures that simultaneously enhance heat removal and contain hydraulic losses [1–3].

Topology optimization (TO) seeks the optimal distribution of material and void within a prescribed design domain to satisfy performance requirements under given constraints, enabling radical topological changes (such as hole creation and merging) beyond traditional shape or size optimization [4–8] and achieve superior bio-inspired design [9].

Originating with the seminal work of Bendsøe and Kikuchi [10] and later generalized to multiple physics [11–16], TO has evolved over the past few decades into a rich family of methods, including the classical density-based approach [6], level-set methods [17–19], bi-directional evolutionary structural optimization (BESO) [20–22], and moving morphable components (MMCs) [23–25]. Despite these advances, TO was long criticized for producing "organic" geometries that were difficult to fabricate by conventional means [26–28]. With the advent of additive manufacturing, however, such freeform structures have become increasingly realizable in practice, catalyzing renewed development and broader application of TO [29–31].

For thermal–fluid problems in TO, directly solving the steady Navier–Stokes equations coupled with convection–diffusion during optimization is often prohibitive [32]; thus, low-fidelity (LF) Darcy–convection surrogates are commonly employed to explore designs efficiently [33–35], while high-fidelity (HF) evaluations are reserved for accurate flow–thermal assessment and final selection. Nonetheless, a modeling gap typically persists between LF and HF formulations—particularly regarding near-wall transport and flow structures—which can impair the direct transfer of LF-optimized designs. Addressing such gaps calls for a multifidelity strategy that encourages broad yet physically meaningful exploration at low cost, followed by rigorous HF screening.

Multifidelity topology design (MFTD) [36–38] provides such a pathway by embedding TO within the broader concept of multifidelity optimization (MFO). MFO combines models of differing fidelity to manage computational cost without sacrificing solution quality and has attracted attention in structural and multidisciplinary optimization [39–41]. While function-based surrogates (e.g., polynomial regression, Kriging, radial basis functions, and support vector regression) are effective for low-dimensional global search [42], their scalability is limited by the high number of design variables inherent to TO. MFTD circumvents this limitation by using LF physics models to generate diverse topology candidates and HF analyses to score and select them; hence, handling high-dimensional design spaces is more effective than conventional function surrogates.

Most LF implementations rely on the density method with penalization (SIMP), which enforces near-binary designs via power-law interpolations between elemental densities and material properties. Since the same element field serves both finite element analysis (FEA) and boundary formation, SIMP often yields blurry, staircase-like interfaces that require shape optimization or other post-processing to recover accurate boundaries [6]. Level-set approaches can produce sharp boundaries, but performance can be sensitive to initialization [43,44]. To provide a more easy-to-use, flexible, and efficient platform, Fu et al. [45,46] proposed the Smooth-Edged Material Distribution for Optimizing Topology (SEMDOT) approach, which combines the smooth geometric representation with the robustness and efficiency of density-based updates. By decoupling geometric smoothness from the analysis density field, SEMDOT yields crisp, CAD-ready boundaries while preserving the computational advantages of density-based TO.

In summary, while Darcy-based LF thermal–fluid topology optimization followed by HF validation is validated, existing pipelines commonly adopt density-based formulations in the LF stage, which often yield blurry or staircase-like material interfaces. Such artifacts typically require post-processing to recover accurate, manufacturable boundaries, thereby introducing additional uncertainty in geometry transfer and HF remeshing. To address this limitation, we integrate SEMDOT into the LF stage to decouple boundary representation from the analysis field, producing smooth, CAD-ready boundaries that can be transferred to HF evaluation in a more direct and robust manner. The main contributions of this work are summarized as follows:

https://doi.org/10.3390/computation14010019

- Proposing an SEMDOT-based multifidelity TO pipeline for thermal–fluid design that couples an efficient Darcy–convection LF model with Navier–Stokes–convection HF verification, achieving a practical balance between scalability and fidelity.
- Introducing a seeding strategy tailored to thermal–fluid objectives, using inlet pressure and P-norm aggregation as levers to generate diverse, high-potential LF designs that transfer effectively to HF evaluation.
- Demonstrating the framework on representative single- and multi-channel problems, showing improved thermal uniformity and reduced peak temperature at competitive or lower pressure drops, as well as discussions on how multifidelity selection consolidates these gains.

The remainder of the paper is organized as follows. Section 2 presents the governing equations for the HF and LF models. Section 3 describes the SEMDOT representation and multifidelity optimization workflow with seeding. Section 4 details the optimization problem and objective aggregation. Section 5 reports the numerical studies and compares the LF–HF results, followed by the conclusions and outlook in Section 6.

2. Governing Equations

In the design of thermal–fluid devices, high-fidelity models are often required to accurately capture the underlying physics. For instance, the incompressible steady Navier–Stokes equations, coupled with the convection–diffusion heat transfer formulation, are capable of fully representing the essential phenomena of laminar flow and thermal transport. However, employing such models directly in TO is not computationally affordable due to the significant cost associated with repeatedly solving the coupled nonlinear equations. To alleviate this, a multifidelity optimization framework is adopted. Specifically, a low-fidelity model based on Darcy's law for fluid transport combined with the convection–diffusion formulation for heat transfer is utilized during the optimization process, providing a computationally efficient yet physically meaningful approximation. The optimized designs are subsequently validated using the high-fidelity Navier–Stokes (NS) equations model, thereby ensuring both efficiency in the design process and reliability of the final solutions. The schematic illustration of multifidelity topology design is shown in Figure 1.

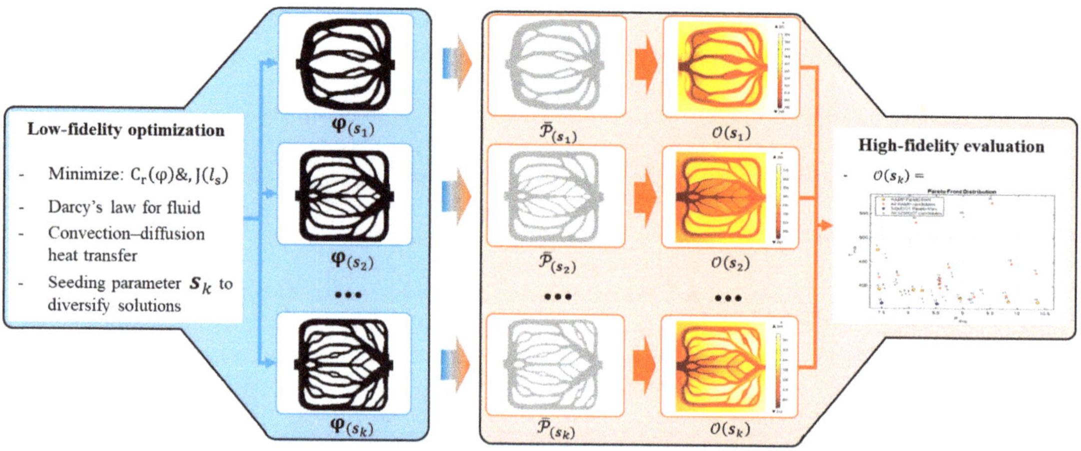

Figure 1. Schematic illustration of multifidelity topology design.

https://doi.org/10.3390/computation14010019

2.1. High-Fidelity Governing Equations

In this work, it is assumed that the designed heat-dissipating components are relatively small in size, and the inlet velocity of the coolant is low. Consequently, the overall Reynolds number of the device remains in a low range. The high-fidelity model employed in this study is based on the incompressible steady-state NS equations coupled with the convection–diffusion equation for heat transfer. The governing equations for the fluid flow are given as follows [47]:

$$\rho(\mathbf{u}\cdot\nabla)\mathbf{u} = -\nabla P + \mu\nabla^2\mathbf{u} \tag{1}$$

where the Equation (1) indicates the momentum conservation equation, $\mathbf{u}$ denotes the velocity vector field of the fluid, and P is the static pressure. The material parameters include the density ρ and the dynamic viscosity μ. It is noted that Equation (1) should be coupled with the continuity equation to make sure the mass conservation:

$$\nabla\cdot\mathbf{u} = 0 \tag{2}$$

The NS equations describe laminar fluid motion by accounting for the balance among inertial, viscous, and pressure forces. Due to the presence of the convective term $\rho(\mathbf{u}\cdot\nabla)\mathbf{u}$, the equations are highly nonlinear. As a result, the solution cannot rely on the principle of superposition and typically requires iterative numerical methods.

For the modeling of heat transfer, the convection–diffusion equation is employed, which captures both advective transport driven by the flow field and conductive diffusion within the medium. The governing equation is given as follows:

$$\rho C_p\mathbf{u}\cdot\nabla T = k\nabla^2 T + Q \tag{3}$$

where T represents the temperature field. The material parameters include the material density ρ, the specific heat capacity C_p, and the thermal conductivity k. The source term Q represents internal heat generation, if present. It should be mentioned that Equations (1)–(3) provide a comprehensive representation of the coupled fluid–thermal behavior in thermal–fluid devices.

2.2. Low-Fidelity Governing Equations

To improve computational efficiency during optimization, a low-fidelity model is adopted in which the fluid motion is governed by Darcy's law rather than the full NS equations. Darcy's formulation assumes a linear relation between the fluid velocity and the pressure gradient, i.e.,

$$\mathbf{u} = -\frac{\kappa}{\mu}\nabla P \tag{4}$$

where κ is the permeability of the porous medium and μ is the fluid viscosity. Inserting this into the continuity equation (Equation (2)) and by ignoring the body force term yields the following model:

$$\nabla\cdot\left(-\frac{\kappa}{\mu}\nabla P\right) = 0 \tag{5}$$

Compared with the full NS equations, the Darcy model eliminates the nonlinear convective acceleration term $\boldsymbol{\rho}(\mathbf{u}\cdot\nabla)\mathbf{u}$ and neglects the detailed resolution of velocity boundary layers. The equation thereby degenerates into a linear elliptic form, which significantly reduces the computational complexity of the solution process. This simplification is reasonable in the present context because the main role of the flow model in the optimization process is to provide an approximate transport mechanism for heat convection,

https://doi.org/10.3390/computation14010019

rather than resolving fine-scale flow structures. Based on the above Darcy flow model, the convective heat transfer model thereby becomes [48] the following:

$$\rho C_p\left(-\frac{\kappa}{\mu}\nabla P\right)\cdot\nabla T = k\nabla^2 T + Q \tag{6}$$

It should be emphasized that this Darcy–convection model is adopted as a low-fidelity transport surrogate and is most appropriate when inertia is secondary at the surrogate scale. If the framework is extended to higher Reynolds numbers where transitional/turbulent effects, separation, and strong inertial transport become important, the Darcy approximation may no longer provide a reliable ranking of candidates. In such regimes, HF validation would require turbulence modeling and potentially unsteady simulations, and the LF surrogate would need to be upgraded (e.g., Brinkman/Forchheimer-type corrections or an NS/Stokes-based penalization model) to preserve LF→HF transferability.

3. Framework of SEMDOT Method

3.1. Formulation of SEMDOT

In the conventional density-based topology optimization framework, the material properties in the governing equations introduced in the previous section are described using a continuous density field φ, which is fully coupled with the finite element mesh. In this context, $\varphi = 1$ denotes a fluid region, while $\varphi = 0$ corresponds to a solid region. The primary motivation for introducing a continuous design variable—typically constrained within the interval [0,1]—is to transform the original discrete 0–1 combinatorial optimization problem into a continuous and differentiable one. This relaxation significantly reduces computational complexity by avoiding the combinatorial explosion inherent to discrete formulations. More importantly, it enables the objective function and constraints to become differentiable with respect to the design variables, allowing the use of sensitivity analysis in conjunction with efficient gradient-based optimization algorithms.

Typically, in the context of the Darcy equation, the relationship between the density variable and the permeability κ of the porous medium is established using the Rational Approximation of Material Properties (RAMP) interpolation scheme [49,50]:

$$\kappa = \kappa_f + (\kappa_s - \kappa_f)\frac{1-\varphi}{(1+q_\kappa\varphi)} \tag{7}$$

In this formulation, κ_s and κ_f denote the permeabilities of the solid and fluid phases, respectively, while q_κ is the corresponding penalization factor that controls the convexity of the interpolation. The fluid viscosity μ is assumed to be constant throughout the domain. Similarly, for the convection–diffusion equation governing heat transfer, a RAMP interpolation scheme is also employed to relate the density variable to the thermal conductivity k:

$$k = k_f + (k_s - k_f)\frac{1-\varphi}{(1+q_k\varphi)} \tag{8}$$

where k_s and k_f represent the thermal conductivities of the solid and fluid phases, respectively, while q_k is the penalization factor controlling the interpolation convexity. In contrast, for the material density ρ and the specific heat capacity C_p, simple linear interpolation schemes are adopted due to their relatively weaker influence on the overall optimization results:

$$\rho = \rho_s + (\rho_f - \rho_s)\varphi \tag{9}$$

$$C_p = C_{pf} + (C_{ps} - C_{pf})(1-\varphi) \tag{10}$$

https://doi.org/10.3390/computation14010019

where ρ is the effective density, ρ_s and ρ_f are the densities of the solid and fluid phases, respectively, C_p is the effective specific heat capacity, and C_{ps} and C_{pf} denote the specific heat capacities of the solid and fluid phases. From Equations (7)–(10), the limiting cases can be verified explicitly as follows:

$$\varphi \to 0 : (\kappa, k, \rho, C_p) \to (\kappa_s, k_s, \rho_s, C_{ps}), \quad \varphi \to 1 : (\kappa, k, \rho, C_p) \to (\kappa_f, k_f, \rho_f, C_{pf}) \tag{11}$$

These limits confirm that the interpolations are consistent with the definition $\varphi = 0$ (solid) and $\varphi = 1$ (fluid).

However, due to the resolution limitation imposed by the finite element mesh, the resulting topology often exhibits jagged, staircase-like boundaries. Such artifacts significantly hinder the quality of the final geometric representation and pose challenges for downstream applications such as CAD reconstruction and manufacturing. To address this issue and to produce a smooth and well-defined structural boundary, the SEMDOT method, whose smooth boundary strategy is demonstrated in Figure 2, is selected for this work.

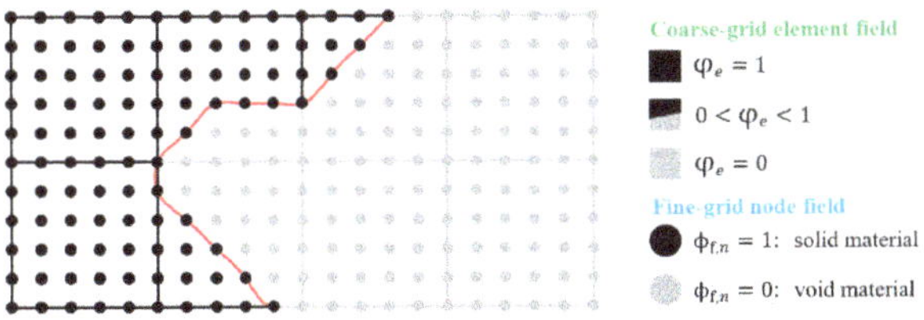

Figure 2. An illustration of the SEMDOT method.

One of the most elegant aspects of the SEMDOT framework lies in its moderate decoupling of the geometric representation (i.e., fine-grid node field $\phi_f \in \mathbb{R}^{N_f}$) and the finite element analysis (FEA) density field (i.e., coarse-grid element field $\varphi \in \mathbb{R}^{N_c}$). In this framework, the low-dimensional density field φ is used for the most computationally intensive tasks, including forward FEA, backward sensitivity analysis, and optimization updates via gradient-based solvers. The coarse-grid element field φ will be firstly smoothed by a convolution filter to avoid some numerical issues like the checkerboard phenomenon:

$$\tilde{\varphi}_m = \frac{1}{\sum_{e \in \mathcal{R}_m} \mathcal{H}_{me}} \sum_{e \in \mathcal{R}_m} \mathcal{H}_{me} \varphi_e \tag{12}$$

where $\mathcal{R}_m$ is the set of elements e for which the center-to-center distance $\Delta(m, e)$ to the element. It is noted that m is smaller than the filter radius $r_{\min}$, and $\mathcal{H}_{me}$ is a weight factor defined as follows:

$$\mathcal{H}_{me} = \max(0, r_{\min} - \Delta(m, e)) \tag{13}$$

After that, the smoothed distribution $\tilde{\varphi}$ is mapped onto the fine-grid ϕ_f, which provides a more refined representation capable of capturing intricate geometrical details. This mapping is carried out using bi-cubic interpolation, where the density value at the fine grid for the nth node x_n is computed as a weighted combination of the values at the surrounding coarse-grid element:

$$\phi_{f,n} = \sum_{m \in \mathcal{N}_n} N(x_n) \tilde{\varphi}_m \tag{14}$$

where $\tilde{\varphi}_m$ denotes the density value at the coarse-grid element m, $N(x_n)$ represents the corresponding bi-cubic interpolation basis function, and $\mathcal{N}_m$ is the set of the neighboring coarse-grid element index associated with the fine-grid node x_n. To alleviate the staircasing artifacts that are inherent to density-based methods, the convolution-based filtering pro-

https://doi.org/10.3390/computation14010019

cedure will apply again to the interpolated fine-grid field, thereby improving boundary smoothness and geometric fidelity.

$$\tilde{\phi}_{f,n} = \frac{1}{\sum_{i \in \mathcal{R}_n} \mathcal{H}_{ni}} \sum_{i \in \mathcal{R}_n} \mathcal{H}_{ni} \phi_{f,i} \tag{15}$$

Subsequently, a smoothed Heaviside projection is employed to obtain a clear $0-1$ representation of the material distribution, where the steepness parameter is progressively updated to sharpen the transition between solid and void regions.

$$\overline{\phi}_f = H(\tilde{\phi}_f, \beta, l_s) = \frac{\tanh(\beta l_s) + \tanh(\beta \tilde{\phi}_f - l_s)}{\tanh(\beta l_s) + \tanh(\beta(1 - l_s))} \tag{16}$$

The structural geometry is further represented by a level-set function, in which the threshold is iteratively determined using a bi-section scheme to strictly satisfy the prescribed volume constraint, which could be expressed as the following 1D optimal problem:

$$\min_{l_s \in [l_{min}, l_{max}]} J(l_s) = \frac{1}{2} \left(\frac{1}{N_f} \sum_{n=1}^{N_f} H(\tilde{\phi}_{f,n}, \beta, l_s) - \frac{1}{N_c} \sum_{m=1}^{N_c} \varphi_m \right)^2 \tag{17}$$

Finally, the updated high-dimensional grid-based field serves as the initial guess for the next optimization cycle, forming a closed-loop process that gradually refines the topological design toward smooth and well-defined boundaries.

3.2. CAD Reconstruction Based on SEMDOT Results

To facilitate downstream CAD modeling and meshing, it is first necessary to convert the SEMDOT-designed density field into an explicit structural boundary. Since the SEMDOT result is represented by the filtered design variable $\overline{\phi}_f$, the solid–void interface can be consistently defined as the isocontour of $\overline{\phi}_f$ at a prescribed threshold l_s:

$$\mathcal{P} = \text{MSA}\left(\overline{\phi}_f, l_s\right) \tag{18}$$

where MSA (*) indicates the Marching Squares Algorithm [51–53], which could be easily realized through the MATLAB 2024a internal function; the details of its formulation are omitted here, and interested readers could refer to the work [54]; $\mathcal{P}$ yields a polyline boundary, which includes point coordinates and topological information. Then, to enable robust CAD modeling and meshing, the non-uniformly distributed polyline $\mathcal{P}$ is resampled to obtain a uniformly spaced point set $\overline{\mathcal{P}}$, and the arc-length interval of the polyline $\overline{\mathcal{P}}$ could be fixed as Δs. The Equal Arc-Length Resampling Algorithm proposed in [55] is adopted here to achieve this goal:

$$\overline{\mathcal{P}} = \text{EAR}(\mathcal{P}, \Delta s) \tag{19}$$

Similarly, the procedure is readily implemented via MATLAB's built-in functions; the implementation details are omitted for brevity. The final resampled polyline $\overline{\mathcal{P}}$ could then be directly exported into a $.dxf$ format, encoding the point coordinates and connectivity in a CAD-compatible structure. These files are subsequently imported into commercial CAE software, where the closed contours are meshed for high-fidelity finite element simulations. During the meshing phase, a third-party mesh generation software (such as COMSOL Multiphysics 6.3 [56]) is employed to discretize the extracted geometry using free triangular elements. To ensure controllability and consistency, the minimum edge

https://doi.org/10.3390/computation14010019

length of the generated triangular mesh is set equal to the arc-length interval Δs defined during the resampling process. As a result, by adjusting the control parameter Δs, which specifies the number of resampled boundary points, both the geometric accuracy and the final number of mesh elements can be directly regulated.

It is worth noting that the SEMDOT framework ultimately produces a high-resolution and smoothly distributed field $\overline{\phi}_f$. Consequently, during the processes described in Equations (18) and (19), the reconstruction of smooth polylines can be achieved in a straightforward and accurate manner. In contrast, the conventional density-based method extracts polylines directly from the low-resolution density field φ, which inherently limits the smoothness of the reconstructed boundaries. This fundamental distinction is illustrated in Figure 3a, where SEMDOT enables the generation of smooth polylines, whereas the traditional approach leads to jagged or staircase boundary representations shown in Figure 3b.

Figure 3. An illustration of boundary expression for word 'SEMDOT' between SEMDOT algorithm and conventional method, (**a**) dense-mesh case; (**b**) sparse-mesh case.

4. Formulations of Optimization Model

4.1. Formulation of Low-Fidelity Optimization Model

For thermal–fluid device design, our primary focus is to achieve the optimal design of structural performance under the constraint of a structural weight ratio. Within the SEMDOT framework, the optimization model for this can be expressed as follows:

$$\begin{cases} \text{find} : \varphi, l_s \\ \text{minimize} : C_r(\varphi),\ J(l_s) \\ \text{subject to} : \begin{cases} \nabla\cdot\left(-\frac{\kappa}{\mu}\nabla P\right) = 0 \\ \rho C_p \mathbf{u}\cdot\nabla T = k\nabla^2 T + Q \\ \frac{1}{N_c}\sum\limits_{m=1}^{N_c} \varphi_m \le V_{tol} \\ \varphi_{\min} \le \forall\varphi_e \le 1 \end{cases} \end{cases} \tag{20}$$

where $\varphi_{\min}$ is set as 1×10^{-9}, which could be used to avoid matrix singularity, and $C_r(*)$ represents the general objective function. In this work, the objective is to minimize the maximum temperature within the design domain. This constraint could be restated in terms of a single differentiable global expression through the aggregation method. The

P-norm aggregation function is adopted [57], and T_{max} could be approximately expressed by the following:

$$T_{max} \approx T_{PN} = \left(\sum_{e=1}^{N_c} (T_e)^p \right)^{\frac{1}{p}} \tag{21}$$

where T_{PN} is the global P-norm measure,T_e is the temperature value for the eth element, and p is the aggregation parameter. Note that the P-norm approaches the real maximum value when $p \to \infty$. However, a large p value tends to make the problem ill-conditioned. A relatively small p value is preferred in practice given the convergence stability, leading to the gap between the exact and the approximated maximum temperature. Therefore, the aggregation parameter p is taken as a seed parameter and could be optimized.

4.2. Formulation of Multifidelity Optimization Model

As shown in Figure 1, an LF model is constructed. This model must be able to be optimized by the gradient method and generate promising design solutions to the original optimization problem. The next step is selecting the seeding parameters. LF optimization generates a number of design solutions by varying the combinations of these parameters. In LF optimization, candidate solutions are generated by solving the following LF optimization problem for K seeding parameter combinations:

$$\begin{cases} find: J = \{s_1, s_2, \ldots, s_k\} \\ minimize: O(s_k) = [P_{drop}, (s_k) T_{max}(s_k)] \\ subject\ to: s_k \in \Omega \end{cases} \tag{22}$$

where J represents the design population and s_k represents the kth seeding parameters combination. In heat transfer problems, a trade-off exists between pressure drop P_{drop} and heat dissipation performance. In the HF evaluation, the maximum temperature T_{max} is adopted as the performance metric for the heat dissipation. This metric is crucial in engineering applications such as electronic device cooling, as it directly affects component reliability, lifespan, and failure risk.

5. Case Studies and Discussions

All numerical examples presented here were implemented using a combination of MATLAB and COMSOL. Specifically, the low-fidelity optimization and the subsequent CAD-based post-processing were carried out in MATLAB, whereas the high-fidelity simulations and the visualization of the corresponding results were performed in COMSOL. All simulations and computations were executed on a high-performance workstation equipped with dual AMD EPYC 7763 CPUs (128 cores, 2.45–3.5 GHz), 1 TB of RAM, and two NVIDIA RTX A6000 GPUs.

The LF iterations are terminated when either (i) the relative change in the objective function between two successive iterations falls below 0.001, indicating that the objective has effectively stabilized, or (ii) the maximum number of iterations reaches 200, which serves as a practical upper bound to control the computational cost.

5.1. Single-Channel Design

5.1.1. Boundary Conditions and Parameter Settings for Single-Channel Design

The most common case of a parallel channel with a single inlet and a single outlet is used as the first case study. The corresponding boundary conditions and geometric dimensions are illustrated in Figure 4.

https://doi.org/10.3390/computation14010019

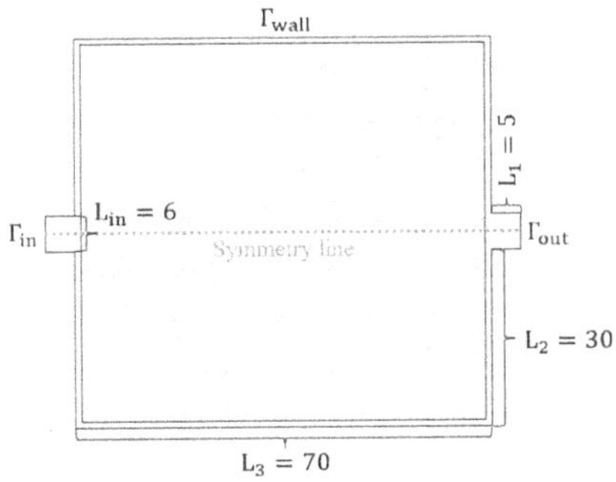

Figure 4. Boundary condition and its corresponding geometry configuration for single-channel design (all lengths are in meters, m).

In this case, the inlet and outlet positions are fixed. Owing to symmetry, only half of the domain is considered, which is discretized into a 300 × 150 element mesh. For the SEMDOT nodal field, a finer resolution of a 3000 × 1500 node is employed. Regarding the boundary conditions, a Dirichlet pressure condition P_{in} is prescribed at the fluid inlet, with zero pressure at the outlet. For the heat transfer problem, the inlet temperature is set to T = 280 K, and the input pressure P_{in} = 200 Pa. For the projection parameters, the β is initially set to 2 and double in every 30 iterations until it reaches 32. The prescribed volume fraction is 0.5. The optimization and material parameters used in the LF topology optimization and HF simulations are summarized in Table 1.

Table 1. Parameters of LF optimization.

Parameter	Value	Parameter	Value
Solid permeabilities	$\kappa_s = 10^{-15}[m^2]$	Fluid heat capacity	$C_{pf} = 871\ [J/kg{\cdot}K^{-1}]$
Fluid permeabilities	$\kappa_f = 2.35 \times 10^{-7}[m^2]$	Penalization factor for κ	$q_\kappa = 8$
Solid thermal conductivities	$k_s = 202\ [W/m{\cdot}K^{-1}]$	Penalization factor for k	$q_k = 8$
Fluid thermal conductivities	$k_f = 0.6\ [W/m{\cdot}K^{-1}]$	Heat source	$Q = 10^4\ [W/m^3]$
Solid density	$\rho_s = 2713\ [kg/m^3]$	Aggregation factor	$p = 4$
Fluid density	$\rho_f = 1000\ [kg/m^3]$	Filter radius	$r_{min} = 3$
Solid heat capacity	$C_{ps} = 4200\ [J/kg{\cdot}K^{-1}]$	Dynamic viscosity	$\mu = 0.001[Pa{\cdot}s]$

5.1.2. Validation of Low-Fidelity Optimization Results for Single-Channel Design

After 200 iterations, the topologically optimized structure could be obtained. The convergence history of the proposed optimization procedure is shown in Figure 5a. The objective function decreases rapidly in the early iterations, followed by a gradual decline with minor oscillations until convergence around iteration 120. The constraint function $g1(k)$ remains negative throughout optimization, ensuring feasibility within the admissible design space. Meanwhile, the threshold parameter ls evolves adaptively, rising from its initial value and stabilizing near 0.53, which sharpens the transition from intermediate densities to a distinct 0–1 boundary. Figure 5b illustrates the evolutionary process of the structure at different iterations. At the initial stage (Itr. 1–10), the design exhibits coarse and irregular material distributions without clear flow passages. By iteration 20–30, the structure gradually forms primitive channel-like features, though still fragmented. As the optimization proceeds (Itr. 40–60), a more connected and branching network emerges, providing preliminary flow paths. Finally, after about 120 iterations, the topological design stabilizes into a well-defined branched structure, which remains consistent until the final iteration (Itr. 200). Overall, the results demonstrate fast convergence, strict

https://doi.org/10.3390/computation14010019

constraint satisfaction, and stable boundary evaluation, highlighting the robustness of the proposed framework.

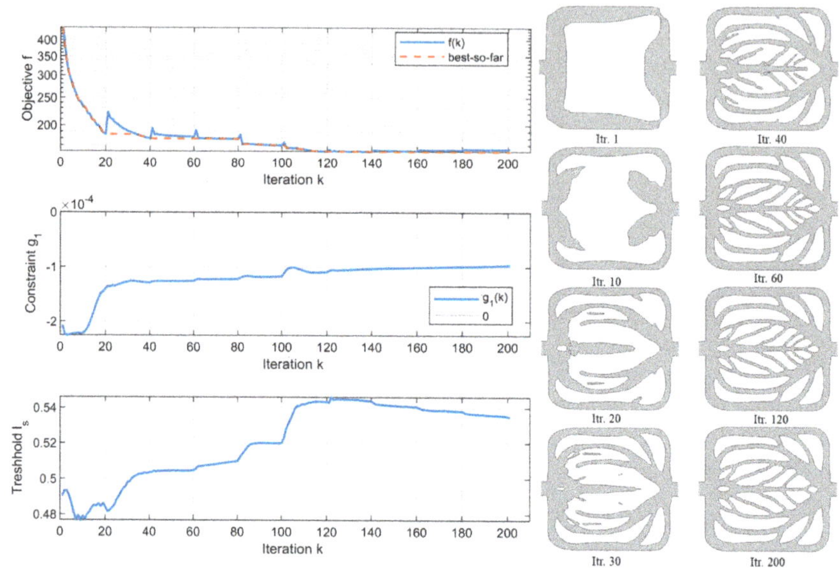

(**a**) (**b**)

Figure 5. Single-Channel Design. (**a**) Convergence history and (**b**) evolutionary history for fluid channel distribution during optimization.

Figure 6 presents a comparative analysis between the SEMDOT-based topology-optimized design (top row, a-1 to a-4) and the conventional channel design (bottom row, b-1 to b-4) under the HF simulation framework. In the HF simulations, a fixed inlet flow rate corresponding to an average inlet velocity of 0.1 m/s is prescribed. Unless otherwise specified, all remaining boundary conditions and material properties are identical for all cases, ensuring a consistent operating condition for performance comparison.

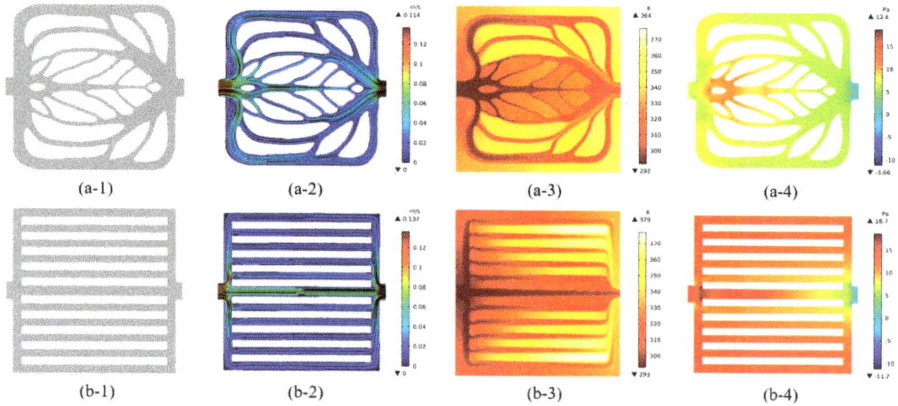

Figure 6. Comparison between SEMDOT design (**a-1~4**) and conventional straight-line design (**b-1~4**).

A mesh-independence analysis is performed for the SEMDOT-based design (Figure 6, a-1) to determine an appropriate mesh resolution Δs for the high-fidelity simulations. Five progressively refined values of Δs are examined to assess mesh convergence, and

https://doi.org/10.3390/computation14010019

the corresponding results are summarized in Table 2. It is observed that further mesh refinement leads to only marginal changes in the monitored quantities, indicating that mesh-independent solutions have been reached. Considering both geometric accuracy and computational cost, $\Delta s = 5 \times 10^{-4}$ is selected, and this mesh resolution is consistently adopted in all subsequent HF simulations.

Table 2. The mesh-independence analysis.

Δs	Pressure Drops	Maximum Temperature	Element Number and Geometry Accuracy [58]
5×10^{-3}	12.88	334	6563, 92.0%
1×10^{-3}	14.05	342	8563, 93.4%
5×10^{-4}	16.62	364	13,563, 96.1%
1×10^{-4}	16.56	369	18,563, 97.8%
5×10^{-5}	17.02	371	21,563, 99.2%

From a geometrical standpoint, the SEMDOT design naturally evolves into a branched, bio-inspired network (a-1), in sharp contrast to the rigid, straight-channel configuration of the conventional design (b-1). The velocity distribution further demonstrates this difference: the SEMDOT structure achieves a more uniform flow allocation across the entire domain (a-2), whereas the conventional straight-channel layout suffers from flow concentration in the central passages and relatively stagnant regions near the side walls (b-2). A similar trend is observed in the temperature field comparison. The SEMDOT structure yields a more homogeneous thermal distribution with a reduced peak temperature (a-3), while the conventional design exhibits steep gradients and local hot spots, particularly in the downstream region (b-3). Pressure drop analysis also highlights the superiority of the SEMDOT design: it achieves a smoother pressure profile with a lower overall loss (~12.6 Pa) compared with the conventional counterpart (~18.7 Pa) (a-4 vs. b-4).

It can be concluded that the SEMDOT framework not only produces adaptive, bio-inspired geometrical layouts but also simultaneously enhances flow uniformity, improves thermal management, and reduces energy consumption, thereby significantly outperforming the conventional straight-channel design.

5.2. Multi-Channel Design

5.2.1. Boundary Conditions and Parameter Settings for Multi-Channel Design

In the second case, a symmetric double-channel configuration is considered, as shown in Figure 7. Two inlets (Γ_{in}) are located on the left and two outlets (Γ_{out}) on the right, both aligned with the horizontal symmetry line. The none unit geometric dimensions are as follows: $L_4 = 70$ (channel length), $L_1 = 5$ (top outlet height), $L_2 = 24$ (distance from the top wall to the upper outlet centerline), $L_3 = 16$ (distance from the bottom wall to the lower outlet centerline), and $L_{\text{in}} = 6$ (inlet length). The same mesh and boundary settings as in the single-channel case are used.

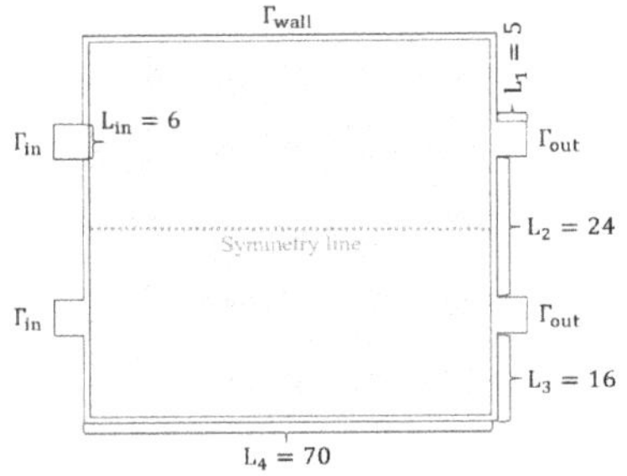

Figure 7. Boundary condition and its corresponding geometry configuration for double-channel design.

5.2.2. Validation of Low-Fidelity Optimization Results for Single-Channel Design

After 200 iterations, a converged topological design is obtained, as illustrated in Figure 8. In Figure 8a, the convergence history shows that the objective function decreases sharply during the early iterations, then gradually declines with minor fluctuations and stabilizes around iteration 120, while the constraint function g1(k) remains negative throughout, confirming feasibility within the design space. At the same time, the threshold parameter ls increases adaptively and stabilizes at near 0.54, which promotes a smooth transition from intermediate densities to a distinct 0–1 boundary. In Figure 8b, the structural evolution reveals that the initial layouts (Itr. 1–10) are irregular and fragmented, but by iterations 20–30, primitive channel-like features appear, followed by progressively connected and branched networks during iterations 40–60. From iteration 120 onward, the structure stabilizes into a well-defined branched topology that persists until the final iteration (Itr. 200). These results collectively demonstrate rapid convergence, reliable constraint handling, and robust structural refinement, highlighting the effectiveness of the proposed framework in generating stable and physically meaningful designs.

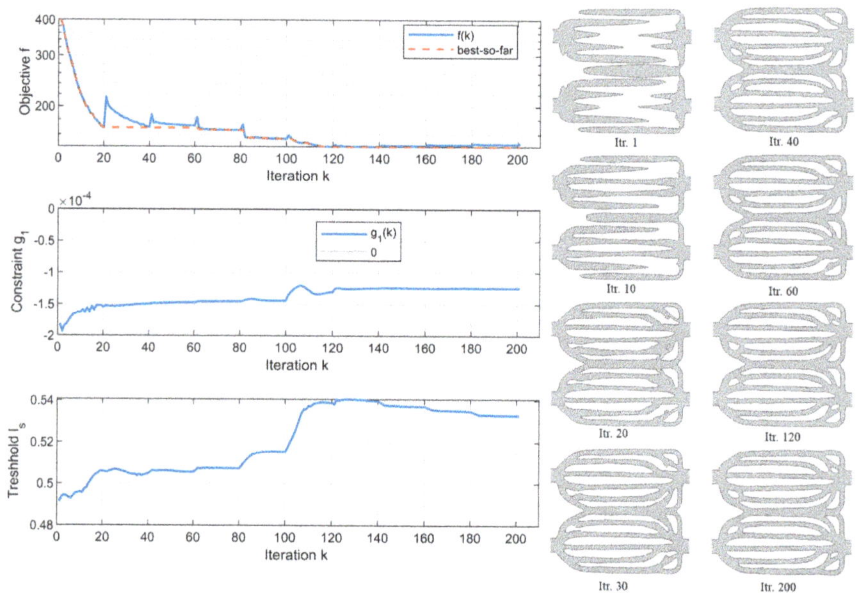

Figure 8. (**a**) Convergence history and (**b**) evolutionary history for fluid channel distribution during optimization.

As illustrated in Figure 9, both the SEMDOT-optimized design (top row) and the conventional parallel-channel design (bottom row) achieve continuous flow passages that enable fluid transport and heat dissipation, with similar global flow directions, a temperature rise along the flow path, and pressure drop trends from inlet to outlet. Despite these commonalities, the SEMDOT result demonstrates clear superiority in multiple aspects. The optimized structure forms branched, bio-inspired flow channels that allow more uniform fluid distribution, whereas the conventional design relies on rigid parallel passages with less flexibility. Consequently, the SEMDOT design achieves a lower maximum temperature (~323 K compared to ~337 K), a more homogeneous thermal field without large hot spots, and smoother velocity streamlines that better utilize the entire cooling domain. In addition, the pressure drop is slightly reduced (21.9 Pa vs. 23.9 Pa) and more evenly distributed, avoiding localized losses observed in the conventional layout. Overall, the SEMDOT

https://doi.org/10.3390/computation14010019

framework not only preserves the basic functionality of flow and heat transfer but also significantly improves cooling uniformity, thermal efficiency, and hydraulic performance compared with the traditional design.

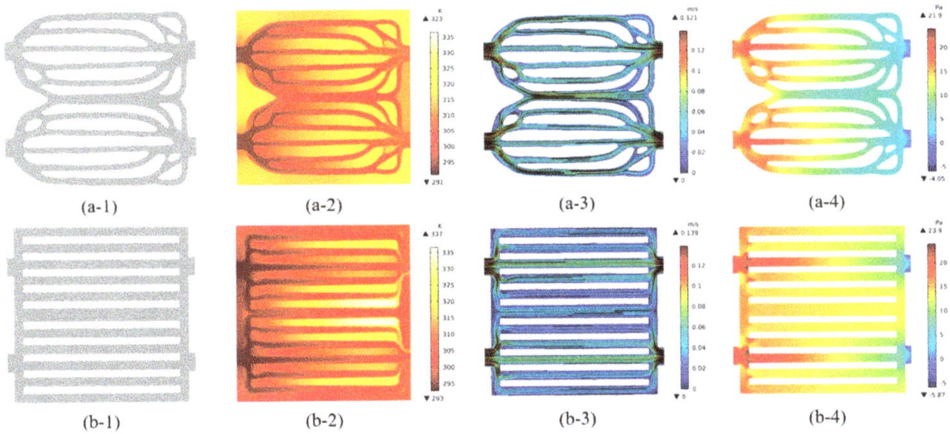

Figure 9. Comparison between SEMDOT design (**a-1~4**) and conventional straight-line design (**b-1~4**).

5.3. Multifidelity Single-Channel Design

In this case study, we further investigate the impact of discrepancies between low- and high-fidelity models on the optimization results. Due to the modeling gap between the LF and HF models, directly adopting low-fidelity solutions does not necessarily guarantee superior performance in HF simulations. To address this issue, two adjustable feeding parameters are introduced to enhance cross-fidelity consistency. The first is the inlet pressure, which compensates for deviations in the flow rate, pressure drop, and heat transfer response between the two models. The second is the aggregation factor, which regulates the conservativeness and smoothness of the constraint functions, thereby enabling the LF optimization to better capture hot spot regions under HF evaluation. By systematically tuning these parameters within the LF optimization and calibrating them at critical points through HF simulations, the transferability of the LF results is significantly improved, leading to a more robust multifidelity optimization process.

The seeding parameters for the LF optimization based on SEMDOT are summarized in Table 3. A total of 20 cases are considered, with P_{in} varied over {50,100,150,200} and P varied over {1,2,4,8,16}. Figure 10 presents the distribution of flow channels generated by the SEMDOT algorithm under varying optimization parameters. From left to right, as the aggregation factor P increases from 1 to 16, the optimized geometries evolve from relatively coarse and sparsely branched channels toward finer and more intricate branching networks, indicating that a larger P promotes higher structural complexity. From top to bottom, as the imposed inlet–outlet pressure difference increases from 50 to 200, the channel networks gradually develop additional secondary branches, enabling more uniform fluid coverage under higher driving forces. Overall, the combined effect of P and the pressure difference governs the balance between channel coarseness and branching density, leading to a rich variety of flow topologies ranging from simple main conduits to highly branched tree-like structures.

https://doi.org/10.3390/computation14010019

Table 3. Seeding parameters for LF optimization in SEMDOT.

Case Number	P_{in}	p	Case Number	P_{in}	p
SEMDOT#1	50	1	SEMDOT#11	150	1
SEMDOT#2	50	2	SEMDOT#12	150	2
SEMDOT#3	50	4	SEMDOT#13	150	4
SEMDOT#4	50	8	SEMDOT#14	150	8
SEMDOT#5	50	16	SEMDOT#15	150	16
SEMDOT#6	100	1	SEMDOT#16	200	1
SEMDOT#7	100	2	SEMDOT#17	200	2
SEMDOT#8	100	4	SEMDOT#18	200	4
SEMDOT#9	100	8	SEMDOT#19	200	8
SEMDOT#10	100	16	SEMDOT#20	200	16

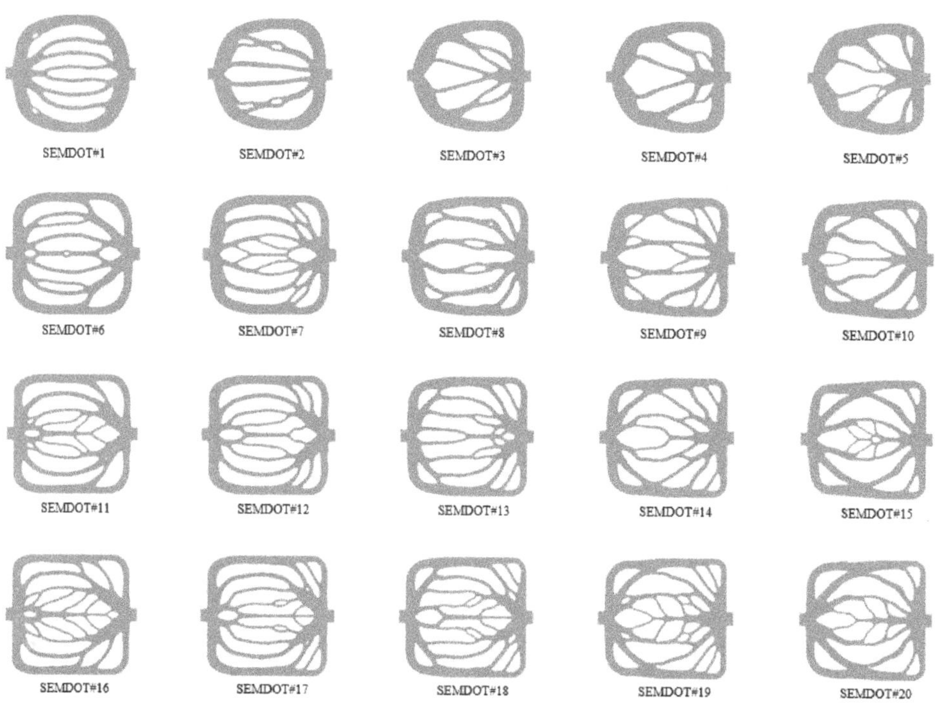

Figure 10. Twenty flow channel designs generated by SEMDOT subjected to different P_{in} and P.

Figure 11 illustrates the Pareto distribution of the SEMDOT-optimized designs with respect to the maximum temperature and pressure drop, together with the representative flow–thermal results. The scatter plot shows a clear Pareto front, indicating the inherent trade-off between cooling performance and hydraulic resistance. Two Rank-1 results are selected (SEMDOT#13 and SEMDOT#16). SEMDOT#13 maintains the lowest maximum temperature (≈363 K) while exhibiting a higher pressure drop. In contrast, Design #16 achieves the very lowest maximum temperature (≈364 K) and the lowest pressure drop (7.502 Pa) by forming a dense and uniformly branched channel network. This reveals an interesting phenomenon: within the proposed case, when the high-fidelity simulation is conducted under low Reynolds number boundary conditions, the low-fidelity optimization yields better performance if a larger pressure drop boundary condition and a smaller aggregation factor (approaching an average-temperature evaluation) are adopted. However,

https://doi.org/10.3390/computation14010019

no clear trend can be identified to confirm that this observation holds universally across all cases.

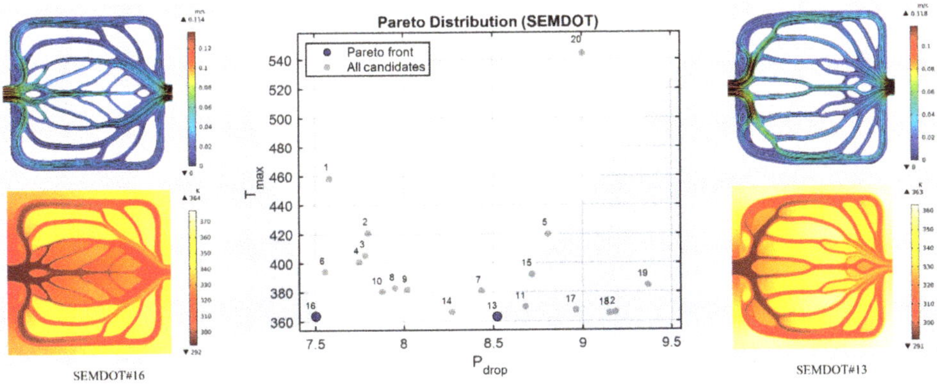

Figure 11. Pareto distribution for 20 SEMDOT designs and two RANK-1 results selected to show fluid velocity and temperature distributions.

5.4. Comparisons with Conventional Methods

In this subsection, the SEMDOT algorithm is compared with the RAMP method. For the RAMP formulation, an additional projection is applied to the density field to obtain clearer boundaries, with the parameter settings and evolution consistent with Equation (16), except that the threshold is fixed at 0.5. The boundaries are then post-processed and extracted using the procedure described in Section 3.2, before being imported into COMSOL for high-fidelity simulations. All other parameters remain consistent with those used in the SEMDOT algorithm.

The seeding parameters for the LF optimization based on RAMP are summarized in Table 4. As with Section 5.3, a total of 20 cases are considered, with P_{in} varied over {50,100,150,200} and P varied over {1,2,4,8,16}. Figure 12 presents the distribution of flow channels generated by the RAMP algorithm under varying optimization parameters. Similar to SEMDOT, the geometrical patterns in the RAMP results exhibit a strong correlation with the values of P_{in} and P. However, in the cases with a larger P, the final shapes are less satisfactory: several designs fail to converge (for example, the unresolved bifurcation in RAMP#19) or exhibit locally oversized channels (such as RAMP#15 and RAMP#20).

Table 4. Seeding parameters for LF optimization in RAMP.

Case Number	P_{in}	p	Case Number	P_{in}	p
RAMP#1	50	1	RAMP#11	150	1
RAMP#2	50	2	RAMP#12	150	2
RAMP#3	50	4	RAMP#13	150	4
RAMP#4	50	8	RAMP#14	150	8
RAMP#5	50	16	RAMP#15	150	16
RAMP#6	100	1	RAMP#16	200	1
RAMP#7	100	2	RAMP#17	200	2
RAMP#8	100	4	RAMP#18	200	4
RAMP#9	100	8	RAMP#19	200	8
RAMP#10	100	16	RAMP#20	200	16

https://doi.org/10.3390/computation14010019

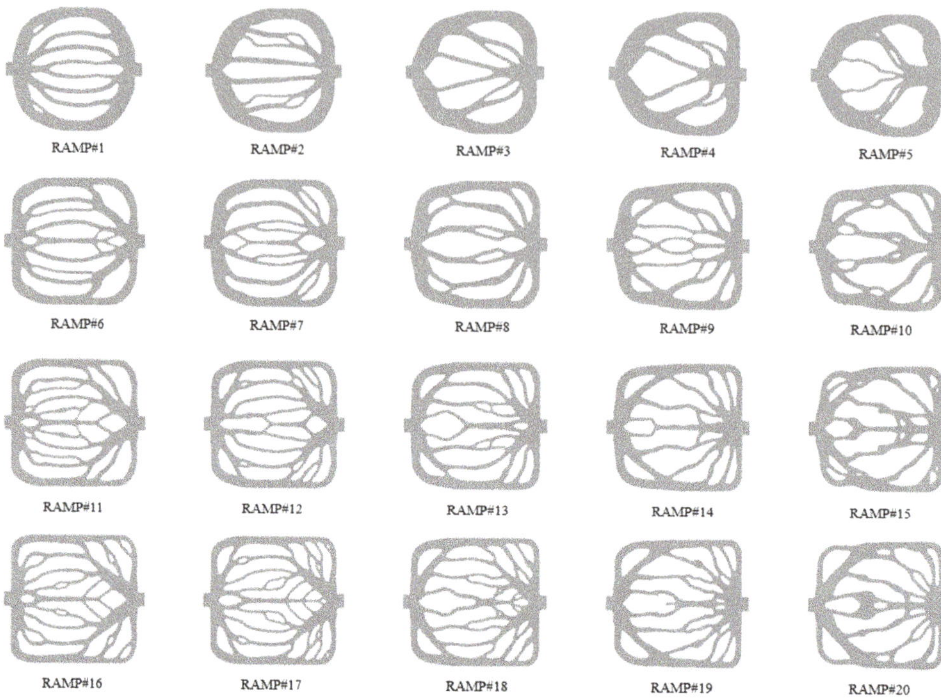

Figure 12. Twenty flow channel designs generated by RAMP with different P_{in} and P.

Subsequently, the series of SEMDOT designs are compared with those obtained using RAMP (see Figure 13). While certain RAMP results achieve lower pressure drops than SEMDOT, they generally perform worse in terms of maximum temperature reduction. Quantitatively, if the hypervolume value of SEMDOT is normalized to 1, the corresponding value for RAMP is 0.923. This indicates that, under the design conditions considered in this study, SEMDOT yields overall better performance in comparison with RAMP.

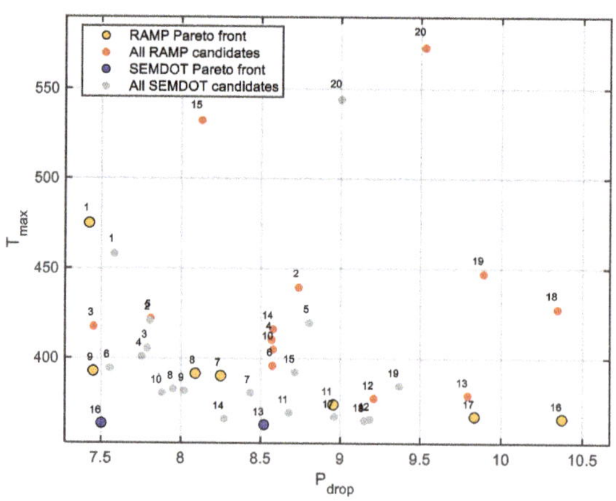

Figure 13. Comparison of Pareto distribution between SEMDOT and RAMP designs.

Four sets of results were randomly selected for pairwise comparison under identical optimization parameters. Specifically, the comparisons were conducted between SEM-

https://doi.org/10.3390/computation14010019

DOT#8 and RAMP#8, as well as SEMDOT#16 and RAMP#16, with each pair representing the corresponding RANK-1 design from the two methods.

The detailed comparison is shown in Figure 14. It can be observed that, for the selected cases, the overall material distributions obtained by the two methods are in close agreement, differing only in a few localized regions.

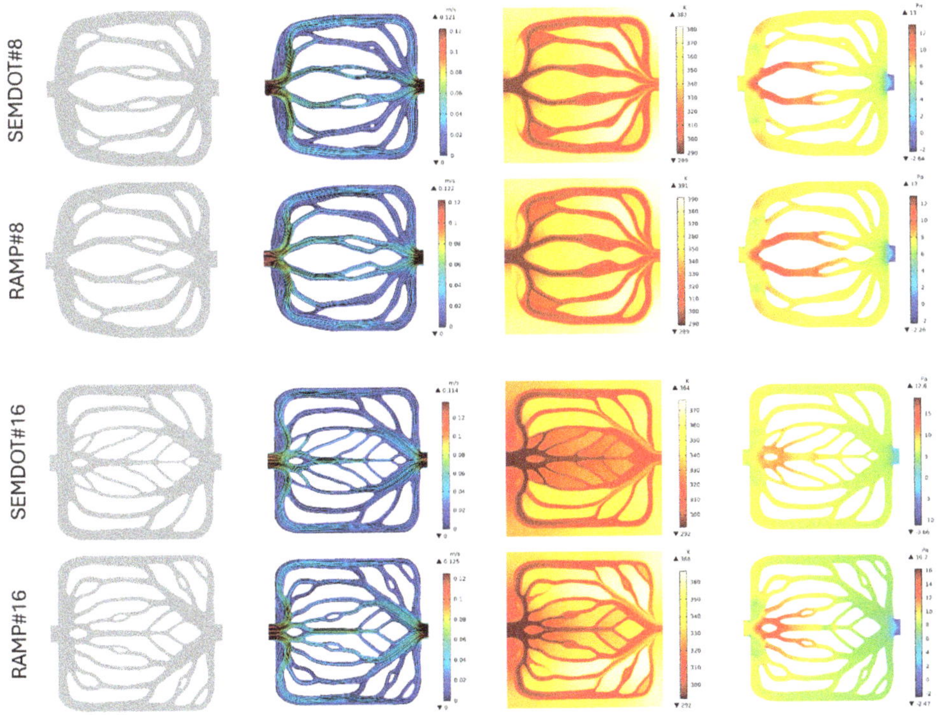

Figure 14. Comparison of SEMDOT and RAMP results subjected to the same seeding parameters.

6. Conclusions

In this work, a multifidelity topology optimization framework for thermal–fluid devices was proposed by integrating a low-fidelity Darcy-based model with a high-fidelity Navier–Stokes formulation, in conjunction with the SEMDOT method. The SEMDOT framework enables the generation of smooth and well-defined structural boundaries through the decoupling of finite element analysis and geometric representation, thereby facilitating robust CAD reconstruction and high-fidelity validation.

Numerical studies on single- and multi-channel heat dissipation devices show that the proposed approach can efficiently generate bio-inspired branched channel layouts that improve heat dissipation and hydraulic performance relative to conventional straight-channel designs under a consistent comparison condition. In a representative single-channel case, the selected SEMDOT design reduced the HF peak temperature from approximately 337 K to 323 K (about 4% reduction in T_{max}) while also reducing the HF pressure drop from approximately 18.7 Pa to 12.6 Pa (about 33% reduction in Δp) at the same operating point. Moreover, when compared with a conventional density-based (RAMP) pipeline under the tested settings, SEMDOT yielded a more favorable Pareto performance in the presented examples (e.g., higher normalized hypervolume).

The framework is particularly relevant to forced-convection cooling components where geometry needs to be exported and manufactured, such as cold plates and compact heat exchangers for electronics and battery thermal management, and additively manufactured cooling inserts, because the LF stage directly produces CAD-ready boundaries and the final selection is based on HF CFD validation. In its current form, the method is immediately applicable to 2D, steady, laminar, low-to-moderate Reynolds number design scenarios where steady HF simulations are an appropriate qualification tool and where a rapid LF-to-CAD-to-HF loop provides practical engineering value.

However, the current study is still limited to (i) 2D, steady, laminar flow and heat transfer, (ii) the specific seeding ranges and aggregation parameter choices explored herein, and (iii) reconstruction and remeshing procedures that can influence Δp and hot spot metrics, particularly when performance differences are small. Extending the conclusions beyond this scope (e.g., to turbulence, transients, or fully 3D devices) requires additional verification.

Accordingly, future work will extend the proposed framework to turbulent flow regimes, transient thermal management problems, and investigate hybrid LF surrogates such as Brinkman (Darcy–Brinkman) or related extensions to incorporate viscous diffusion and improve near-wall accuracy when inertia becomes non-negligible. In addition, we will pursue large-scale three-dimensional designs to broaden the applicability of the framework to advanced cooling system design and manufacturing-oriented topology optimization.

Author Contributions: Conceptualization, Y.S. and Y.-F.F.; methodology, Y.G. and S.X.; software, Y.G.; validation, Y.S., S.X. and Y.G.; formal analysis, Y.S. and S.X.; investigation, Y.S. and S.X.; resources, Y.-F.F. and S.X.; data curation, Y.S. and Y.G.; writing—original draft preparation, S.X. and Y.S.; writing—review and editing, S.X., Y.G. and Y.-F.F.; visualization, Y.S. and S.X.; supervision, S.X.; project administration, S.X.; funding acquisition, Y.-F.F. All authors have read and agreed to the published version of the manuscript.

Funding: This research received no external funding.

Data Availability Statement: The original contributions presented in this study are included in the article. Further inquiries can be directed to the corresponding authors.

Conflicts of Interest: The authors declare no conflicts of interest.

References

1. Ahmed, H.E.; Salman, B.H.; Kherbeet, A.S.; Ahmed, M. Optimization of thermal design of heat sinks: A review. *Int. J. Heat Mass Transf.* **2018**, *118*, 129–153. [CrossRef]
2. Alexandersen, J.; Sigmund, O.; Aage, N. Large scale three-dimensional topology optimisation of heat sinks cooled by natural convection. *Int. J. Heat Mass Transf.* **2016**, *100*, 876–891. [CrossRef]
3. Alexandersen, J.; Aage, N.; Andreasen, C.S.; Sigmund, O. Topology optimisation for natural convection problems. *Int. J. Numer. Methods Fluids* **2014**, *76*, 699–721. [CrossRef]
4. Sigmund, O.; Maute, K. Topology optimization approaches: A comparative review. *Struct. Multidiscip. Optim.* **2013**, *48*, 1031–1055. [CrossRef]
5. Guo, Y.; Xu, S.; Wang, Y.; Liu, J.; Ahmad, R.; Ma, Y. DGTO: Derivable geodesics-coupled topology optimization for multi-axis hybrid additive and subtractive manufacturing with curved layer generation. *Addit. Manuf.* **2025**, *105*, 104786. [CrossRef]
6. Bendsøe, M.P.; Sigmund, O. Material interpolation schemes in topology optimization. *Arch. Appl. Mech.* **1999**, *69*, 635–654. [CrossRef]
7. Sigmund, O. A 99 line topology optimization code written in Matlab. *Struct. Multidiscip. Optim.* **2001**, *21*, 120–127. [CrossRef]
8. Liu, J.; Zou, Z.; Li, Z.; Zhang, M.; Yang, J.; Gao, K.; Wu, Z. A clustering-based multiscale topology optimization framework for efficient design of porous composite structures. *Comput. Methods Appl. Mech. Eng.* **2025**, *439*, 117881. [CrossRef]
9. Liu, J.; Liu, J.; Gao, K.; Mohagheghian, I.; Fan, W.; Yang, J.; Wu, Z. A bioinspired gradient curved auxetic honeycombs with enhanced energy absorption. *Int. J. Mech. Sci.* **2025**, *291*, 110189. [CrossRef]
10. Bendsøe, M.P.; Kikuchi, N. Generating optimal topologies in structural design using a homogenization method. *Comput. Methods Appl. Mech. Eng.* **1988**, *71*, 197–224. [CrossRef]
11. Xu, S.; Liu, J.; Li, X.; Ma, Y. A full-scale topology optimization method for surface fiber reinforced additive manufacturing parts. *Comput. Methods Appl. Mech. Eng.* **2022**, *401*, 115632. [CrossRef]

https://doi.org/10.3390/computation14010019

12. Xu, S.; Liu, J.; Ma, Y. Residual stress constrained self-support topology optimization for metal additive manufacturing. *Comput. Methods Appl. Mech. Eng.* **2022**, *389*, 114380. [CrossRef]
13. Deaton, J.D.; Grandhi, R.V. A survey of structural and multidisciplinary continuum topology optimization: Post 2000. *Struct. Multidiscip. Optim.* **2014**, *49*, 1–38. [CrossRef]
14. Meng, K.; Liu, J.; Yu, H. Multi-material topology optimization considering interface stresses under coupled thermal and dynamic loads. *Comput. Methods Appl. Mech. Eng.* **2025**, *446*, 118312. [CrossRef]
15. Muayad, H.; Raffaele, C.; Marco, D.; Hamed, F.; Movahedi Rad, M. Thermo-mechanical reliability-based topology optimization for imperfect elasto-plastic materials. *Int. J. Mech. Mater. Des.* **2025**, *21*, 1755–1776. [CrossRef]
16. Habashneh, M.; Cucuzza, R.; Domaneschi, M.; Rad, M.M. Advanced elasto-plastic topology optimization of steel beams under elevated temperatures. *Adv. Eng. Softw.* **2024**, *190*, 103596. [CrossRef]
17. Wang, M.Y.; Wang, X.; Guo, D. A level set method for structural topology optimization. *Comput. Methods Appl. Mech. Eng.* **2003**, *192*, 227–246. [CrossRef]
18. Wang, S.; Lim, K.M.; Khoo, B.C.; Wang, M.Y. An extended level set method for shape and topology optimization. *J. Comput. Phys.* **2007**, *221*, 395–421. [CrossRef]
19. Yaji, K.; Yamada, T.; Kubo, S.; Izui, K.; Nishiwaki, S. A topology optimization method for a coupled thermal–fluid problem using level set boundary expressions. *Int. J. Heat Mass Transf.* **2015**, *81*, 878–888. [CrossRef]
20. Huang, X.; Xie, Y.-M. A further review of ESO type methods for topology optimization. *Struct. Multidiscip. Optim.* **2010**, *41*, 671–683. [CrossRef]
21. Huang, X.; Xie, Y.M. Bi-directional evolutionary topology optimization of continuum structures with one or multiple materials. *Comput. Mech.* **2009**, *43*, 393–401. [CrossRef]
22. Xiong, Y.; Zhao, Z.-L.; Lu, H.; Shen, W.; Xie, Y.M. Parallel BESO framework for solving high-resolution topology optimisation problems. *Adv. Eng. Softw.* **2023**, *176*, 103389. [CrossRef]
23. Zhang, W.; Yuan, J.; Zhang, J.; Guo, X. A new topology optimization approach based on Moving Morphable Components (MMC) and the ersatz material model. *Struct. Multidiscip. Optim.* **2016**, *53*, 1243–1260. [CrossRef]
24. Zhang, W.; Song, J.; Zhou, J.; Du, Z.; Zhu, Y.; Sun, Z.; Guo, X. Topology optimization with multiple materials via moving morphable component (MMC) method. *Int. J. Numer. Methods Eng.* **2018**, *113*, 1653–1675. [CrossRef]
25. Du, Z.; Cui, T.; Liu, C.; Zhang, W.; Guo, Y.; Guo, X. An efficient and easy-to-extend Matlab code of the Moving Morphable Component (MMC) method for three-dimensional topology optimization. *Struct. Multidiscip. Optim.* **2022**, *65*, 158. [CrossRef]
26. Xu, S.; Liu, J.; Yaji, K.; Lu, L. Topology optimization for hybrid additive-subtractive manufacturing incorporating dynamic process planning. *Comput. Methods Appl. Mech. Eng.* **2024**, *431*, 117270. [CrossRef]
27. Liu, J.; Huang, J.; Zheng, Y.; Hou, S.; Xu, S.; Ma, Y.; Huang, C.; Zou, B.; Li, L. Challenges in topology optimization for hybrid additive–subtractive manufacturing: A review. *Comput.-Aided Des.* **2023**, *161*, 103531. [CrossRef]
28. Liu, J.; Ma, Y. A survey of manufacturing oriented topology optimization methods. *Adv. Eng. Softw.* **2016**, *100*, 161–175. [CrossRef]
29. Xu, S.; Liu, J.; He, D.; Tang, K.; Yaji, K. Self-support structure topology optimization for multi-axis additive manufacturing incorporated with curved layer slicing. *Comput. Methods Appl. Mech. Eng.* **2025**, *438*, 117841. [CrossRef]
30. Guo, Y.; Liu, J.; Ahmad, R.; Ma, Y. Concurrent structural topology and fabrication sequence optimization for multi-axis additive manufacturing. *Comput. Methods Appl. Mech. Eng.* **2025**, *435*, 117627. [CrossRef]
31. Ren, H.; Chen, Z.; Shen, X.; Xiong, Y. Manufacturability-aware topology and toolpath co-design for continuous fiber-reinforced composites additive manufacturing. *Comput. Methods Appl. Mech. Eng.* **2025**, *444*, 118162. [CrossRef]
32. Dilgen, S.B.; Dilgen, C.B.; Fuhrman, D.R.; Sigmund, O.; Lazarov, B.S. Density based topology optimization of turbulent flow heat transfer systems. *Struct. Multidiscip. Optim.* **2018**, *57*, 1905–1918. [CrossRef]
33. Zhao, X.; Zhou, M.; Sigmund, O.; Andreasen, C.S. A "poor man's approach" to topology optimization of cooling channels based on a Darcy flow model. *Int. J. Heat Mass Transf.* **2018**, *116*, 1108–1123. [CrossRef]
34. Luo, J.-W.; Yaji, K.; Chen, L.; Tao, W.-Q. Data-driven multifidelity topology design for enhancing turbulent natural convection cooling. *Int. J. Heat Mass Transf.* **2025**, *240*, 126659. [CrossRef]
35. Schewe, F.; Fleischer, D.; Elham, A. Industrial application of thermofluid topology optimization to rollbonding cold plates with dedicated manufacturing constraints. *Struct. Multidiscip. Optim.* **2023**, *66*, 230. [CrossRef]
36. Yaji, K.; Yamasaki, S.; Fujita, K. Multifidelity design guided by topology optimization. *Struct. Multidiscip. Optim.* **2020**, *61*, 1071–1085. [CrossRef]
37. Kii, T.; Yaji, K.; Fujita, K.; Sha, Z.; Conner Seepersad, C. Latent crossover for data-driven multifidelity topology design. *J. Mech. Des.* **2024**, *146*, 051713. [CrossRef]
38. Kato, M.; Kii, T.; Yaji, K.; Fujita, K. Maximum stress minimization via data-driven multifidelity topology design. *J. Mech. Des.* **2025**, *147*, 081702. [CrossRef]
39. Peherstorfer, B.; Willcox, K.; Gunzburger, M. Survey of multifidelity methods in uncertainty propagation, inference, and optimization. *Siam Rev.* **2018**, *60*, 550–591. [CrossRef]

https://doi.org/10.3390/computation14010019

40. Park, C.; Haftka, R.T.; Kim, N.H. Remarks on multi-fidelity surrogates. *Struct. Multidiscip. Optim.* **2017**, *55*, 1029–1050. [CrossRef]
41. March, A.; Willcox, K. Constrained multifidelity optimization using model calibration. *Struct. Multidiscip. Optim.* **2012**, *46*, 93–109. [CrossRef]
42. Forrester, A.; Sobester, A.; Keane, A. *Engineering Design via Surrogate Modelling: A Practical Guide*; John Wiley & Sons: Hoboken, NJ, USA, 2008.
43. Van Dijk, N.P.; Maute, K.; Langelaar, M.; Van Keulen, F. Level-set methods for structural topology optimization: A review. *Struct. Multidiscip. Optim.* **2013**, *48*, 437–472. [CrossRef]
44. Yamada, T.; Izui, K.; Nishiwaki, S.; Takezawa, A. A topology optimization method based on the level set method incorporating a fictitious interface energy. *Comput. Methods Appl. Mech. Eng.* **2010**, *199*, 2876–2891. [CrossRef]
45. Fu, Y.-F.; Rolfe, B.; Chiu, L.N.; Wang, Y.; Huang, X.; Ghabraie, K. SEMDOT: Smooth-edged material distribution for optimizing topology algorithm. *Adv. Eng. Softw.* **2020**, *150*, 102921. [CrossRef]
46. Fu, Y.-F.; Rolfe, B. *Smooth Topological Design of Continuum Structures*; CRC Press: Boca Raton, FL, USA, 2025.
47. Alexandersen, J.; Andreasen, C.S. A review of topology optimisation for fluid-based problems. *Fluids* **2020**, *5*, 29. [CrossRef]
48. Qian, X.; Dede, E.M. Topology optimization of a coupled thermal-fluid system under a tangential thermal gradient constraint. *Struct. Multidiscip. Optim.* **2016**, *54*, 531–551. [CrossRef]
49. Osanov, M.; Guest, J.K. Topology optimization for architected materials design. *Annu. Rev. Mater. Res.* **2016**, *46*, 211–233. [CrossRef]
50. Gao, T.; Xu, P.; Zhang, W. Topology optimization of thermo-elastic structures with multiple materials under mass constraint. *Comput. Struct.* **2016**, *173*, 150–160. [CrossRef]
51. Mantz, H.; Jacobs, K.; Mecke, K. Utilizing Minkowski functionals for image analysis: A marching square algorithm. *J. Stat. Mech. Theory Exp.* **2008**, *2008*, P12015. [CrossRef]
52. Ho, C.-C.; Wu, F.-C.; Chen, B.-Y.; Chuang, Y.-Y.; Ouhyoung, M. Cubical marching squares: Adaptive feature preserving surface extraction from volume data. *Comput. Graph. Forum* **2005**, *24*, 537–545. [CrossRef]
53. Gómez, J.V.; Lumbier, A.; Garrido, S.; Moreno, L. Planning robot formations with fast marching square including uncertainty conditions. *Robot. Auton. Syst.* **2013**, *61*, 137–152. [CrossRef]
54. Maple, C. Geometric design and space planning using the marching squares and marching cube algorithms. In Proceedings of the 2003 International Conference on Geometric Modeling and Graphics, 2003. Proceedings, London, UK, 16–18 July 2003; pp. 90–95.
55. Xu, C.; Chen, J.; Ge, Y.; Li, M. Theoretical formulation/development of signal sampling with an equal arc length using the frame theorem. *EURASIP J. Adv. Signal Process.* **2022**, *2022*, 59. [CrossRef]
56. Multiphysics, C. *Introduction to COMSOL Multiphysics®*; COMSOL Multiphysics: Burlington, MA, USA, 1998; Volume 9, p. 32.
57. Kiyono, C.Y.; Vatanabe, S.L.; Silva, E.C.N.; Reddy, J. A new multi-p-norm formulation approach for stress-based topology optimization design. *Compos. Struct.* **2016**, *156*, 10–19. [CrossRef]
58. Xu, S.; Kawabe, H.; Yaji, K. Evolutionary de-homogenization using a generative model for optimizing solid-porous infill structures considering the stress concentration issue. *arXiv* **2024**, arXiv:2412.19154. [CrossRef]

https://doi.org/10.3390/computation14010019

computation

MDPI

Article

A CAD-Integrated Framework for Dynamic Structural Topology Optimisation via Visual Programming

Laura Sardone [1,*], Stefanos Sotiropoulos [2] and Alessandra Fiore [3]

1 Department of Structural, Geotechnical, and Building Engineering, Polytechnic of Turin, 10129 Turin, Italy
2 School of Civil Engineering, National Technical University of Athens, 15780 Athens, Greece; st.sotirop@gmail.com
3 Department of Architecture, Construction, and Design, Polytechnic of Bari, 70126 Bari, Italy; alessandra.fiore@poliba.it
* Correspondence: laura.sardone@polito.it

Abstract: Structural Topology Optimisation (STO) plays a critical role in computational engineering, enabling the creation of material-efficient, performance-driven structures. However, dynamic STO workflows, particularly those involving time-varying or seismic excitations, are often inaccessible to architects and engineers due to their reliance on standalone solvers, large-scale data handling, and advanced programming skills. This paper introduces a Computer-Aided Design (CAD)-embedded, time-dependent STO framework built upon a modular, adjoint-based optimisation core integrated into a Visual Programming Language (VPL) interface. Implemented within a parametric CAD environment through a custom C# component, the framework embeds a MATLAB-based solver to support geometry definition, boundary condition control, and dynamic finite element analysis under harmonic and seismic loading. The resulting Graphical User Interface (GUI) lowers technical barriers by enabling users to iteratively configure STO parameters, manage meshing, and visualise real-time results. Case studies on tall building façades under earthquake excitation validate the framework's ability to minimise displacement at targeted Degrees of Freedom (DOFs), dynamically adapt material distributions, and enhance structural resilience. By bridging high-fidelity computational methods with accessible visual workflows, the proposed system advances the integration of dynamic STO into both architectural and engineering practice.

Keywords: Visual Programming Language; Graphical User Interface; Algorithm-Aided Design; computational design; Structural Topology Optimisation

1. Introduction

Designers and engineers increasingly rely on CAD environments to develop, analyse, and refine complex geometries. Tools such as Rhinoceros3D and its Grasshopper (GH) add-on facilitate a VPL approach, wherein users can expeditiously explore parametric forms without extensive or complex scripting. Notwithstanding these advancements, the integration of high-level Structural Optimisation (SO), particularly under dynamic loading conditions, remains an unresolved challenge. The majority of Topology Optimisation (TO) methods operate in stand-alone solvers, necessitating advanced coding skills and intricate data exchanges that impede iterative design processes [1–3]. Recent studies underscore the value of TO for material efficiency, lightweight structures, and performance-driven design [4], enabling the efficient distribution of material within a given design domain to achieve optimal structural performance under defined constraints. Originally developed in

https://doi.org/10.3390/computation13110267

the field of mechanical and aerospace engineering, TO has gained increasing relevance in the Architecture, Engineering, and Construction (AEC) industry, particularly with the rise of computational design tools and parametric modelling platforms [5,6].

Over the past decade, several GH plug-ins have been developed to provide TO capabilities, bridging the gap between advanced computational techniques and practical design applications [7]. However, despite their initial promise, the majority of these plug-ins suffer from two major limitations: (i) most TO plug-ins available for GH focus on static loading conditions, limiting their applicability to real-world structural scenarios that involve dynamic loads, seismic forces, or transient responses; (ii) many TO plug-ins, once actively developed, have become outdated, unsupported, or incompatible with newer versions of GH and Rhino3D, reducing their usability in modern design workflows.

Among the plug-ins developed to perform TO can be found *Millipede*, *Ameba*, *TopOpt*, *tOpos*, and *Peregrine*. Each of these tools provided a unique approach to SO, but they also faced significant limitations. For instance, *Millipede*, one of the earliest TO plug-ins for GH, implemented a Solid Isotropic Material Penalisation (SIMP)-based TO algorithm; however, it primarily focused on static structural problems and is no longer actively maintained [8]. *Ameba*, developed by researchers at Tongji University, introduced a biologically inspired TO method and supported Multi-Objective Optimisation (MOO) [9,10]. While it provides enhanced capabilities, it still lacks dynamic loading analysis and has a limited update cycle. *TopOpt*, based on the well-known research project at the Technical University of Denmark (DTU), implements static TO using SIMP [11]. However, it lacks flexibility for complex parametric workflows and has not been significantly updated for the latest GH versions. Another well-known plug-in is *tOpos*; the latter one has been developed for architectural applications introducing a structural growth-based TO method [12], but was not widely adopted due to performance limitations and lack of updates. Finally, *Peregrine* focuses on truss optimisation [13], making it more applicable to structural form generation rather than freeform TO. Despite the availability of the aforementioned tools, the AEC industry increasingly requires TO methods that account for dynamic loading conditions, including seismic forces, wind loads, vibrations, and transient structural responses. Existing plug-ins lack this capability, creating a gap between research-driven TO methodologies and real-world engineering applications [14]. Additionally, the obsolescence of many TO tools presents practical barriers for designers and engineers who seek reliable, well-maintained software solutions that can integrate seamlessly into modern computational workflows.

STO was initially investigated by automotive–aeronautical research groups and Computer-Aided Engineering (CAE) software companies in its early stages of development [5,6], but significant progress has been made in its application in architecture and civil engineering over the past 15 years [15,16]. Nevertheless, most STO research still focuses on static and deterministic loading conditions, and most open-source codes solve linear elasticity problems that demand manual coding for defining structures, making them inaccessible to non-programmers [17,18]. The dynamic response of a structure is significantly more complex and often aligns closely with real-world conditions, requiring methods such as direct or indirect time integration analyses. Integrating such methodologies into CAD-based parametric modelling environments remains a major challenge, as traditional STO workflows involve high computational costs and complex scripting.

Direct time integration methods, such as those proposed by Min et al. (1999) [19] and Bendsøe and Sigmund (2004) [20], show promise in transient analysis but are computationally expensive when applied iteratively in TO processes. Kang et al. (2006) [21] conducted a review of STO problems under transient loads, which included time-dependent constraints (utilising both direct and transformation methods), design sensitivity calculations (using Direct Differentiation Methods (DDM) and Adjoint Variable Methods (AVM)), and various approximations. Despite this, their practical implementation in CAD-friendly environments remains rare [22–24].

Model reduction techniques, such as mode superposition and Ritz vectors [25], provide solutions to computational demands but require complex programming to integrate them into CAD workflows. Several notable implementations have been presented. For instance, Giraldo-Londoño and Paulino (2021) [26] offered a comprehensive MATLAB implementation for dynamic STO problems, allowing for dynamic loads to be applied to both structured and unstructured meshes. Filipov et al. (2016) [27] utilised high-resolution polygonal finite elements to tackle dynamic STO problems, focusing on eigenfrequency optimisation and compliance-based optimisation for structures subjected to forced vibrations. Additionally, Martin and Deierlein (2020) [28] examined the dynamic response of tall buildings to STO problems under seismic excitation using response spectrum analyses to minimise structural vibrations, although they lack CAD-compatible, interactive tools for broader adoption. Recent advances in dynamic STO have demonstrated the feasibility of adjoint-based sensitivity analysis and time-integration schemes for transient and seismic excitation scenarios [19,20]. However, existing implementations remain primarily confined to research-oriented or MATLAB-based environments, limiting accessibility for design practitioners. Currently, no CAD-integrated or VPL-based framework has been presented that enables dynamic STO with time-varying loads and adjoint sensitivities directly within an architectural modelling ecosystem. This context underlines the need for CAD-compatible dynamic STO methods, which motivates the development of the framework proposed in this study. To address this gap, we present a comprehensive Visual Programming Language (VPL) framework for dynamic STO within Grasshopper (GH) for Rhino3D. The framework integrates an open-source MATLAB-based solver adapted from Giraldo-Londoño et al. (2021) [26], embedded through a C# plug-in, enabling users to define geometry and boundary conditions with familiar GH components, compute optimised material distributions without external scripting, and generate CAD-ready geometry that can be further manipulated or exported for fabrication. Unlike conventional approaches that produce only images, our method returns tessellated CAD models, allowing detailed study and optimisation of both structured and unstructured meshes. The system supports realistic scenarios by accommodating multiple lumped masses (MDOF systems) and ground acceleration time history data, thereby simulating the dynamic response of tall buildings under real earthquake excitations. By lowering technical barriers and embedding adjoint-based optimisation for time-varying loads directly in GH, the framework enhances accessibility and enables iterative, performance-driven seismic design in parametric workflows.

2. Formulation of the Topology Optimisation Problem

STO is a mathematical method used in engineering design to optimise the layout or distribution of materials within a given design space, subject to certain constraints, to achieve the best performance of a structure or system [29]. The goal is to determine the optimal configuration of material distribution that minimises or maximises certain Objective Functions (OFs), such as minimising weight while maintaining structural integrity, maximising stiffness while minimising material usage, or optimising heat dissipation in a system [30,31].

2.1. Formulation of the Dynamic STO

In this study, the dynamic optimisation problem incorporating time history analysis is addressed, where the external forces can be represented as sinusoidal functions or data from real earthquake ground motions. The objective is defined as the minimisation of the squared displacement at selected DOFs (Equation (1)). This choice, rather than the more common dynamic compliance, directly addresses façade drift under seismic and dynamic excitation, a key performance indicator in engineering and architectural design. By focusing on critical DOFs, the objective provides a physically meaningful link to serviceability criteria (e.g., inter-story drift limits), ensuring that the optimised topology is directly interpretable in practice. The dynamic STO problem is formulated as follows:

$$\min f = \frac{1}{N_t}\sum_{i=0}^{N_t} ||\mathbf{L}^T \mathbf{u}_i||^2 \quad (1)$$

where $||\cdot||$ denotes the Euclidean L_2 norm. Equation (1) represents the time-averaged squared displacement at the selected DOF(s). Here, $\mathbf{L}$ is a selector vector (a sparse binary vector) that isolates the displacement at the target DOF, N_t is the number of time steps, and $\mathbf{u}_i$ is the displacement vector at time step i.

Equation (1) is subjected to the following equation of motion:

$$\mathbf{M}(\rho_e)\ddot{\mathbf{u}}_t + \mathbf{C}(\rho_e)\dot{\mathbf{u}}_t + \mathbf{K}(\rho_e)\mathbf{u}_t = \mathbf{F}_t \quad (2)$$

where $\ddot{\mathbf{u}}_t$, $\dot{\mathbf{u}}_t$, $\mathbf{u}_t$ are, respectively, the acceleration, velocity, and displacement vectors. The matrices $\mathbf{M}$, $\mathbf{C}$, and $\mathbf{K}$ denote the mass, damping, and stiffness matrices, respectively, while $\mathbf{F}_t$ represents the external dynamic forces (e.g., seismic ground motion) [32–34]. In this formulation, the imposed ground acceleration acts through the external load vector $\mathbf{F}_t$, which represents the equivalent inertial forces transmitted from the foundations to the structure

$$\mathbf{F}_t = -\mathbf{M}\cdot a_g(t) \quad (3)$$

Therefore, the base nodes are kinematically fixed relative to the ground, moving coherently with the prescribed base acceleration but having zero relative displacement, consistent with the physical behaviour of a rigidly founded structure.

The material density field is defined at the element level by the following:

$$0 \le \rho_e \le 1 \quad (4)$$

where ρ_e is the element-wise material density field.

Finally, the volume constraint is enforced as follows:

$$\sum\nolimits_{e\in\Omega} \rho_e V_e \le V_{allowed} \quad (5)$$

where V_e is the volume of the element e in the design domain Ω, and $V_{allowed}$ is the prescribed maximum material volume.

The damping parameters is given by

$$\mathbf{C} = \alpha_r\mathbf{M} + \beta_r\mathbf{K} \quad (6)$$

using Rayleigh damping, a linear combination of the $\mathbf{M}$ and $\mathbf{K}$ where α_r is the mass-proportional damping coefficient and β_r is the stiffness-proportional damping coefficient [35,36]. This model ensures that higher frequency modes experience greater damping while lower frequency modes remain less affected [37].

2.2. Structural Dynamic Resolution in STO

The structural dynamic problem resolution is based on the HHT-α method introduced by Hilber et al. (1977) [38]. This approach extends the Newmark–β method [39] to address structural dynamics issues, adjusting the equation of motion by incorporating the parameter

α, which accounts for a numerical lag among the damping, stiffness, and external force vectors, leading to a modified equation of motion:

$$\mathbf{M}\ddot{\mathbf{u}}_i + (1-\alpha)\mathbf{C}\dot{\mathbf{u}}_i + \alpha\mathbf{C}\dot{\mathbf{u}}_{i-1} + (1-\alpha)\mathbf{K}\mathbf{u}_i + \alpha\mathbf{K}\mathbf{u}_{i-1} = (1-\alpha)\mathbf{f}_i + \alpha\mathbf{f}_{i-1}, \; i = 1,\ldots,N_t \quad (7)$$

This condition maintains unconditional stability while ensuring second-order accuracy when $0 \le \alpha \le \frac{1}{3}$, $\beta = \frac{(1+\alpha)^2}{4}$ and $\gamma = \frac{1+2\alpha}{2}$ are satisfied; if $\alpha = 0$, the standard Newmark-β method (no numerical damping) is recovered; if $\alpha > 0$, high-frequency numerical damping is introduced, reducing spurious oscillations, and the upper limit $\alpha = \frac{1}{3}$ provides the maximum numerical dissipation without affecting low-frequency modes.

To compute the displacements and velocities at each time step, the Newmark–β Finite Difference (FD) approximations are applied [26,40]:

$$\mathbf{u}_i = \mathbf{u}_{i-1} + \Delta t\dot{\mathbf{u}}_{i-1} + \Delta t^2\left[\left(\frac{1}{2}-\beta\right)\ddot{\mathbf{u}}_{i-1} + \beta\ddot{\mathbf{u}}_i\right]$$

$$\dot{\mathbf{u}}_i = \dot{\mathbf{u}}_{i-1} + \Delta t[(1-\gamma)\ddot{\mathbf{u}}_{i-1} + \gamma\ddot{\mathbf{u}}_i] \quad (8)$$

where β controls the numerical accuracy and γ the numerical stability.

The dynamic problem is addressed at each time step $i = 1,\ldots,N_t$ by updating the terms $\dot{u}_i$ and u_i for $\ddot{u}_i$. The initial time step is settled as $i = 0$, corresponding to the initial conditions u_0 and $\dot{u}_0$. From the latter, it is possible to compute $\ddot{u}_0 = M^{-1}(f_0 - C\dot{u}_0 - Ku_0)$. The dynamic analysis starts from equilibrium at rest, assuming null initial displacement and velocity vectors, $\mathbf{u}_0 = \dot{\mathbf{u}}_0 = 0$.

2.3. Material Interpolation

In density-based methods, the shape of the structure is characterised by a density function, where $\rho = 0$ denotes void regions, and $\rho = 1$ signifies solid material. In the literature, there are three approaches for solving STO problems in the continuum: density-, boundary evolution-, and explicit geometry-based methods; in this context, we consider density-based STO. The homogenisation method and SIMP method are the most popular density-based STO approaches, with the latter being the most implemented method in commercial software, owing to its simplicity and feasibility [41–43]. In this contribution, an alternative methodology known as the Rational Approximation of Material Properties (RAMP) is employed, which presents distinct advantages, particularly in scenarios characterised by near-zero material densities [20,44,45].

The stiffness of each element (m_E) is interpolated as a function of its density (ρ_e) through the following RAMP scheme [44]:

$$m_E(\rho_e) = \frac{m_V(\rho_e)}{1 + p_0\,[1 - m_V(\rho_e)]} \quad (9)$$

where p_0 is the RAMP penalisation parameter that enhances convergence toward solid-void solutions, and m_V is the volume interpolation function of each element as a function of its density [46–48]:

$$m_V(\rho_e) = \frac{\tanh(\overline{\beta}\overline{\eta}) + \tanh(\overline{\beta}\,(\rho_e - \overline{\eta}))}{\tanh(\overline{\beta}\overline{\eta}) + \tanh(\overline{\beta}\,(1 - \overline{\eta}))} \quad (10)$$

where $\overline{\eta}$ denotes the projection threshold (typically $\overline{\eta} = 0.5$), while $\overline{\beta}$ controls the sharpness of the projection. In practice, $\overline{\beta}$ is progressively increased during the optimisation (e.g., from 1 to 8) to promote near-binary solutions.

The adopted RAMP interpolation follows the formulation by Stolpe & Svanberg (2001), as implemented in the MATLAB framework [49]. In the present implementation, the continuation of the projection parameter $\overline{\beta}$ follows a linear schedule, gradually increasing throughout the optimisation according to the following:

$$\overline{\beta}_{k+1} = \overline{\beta}_k + \frac{\overline{\beta}_{max} - \overline{\beta}_{min}}{N_{iter}}, \tag{11}$$

where $\overline{\beta}_{min} = 1$, $\overline{\beta}_{max} = 8$, k is the iteration index, and N_{iter} is the maximum number of iterations. The optimisation process terminates when the relative variation of the OF between consecutive iterations falls below 10^{-4}, or when the maximum number of iterations ($N_{iter} = 200$) is reached. These settings follow the standard practices in density-based TO [9,20,49].

The RAMP penalisation parameter is fixed at $p_0 = 3$, and an ersatz parameter $\varepsilon = 10^{-3}$ is adopted for stability when densities approach zero. Here, $m_E(\rho_e)$ interpolates the Young's modulus of the solid material, i.e., $E_e = m_E(\rho_e)E_0$, with E_0 as the modulus of the solid phase. The physical material density ρ_0 remains constant, while the design dependence of the elemental mass matrices is introduced exclusively through the interpolation function $m_V(\rho_e)$. This choice avoids ill-conditioning that may arise when both stiffness and density are interpolated in dynamic topology optimisation. Following the convention adopted in [26], the elemental physical density ρ_e and the filtered design variable y_e are distinct but related quantities. The normalised design variable y_e (ranging from 0 to 1) results from the filtering operation described in Equation (12) and is used in the interpolation functions $\widetilde{m}_E(y_e)$ and $\widetilde{m}_V(y_e)$. The corresponding physical density of each finite element is $\rho_e = y_e\rho_0$, where ρ_0 is the base material density.

For the time integration scheme, the generalised α parameters are set to $\alpha = 0.25$, $\beta = (1 + \alpha)^2/4 = 0.39$, and $\gamma = (1 + 2\alpha)/2 = 0.75$, which guarantee unconditional stability and controlled high-frequency dissipation. The time step Δt is chosen as a fraction of the fundamental period (typically 1/10–1/20) to ensure accuracy and stability.

In the implementation, the interpolation functions are applied consistently to the assembly of the FE mass and stiffness matrices. The global matrices are written as follows [26]:

$$\mathbf{M} = \sum_{e=1}^{N} \widetilde{m}_V(y_e)\mathbf{m}_e, \qquad \mathbf{K} = \sum_{e=1}^{N} \widetilde{m}_E(y_E)\mathbf{k}_e \tag{12}$$

where $\mathbf{m}_e$ and $\mathbf{k}_e$ are the elemental mass and stiffness matrices, respectively. The elemental mass and stiffness matrices $\mathbf{m}_e$ and $\mathbf{k}_e$ are evaluated at unit material density, according to $\mathbf{m}_e = \int \Omega_e \rho_0 N_e^T N_e dx$ and $\mathbf{k}_e = \int \Omega_e B_e^T D_0 B_e dx$, where N_e and B_e are the shape-function and strain–displacement matrices, respectively. In Equation (10) $\widetilde{m}_V$, $\widetilde{m}_E$ denote the filtered and projected interpolation functions including the ersatz parameter $\varepsilon \ll 1$:

$$\widetilde{m}_V(y_e) = \varepsilon + (1-\varepsilon)m_V(y_e), \qquad \widetilde{m}_E(y_E) = \varepsilon + (1-\varepsilon)m_E(y_e) \tag{13}$$

Here, $\widetilde{m}_V(y_e)$ and $\widetilde{m}_E(y_E)$ are the filtered and projected interpolation functions defined in Equations (9) and (10), respectively. The physical material density ρ_0 remains constant in the definition of the elemental mass matrices $\mathbf{m}_e$, while the design dependence of the mass matrix is introduced exclusively through the function m_V.

A filtering function is applied to prevent numerical instabilities and mitigate the checkerboard pattern. The filtered design variables are defined as follows:

$$\mathbf{y} = \mathbf{Pz}, \; P_{e_k} = \frac{w_{ek}\boldsymbol{A}_k}{\sum_{j=1}^{N} w_{e_j}\boldsymbol{A}_j}, \qquad w_{ek} = \max\left(0, 1 - \frac{\|\mathbf{x}_e^* - \mathbf{x}_k\|}{r_{min}}\right)^q \tag{14}$$

where $\mathbf{y}$ are the filtered values, $\mathbf{z}$ the raw design variables, $\mathbf{x}_e^*$ the centroid of element e, $\mathbf{A}_k$ the area of element k, r_{min} the filter radius, and q the weighting exponent (set to q = 2). This formulation corresponds to the classical density filter that suppresses checkerboard patterns and mesh dependency by averaging design variables within the neighbourhood defined by r_{min} [50,51].

2.4. Sensitivity Analysis—Update Scheme

In most STO problems, gradient-based optimisation algorithms are applied; thus, the sensitivity analysis plays a critical role in guiding the iterative update of the material distribution. The solver that is used in the present framework employs the Zhang–Paulino–Ramos (ZPR) algorithm [52], so the derivative of the OF with respect to the design variable is evaluated. Direct computation of sensitivities can be computationally expensive, particularly for time-dependent problems where solving the forward problem is already costly. To overcome this, the adjoint method is commonly employed, significantly reducing computational cost by solving an auxiliary adjoint equation rather than differentiating the full forward problem directly [53,54]. In our problem, the derivative of the OF with respect to the density ρ_e is expressed as follows:

$$\frac{df}{d\rho_e} = \frac{\delta f}{\delta \rho_e} + \sum_{i=0}^{N_t} \frac{\delta f}{\delta \mathbf{u}_i} \times \frac{\delta \mathbf{u}_i}{\delta \rho_e} \tag{15}$$

where $\frac{\delta f}{\delta \rho_e}$ is the explicit dependency of the OF on the design variables ρ_e, and $\sum_{i=0}^{N_t} \frac{\delta f}{\delta \mathbf{u}_i} \times \frac{\delta \mathbf{u}_i}{\delta \rho_e}$ accounts for the implicit dependency through the state variables $\mathbf{u}_i$.

Since the OF in Equation (1) depends only on the displacement, there is no explicit dependency on the design variables ρ_e; therefore, the first term vanishes.

It is worth noting that, in the case of base-acceleration excitation, the external load vector depends on the elemental mass matrix (see Equation (3)). Accordingly, its derivative with respect to the elemental density is non-zero and contributes to the sensitivity analysis as $\frac{\partial \mathbf{F}_t}{\partial \rho_e} = -\mathbf{m}_e \cdot a_g(t)$, where $\mathbf{m}_e$ denotes the elemental mass matrix [32,34,36].

The partial derivative with respect to displacement at time step i is

$$\frac{\partial f}{\partial_{\mathbf{u}i}} = \frac{2}{N_t} (\mathbf{L}^\top \mathbf{u}_i) \mathbf{L} \tag{16}$$

For the computation of $\frac{\delta \mathbf{u}_i}{\delta \rho_e}$, the adjoint method is applied, making use of the residual form of the HHT-a method. Using the adjoint variables, the gradient with respect to the design variables $\mathbf{z}$ is obtained through the filter–projection–RAMP chain as follows:

$$\frac{df}{d\mathbf{z}} = \mathbf{P}^\top \mathbf{J}_{\tilde{m}_E}(\mathbf{P}_\mathbf{z}) \frac{df}{d\mathbf{E}} + \mathbf{P}^\top \mathbf{J}_{\tilde{m}_V}(\mathbf{Pz}) \frac{df}{d\mathbf{V}} \tag{17}$$

where $\mathbf{P}$ is the density filter operator and $\mathbf{J}_{\tilde{m}_E}, \mathbf{J}_{\tilde{m}_V}$ are diagonal matrices with entries given by the derivatives of the stiffness and volume interpolation functions (including the ersatz). For the global volume constraint (Equation (4)), the sensitivity with respect to the design variables is as follows:

$$\frac{d\mathbf{V}}{d\mathbf{z}} = \mathbf{P}^\mathrm{T} \left(\mathbf{J}_{\tilde{\mathrm{m}}_\mathrm{V}}(\mathbf{Pz}) \mathbf{A} \right) \tag{18}$$

where $\mathbf{A}$ is the vector collecting the element areas $\mathrm{A_e}$. The inequality is then imposed as $\mathrm{V(z)} \leq \mathrm{V_{allowed}}$. For regional volume constraints, the same expression applies with A restricted to the elements of the considered sub-domain. The computed sensitivities are subsequently employed within the gradient-based update scheme of the optimiser to iteratively adjust the element densities, driving the design toward the optimal material distribution under dynamic loading. To ensure the correctness of the implemented sensitivity formulation, the analytical derivatives employed in this paper follow the adjoint-based derivation introduced in the MATLAB framework developed by Giraldo-Londoño & Paulino, (2021) [26]. This formulation was previously validated by comparison with finite-difference estimations, confirming the correctness of the analytical gradients. Therefore, the same verified expressions are adopted here without further numerical verification.

3. VPL–GUI Development

GH is a node-based programming paradigm that has gained widespread acceptance in architectural and product design communities, enabling users to manipulate geometry and control parametric parameters through a graphical interface rather than raw scripting. Previous GH plugins have explored static TO or simple shape optimisation; however, dynamic load scenarios typically require advanced solvers and additional coding skills. Furthermore, most of the available plug-ins are no longer updated, rendering them obsolete. The objective of this research was to unify geometric modelling, a dynamic STO solver, and real-time visualisation into a single, coherent workflow. The framework presented in this document consists of the following:

- *Geometry Definition and Meshing*: Users define the design domain in GH and generate structured or unstructured meshes (e.g., quad-mesh, triangular mesh, Voronoi tessellations).
- *Boundary Conditions and Load Input*: Users specify fixed supports, lumped masses, and external dynamic forces (e.g., earthquake time-history data, sinusoidal Simple Harmonic Motion (SHM)).
- *Solver Execution*: The MATLAB-based STO solver runs through a C#-compiled DLL, computing the optimised topology.
- *Results Visualisation and Export*: Optimised structures are displayed in GH-Rhino3D and can be baked into CAD files for further analysis.

Initially, the user must determine the initial design space Ω (e.g., façade of a tall building) to be optimised and create the mesh system using the VPL-CAD linked tool. Consequently, from the generated mesh, the nodes and the system's connectivity are retrieved like in a typical FEM formulation. It is then required to define the boundary conditions, i.e., type and location of supports, lumped mass in the system, and ground acceleration-related data. Additional design functionalities are provided by selecting specific areas to be maintained as solid ($\rho = 1 \in \Omega$) in the optimisation process (i.e., passive areas) and by controlling the final volume ratio in predefined subsets of the initial design space. The next step is defining the FEM and optimisation properties; major details can be found in Section 3.1. The optimised layout visualisation is carried out by setting a threshold (Thr), which is defining the existence or not of a mesh element in the final structure. By culling only the existing elements post-STO from the initial configuration, it is possible to retrieve the FEs in the VPL (Section 3.2). The described workflow is shown in Figure 1.

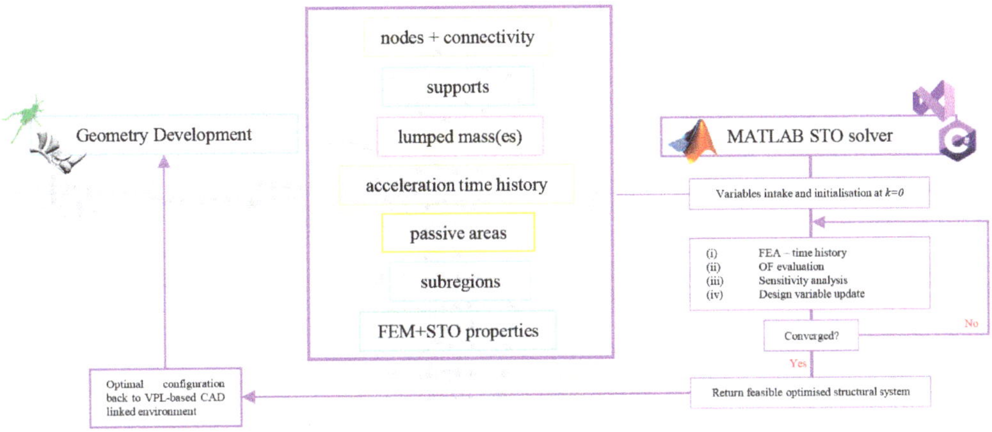

Figure 1. VPL workflow and MATLAB-based STO tool's connection.

3.1. User-Level Details

The plugin was developed in the C# programming language using the vs. Integrated Development Environment (IDE), with the MATLAB (v.2018b)-based code integrated into vs. as a .dll format. Initially, the user can create any desired geometry in the VPL environment and generate a mesh. The primary inputs of the plug-in are the coordinates of the nodes (Point List) and connectivity of the FE mesh (Data Tree). The subsequent inputs are the boundary conditions of the problem, which must be a Point List for which all Degrees Of Freedom (DOFs) are to be constrained, specifically translations in the X and Y directions. Subsequently, the coordinates of the nodes in which the concentrated masses are considered must be provided (Point List). This constitutes the minimum geometrical information required to formulate the STO problem.

The input data structure for the FEM problem comprises the following properties in this specific order: (i) OF, (ii) Simulation Time (T_max), (iii) Mass Magnitude (M_i), (iv) Young's modulus (E), (v) Poisson's ratio (v), (vi) Mass Density (ρ), (vii) Element Thickness (th), (viii) Rayleigh Damping (Ag), and (ix) Tag for Regular Meshes. The subsequent input is the ground acceleration applied to the STO problem, provided in .txt format with each row representing the acceleration for each time step (t_i). Subsequently, all parameters for the optimisation formulation should be provided in the following order: (i) filter radius (r_{min}), (ii) VolFrac, (iii) symmetry axis, and (iv) maximum number of iterations. The local file path, where the STO problem results will be stored, is also required. Lastly, a Boolean parameter determines whether the optimisation procedure will commence (Toggle). At the base of the component, as shown in Figure 2, optional geometric inputs may be included to impose constraints on the final output. The input PassiveEl comprises a Data Tree of points that defines the FE to be retained with ρ = 1 (the density of these elements is considered solid). The subsequent inputs pertain to potential sub-region constraints that may be imposed to regulate the maximum member size of the optimised structures, as described by Sanders et al. (2018) [55] and Giraldo-Londoño and Paulino (2020) [56,57]. Based on the empirical number of distinct sub-regions into which the initial structure is divided, an equivalent number of data points must be provided. In the absence of sub-region specifications, the STO solver will proceed without considering of any passive areas and/or sub-regions (g). Finally, to visualise the optimised structure, it is necessary for the user to define the Thr, which delineates the boundary between void and solid FEs.

3.2. Developer-Level Details

The development and the execution of the plug-in was performed using an Intel Core i7-7800X CPU @ 3.50GHz and 16 GB RAM. The OS was Windows 10 Pro, version 22H2, while the software used were Matlab2018b, Rhino V6.5, and Visual Studio 2019. The initial process phase involved collecting all user inputs employing the GH SDK [58] and transforming them into C# objects. Consequently, a preprocessing step was necessary to appropriately format the collected data for utilisation in the MATLAB function. When extracting nodes from a GH file (.gh) containing mesh elements, it is common to encounter duplicated points. This redundancy arises from the mesh generation process, where nodes associated with multiple elements can share identical coordinates. Thus, to maintain an accurate representation of the geometry in designs featuring consequential FE, it is essential to identify and remove these duplicate nodes from the list. Next, the connectivity information is modified to transform a collection of point coordinates into a matrix. Each row of the matrix contains unique identifiers (IDs) of the nodes constituting each element. Subsequently, the Data Trees containing nodes and elements are converted into arrays, with each row containing a node ID or element belonging to the corresponding group of nodes or elements (e.g., support nodes and passive elements). Finally, before invoking the MATLAB function, MWNumericArray and MWArray are employed to convert all the data into a format compatible with the MATLAB platform.

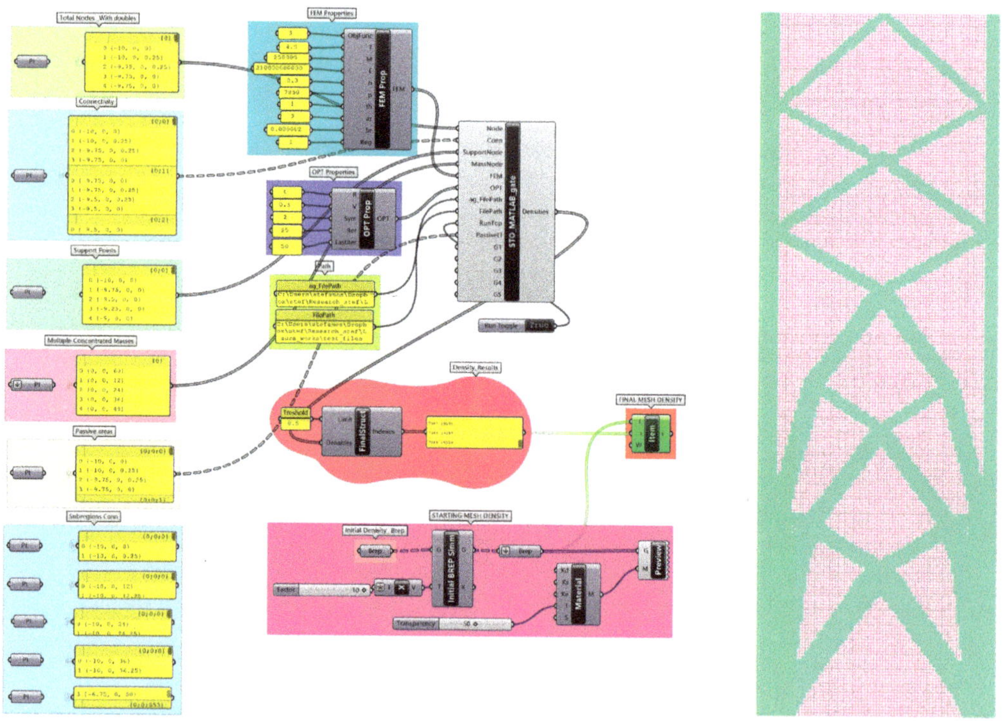

Figure 2. GH canvas—wired elements for the STO problem's resolution and TO solution in Rhino3D Viewport Front Area.

As previously stated, the primary core of the dynamic STO solver is implemented in MATLAB [26], and additional preprocessing calculations must be performed in the same environment. Of particular significance is the requirement to arrange the nodes of the element connectivity in an anticlockwise order, as this information is retrieved from .gh, which does not guarantee this specific condition (necessary for FEA). All pre-processing calculations, in conjunction with the script that invokes the STO solver, are encapsulated within a function that receives GH component input. Subsequently, utilising the MATLAB Compiler SDK (Library Compiler), all requisite functions are wrapped into a .dll file that can be imported into the VS. Through this method, the primary MATLAB function is called from the C# script, which is compiled in a GH Assembly file, and the GH component is generated. (Figure 2). In order to execute the components in the VPL environment, both the .gh and .dll files must be inserted into the *Library folder* of the GH installation (Rhino→Grasshopper→File→Special Folder→Library), enabling it to function akin to any other GH add-on.

A complete demonstration of the user interaction within the developed GUI is illustrated in Figures 1 and 2, showing the entire workflow—from geometry creation and FEM setup in the VPL environment to TO and visualisation in Rhino 3D. To ensure transparency and reproducibility, all Grasshopper definitions, MATLAB solver scripts, and resulting optimised geometries have been made openly available in the public GitHub repository linked to this research. The repository also includes a detailed README file describing each step of the process, from input preparation and solver execution to result post-processing and export in Rhino 3D.

3.3. Generation of the Initial Geometries of the Case Studies

Prior to executing the STO solver, the initial geometries were obtained through a parametric modelling workflow. The process was segmented into several phases, including the definition of the design domain that was modelled in the VPL environment—GH for Rhino (v.7). The initial geometry is defined through points, curves, or surfaces (Figure A1). The mesh may vary (structured or unstructured) in the two primary categories that represent the base test cases; however, the workflow logic remains consistent. The design domain is discretised through specific GH components with outputs organised in ordered lists; for the structured mesh, a quadrangular mesh system obtained through the *Lunchbox* add- will be adopted on [59], whilst for the unstructured mesh, a GH construction of a 2D Voronoi diagram will be employed.

Passive areas, i.e., regions that must maintain a density $\rho = 1$, are selected manually or through geometric criteria developed through VPL scripting. The passive elements are subsequently returned in the form of Data Trees, wherein each branch contains the list of linked points that are creating each passive FE (Figure A2).

Support points corresponding to constrained nodes, are identified and organised as separate inputs. In VPL, this process is accomplished through node coordinate selection components, which are subsequently filtered and converted into structured lists (Figure A3). The concentrated masses are determined on specific nodes through a coordinate ID system and mass magnitude assignment. By identifying the appropriate location for the lumped mass assignment, the specific coordinate for the application is retrieved from the total Point List derived from the mesh system. In Figure A4, the selection is based on the total point coordinates deconstruction such that the masses are situated at specific heights on the z-axis.

To ensure control over the material distribution within the design domain, Ω is divided into sub-regions. Each sub-region is defined as a distinct subset by dividing the total height of the building into equal parts, thus creating a series of sub-elements. The list of FEs belonging to each sub-region is subsequently organised in separate Data Trees containing the IDs of the individual FEs and the nodes belonging to them, thereby facilitating management during data transfer (Figure A5).

The close integration of VPL and MATLAB facilitates an automated workflow. Geometric data and boundary conditions are input into the GH environment (VPL) and organised into compatible matrices. Subsequently, the solver computes mass, damping, and stiffness matrices, solving the dynamic problem. The final density distribution map is returned to the .gh, where it can be visualised or exported with the "*Bake*" command into the CAD program.

3.4. Post-Processing and Export Features

After the optimisation process, the CAD-integrated framework (Rhino + GH V6.5 and later) provides post-processing functionalities to transform the density field into a clean, buildable geometry. The optimised density field is transmitted from MATLAB to Grasshopper as an indexed list of finite elements, where each index corresponds to a specific mesh element of the initial discretisation. This information is received by the Densities results output component (see Figure 2), which associates each element index with its corresponding density value.

A threshold parameter (Thr) is then applied within GH to distinguish solid and void regions. Elements whose density values exceed the threshold are identified as active members and extracted from the complete mesh from the initial density; this process isolates the subset of structural elements that define the final optimised layout.

Each selected element preserves its original nodal connectivity and geometric position, as imported from MATLAB, ensuring full consistency between the numerical model and the visualised mesh in Rhino 3D.

To enhance the readability of the optimised topology, edge detection and smoothing can be applied to the selected mesh. In practice, these operations can be implemented using native and plugin-based GH components such as Mesh Edges, Weaverbird Laplacian Smoothing, and Remesh, which remove irregularities and improve the visual continuity of the structure. Connectivity repair between adjacent elements can automatically be performed through the Join Meshes and Weld components, merging coincident vertices and eliminating small gaps along shared edges.

Finally, the refined mesh can be subdivided using the components such as Rhino's QuadRemesh tools to improve the resolution of the final layout before export.

Then, the final mesh can be baked into Rhino 3D and exported to standard CAD formats (.3dm, .stl, .obj) or text-based files (.csv, .txt) for further analysis or fabrication. This integration ensures a continuous workflow from density-based optimisation to editable, fabrication-ready geometry, demonstrating the interoperability between the MATLAB solver and the visual programming interface.

In the next sections, several test cases are presented to assess the framework's capability; specifically, two distinct geometries and mesh systems for the structural system of tall buildings are investigated under different dynamic loading conditions.

4. Numerical Case Studies

This section presents case studies on the dynamic STO application in tall buildings employing the developed VPL framework. All numerical examples are restricted to 2D plane-stress models, consistent with façade-like geometries on the XZ plane. Therefore, the current release is limited to two-dimensional meshes. The focus is minimising the square displacement at a target DOF, as outlined in Equation (1) for Single Degree of Freedom (SDOF) systems. In Multi-Degrees of Freedom (MDOFs), the OF minimises the sum of the square displacements of each DOF. The numerical test cases in Sections 4.1 and 4.2 involve a tall building with a quadrangular base measuring 20×20 m and a height of 60 m. Various parameters and filters are varied during the analysis. The building's façade is initially defined as a surface, then divided into regular quadrangular FEs using the *Lunchbox©* plug-in in GH. In this case, the surface is divided into 80 × 240 quad-panels, generating 19,200 FEs (Figure 3).

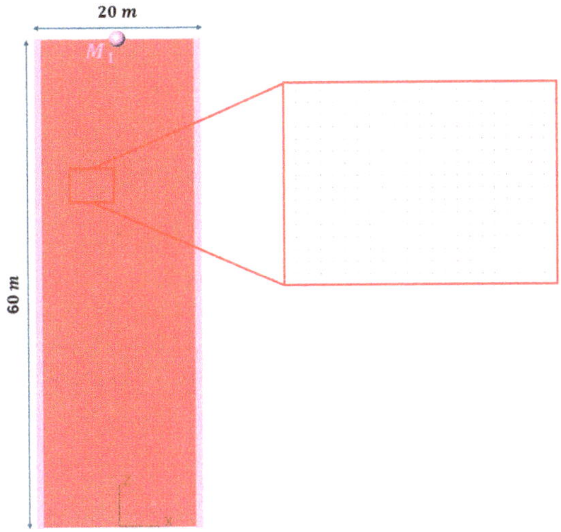

Figure 3. Façade1, quad-mesh, 19,200 FEs.

This subdivision is empirically calibrated to ensure satisfactory mesh discretisation, yielding accurate results during the optimisation. Additionally, the filter radius size setting (r_{min}) is also taken into account. The r_{min} is applied after computing the elemental criterion to mitigate the occurrence of a checkerboard pattern in the optimised solution. This filter modifies the elemental criterion of a specific element by calculating a weighted average value within a specified neighbourhood. The user determines the r_{min}, which should exceed the size of the smallest FE to be effective (Figure 4). Adjusting the filter radius size enables control over the minimum size of the resulting features within the design domain [60], generally preventing compression-dominated regions from becoming overly thin.

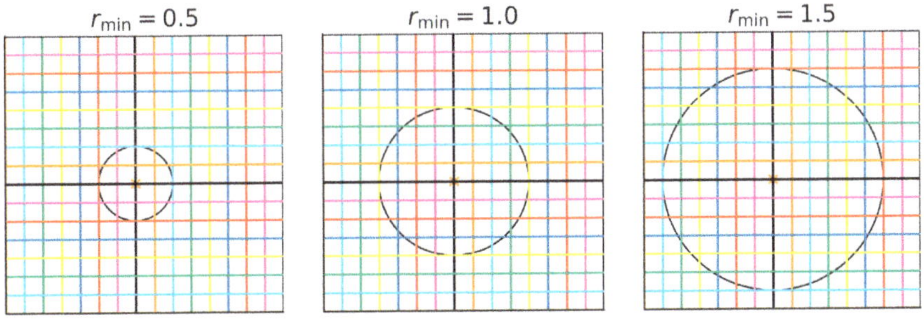

Figure 4. Filter radius r_{min} representation with a single cell base = height, 0.25 × 0.25 cm.

Passive areas are incorporated into the model; these specific elements are designated as non-optimisable by the solver (see Figure 5). For convenience, the configuration shown in the following figure and in Figure 3 will be referred to as "Façade1" throughout the rest of the document.

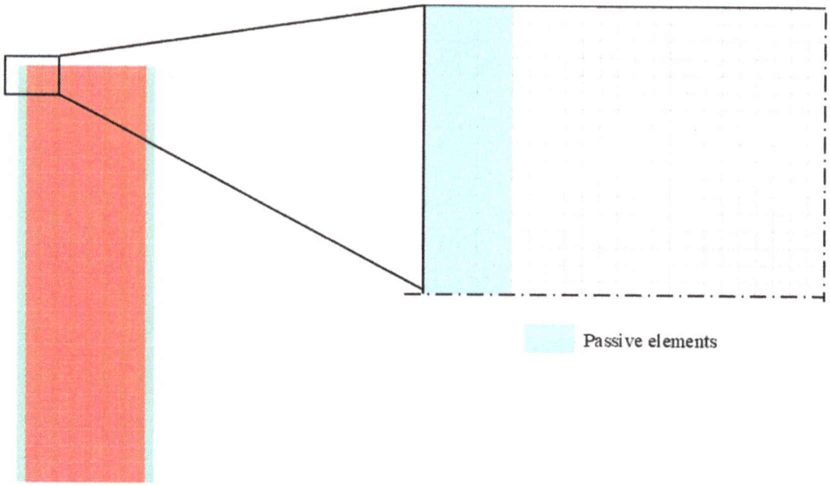

Figure 5. Façade1: Passive areas definition and quad-mesh FE.

The building inter-storey is set at I = 3 m, so the tall building is hypothesised with a total of 20 floors. To simplify the problem, a single lumped mass M_i is initially considered on top of the building (Figure 3). The magnitude of M_1 is defined considering the building footprint as follows:

$$B = l_x \times l_y = 400\ \text{m}^2 \tag{19}$$

where B represents the building footprint (m^2).

Reliable values regarding the floor thickness Θ were considered according to Eurocode 2 as follows [61]:

$$\theta_{min,\ max} = [12.5,\ 30](\text{cm}) \tag{20}$$

This allows calculation of the slab volume S per each floor by considering the following building footprint B:

$$S = B\ \times [\theta_{min,\ max}] = [50, 120]\ (\text{m}^3) \tag{21}$$

By assuming the concrete density as γ_{cr} = 2400 kg/m^3, a single slab mass value ranges from 0.12×10^6 kg to 0.288×10^6 kg:

$$S \times \gamma_{cr} = [0.12,\ 0.288] \times 10^6\ (\text{kg}) \tag{22}$$

Considering γ_{s} = 100 kg/m^3 for the steel reinforcement, the mass value to be added varies as [5000, 12,000] (kg). Therefore, the total mass of the single floor lies in the range $[0.125 \times 10^6, 0.3 \times 10^6]$ (kg) ($\text{Mass}_{\Theta\text{min}}$, $\text{Mass}_{\Theta\text{max}}$).

Two different values for the lumped masses are considered in the numerical test cases, corresponding to Θ_{min} and Θ_{max}. Therefore, by fixing a total number of twenty floors, the total mass magnitudes for the case studies are calculated as $M_{min} = Mass_{\Theta_{min}} \times 20 = 2.5 \times 10^6$ kg and $M_{max} = Mass_{\Theta_{max}} \times 20 =\ 6 \times 10^6$ kg. Having considered four areas of influence, since the optimisation phase contemplates only the two-dimensional development, the mass magnitudes are $\boldsymbol{M_{min'}} = \frac{M_{\text{min}}}{2} = 1.25 \times 10^6$ kg and $\boldsymbol{M_{max'}} = \frac{M_{\text{max}}}{2} = 3 \times 10^6$ kg.

For all the subsequent case studies, the following parameters were settled as follows: (i) E = 210,000 MPa; (ii) ν = 0.3; (iii) ρ = 7800 kg/m^3; (iv) th = 1 m; (v) Ag = $[2, 2 \times 10^{-6}]$; (vi) OF as in Equation (1); (vii) VolFrac = [0.3; 0.4]; (viii) r_{min} = [1]; (ix) Thr = 0.5; (x) $M_i = [M_{min'}, M_{max'}]$. The façade thickness does not correspond to the physical cladding thickness but represents an equivalent homogenised depth that accounts for the tributary contribution of mullions, spandrels, and secondary framing. For consistency, a reference value th = 1 m is adopted as a normalisation choice, ensuring proportional scaling of stiffness and mass per unit area.

While Sections 4.1 and 4.2 focus on the application of the STO on the structured quad-mesh, Section 4.3 will analyse a special case of an unstructured mesh within a complex design domain. However, all the parameters listed above will remain unchanged. More information about the geometrical model is provided in the dedicated subsection.

4.1. Simple Harmonic Motion in Structured Mesh

In this subsection, the initial set of case studies focuses on applying SHM to evaluate the initial response of the VPL framework in a simplified scenario. In all dynamic simulations, the excitation is introduced as a ground motion imposed at the base of the façade domain. In the harmonic case, the ground acceleration is defined as a sinusoidal input with angular frequency ω. In the earthquake cases, the excitation corresponds to recorded accelerograms applied as base accelerations at the support nodes.

Although only single-excitation results are reported herein for clarity, the proposed framework inherently supports multiple dynamic load cases. Owing to the linear nature of the equilibrium equation, different excitation windows or SHM frequencies can be superimposed to perform multi-load analyses, allowing robustness assessments without modifying the optimisation algorithm.

In this context, the imposed base acceleration for the harmonic case is defined as follows:

$$\ddot{\mu}_g(t) = 5\sin(2.5\pi t) \tag{23}$$

where the peak acceleration is 5 m/s^2, T_max is capped at 4.8 s with 80 time-steps, and the angular frequency is ω = 2.5π rad/s (Figure 6).

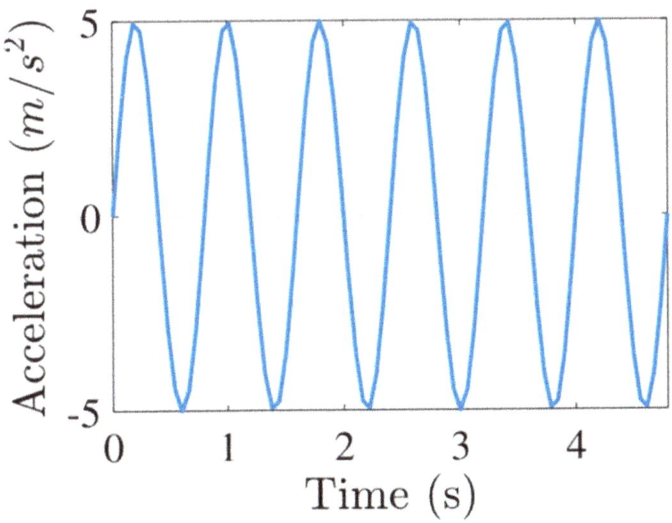

Figure 6. SHM application—f_i in the dynamic problem.

4.1.1. Case Study No. 1 Imposing SDOF, 1 g, SHM

The first results are obtained solving the minimisation problem in Equation (1), by imposing one sub-region g_1 as constraint in Façade1 in the XZ plane under SHM (Figure 6). The fixed support points are located at the base (Figure 7). Two different tests were carried out by varying $M_{1[min', max']}$ while maintaining constant the *VolFrac* = 0.3 for the sub-region g_1 (no sub-region is developed in the GH workflow).

Figure 7. Façade1 definition, single concentrated mass M_1, single sub-region g_1.

Figure 8 displays the evolution of the bracing system developed by the VPL solver using a unified design domain. The complete optimisation of Test Case 1 required approximately 15 min on a standard workstation (Intel i7, 32 GB RAM), with a peak memory usage of about 2.6 GB.

In this scenario, M_1 is set as $M_{min'}$ for the left configuration (Figure 8a) and $M_{max'}$ for the right configuration (Figure 8b). Applying SHM excitation, the results revealed a significant dependence of bracing system topology on M_1; the optimised design demonstrated for $M_{1,\text{min}'}$ a uniform diagonal bracing pattern, while for $M_{1,\text{max}'}$ a denser bracing structure to counteract increased inertial forces. Despite the design codes not providing a direct horizontal deflection limit, recent research has demonstrated that most of the δ_{max} for tall buildings varies in the range of values $\left[\frac{h}{200}, \frac{h}{600}\right]$ [15,62]. In our case, the optimised designs demonstrated for $M_{1,\text{min}'}$ a maximum horizontal displacement located at the position of the targeted DOF equal to $\delta_{\text{max}} = 0.031$ m, and for $M_{1,\text{max}'}$ a larger displacement such as $\delta_{\text{max}} = 0.082$ m. The results show a realistic outcome in terms of practical application, since δ_{max} for $M_{1,\text{max}'}$ is slightly smaller than $\frac{h}{600} = 0.1$. The δ_{max} increased with mass magnitude, confirming the solver's ability to adjust material distribution based on dynamic demand. The r_{min} helped smooth out density variations, preventing unrealistic checkerboarding effects in the optimised topology. The test case confirms that larger mass magnitudes require denser bracing, particularly in the lower regions of the structure.

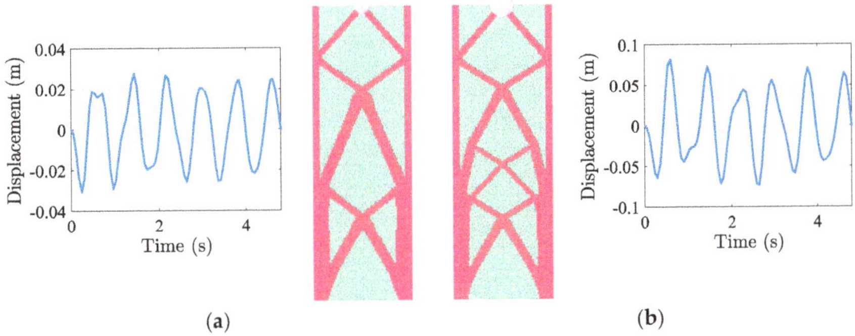

Figure 8. Façade1, dynamic STO results, SDOF, 1 g; δ_{max} over time and final configuration for (**a**) $M_{1min'}$, (**b**) $M_{1max'}$.

4.1.2. Case Study No. 2 Imposing SDOF, 5 g, SHM

The second analysis carried out on Façade1 consists of applying five distinct sub-regions denoted as $g_{[1, 5]}$ (Figure 9). Each sub-region is evaluated in the STO problem separately, considering the value *VolFrac* = 0.4. Support points and passive areas are equal to Test No.1, as indicated in the following picture.

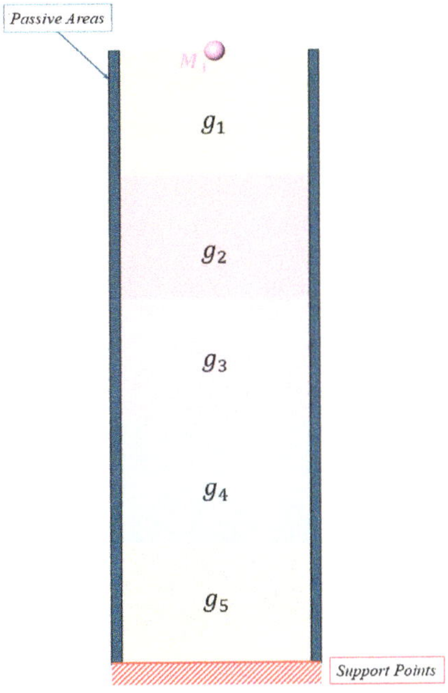

Figure 9. Façade1, inclusion of 5 sub-regions $g_{[1, 5]}$; SDOF, M_1 variable.

After applying the SHM in Equation (23) and illustrated in Figure 6, by minimising the square displacement located at M_1, the following results were observed. Figure 10 illustrates the evolution of the bracing system post-optimisation relating to a value of M_1 equal to $M_{min'}$ (Figure 10a) and to $M_{max'}$ (Figure 10b) based on the above-described calculations involving Eurocode 2. The results show the maximum lateral displacement obtained by applying SHM as δ_{max} = 0.031 m with $M_{1,min'}$ and δ_{max} = 0.068 m by applying $M_{1,max'}$. The introduction of five sub-regions resulted in a more stable, evenly distributed bracing layout compared to the single-region case. As mass increased, the material remained concentrated along the main lateral force transmission paths, confirming the stability and robustness of the STO solver. The results highlight the importance of introducing a filtering scheme that simultaneously imposes a target length scale in both solid and void phases, as they ensure better material allocation across different load conditions [63]. In this scenario can be noticed the sensitivity of the system to the VolFrac parameter. By observing Case Study No.1 in Figure 8, the change in the lateral bracing system topology clearly emerges as the VolFrac increases, despite r_{min} not varying in both cases. The δ_{max} in $M_{1max'}$ was reduced due to the increased material retention across the sub-regions resulting from the imposition of a higher VolFrac value. However, considering the actual results pertaining to δ_{max} and the general indication provided by Smith, R. (2011) [62], achieving such a low lateral displacement value is not necessary. Consequently, in the subsequent case studies applying SHM, VolFrac = 0.3 is utilised.

(a) (b)

Figure 10. Façade1, dynamic STO results, SDOF, 5 g; δ_{max} over time and final configuration for (**a**) $M_{1min'}$, (**b**) $M_{1max'}$.

4.1.3. Case Study No. 3 Imposing MDOFs, 1 g, SHM

The third case study extends the SDOF case by distributing five concentrated masses at different heights and analysing how the material distribution adapts. The lumped massed $M_{[1,5]}$ are located at specific coordinates along the height of the building, as follows {x, y, z}: M_5 = {0, 0, 12}; M_4 = {0, 0, 24}; M_3 = {0, 0, 36}; M_2 = {0, 0, 48}; M_1 = {0, 0, 60} (Figure 11). The different applied mass magnitudes are derived by equally subdividing the total magnitude defined as $\boldsymbol{M_{min'}} \veebar \boldsymbol{M_{max'}}$, such as $M_1 = M_2 = M_3 = M_4 = M_5 = \frac{M_{min'}}{5} \veebar \frac{M_{max'}}{5}$. Also in this case, the STO problem is addressed by applying dynamic forces in the form of SHM while VolFrac = 0.3. In order to simplify the problem, a single region is contemplated (g = 1). Since it is considered an MDOF system, it is minimised as the sum of square displacements at the targeted DOFs.

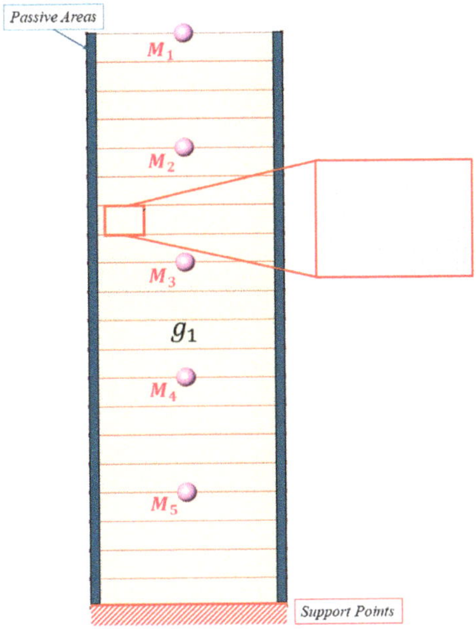

Figure 11. Façade1, Numerical Test Case No. 3. MDOFs, 1 g.

The findings in Figure 12 indicate that including the five lumped masses $M_{[1,5]}$ brings about a more even distribution of diagonal members throughout the height, notably linked to their location. In this case, at the structure's tip is obtained δ_{max} = 0.062 m by applying $M_{[1,5]min}$, while applying $M_{[1,5]max}$, leads to δ_{max} = 0.205 m. The results show that the STO solver distributed diagonal bracing evenly across the entire height, reflecting the contributions of multiple mass locations. Increased masses resulted in thicker diagonal members near mid-height, as inertia forces accumulated in the middle levels. In comparison with Case Study No. 1, the presence of MDOFs led to a more uniformly distributed bracing system in the height of Façade1. The introduction of MDOFs simulates a more realistic representation of the mass distribution within a tall building. The higher value of δ_{max}, compared to a SDOF system, resulted in improved accuracy of the maximum lateral displacement, particularly evident in the $M_{[1,5]max}$, application, falling within the suggested range $\left[\frac{h}{200}, \frac{h}{600}\right]$ [62], such as $\delta_{max} \approx \frac{h}{300}$. These results demonstrate strong alignment with real-world bracing strategies, highlighting the significance of incorporating MDOFs compared to the simplified assumption made in SDOF adoption.

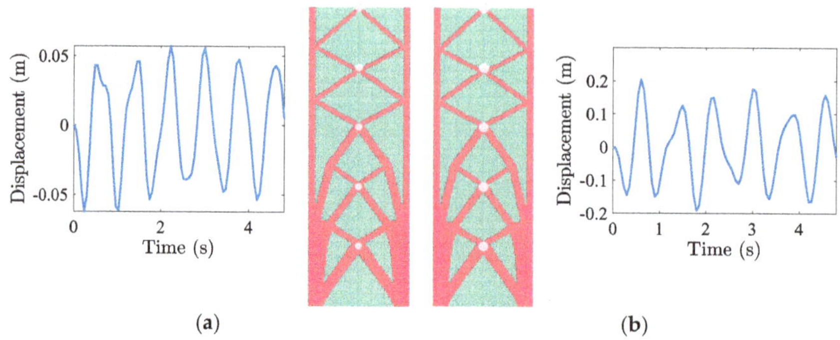

Figure 12. Façade1, dynamic STO results, MDOFs, 1 g. δ_{max} over time, final configuration for (**a**) $M_{[1,5]min'}$, (**b**) $M_{[1,5]max'}$.

4.1.4. Case Study No. 4 Imposing MDOFs, 5 g, SHM

The following numerical test for applying SHM in the STO problem was carried out on Façade1 by applying five simplifications of sub-regions within the total design domain Ω, setting the parameter related to $g = 5$. In this scenario, we maintain VolFrac = 0.3 and $r_{min} = 1$, while applying five lumped masses $M_{[1,5]}$ to create an MDOF system, as shown in the accompanying illustrative image (Figure 13).

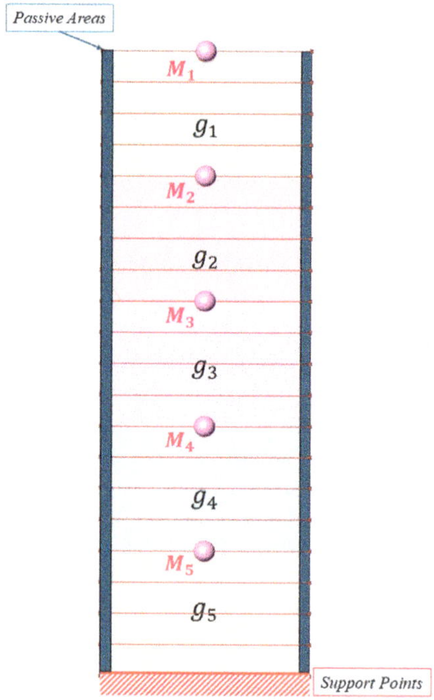

Figure 13. Façade1, MDOFs, 5 g.

The outcomes in Figure 14 indicate that the introduction of $g_{[1,...,5]}$ results in a uniform distribution of the material within each imposed sub-region. This contrasts with the observations from the previous Case Study No. 3, where the material percentage defined by the VolFrac parameter is predominantly located at the base of the tall building. The maximum horizontal displacement proportionally follows the applied magnitude as

$\delta_{max} = 0.071$ m in $M_{[1,5]min'}$, while $\delta_{max} = 0.255$ m in $M_{[1,5]max'}$. Significant observations from the latest results can be made, noting that the bracing members became more uniform in thickness, demonstrating that multiple sub-regions enhance material allocation efficiency. Consequently, δ_{max} is increased compared to Case Study No. 3, indicating that subdividing the design domain into sub-regions led to equal material distribution within the lower and upper sections. Considering that for $M_{[1,5]max'}$, $\delta_{max} \approx \frac{h}{250}$, the outcome still meets the general range of lateral displacements found in the real data concerning tall buildings. Thus, combining MDOFs and multiple sub-regions not only results in a well-distributed bracing system that provides enhanced resistance against lateral forces while maintaining material efficiency, but also can assist designers involved in the architectural, engineering, and construction (AEC) industry in the decision-making process, offering the possibility to consider the same material distribution within the sub-region to meet constructability criteria using fewer different cross-sections to produce bracing systems.

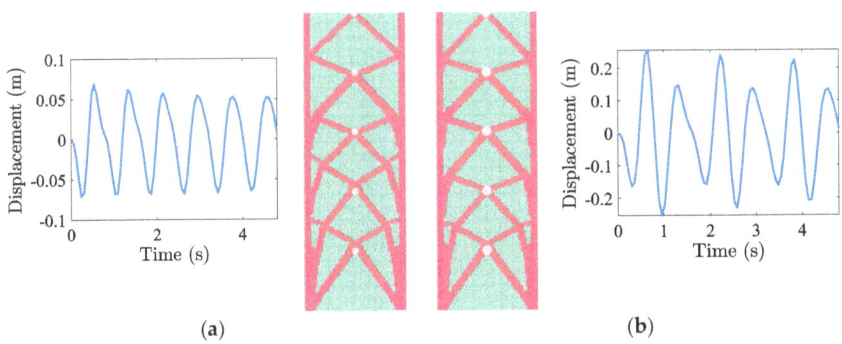

Figure 14. Façade1, STO results, SHM, MDOFs, 5 g. δ_{max} over time and final configuration for (**a**) $M_{[1,5]min'}$, (**b**) $M_{[1,5]max'}$.

4.2. Real Earthquake Data in STO

In this study, appropriate recorded earthquake data from ground motion time histories were utilised to simulate seismic excitations for optimising structural dynamic design, with the objective of enhancing structural resilience in highly seismic regions. Two distinct ground motion accelerations ($\ddot{u}_g$) were employed, namely the L'Aquila earthquake (Italy, 2009) and the Athens earthquake (Greece, 1999). In the subsequent test cases, the same design domain configuration as Façade1 is adopted; the accelerogram is integrated into the solution for the earthquake response spectrum, while the parameters E, v, ρ, th, Ag, r_{min}, and Thr remain consistent across both the SHM and earthquake simulations.

4.2.1. Case Study No. 5—L'Aquila Earthquake

The first test deals with the L'Aquila earthquake, which occurred in Italy in 2009. The recording source of the event and the characteristics of the earthquake are herein summarised: Station Code: AQK; source ITACA ID IT-2009-0009; Processing manual [64], Event time: 6 April 2009 01:32:40 [65]. In order to reduce the computational cost, the time interval [30.4, 42.9] (s) was chosen for a total duration of T_max = 12.5 (s), while the discretisation referring to the time step is equal to $t_i = 0.01$ (s) (Figure 15).

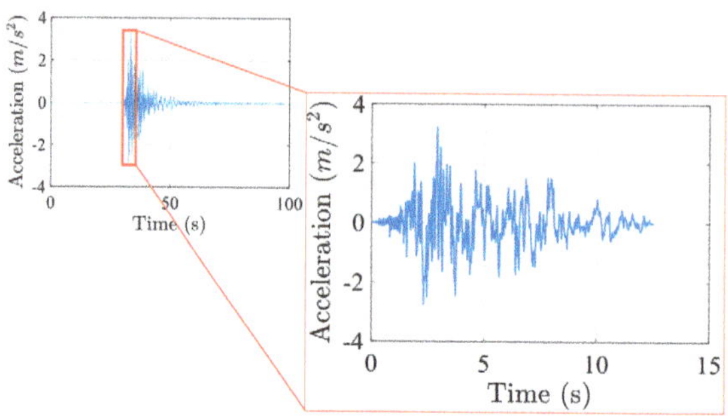

Figure 15. L'Aquila Earthquake (2009); zoom on time interval [30.4, 42.9] (s).

To compare the results by applying the same external excitation, two primary test cases were developed by varying the number of lumped masses applied and their magnitude, the VolFrac, and the number of sub-regions. Specifically, the first test case is initially simplified by applying a single lumped mass $M_1 = M_{min'}$ while adopting five sub-regions (see Figure 9) with VolFrac = 0.4. Subsequently, another configuration was created with the incorporation of five DOFs ($M_{[1,5]}$) into Façade1 within the VPL environment; in this instance, the design domain was treated as a single region, denoted as g = 1 (see Figure 11) while the magnitude of $M_{[1,5]} = M_{max'}$ and VolFrac = 0.3. The comparative results presented in Figure 16 illustrate the optimised structure under the seismic activity that occurred in L'Aquila in 2009, adopting different parameter settings.

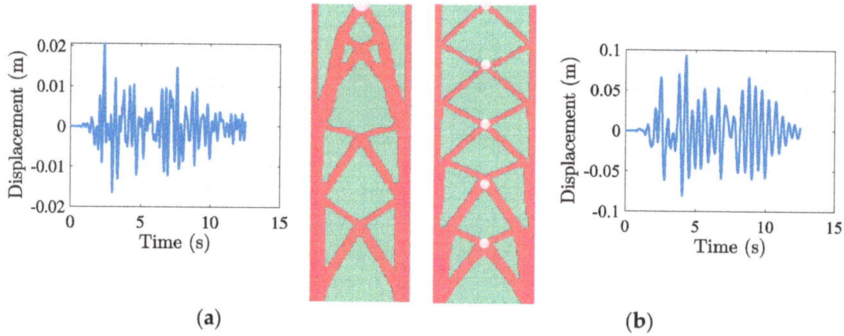

Figure 16. Results of dynamic STO, L'Aquila Earthquake (2009). (**a**) SDOF, $M_1 = M_{min'}$, VolFrac = 0.4, 5 g, (**b**) (5) MDOFs, $M_{[1,5]} = M_{max'}$, VolFrac = 0.3, 1 g.

The upper figure, illustrating the results for the two distinct test cases subjected to identical external forces, demonstrates the solver's efficacy in developing bracing-like material patterns in response to authentic seismic motions, thus indicating practical applicability in the field of seismic engineering. The δ_{max} observed during the optimisation process for the SDOF (a) was $\delta_{max} = 0.020$ m, while the MDOF system (b) recorded a higher maximum displacement of $\delta_{max} = 0.093$ m.

In configuration (a), the material distribution in the façade deviates from the typical expected outcome, particularly when compared to (b). This discrepancy arises from the contrast between the realistic seismic force and the unlikely simplified representation of the tall building as a single lumped mass system with a total height of 60 m. Moreover, the introduction of multiple sub-regions resulted in a more uniform material distribution along the structure's height, without differentiating the impact of the seismic action at different heights of the building. Extending the L'Aquila test to incorporate the MDOF system yielded several notable findings: lateral bracing became evenly distributed, reducing stress concentrations near mass points, and diagonal bracing patterns emerged predominantly in the lower half of the structure. The observed differences in material distribution in (b) are attributed to the single sub-region application, demonstrating the solver's adaptability in the absence of specific constraints; additionally, the larger displacement can be linked to the higher total mass and lower VolFrac. The optimised structures demonstrated improved resilience against earthquake-induced displacements, since the δ_{max} obtained remained within anticipated seismic performance thresholds. Both designs demonstrate adaptation to the earthquake loading, with diagonal bracing patterns emerging to resist lateral forces.

4.2.2. Case Study No. 6—Athens Earthquake

With the aim of further investigating the impact of significant seismic ground motions on the previous geometry, the case of the earthquake that occurred in Athens, Greece, on 7 September 1999, was also examined. Despite its moderate magnitude and the low seismic risk of the corresponding zone, the earthquake caused severe damage [66]. In this instance, to reduce computational cost, the time interval [2.00, 7.00] (s) was chosen for a total duration of T_max = 5.00 (s) (Figure 17). The discretisation referring to the time step is equal to t_i = 0.01 (s) [67].

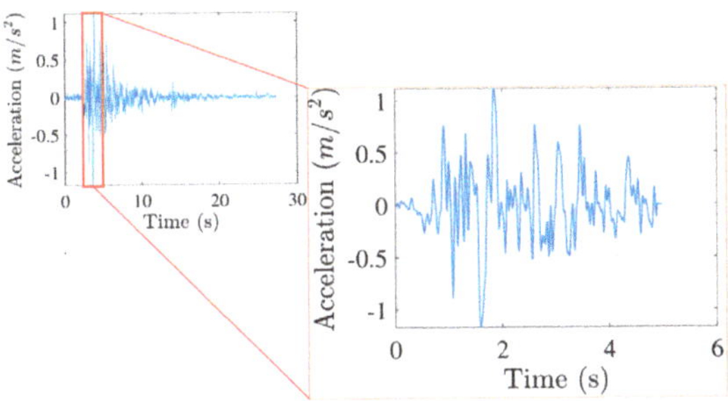

Figure 17. Athens Earthquake (1999); zoom on time interval [2, 7] (s).

As for the previous case study, two comparative applications were developed. The set of results depicted in Figure 18 pertains to the MDOF system with $M_{[1,5]} = M_{min'}$, VolFrac = 0.3, and r_{min} = 1. Specifically, configuration (a) focuses on a single region (g = 1) and relates to Façade1 illustrated in Figure 11, while in (b) the results refer to the application of five different sub-regions, i.e., g = 5 (see Figure 13).

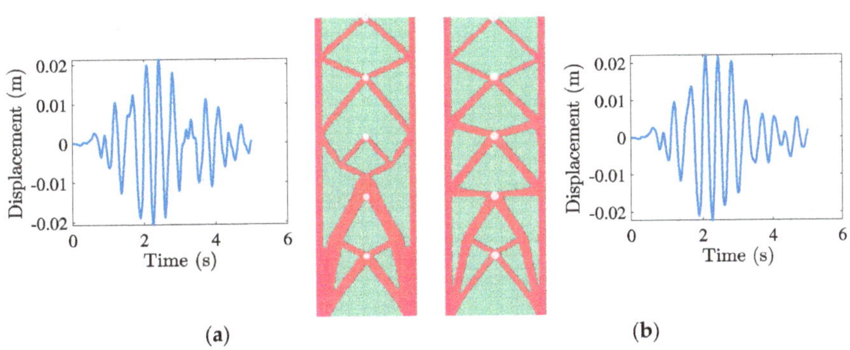

Figure 18. Results of Dynamic STO, Athens Earthquake (1999). MDOFs, $M_{[1-5]} = M_{min'}$, VolFrac = 0.3. (**a**) 1 g. (**b**) 5 g.

In the left configuration (Figure 18a), $\delta_{max} = 0.021$ m was recorded on the x-axis. The results also indicate that diagonal members are distributed with increasing thickness progressing from the apex to the base of the tower due to the presence of a single sub-region. In the right configuration (Figure 18b), with the application of multiple sub-regions, the optimised bracing was uniformly distributed, preventing localised stress accumulation. $\delta_{max} = 0.022$ m remained stable compared to (a) due to the same mass magnitude application, demonstrating further refinement in material utilisation. Compared to the MDOF L'Aquila earthquake results (Figure 16b), the topology (a) displayed alterations due to variations in frequency content. The solver demonstrated effective adaptation to various earthquake stimuli while balancing material usage and displacement control, highlighting its practical applicability across different seismic regions.

4.3. SHM in Unstructured Mesh

In this subsection, the proposed VPL framework was used to tackle the dynamic STO problem for irregular geometries. This updated application enables the creation of geometry within a complex design domain, which includes various mesh cell geometries, such as Voronoi tessellations. To assess the VPL framework effectiveness with irregular geometries, an initial configuration of the design domain Ω was set up. This configuration features a circular structure on the XZ plane, supported at its base. The base structure has a height h = 90 m and a base width b = 20 m. The mesh is discretised into Voronoi cells directly created in the VPL-CAD linked environment based on empirical determination, in order to ensure accurate evaluation while maintaining computational efficiency. A total of 7984 Voronoi elements were utilised in the discretisation (Figure 19); for clarity, we shall refer to the specific geometry characterised by unstructured mesh as "Façade2".

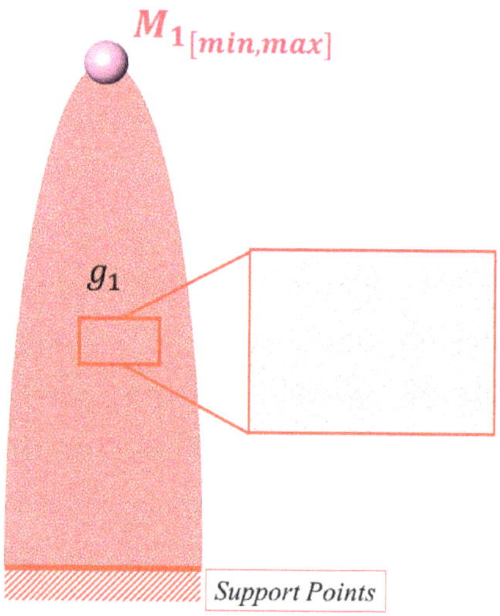

Figure 19. Unstructured Mesh Development—Voronoi tessellation and lumped mass variation.

The following tests evaluated the behaviour of the VPL—STO solver for a tall building subjected to SHM excitation following the external force characteristics listed in Section 4.1 (Figure 6). A concentrated single lumped mass with variable magnitudes given by M_{1min}, and M_{1max}, is considered. In this particular scenario, no passive areas and sub-regions (g = 1) were designated to assess the outcome of the STO with minimal constraints. The minimum filter radius size was established as $r_{min} = 1$.

In Figure 20 are reported the results obtained by imposing Equation (1) and employing the produced add-on in VPL, according to Section 3; specifically, in the STO setting, a pattern of variable conditions imposed is listed as follows: (a) VolFrac = 0.3, $M_{1min'}$; (b) VolFrac = 0.3, $M_{1max'}$; (c) VolFrac = 0.4, $M_{1min'}$; (d) VolFrac = 0.4, $M_{1max'}$.

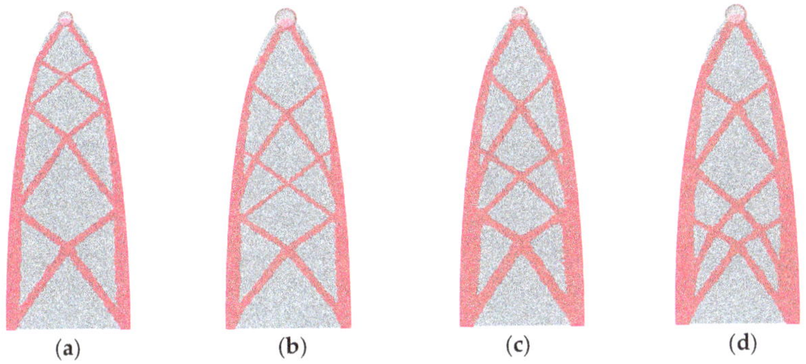

Figure 20. Post-STO Voronoi tessellation. VolFrac = 0.3 (**a**) $M_{1,min'}$, (**b**) $M_{1,max'}$; VolFrac = 0.4 (**c**) $M_{1,min'}$, (**d**) $M_{1,max'}$.

As variations in VolFrac and mass magnitude occur, distinct lateral deflection values and topological characteristics emerge in the two systems under consideration. The diagrams in Figure 21 illustrate, in both instances, the displacement trend as a function of time. Specifically, in Figure 20a, δ_{max} = 0.041 m is obtained, while in Figure 20b δ_{max} = 0.107 m is recorded. Similarly, by setting VolFrac = 0.4 in Figure 20c,d, different results concerning both the topological configuration and the lateral displacement values are obtained, as demonstrated from (c) in which δ_{max} = 0.033 m and in (d) where δ_{max} = 0.068.

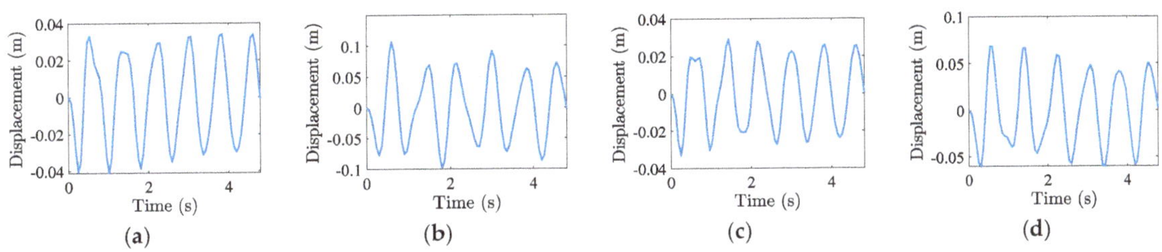

Figure 21. Post-STO δ_{max}. VolFrac = 0.3 (**a**) $M_{1,min'}$, (**b**) $M_{1,max'}$; VolFrac = 0.4 (**c**) $M_{1,min'}$, (**d**) $M_{1,max'}$.

The observed δ_{max} in both instances correlates with the mass magnitude variation, as well as the modifications in material allocation with additional bracing systems incorporated as the mass increases, thereby facilitating the transfer of inertial forces to the supports. In addition to the mass magnitude variation, the sensitivity to the VolFrac is also examined. In the case of the unstructured mesh, the structure exhibits a response to the filter variation, indicating that the data transmission from VPL to the STO solver is comprehensive. The bracing structure adapted to the irregular mesh and design domain, demonstrating flexibility in accommodating non-standard geometries. The material distribution remained stable despite the complex Voronoi tessellation, confirming the solver's connection robustness. The displacement values results aligned well with structured-mesh cases, ensuring accuracy regardless of meshing strategy.

5. Conclusions and Discussion

This research advances STO in the context of earthquake engineering, demonstrating an integrated computational framework that enhances structural resilience under dynamic loading. By integrating time history ground motion data into the STO framework, a VPL tool within GH for Rhino3D was developed, enabling design of structures that are material efficient and highly resistant to seismic forces. This integration addresses the need for structures to withstand complex forces generated by earthquakes, ensuring optimisation techniques are directly applicable to real-world engineering problems. A key achievement is the seamless connection between the VPL-CAD linked tools and MATLAB-based programming. The integration within a VPL environment enhances STO accessibility for engineers and architects, allowing users to define geometries, set optimisation constraints, and visualise results within a single workflow. By embedding numerical optimisation techniques into the VPL environment, the approach reduces the gap between analysis and design, enabling an iterative process that ensures optimal structural performance under dynamic loads.

The numerical test cases confirm that material distribution, mass magnitude, and sub-region constraints significantly influence bracing topology, highlighting the importance of considering concentrated mass locations and dynamic excitation characteristics. The integrated VPL framework effectively adapts to varying conditions, redistributing material in response to seismic and harmonic loading, thereby ensuring optimal stiffness and structural efficiency. The application of real earthquake data, including L'Aquila (2009) and Athens (1999) ground motion records, validates the approach's ability to minimise the displacements at a target DOF while maintaining efficient material use, demonstrating its potential for compliance with modern seismic engineering standards. The observed variations in bracing topologies between the two earthquakes emphasise the need for a data-driven, site-specific approach to seismic-resistant design, as different frequency contents and intensities demand tailored optimisation solutions. Furthermore, the implementation of STO on an unstructured Voronoi tessellation extends the method's versatility, proving its capability to handle complex, irregular geometries while maintaining structural stability. The ability to optimise both structured and unstructured mesh systems ensures that engineers and designers have the flexibility to explore innovative structural forms while maintaining high efficiency and safety employing a CAD-friendly environment.

This study confirms that integrating STO within a CAD-based VPL enhances accessibility, efficiency, and practicality. The combination of parametric design tools, numerical optimisation techniques, and real-time visualisation allows for rapid generation and refinement of optimised structural layouts, ensuring engineering accuracy without extensive manual intervention. The research highlights the value of integrating coding-based methodologies with CAD platforms, transforming STO into a powerful, practical solution for real-world engineering challenges. Future research will refine optimisation algorithms to enhance computational efficiency, especially for large-scale and three-dimensional structures. Studies will extend the methodology to multi-hazard scenarios, incorporating seismic, wind, and impact loads for more resilient designs. Expanding the problem library to include diverse structural typologies, materials, and load conditions would further validate the solver's efficacy in various engineering contexts. Enhancing VPL-CAD integration and expanding STO capabilities will help develop safer, more resilient, and sustainable infrastructure to withstand extreme dynamic events, advancing seismic-resistant structural design.

Author Contributions: Conceptualisation: L.S., S.S.; Data curation: L.S.; Formal analysis and investigation: L.S., S.S.; Funding acquisition: L.S.; Methodology: L.S., S.S.; Project administration: L.S.; Resources: L.S., S.S.; Software: L.S., S.S.; Supervision: A.F.; Validation and Visualisation: L.S.,

S.S.; Writing—original draft preparation: L.S.; Writing—review and editing: L.S. All authors have read and agreed to the published version of the manuscript.

Funding: Dr. Laura Sardone carried out this study within the RETURN Extended Partnership and received funding from the European Union Next-GenerationEU (National Recovery and Resilience Plan—NRRP, Mission 4, Component 2, Investment 1.3—D.D. 1243 2/8/2022, PE0000005). Dr. Alessandra Fiore acknowledges the research projects: PRIN PNRR 2022 "Artificial Intelligence for ENVIronmental impact minimisation of SEismic Retrofitting of Structures (AI-ENVISERS)"; PRIN 2022 "Digitalised life-cycle management of historic bridges by an integrated monitoring and modelling CDE platform—HBridgeIM (Historic Bridge Information Modelling)" (2022744YM9).

Data Availability Statement: The data are openly accessible in the following GitHub repository: https://github.com/stsotirop/VPL_DTO/tree/main (accessed on 28 October 2025). The verifiability and replicability of the results are ensured through the open-access publication of the case studies presented in this paper, as well as the software for the Visual Programming Language (VPL) and the associated environment (Grasshopper® for Rhinoceros 3D). The implementation requires licensed (or trial) versions of Rhinoceros 3D (v6.0 or later) with Grasshopper, and MATLAB2018b. The framework has been tested on Windows 10; compatibility with other operating systems has not yet been verified. For installation, copy the Grasshopper definition (.gh) and the compiled plugin (.dll) into the Grasshopper Libraries folder; the new components will be automatically loaded at Rhino startup. The repository also provides a README with detailed setup and execution instructions, enabling step-by-step reproduction of the results.

Conflicts of Interest: All authors certify that they have no affiliations with or involvement in any organisation or entity with any financial interest or non-financial interest in the subject matter or materials discussed in this manuscript.

Abbreviations

The following abbreviations are used in this manuscript:

STO	Structural Topology Optimisation
CAD	Computer-Aided Design
VPL	Visual Programming Language
GUI	Graphical User Interface
DOF	Degrees of Freedom
SDOF	Single Degree Of Freedom
SO	Structural Optimisation
TO	Topology Optimisation
GH	Grasshopper
AEC	Architecture, Engineering, and Construction
SIMP	Solid Isotropic Material Penalisation
CAE	Computer-Aided Engineering
DDM	Direct Differentiation Methods
AVM	Adjoint Variable Methods
MDOF	Multi-Degree Of Freedom
OF	Objective Function
RAMP	Rational Approximation of Material Properties
SHM	Simple Harmonic Motion
FEM	Finite Element Model

Appendix A

Figures A1–A5 show the step-by-step Grasshopper workflow used to generate the façade models based on a quadrangular mesh system. These screenshots complement the GitHub repository and are provided to guide readers through the implementation.

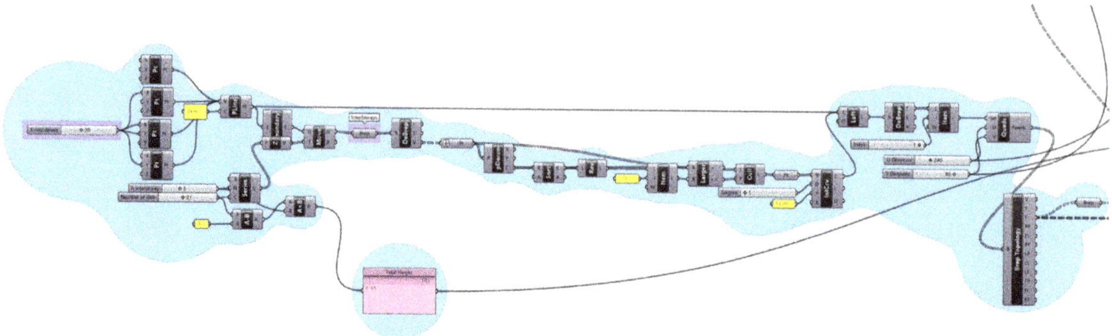

Figure A1. Geometry development in VPL—Tall Building 20 × 60 (m).

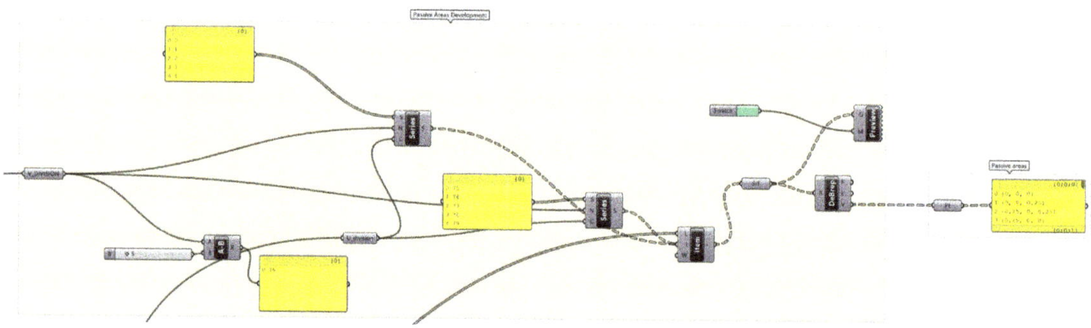

Figure A2. Passive areas selection in GH canvas.

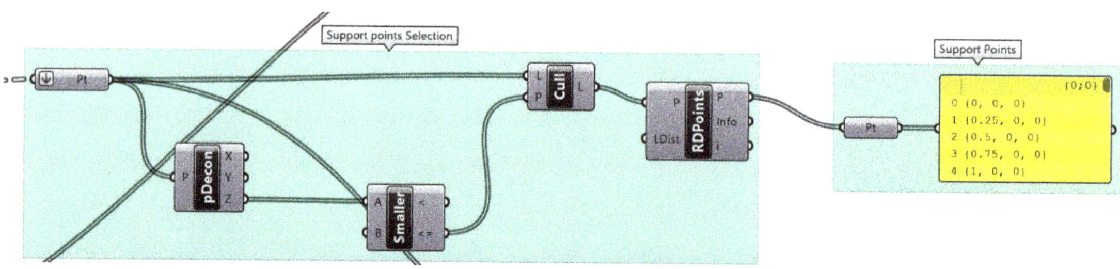

Figure A3. Support points in GH canvas.

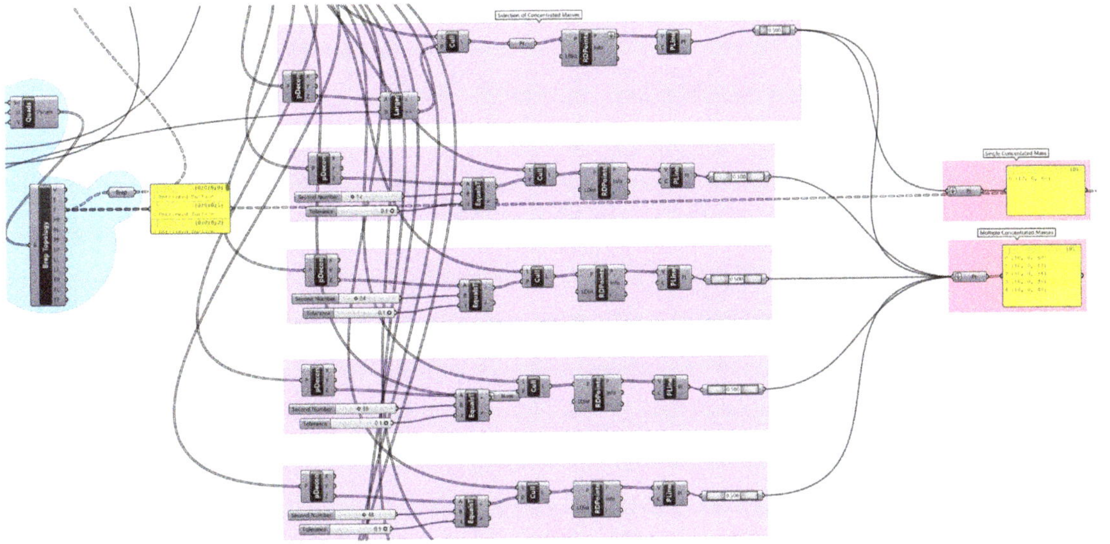

Figure A4. Lumped masses in GH canvas.

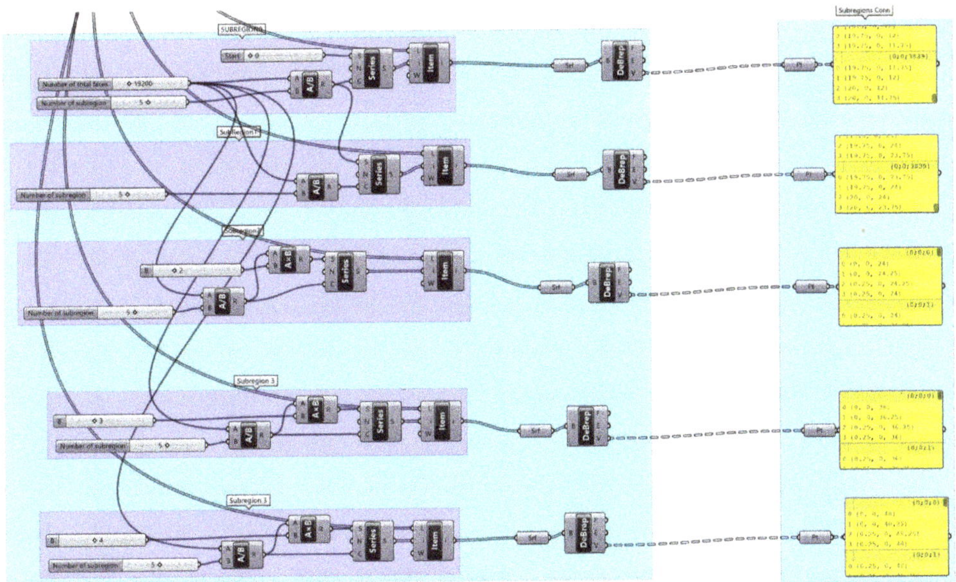

Figure A5. Sub-regions definition in GH canvas.

References

1. Duarte, L.S.; Celes, W.; Pereira, A.; Menezes, I.F.M. PolyTop++: An efficient alternative for serial and parallel topology optimization on CPUs & GPUs. *Struct. Multidiscip. Optim.* **2015**, *52*, 845–859.
2. Mukherjee, S.; Breitkopf, P.; Zhang, W.; Dutta, S.; Xiao, M.; Lu, D.; Raghavan, B. Accelerating Large-scale Topology Optimization: State-of-the-Art and Challenges. *Arch. Comput. Methods Eng.* **2021**, *28*, 4549–4571. [CrossRef]
3. Bendsøe, M.P.; Kikuchi, N. Generating optimal topologies in structural design using a homogenization method. *Comput. Methods Appl. Mech. Eng.* **1988**, *71*, 197–224. [CrossRef]
4. Zhang, J.; Sato, Y.; Yanagimoto, J. Homogenization-based topology optimization integrated with elastically isotropic lattices for additive manufacturing of ultralight and ultrastiff structures. *CIRP Ann.* **2021**, *70*, 111–114. [CrossRef]

5. Altair. Altair® OptiStruct®. Available online: https://altair.com/optistruct/ (accessed on 15 January 2025).
6. Yang, R.-J.; Chahande, A.I. Automotive applications of topology optimization. *Struct. Optim.* **1995**, *9*, 245–249. [CrossRef]
7. Abualigah, L.; Diabat, A. A comprehensive survey of the Grasshopper optimization algorithm: Results, variants, and applications. *Neural Comput. Appl.* **2020**, *32*, 15533–15556. [CrossRef]
8. CREATIVE MUTATION. Millipede. Available online: https://www.creativemutation.com/millipede (accessed on 14 January 2025).
9. Sigmund, O. A 99 line topology optimization code written in Matlab. *Struct. Multidiscip. Optim.* **2001**, *21*, 120–127. [CrossRef]
10. Zhou, Q.; Shen, W.; Wang, J.; Zhou, Y.; Xie, Y. Ameba: A new topology optimization tool for architectural design. In Proceedings of the IASS Symposium 2018, Creativity in Structural Design, Boston, MA, USA, 16–20 July 2018.
11. Aage, N.; Nobel-Jørgensen, M.; Andreasen, C.; Sigmund, O. Interactive topology optimization on hand-held devices. *Struct. Multidiscip. Optim.* **2013**, *47*, 1–6. [CrossRef]
12. Białkowski, S. Topology Optimisation Influence on Architectural Design Process—Enhancing Form Finding Routine by tOpos Toolset utilisation. In Proceedings of the eCAADe 2018, Lodz, Poland, 17–21 September 2018.
13. He, L.; Li, Q.; Gilbert, M.; Shepherd, P.; Rankine, C.; Pritchard, T.; Reale, V. Optimization-driven conceptual design of truss structures in a parametric modelling environment. *Structures* **2022**, *37*, 469–482. [CrossRef]
14. Selmı, M.; İlerisoy, Z.Y. A Comparative Study of Different Grasshopper Plugins for Topology Optimization in Architectural Design. *Gazi Univ. J. Sci. Part B Art Humanit. Des. Plan.* **2022**, *10*, 323–334.
15. Stromberg, L.L.; Beghini, A.; Baker, W.F.; Paulino, G.H. Topology optimization for braced frames: Combining continuum and beam/column elements. *Eng. Struct.* **2012**, *37*, 106–124. [CrossRef]
16. Sotiropoulos, S.; Lagaros, N.D. A two-stage structural optimization-based design procedure of structural systems. *Struct. Des. Tall Spec. Build.* **2022**, *31*, e1909. [CrossRef]
17. Andreassen, E.; Clausen, A.; Schevenels, M.; Lazarov, B.S.; Sigmund, O. Efficient topology optimization in MATLAB using 88 lines of code. *Struct. Multidiscip. Optim.* **2011**, *43*, 1–16. [CrossRef]
18. Talischi, C.; Paulino, G.; Pereira, A.; Menezes, I. PolyTop: A Matlab implementation of a general topology optimization framework using unstructured polygonal finite element meshes. *Struct. Multidiscip. Optim.* **2012**, *45*, 329–357. [CrossRef]
19. Min, S.; Kikuchi, N.; Park, Y.C.; Kim, S.; Chang, S. Optimal topology design of structures under dynamic loads. *Struct. Optim.* **1999**, *17*, 208–218. [CrossRef]
20. Bendsøe, M.; Sigmund, O. *Topology Optimization: Theory, Methods and Applications*; Springer: Berlin/Heidelberg, Germany, 2004.
21. Kang, B.-S.; Park, G.-J.; Arora, J.S. A review of optimization of structures subjected to transient loads. *Struct. Multidiscip. Optim.* **2006**, *31*, 81–95. [CrossRef]
22. Fleury, C.; Braibant, V. Structural optimization: A new dual method using mixed variables. *Numer. Methods Eng.* **1986**, *23*, 409–428. [CrossRef]
23. Dennis, J.E.; Schnabel, R.B. *Numerical Methods for Unconstrained Optimization and Nonlinear Equations*; SIAM: Philadelphia, PA, USA, 1996.
24. Byrd, R.H.; Nocedal, J.; Yuan, Y.-X. Global Convergence of a Cass of Quasi-Newton Methods on Convex Problems. *SIAM J. Numer. Anal.* **1987**, *24*, 1171–1190. [CrossRef]
25. Yoon, G.H. Structural topology optimization for frequency response problem using model reduction schemes. *Comput. Methods Appl. Mech. Eng.* **2010**, *199*, 1744–1763. [CrossRef]
26. Giraldo-Londoño, O.; Paulino, G.H. PolyDyna: A Matlab implementation for topology optimization of structures subjected to dynamic loads. *Struct. Multidiscip. Optim.* **2021**, *64*, 957–990. [CrossRef]
27. Filipov, E.T.; Chun, J.; Paulino, G.H.; Song, J. Polygonal multiresolution topology optimization (PolyMTOP) for structural dynamics. *Struct. Multidiscip. Optim.* **2016**, *53*, 673–694. [CrossRef]
28. Martin, A.; Deierlein, G.G. Structural Topology Optimization of Tall Buildings for Dynamic Seismic Excitation Using Modal Decomposition. *Eng. Struct.* **2020**, *216*, 110717. [CrossRef]
29. Jin, F.; Yang, Y.; Xiao, Z.; Gao, B.; Lou, H. Shear wall layout optimization of multi-tower buildings based on conceptual design and extended evolutionary structural optimization method. *Eng. Optim.* **2023**, *56*, 486–505. [CrossRef]
30. Du, Y.; Li, H.; Luo, Z.; Tian, Q. Topological design optimization of lattice structures to maximize shear stiffness. *Adv. Eng. Softw.* **2017**, *112*, 211–221. [CrossRef]
31. Wang, B.; Cheng, G. Design of cellular structures for optimum efficiency of heat dissipation. *Struct. Multidiscip. Optim.* **2005**, *30*, 447–458. [CrossRef]
32. Chopra, A.K. *Dynamics of Structures: Theory and Applications to Earthquake Engineering*, 4th illustrated ed.; Prentice Hall: Upper Saddle River, NJ, USA, 2012.
33. Clough, R.; Penzien, J. *Dynamics of Structures*, 2nd ed.; McGraw-Hill: New York, NY, USA, 1993.
34. Wilson, E.L. *Three-Dimensional Static and Dynamic Analysis of Structures: A Physical Approach With Emphasis on Earthquake Engineering*, 3rd ed.; Computers and Structures, Inc.: Berkeley, CA, USA, 2002.
35. Rayleigh, J.W.S. *The Theory of Sound*; Macmillan: London, UK, 1877.

36. Craig, R.R., Jr.; Kurdila, A.J. *Fundamentals of Structural Dynamics*, 2nd ed.; John Wiley & Sons: Hoboken, NY, USA, 2006.
37. Jog, C.S. Topology design of structures subjected to periodic loading. *J. Sound Vib.* **2022**, *253*, 687–709. [CrossRef]
38. Hilber, H.M.; Hughes, T.J.; Taylor, R.L. Improved numerical dissipation for time integration algorithms in structural dynamics. *Earthq. Eng. Struct. Dyn.* **1977**, *5*, 283–292. [CrossRef]
39. Newmark, N. A method of computation for structural dynamics. *J. Eng. Mech. Div.* **1959**, *85*, 67–94. [CrossRef]
40. Li, X.D.; Wiberg, N.-E. Structural Dynamic Analysis by a Time-Discontinuous Galerkin Finite Element Method. *Numer. Methods Eng.* **1996**, *39*, 2131–2152. [CrossRef]
41. Herrero-Pérez, D.; Picó-Vicente, S.G.; Martínez-Barberá, H. Efficient distributed approach for density-based topology optimization using coarsening and h-refinement. *Comput. Struct.* **2022**, *265*, 106770. [CrossRef]
42. Wang, Y.; Kang, Z.; He, Q. Adaptive topology optimization with independent error control for separated displacement and density fields. *Comput. Struct.* **2014**, *135*, 50–61. [CrossRef]
43. de Troya, M.A.S.; Tortorelli, D.A. Adaptive mesh refinement in stress-constrained topology optimization. *Struct. Multidiscip. Optim.* **2018**, *58*, 2369–2386. [CrossRef]
44. Stolpe, M.; Svanberg, K. An alternative interpolation scheme for minimum compliance optimization. *Struct. Multidiscip. Optim.* **2001**, *22*, 116–124. [CrossRef]
45. Sui, Y.; Peng, X. Chapter 1—Exordium. In *Modelling, Solving and Application for Topology Optimization of Continuum Structures: ICM Method Based on Step Function*; Butterworth-Heinemann: Oxford, UK, 2018; pp. 1–36.
46. Wang, F.; Lazarov, B.; Sigmund, O. On projection methods, convergence and robust formulations in topology optimization. *Struct. Multidiscip. Optim.* **2011**, *43*, 767–784. [CrossRef]
47. Wadbro, E.; Hägg, L. On quasi-arithmetic mean based filters and their fast evaluation for large-scale topology optimization. *Struct. Multidiscip. Optim.* **2015**, *52*, 879–888. [CrossRef]
48. Li, L.; Khandelwal, K. Volume preserving projection filters and continuation methods in topology optimization. *Eng. Struct.* **2015**, *85*, 144–161. [CrossRef]
49. Stolpe, M.; Svanberg, K. On the trajectories of penalization methods for topology optimization. *Struct. Multidiscip. Optim.* **2001**, *21*, 128–139. [CrossRef]
50. Sigmund, O. Morphology-based black and white filters for topology optimization. *Struct. Multidiscip. Optim.* **2007**, *33*, 401–424. [CrossRef]
51. Xing, J.; Qie, L. A Weighted Control Scheme for Topology Optimization. *J. Phys. Conf. Ser.* **2021**, *1838*, 012067. [CrossRef]
52. Zhang, X.; Paulino, G.; Ramos, A.S., Jr. Multi-material topology optimization with multiple volume constraints: A general approach applied to ground structures with material nonlinearity. *Struct. Multidiscip. Optim.* **2017**, *57*, 161–182. [CrossRef]
53. Jensen, J.S.; Nakshatrala, P.B.; Tortorelli, D.A. On the consistency of adjoint sensitivity analysis for structural optimization of linear dynamic problems. *Struct. Multidiscip. Optim.* **2014**, *49*, 831–837. [CrossRef]
54. Fernandez, F.; Tortorelli, D.A. Semi-analytical sensitivity analysis for nonlinear transient problems. *Struct. Multidiscip. Optim.* **2018**, *58*, 2387–2410. [CrossRef]
55. Sanders, E.; Pereira, A.; Aguiló, M.; Paulino, G. PolyMat: An efficient matlab code for multi-material topology optimization. *Struct. Multidiscip. Optim.* **2018**, *58*, 2727–2759. [CrossRef]
56. Giraldo-Londoño, O.; Paulino, G. PolyStress: A Matlab implementation for local stress-constrained topology optimization using the augmented Lagrangian method. *Struct. Multidiscip. Optim.* **2020**, *63*, 2065–2097. [CrossRef]
57. Giraldo-Londoño, O.; Paulino, G.H. A unified approach for topology optimization with local stress constraints considering various failure criteria: Von Mises, Drucker–Prager, Tresca, Mohr–Coulomb, Bresler– Pister and Willam–Warnke. *Proc. R. Soc. A* **2020**, *476*, 20190861. [CrossRef]
58. McNeel. Grasshopper SDK. Grasshopper API. Available online: https://mcneel.github.io/grasshopper-api-docs/api/grasshopper/html/723c01da-9986-4db2-8f53-6f3a7494df75.htm (accessed on 20 August 2024).
59. Miller, N. LunchBox. food4Rhino. 2023. Available online: https://www.food4rhino.com/en/app/lunchbox (accessed on 12 December 2024).
60. Querin, O.M.; Victoria, M.; Alonso, C.; Ansola, R.; Martí, P. Discrete Method of Structural Optimization. In *Topology Design Methods for Structural Optimization*; Academic Press: Cambridge, MA, USA, 2017; pp. 27–46.
61. *1_BS EN 1992-1-1:2004*; Eurocode 2: Design of concrete structures. British Standards Institution: London, UK, 2004.
62. Smith, R. Deflection Limits in Tall Buildings—Are They Useful? In Proceedings of the Structures Congress 2011, Las Vegas, NV, USA, 14–16 April 2011.
63. Pellens, J.; Lombaert, G.; Lazarov, B.; Schevenels, M. Combined length scale and overhang angle control in minimum compliance topology optimization for additive manufacturing. *Struct. Multidiscip. Optim.* **2019**, *59*, 2005–2022. [CrossRef]
64. Paolucci, R.; Pacor, F.; Puglia, R.; Ameri, G.; Cauzzi, C.; Massa, M. Record Processing in ITACA, the New Italian Strong-Motion Database. In *Earthquake Data in Engineering Seismology*; Geotechnical, Geological and Earthquake Engineering; Springer: Dordrecht, The Netherlands, 2011; Volume 14.

65. National Institute of Geophysics and Volcanology. INGV. 6 April 2009. Available online: https://itaca.mi.ingv.it/ItacaNet_40/#/event/IT-2009-0009 (accessed on 12 December 2024).
66. Sotiropoulos, S.; Lagaros, N.D. Optimum topological bracing design of tall steel frames subjected to dynamic loading. *Comput. Struct.* **2022**, *259*, 106705. [CrossRef]
67. Papadimitriou, P.; Voulgaris, N.; Kassaras, I.; Kaviris, G.; Delibasis, N.; Makropoulos, K. The M_w = 6.0, 7 September 1999 Athens Earthquake. *Nat. Hazards* **2002**, *27*, 15–33. [CrossRef]

computation

MDPI

Article

An Efficient Filter Implementation Method and Its Applications in Topology Optimization Utilizing k-d Tree Data Structure

Jingbo Huang [1], Ayesha Saeed [1], Kai Long [1,*], Yutang Chen [1], Rongrong Geng [1], Jiao Jia [2] and Tao Tao [3]

1 School of New Energy, North China Electric Power University, Beijing 102206, China; jingbohuang2002@163.com (J.H.); ayeshasaeededu@gmail.com (A.S.); cyt5237@163.com (Y.C.); gengrr3642@163.com (R.G.)
2 Flying College, Beihang University, Beijing 100191, China; jiajiao@buaa.edu.cn
3 China Southern Power Grid Technology Co., Ltd., Guangzhou 510080, China; taot0804@163.com
* Correspondence: longkai1978@163.com; Tel.: +86-15116910571

Abstract: Topology optimization (TO) with the variable density concept has made significant advancements in academic research and engineering applications; yet it still encounters obstacles associated with computer inefficiencies in the filtering process. This work introduces a novel filter implementation method that significantly enhances the optimization process by adapting the k-d tree data structure. The proposed method converts traditional neighborhood search operations into extremely efficient spatial searches while preserving solution accuracy. This method inherently accommodates a comprehensive array of manufacturability constraints, including symmetry, local volume control, periodic patterning, stamping-oriented overhang control, and more, without compromising computational duration. Extensive numerical examples validate the proposed method's efficiency yielding precise, scalable designs, achieving substantial acceleration relative to conventional methods The method demonstrates specific advantage in large scale optimization challenges and intricate complex geometric restrictions, encompassing unstructured meshes. This study explores a new paradigm for effective constraint integration in topology optimization through advanced data structures, providing extensive applicability in engineering design.

Keywords: topology optimization; density filtering; k-d tree data structure; neighborhood search

1. Introduction

Structural topology optimization (TO) is a potent design methodology that allocates material within a defined design space to either minimize or maximize a given objective function, while conforming to established restrictions for an engineering system. It is widely applied in key industrial fields requiring lightweight, high-performance designs, including aerospace, automotive, renewable energy, and biomedical engineering, which often demand large-scale, high-resolution TO models, making the efficiency of core processes critical to practical implementation. Contemporary TO approaches are often categorized into variable-density or boundary-variation approaches. Prevalent density-based methodologies encompass homogenization [1], solid isotropic material with penalization (SIMP) [2–5], and evolutionary structural optimization (ESO) [6]. Conversely, boundary-variation methodologies, such as level set method [7,8] and the moving morphable components method [9], have been developed more recently. Each method presents distinct advantages across different domains. Recent solutions amalgamate characteristics from both variable-density and boundary-variation methodologies to improve structural performance. The smooth-edged material distribution approach for topology optimization [10–12] produced optimal topologies with smooth boundaries by assigning solid and void element to each element. By combining the level set and SIMP approaches, the level set band concept [13] was able to provide clear border representation.

Checkerboard patterns and mesh dependency are evident in various element-based TO methods [14,15]. Various restrictions have been proposed to address these issues, including the use of high-order elements [16,17], the integration of slope constraints or perimeter controls [18,19], and the implementation of digital image processing technologies [20–23]. Among these tactics, filtering approaches are essential and have been extensively refined in scholarly study. They can be classified into sensitivity filtering and density filtering. Sensitivity filtering [24], an older heuristic method, was subsequently supplanted by the advancement of density filtering [25], commonly referred to as the two-field projection method. The three-field projection method was subsequently developed to resolve the clarity concerns arising from filtering, providing a more advanced approach to these challenges [26,27]. In TO, the filtering process is often conducted in two stages: first, a neighborhood search to ascertain the adjacent cells of a certain design variable, and subsequently, the calculation of the filtered value through the application of a convolution integral over the found neighbors. The convolution integral averages the filtering variables among adjacent cells, hence smoothing the material distribution. The efficacy of the overall filtering operation is significantly contingent upon the efficiency of the preliminary neighborhood search.

Traditional methods for neighborhood search often rely on brute-force techniques, such as for-loops [28], which examine all design variables, calculate pairwise distances, and identify adjacent elements. While these methods are simple, they become a significant bottleneck in complex problems with high-resolution elements, severely hindering the optimization process. Many researchers have proposed new strategies for more efficient filtering, but each comes with its own set of limitations. For instance, the partial differential equation-based filtering method [29] transforms explicit filters into solutions of additional linear systems. This approach requires substantial computational resources, particularly for large 3D problems. Our k-d tree method avoids this issue by optimizing neighborhood search directly and does not require extra system solvers. Vectorization techniques [30] can speed up convolution operations for structured grids. They are ineffective for irregular geometries or non-uniform meshes due to their reliance on regular memory access patterns. Our method maintains efficiency across both structured and unstructured meshes. This is validated in Sections 3.1, 3.3, and 3.6. Subdomain parallelization [31] enables distributed processing. Its performance is often limited by communication delays between partitions, especially when larger filter radii are used. Our k-d tree reduces data exchange by localizing spatial searches, which complements parallelization. This complementarity is discussed in Section 4. To address these challenges, we propose using a k-d tree (k-dimensional tree) data structure to improve the efficiency of the filtering process, specifically in the neighborhood search phase. This data structure recursively divides the design domain, reducing unnecessary comparisons and speeding up the convolution-based filtering process [32,33]. Our approach preserves the traditional convolution step, ensuring that the core principles of density filtering are maintained. The key innovation of our method lies in its ability to rapidly identify neighboring elements, allowing for more efficient convolution operations without compromising the integrity of the filtered design. Additionally, this approach facilitates the integration of manufacturability constraints through enhanced neighborhood search and sensitivity preprocessing.

The following portions of the paper are structured as outlined below. Section 2 delineates the TO problem statement, followed by the proposed neighborhood search approach employing the k-d tree algorithm, together with its modifications for symmetry constraints and implicit local volume constraints, thereby offering a scalable framework for more extensive manufacturability requirements. Section 3 substantiates the techniques with five numerical examples and an engineering application, illustrating their efficacy and adaptability. The concluding section delineates the findings.

2. Topology Optimization Problem Statement

2.1. Problem Formulation

In a design domain comprising NE finite elements, the objective is to maximize stiffness while conforming to a certain volume fraction constraint. The TO formulation for the continuum structure is formally expressed as follows:

$$\begin{aligned} &\text{find} : \boldsymbol{\rho} = \{\rho_1, \rho_2, \ldots \rho_{NE}\} \\ &\min : c = \boldsymbol{F}^{\mathrm{T}}\boldsymbol{U} \\ &s.t. : V/V_0 \leq f \\ &\quad \boldsymbol{K}\boldsymbol{U} = \boldsymbol{F} \\ &\quad 0 \leq \rho_e \leq 1 \quad (e = 1, 2, \ldots, NE) \end{aligned} \tag{1}$$

where vector $\boldsymbol{\rho}$ consists of the design variables exclusively pertinent to each element; The static compliance c quantifies structural stiffness, while $\boldsymbol{K}$ represents the global stiffness matrix. The symbols $\boldsymbol{U}$ and $\boldsymbol{F}$ denote the displacement and external load vector, respectively. V and V_0 are the total material volume and permissible volume, respectively. The variable f denotes the specified volume fraction.

2.2. Material Interpolation with Three-Phase SIMP Method

The SIMP model is commonly utilized to interpolate material properties between solid and void states [34]. The Young's modulus, denoted as E_e, is defined as:

$$E_e = E_{\min} + \overline{\rho}_e^{p}(E_0 - E_{\min}) \tag{2}$$

where E_0 and $E_{\min}$ represent the Young's modulus of the solid material and to void phase, respectively. The penalty factor p generally satisfied the inequality $p \geq 1$.

It is noteworthy that Equation (2) employs physical density, which is utilized in finite element analyses and volume computations, and possesses authentic physical relevance. The physical density values are generated at the results' post-processing phase. Conversely, the symbol ρ_e in Equation (1) functions as a design variable and lacks substantial physical significance.

2.3. Filtering and Threshold Projection

In the three-field SIMP approach, a mapping relationship exists between the design variable ρ_e to the physical density $\overline{\rho}_e$, incorporating the filtered density $\widetilde{\rho}_e$. As previously discussed, filtering techniques are employed to avert numerical instabilities, including checkerboard patterns and mesh dependency. The mathematical relationship between the design variable and the filtered density can be given by:

$$\widetilde{\rho}_e = \frac{\sum\limits_{i \in \Phi_r} \kappa(r_{ei})\rho_i}{\sum\limits_{i \in \Phi_r} \kappa(r_{ei})} \tag{3}$$

where Φ_r represents a sphere in three dimensions or a circle in two dimensions, centered at e with a radius of r. r_{ei} is the distance from unit i to the center of unit e, where i is the element in the domain Φ_r; The weighting factor $\kappa(r_{ei})$ is mathematically expressed as

$$\kappa(r_{ei}) = \max(r - r_{ei}, 0) \tag{4}$$

Threshold projection techniques, such as the Heaviside projection, are employed to achieve clearly defined structural boundaries. These methods map the filtered density field onto a physical density field, ensuring a distinct transition between solid and void regions. The Heaviside projection can be defined as [27,35]:

$$\bar{\rho}_e = \frac{\tanh(\beta\eta) + \tanh[\beta(\tilde{\rho}_e - \eta)]}{\tanh(\beta\eta) + \tanh[\beta(1-\eta)]} \tag{5}$$

where β is a parameter that regulates the sharpness of the projection, and η is a threshold with values ranging from 0 to 1. As the projection parameter escalates, the filtered density values converge towards 0 and 1. In practical application, a strategy of gradually increasing the parameter is typically employed to achieve completely distinct topologies. Figure 1 shows the schematic of topology optimization.

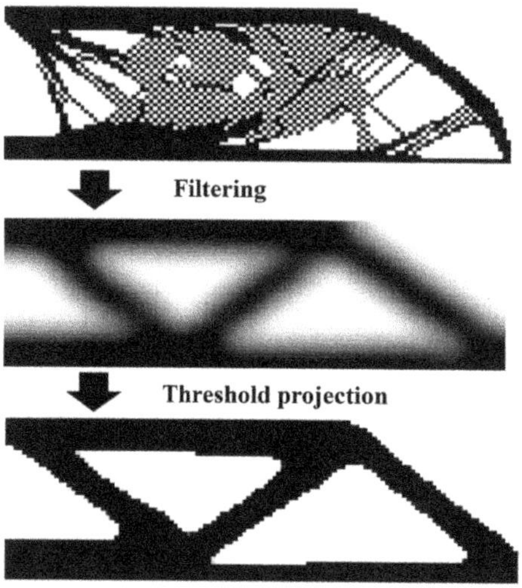

Figure 1. The schematic of topology optimization.

2.4. Sensitivity Analysis

For the compliance minimization problem, the sensitivity of the compliance c with respect to the physical density can be expressed as follows:

$$\frac{\partial c}{\partial \bar{\rho}_e} = -p\bar{\rho}_e^{\,p-1}\boldsymbol{u}_e^{\mathrm{T}}\boldsymbol{k}_0\boldsymbol{u}_e \tag{6}$$

where $\boldsymbol{u}_e$ represents the element displacement vector. $\boldsymbol{k}_0$ denotes the stiffness matrix of solid material. This information is crucial for the TO algorithm to navigate the design space towards an optimal solution.

The sensitivity of the static compliance can be conducted using the chain rule as

$$\alpha_e = \frac{\partial c}{\partial \rho_e} = \sum_{i\in\Phi_r} \frac{\partial c}{\partial \bar{\rho}_i}\frac{\partial \bar{\rho}_i}{\partial \tilde{\rho}_i}\frac{\partial \tilde{\rho}_i}{\partial \rho_e} \tag{7}$$

where α_e denotes the derivative of the static compliance with respect to the e-th design variable.

2.5. Neighborhood Search Based on k-d Tree Algorithm

A k-d tree is formed by iteratively dividing the dataset into two subsets until each subset includes either a single data point or none. Let the coordinates of all m elements constitute a three-dimensional point set $\boldsymbol{\lambda} = \{\boldsymbol{\lambda}_1, \boldsymbol{\lambda}_2, \ldots, \boldsymbol{\lambda}_m\}$, where each point $\boldsymbol{\lambda}_i$ is represented by the three-dimensional vector $\boldsymbol{\lambda}_i = (\lambda_{ix}, \lambda_{iy}, \lambda_{iz})$. This study uses the dimension with the greatest variation as the splitting axis for generating the tree structure incrementally, to maximize tree balance and enhance query efficiency, given the random distribution of element coordinates in practical applications. The precise computations are as follows:

$$\mu_d = \frac{1}{m}\sum_{i=1}^{m}\lambda_{id} \tag{8}$$

$$\sigma_d^2 = \frac{1}{m}\sum_{i=1}^{m}(\lambda_{id} - \mu_d)^2 \tag{9}$$

where d represents the dimension, with its value being $d \in \{1,2,3\}$ (i.e., the x, y, z axes), λ_{id} denotes the value of the vector $\boldsymbol{\lambda}_i$ in the d-th dimension, μ_d represents the mean value in the d-th dimension, and σ_d^2 represents the variance in the d-th dimension.

Identify the dimension exhibiting the greatest variance to serve as the splitting axis, and arrange all points based on the d-th dimension.

$$d = \text{argmax}\left(\sigma_d^2\right) \quad d \in \{1,2,3\} \tag{10}$$

Determine the median, which serves as the splitting point of the current node, segmenting the point set $\boldsymbol{\lambda}$ into two subsets:

$$\lambda_l = \{\lambda_i \in \lambda | \lambda_{id} \leq M_d\} \tag{11}$$

$$\lambda_r = \{\lambda_i \in \lambda | \lambda_{id} > M_d\} \tag{12}$$

where M_d denotes the median value in the d-th dimension, $\boldsymbol{\lambda}_l$ and $\boldsymbol{\lambda}_r$ signify the subsets of points contained are at the left and right subtrees of the splitting point, respectively. Recursively repeat the above steps for $\boldsymbol{\lambda}_l$ and $\boldsymbol{\lambda}_r$ until each subset contains either a single point or none.

The k-d tree constructed can facilitate efficient range queries. To identify all points within a radius of r surrounding a given query point $\boldsymbol{\lambda}_j$ = (λ_{jx}, λ_{jy}, λ_{jz}), the computation procedure is as follows:

$$\|\lambda_t - \lambda_j\|_2 = \sqrt{(\lambda_{tx} - \lambda_{jx})^2 + (\lambda_{ty} - \lambda_{jy})^2 + (\lambda_{tz} - \lambda_{jz})^2} \tag{13}$$

$$\|\lambda_t - \lambda_j\|_2 \leq r \tag{14}$$

where $\|\lambda_t - \lambda_j\|_2$ represents the Euclidean distance between the query point $\boldsymbol{\lambda}_j$ and the current tree node $\boldsymbol{\lambda}_t$ = (λ_{tx}, λ_{ty}, λ_{tz}). If it satisfies Equation (14), the current tree node $\boldsymbol{\lambda}_t$ is incorporated into the result set.

Assume that the query point and the current tree node in the splitting dimension have values of λ_{jd} and λ_{td}, respectively, and that the splitting dimension is d. The recursive criteria are as follows:

$$\lambda_{jd} - r \leq \lambda_{td} \tag{15}$$

$$\lambda_{jd} + r > \lambda_{td} \tag{16}$$

If Equation (15) holds, it signifies that the query neighborhood intersects with the search space of the left subtree, prompting the algorithm recurses into the left subtree. If Equation (16) is satisfied, it indicates that the query neighborhood intersects with the search space of the right subtree, so the algorithm recurses into the right subtree. Repeat the aforementioned process until the current tree node has no subtrees. The processes for constructing a k-d tree and conducting neighborhood searches are outlined in pseudocode as Algorithm 1: Construction of k-d Tree and Neighborhood Search.

Algorithm 1: Construction of k-d Tree and Neighborhood Search

1. Input the initial set of three-dimensional coordinate points: $\boldsymbol{\lambda} = \{\boldsymbol{\lambda}_1, \boldsymbol{\lambda}_2, \ldots, \boldsymbol{\lambda}_m\}$.
2. Initialize dimension $d = 0$ and variance $\sigma_{max}^2 = 0$.
3. **While** $d < 3$, **do**
4. $d = d + 1$;
5. Calculate the mean value μ_d in the d-th dimension according to Equation (8);
6. Calculate the variance σ_d^2 in the d-th dimension according to Equation (9);
7. **if** $\sigma_d^2 > \sigma_{max}^2$
8. **do** Update the largest variance value $\sigma_{max}^2 = \sigma_d^2$;
9. **do** Record the current d as the split axis;
10. **end if**
11. **End while**
12. Calculate the left and right subtrees $\boldsymbol{\lambda}_l$, $\boldsymbol{\lambda}_r$;
13. Replace the $\boldsymbol{\lambda}$ in Step 1 with $\boldsymbol{\lambda}_l$ and $\boldsymbol{\lambda}_r$ and repeat the above steps until $\boldsymbol{\lambda}_l$ and $\boldsymbol{\lambda}_r$ contain only one point or no points;
14. Input the query point $\boldsymbol{\lambda}_j = (\lambda_{jx}, \lambda_{jy}, \lambda_{jz})$ and the current tree node $\boldsymbol{\lambda}_t = (\lambda_{tx}, \lambda_{ty}, \lambda_{tz})$;
15. Find the coordinates in the split dimension of current tree node are λ_{jd} and λ_{td};
16. Calculate the Euclidean distance according to Equation (13);
17. **If** Equation (14) is satisfied
18. **do** add the current tree node $\boldsymbol{\lambda}_t$ to the neighborhood set;
19. **if** Equation (15) is satisfied
20. **do** return to Step 14 to recursively search the left subtree;
21. **else if** Equation (16) is satisfied
22. **do** return to Step 14 to recursively search the right subtree;
23. **end if**
24. **End if**
25. **Return** the final neighborhood set.

A k-d tree recursively divides the space into smaller areas, enabling each node's examination to concentrate solely on a particular subspace rather than the entire space. If the query point is distant from the current node's splitting position, the subtree may be disregarded, significantly decreasing the number of nodes that need assessment. Utilizing brute-force methods like nested for-loops requires comparing each point, resulting in a time complexity of $O(n^2)$, which is exceedingly wasteful for large data searches. In contrast, the ideal time complexity for a k-d tree search is $O(\log n)$, and even in the worst-case scenario, its performance far surpasses $O(n^2)$. Chapter 3 will provide numerical examples to assess the effectiveness of these two strategies.

2.6. The Extension of Neighborhood Search with k-d Tree

Manufacturability constraints in engineering applications encompass a wide spectrum of requirements, including but not limited to planar symmetry, rotational symmetry, local volume control, periodic patterning, stamping-oriented overhang control [36–40]. This section specifically examines planar symmetry, rotational symmetry (shown in Figure 2) and implicit local volume constraint as representative cases, developing corresponding heuristic formulations to demonstrate the method's core capability. Notably, the proposed k-d tree method can be readily extended to implement virtually all other types of symmetry constraints without fundamental algorithmic modifications.

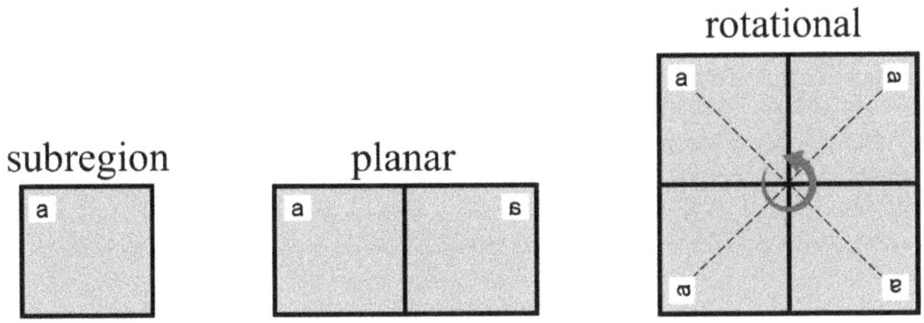

Figure 2. Planar symmetry and rotational symmetry.

2.6.1. Planar Symmetry

Suppose that the design domain is divided into j symmetric sets, and the sensitivity of symmetric elements in each set is averaged, it yields

$$\overline{\alpha}_j = \frac{1}{n}\sum_{i=1}^{n} \alpha_{ji} \tag{17}$$

where α_{ji} is the sensitivity of element i in the jth symmetric set, $\overline{\alpha}_j$ is the sensitivity of each element and its symmetric elements after considering symmetry constraints. This sensitivity updating process is illustrated in Figure 3.

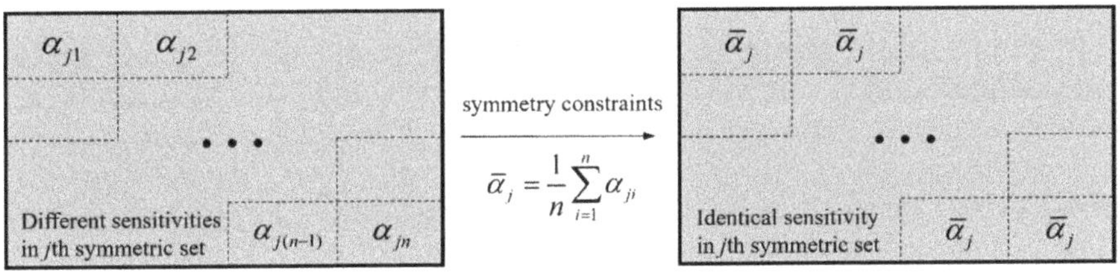

Figure 3. The sensitivity updating process after applying symmetric constraints.

For the planar symmetry constraint, without losing generality, take the planar yoz pair as an example. For an element along coordinates $\boldsymbol{\lambda}_i = (x_i, y_i, z_i)$, its symmetric counterpart satisfies:

$$\lambda_{is} = (-x_i, y_i, z_i) \tag{18}$$

In implementation, we enforce symmetry by taking the absolute value of the x-coordinate, thus symmetric coordinates $\boldsymbol{\lambda}_i$ and $\boldsymbol{\lambda}_{is}$ will map to the same modified coordinate:

$$\lambda_i^* = \lambda_{is}^* = (|x_i|, y_i, z_i) \tag{19}$$

Assume that $S = \{\boldsymbol{\lambda}_1^*, \boldsymbol{\lambda}_{1s}^*, \boldsymbol{\lambda}_2^*, \boldsymbol{\lambda}_{2s}^*, \ldots \boldsymbol{\lambda}_n^*, \boldsymbol{\lambda}_{ns}^*\}$ is the set of all modified element coordinates. For a given tolerance $\varepsilon > 0$, the k-d tree algorithm identifies symmetric element pairs or groups such that

$$\|\lambda_u - \lambda_v\|_2 \leq \varepsilon \tag{20}$$

where $\|\lambda_u - \lambda_v\|_2$ represents the Euclidean distance between any two points $\boldsymbol{\lambda}_u$ and $\boldsymbol{\lambda}_v$ in the set S. It is significant that Equation (20) nearly parallels Equation (14), varying in the substitution of the radius r with a tolerance ε approaching zero. This update ingeniously alters the function of the k-d tree from looking for items within a radius r to identifying symmetrically positioned elements located at the same coordinates. The parameter ε is set to 0.01 times the average element size for regular meshes because symmetric elements in such meshes have uniform spacing equal to the element size—this small tolerance ensures only true symmetric pairs are detected, avoiding false matches from non-symmetric elements. For irregular meshes, element dimensions and spacing vary, so ε is increased to 0.2 times the average element size to accommodate minor coordinate deviations from discretization while still preventing missed symmetric pairs. This choice of ε aligns with the geometric characteristics of the respective mesh types, ensuring symmetry enforcement remains accurate without relying on arbitrary heuristics.

Notably, the consistency of optimized results across regular and irregular meshes (Sections 3.1 and 3.3) further supports the appropriateness of ε: in both cases, the final topologies exhibit clear symmetry and stable compliance values, confirming that the selected ε does not introduce numerical inconsistencies or compromise design quality.

2.6.2. Rotational Symmetry

For the rotational symmetry constraint, the Cartesian coordinates (x, y, z) at the center of the element are first converted into spherical polar coordinates (r_p, θ, φ), i.e.,

$$r_p = \sqrt{x^2 + y^2 + z^2} \tag{21}$$

$$\theta = \arccos\left(\frac{z}{r_p}\right) \tag{22}$$

$$\varphi = \arctan\left(\frac{y}{x}\right) \tag{23}$$

where the radial distance r_p is the distance from the coordinate point to the center of the sphere o, the polar angle θ is the angle between the z axis and r_p, and the azimuth angle φ is the angle between the projection line of r_p onto the xoy plane and the positive direction of the x axis.

Considering the rotational symmetry number n, the azimuth angle increment for each symmetric subregion is

$$\zeta = \frac{2\pi}{n} \tag{24}$$

Consequently, the symmetric element group under this constraint has the following characteristics: The radial distance r and the polar angle θ remain constant, and for the kth symmetric subregion, the azimuth angle is

$$\varphi_k = \varphi_0 + k\zeta \tag{25}$$

where φ_0 is the initial azimuth angle. The elements with a φ value in each subregion are traversed by the programming language, corresponding to the reduced angle $k\zeta$, ensuring that elements under symmetric restrictions are overlapped. Then Equation (20) is used to search for symmetric elements.

2.6.3. Implicit Local Volume Constraint

The suggested filtering technique may also be utilized in the construction of porous structures via the implicit local volume constraint [38]. As illustrated in Figure 4, the primary concept is to prevent the accumulation of material regions by incorporating voids in the physical density.

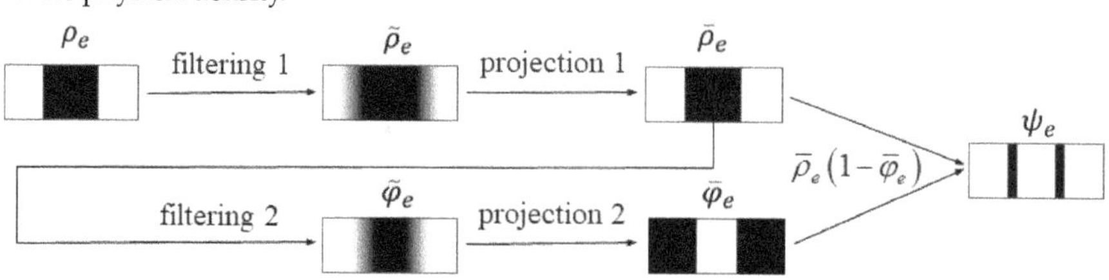

Figure 4. The implementation principle of implicit local volume constraints.

The updated physical density field ψ_e is computed by performing a point-wise multiplication of the two projected fields.

$$\psi_e = \overline{\rho}_e(1 - \overline{\varphi}_e), \forall e \tag{26}$$

where $\overline{\varphi}_e$ is the second projected field. The point-by-point multiplication of two scalar fields facilitates material distribution without violating the local volume limit, and the updated physical density can be incorporated into Equation (2) for material interpolation and stiffness matrix computation.

Similar to Equation (3), the second filtered field $\widetilde{\varphi}_e$ characterizes the local volume fraction of solid material in the scalar field $\overline{\rho}_e$, it yields

$$\widetilde{\varphi}_e = \frac{1}{|\Phi_R|} \sum_{i \in \Phi_R} \overline{\rho}_i \tag{27}$$

where Φ_R denotes the neighborhood set of the element e for the second filter and $|\Phi_R|$ denotes the number of elements in the set. Here, Φ_R is defined in the same way as Φ_r in Equation (1) except r replaced with R, which is usually larger than that of r.

The second projected field $\overline{\varphi}_e$ is constructed by applying a novel projection function to the previously obtained filtered field $\widetilde{\varphi}_e$, expressed as:

$$\overline{\varphi}_e = \frac{\tanh(\beta'\eta') + \tanh[\beta'(\widetilde{\varphi}_e - \eta')]}{\tanh(\beta'\eta') + \tanh[\beta'(1 - \eta')]} \tag{28}$$

where β' represents a parameter controlling the sharpness of the second projection, $\widetilde{\varphi}_e$ is the second filtered filed. The parameter term of this formula closely resembles the initial projection function in Equation (5); however, the second projection solely elevates the lesser value $\widetilde{\varphi}_e$ to 1, resulting in the aforementioned projection function demonstrating a low-pass characteristic, which is precisely contrary to the outcome of the step projection function in Equation (5).

The ensuing optimization solution is congruent with the aforementioned strategy. In assessing sensitivity, it is crucial to acknowledge that the incorporation of the second filtering and projection techniques requires the inclusion of these two factors in the chain derivation formula referenced in Equation (7).

$$\frac{\partial c}{\partial \rho_e} = \sum_{i \in \Phi_r} \frac{\partial c}{\partial \rho_i^*} \frac{\partial \rho_i^*}{\partial \overline{\rho}_i} \frac{\partial \overline{\rho}_i}{\partial \widetilde{\rho}_i} \frac{\partial \widetilde{\rho}_i}{\partial \rho_e} + \sum_{i \in \Phi_r} \left(\sum_{j \in \Phi_R} \frac{\partial c}{\partial \rho_j^*} \frac{\partial \rho_j^*}{\partial \overline{\varphi}_j} \frac{\partial \overline{\varphi}_j}{\partial \widetilde{\varphi}_j} \frac{\partial \widetilde{\varphi}_j}{\partial \overline{\rho}_i} \right) \frac{\partial \overline{\rho}_i}{\partial \widetilde{\rho}_i} \frac{\partial \widetilde{\rho}_i}{\partial \rho_e} \tag{29}$$

This method necessitates two neighborhood searches due to the two filter radii, with the second search encompassing a larger range than the first. This complexity may pose challenges for large-scale applications. The k-d tree algorithm proposed in this work efficiently performs both neighborhood searches, hence improving the efficiency of addressing porous structure issues.

3. Numerical Examples and Discussion

In the absence of contrary indications, an elastic modulus of 1 and a Poisson's ratio of 0.3 are assigned, respectively. The convention TO problem, as articulated in Equation (1), can be addressed through moving morphable asymptotes (MMA) technique [41]. A supplementary parameter for the movement limit is established at 0.05. Due to the establishment of low thresholds for convergence criteria, the optimizations conducted in Section 3 consistently concluded upon reaching the maximum of 350 iterations. β commences at a value of 1 and doubles at every 50 steps until it reaches a maximum of 64. All numerical tests are conducted on a desktop computer using an Intel i7 2.93 GHz CPU and 64 GB of RAM.

3.1. Example 1

The benchmark Messerschmitt–Bölkow–Blohm (MBB) structure as depicted in Figure 5, with a design domain measuring 120 × 40, is optimized to validate the efficacy of the proposed *k*-d tree density filtering technique. The design realm was discretized into regular elements of dimensions 120 × 40, 240 × 80, 360 × 120, and 480 × 160, respectively. The left boundary is fully constrained in the horizontal direction, while vertical support is applied at the bottom-right corner. A vertical force $F = 1$ is exerted at the upper left corner. The target volume fraction and the filter radius r is set to 50% and 5, respectively.

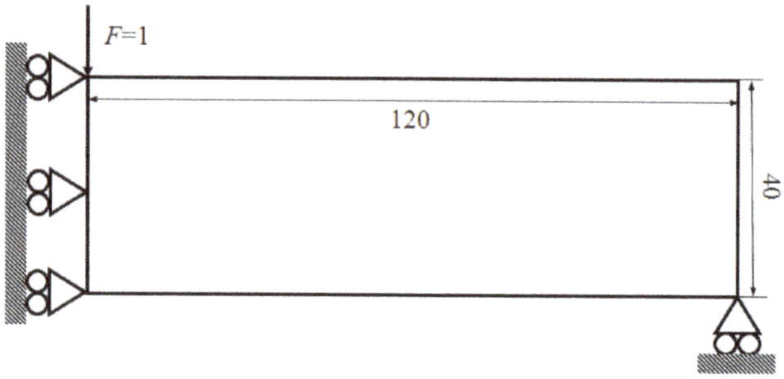

Figure 5. Design domain of MBB structure.

No checkerboard patterns are present in any of the optimized topologies, hence validating the efficacy of the utilized filtering method in eliminating such numerical aberrations. The above Figure 6 depicts the outcomes obtained from the proposed density filtering method. The study of these data demonstrates a strong consistency in various optimized topologies across different mesh densities, signifying the efficacy of the proposed strategy in attaining mesh-independent solutions. The compliance values of the final design show a slight upward trend with higher element resolution. This is expected, as finer discretization captures more intricate structural details, which can result in higher compliance values.

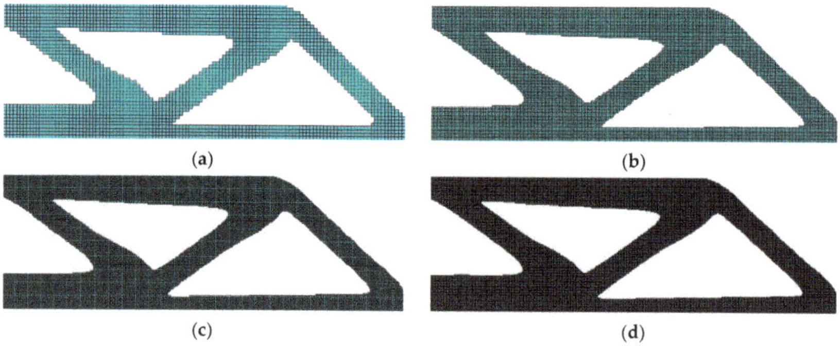

Figure 6. Optimized structures were obtained by (**a**) 120 × 40 elements, $c = 228.345$, (**b**) 240 × 80 elements, $c = 229.803$, (**c**) 360 × 120 elements, $c = 232.363$ and (**d**) 480 × 160 elements, $c = 234.799$.

3.2. Example 2

This example optimizes a 3D L-shaped structure, aiming to validate the advantages of the *k*-d tree search algorithm over the traditional brute-force search algorithms. The structure is clamped at its top edge and a concentrated force $F = 0.1$ is exerted on the upper sideline of the right side, as illustrated in Figure 7a. The design domain is discretized using brick elements with elemental sizes of 2, 1, and 0.5, resulting in total elemental counts of 2500, 20,000, and 160,000, respectively. The desired volume fraction is set to 50%. Table 1 shows the computation times spent in neighborhood search and overall optimization between the brute-force and *k*-d tree algorithms.

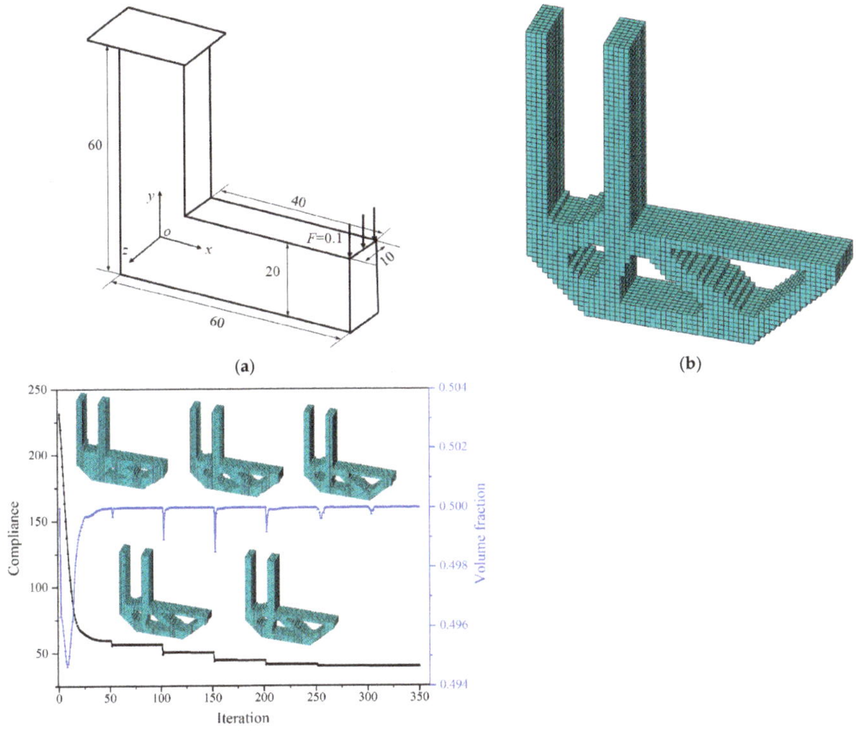

Figure 7. Optimization of the L-shaped structure. (**a**) loading and boundary conditions, (**b**) optimized design, and (**c**) iteration histories of compliance and volume fraction.

Table 1. Computation times spent in neighborhood search and overall optimization between the brute-force and *k*-d tree algorithms.

Number of Elements	Element Size	Filter Radius	Brute-Force (Search/Overall Time)	*k*-d Tree (Search/Overall Time)
2500	$2 \times 2 \times 2$	10	13.72/1598.54	0.76/1563.11
20,000	$1 \times 1 \times 1$	5	1175.47/3689.21	8.74/2491.73
160,000	$0.5 \times 0.5 \times 0.5$	2.5	-	78.41/31,038.53

Both the *k*-d tree and brute-force search approaches follow the same iterative processes and yield the same results, with the only difference being computational efficiency. The optimization problem is addressed inside the same hardware environment to guarantee that the comparison of algorithm efficiency remains unaffected by hardware discrepancies. Using the model with 20,000 elements as an example, its topological optimization results and iteration histories are depicted in Figures 7b and 7c, respectively. The graph illustrates compliance as a stepwise sequence of possessive decline. The parameter β updates every 50 steps, resulting in a sudden drop followed by a plateau until the subsequent update. This procedure demonstrates the effect of progressively augmenting the beta value to enhance material configuration. The volume is consistently controlled within the volume fraction.

Table 1 demonstrates that *k*-d tree algorithms significantly outperform the brute-force method in computational efficiency, particularly as the number of elements increases. For a limited number of elements (2500 elements), both methodologies are feasible. Nonetheless, the k-d tree demonstrates a significant speed advantage. As the element count increases to 20,000, the k-d tree maintains its efficiency, decreasing both neighborhood search time and overall optimization time compared to the brute-force method. As the element count nears 160,000, the brute-force method becomes impractical due to memory constraints; however, the k-d tree continues to exhibit efficient performance. This underscores the scalability of the k-d tree technique and its adeptness efficiently addressing large-scale optimization problems. Thus, the increasing computational efficiency of k-d tree makes them a preferable choice for intricate, large-scale applications, whereas conventional methods are inadequate.

3.3. Example 3

This example features a double L-shaped structure, intended to demonstrate the proposed approach's capability to attain a planar symmetry design, despite the presence of irregular elements. The design domain is discretized utilizing quadrilateral and triangular elements; each elemental size is 1, respectively. The boundary conditions are depicted in Figure 8, illustrate the combination of two L-shaped beams, fixed at the top, subject to vertical downward loads of magnitude 1 applied to the left and right corners. Additionally, a horizontal leftward load of magnitude 0.3 is applied to the left corner to introduce asymmetry in the topology optimization results. The target volume fraction and the filter radius r are set to 50% and 3, respectively. Figure 9 illustrates various optimized topologies prior to and subsequent to the implementation of the planar symmetry constraint.

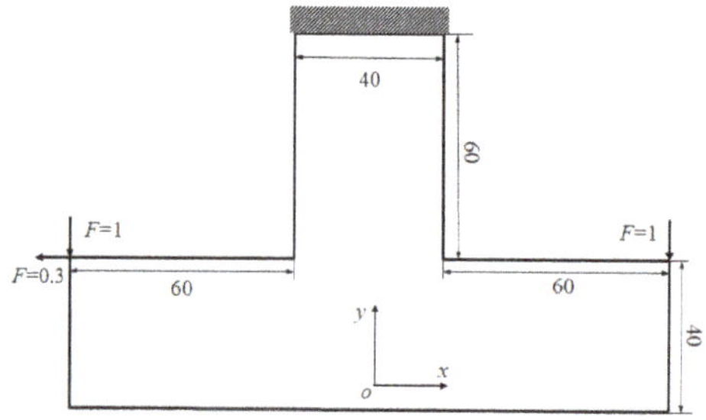

Figure 8. Design domain of double L-shaped structure.

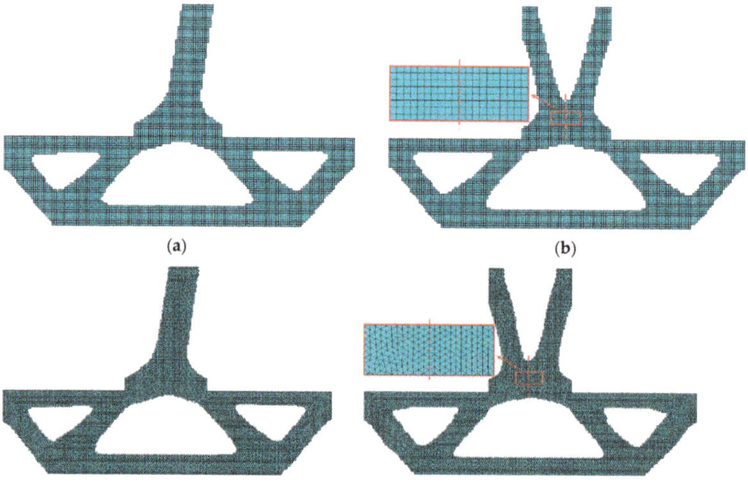

Figure 9. Optimized structures were obtained by (**a**) regular elements without planar symmetry constrained, (**b**) regular elements with planar symmetry constraint, (**c**) irregular elements without planar symmetry constrained and (**d**) irregular elements with planar symmetry constraint.

3.4. Example 4

This example depicts a gear design featuring a circular shaped design domain and non-designable inner- and outer-rings, aiming to validate the rotational symmetry design using the proposed approach. The blue-designated region is attached to the white non-designable area. The boundary conditions are depicted in Figure 10. A concentrated force of magnitude 1 is exerted tangentially along the outside circumference as surface traction. The inner bearing of the inner ring is fully restricted. The target volume percentage is established at 50%, with the filter radius set at 4. When the rotational symmetry number is designated as n, the optimized material distribution results are illustrated in Figure 11.

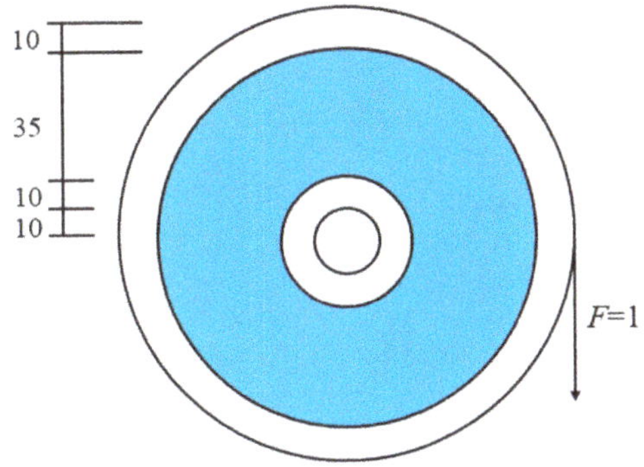

Figure 10. The design domain and the boundary conditions.

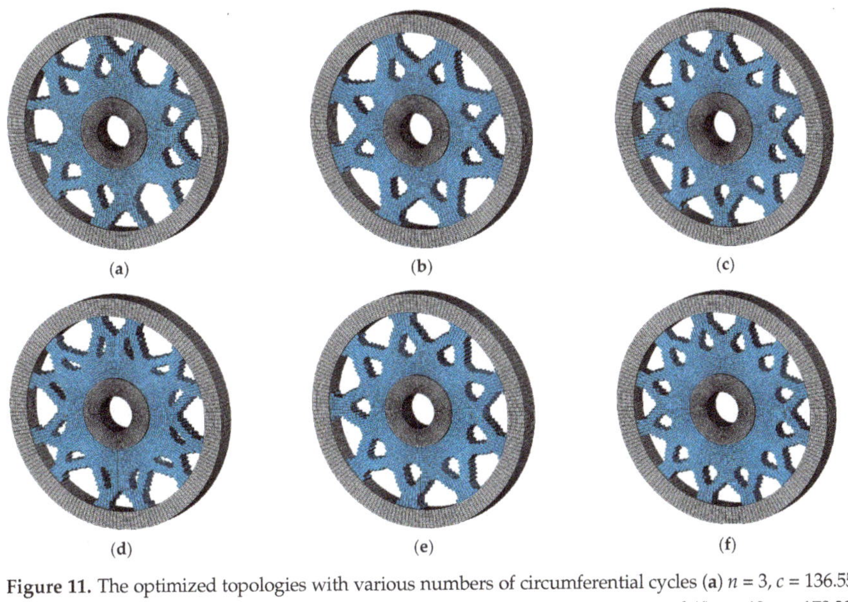

Figure 11. The optimized topologies with various numbers of circumferential cycles (**a**) $n = 3$, $c = 136.55$, (**b**) $n = 4$, $c = 136.46$, (**c**) $n = 5$, $c = 142.94$ (**d**) $n = 6$, $c = 144.32$ (**e**) $n = 9$, $c = 157.44$ and (**f**) $n = 12$, $c = 178.23$.

Figure 11 demonstrates that the application of rotational symmetry as an additional constraint in the optimization problem generally diminishes the structure's performance. When the cycle count is low, the constraint effect is nuanced, seen only in modifications to the topological pattern. As the quantity escalates, the rotational symmetry requirement becomes paramount in the optimization problem, affecting both performance and the ultimate topology. The structure achieves the limitation by compromising rigidity, leading to an increase in compliance. Through coordinate translation, the k-d tree can convert the symmetric constraint problem into a defined neighborhood search problem, hence enabling the implementation of circumferential constraints. The numerical findings underscore the efficacy of the proposed method in addressing rotational symmetry constraints.

3.5. Example 5

A 2D bone-like structure was optimized to assess the viability of the local volume fraction approach augmented by the proposed *k*-d tree algorithm [42]. The finite element model comprises 29,854 elements and 29,792 nodes, with three layers of elements kept as the non-design domain. The bottom edge was entirely fixed, while concentrated loads were applied at both top corners with a downward 45° inclination ($\theta = 45°$), as depicted in Figure 12. The magnitude of the left and right load $\sqrt{2}$. Set the volume fraction to 0.5 and the maximum number of iteration steps to 350. Specify the filter parameters $r = 4.5$ and $R = 10$, the projection parameters $\beta_1 = 1$ and $\beta_2 = 8$, and the projection parameters $\eta_1 = 0.5$ and $\eta_2 = 0.6$. The optimized infill structure is drawn in Figure 13.

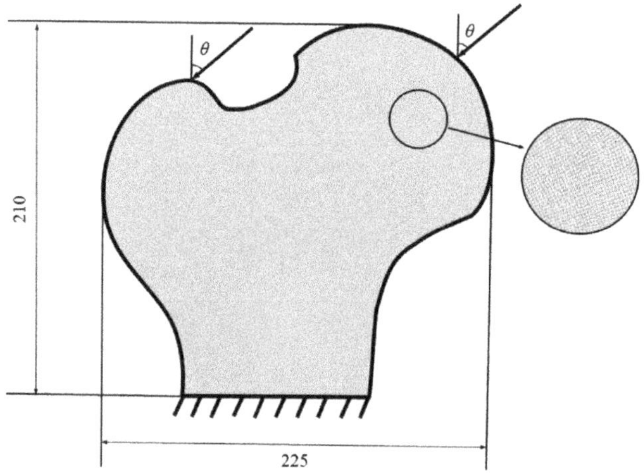

Figure 12. The boundary conditions of the bone-like structure.

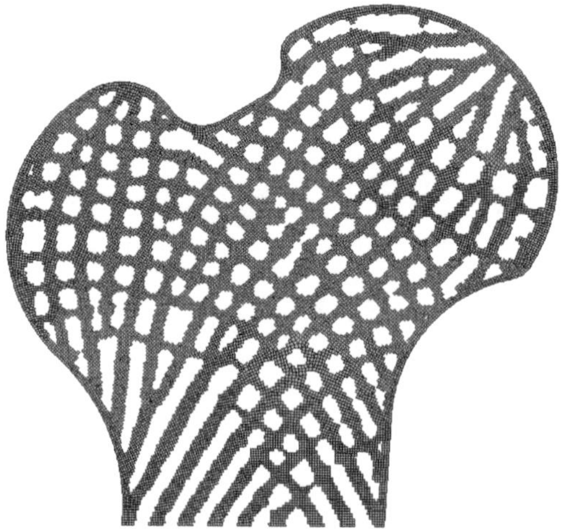

Figure 13. The optimized bone-like structure.

As expected, a porous structure is generated to satisfy the given design criteria, while all constraints are nearly rigorously fulfilled. This challenge requires the implementation of two neighborhood searches with radius r and R need to be implemented. The k-d tree technique can accurately execute two neighborhood searches, which usually demand considerable time using traditional techniques. Additionally, the results demonstrate the k-d tree algorithm's practicality under the local volume constraint.

3.6. Engineering Application

In recent years, structural optimization technology has gained prominence in the wind power industry. TO method serves as an innovative design tool during the conceptual design phase, as evidenced in the structural design of blades [43,44], jackets [45–47] and tripod supports [48]. This example demonstrates the TO of the front framework of a wind turbine validate the feasibility and superiority of the k-d tree algorithm for large-scale engineering challenges. The finite element of assembly model comprises 764,477 nodes and 824,573 elements, in which the front framework is predominately discretized using hexahedral solid elements. Figure 14 illustrates the finite element model of the assembly. The material possesses an elastic modulus of 169,000 MPa and a Poisson's ratio of 0.275. The target volume fraction is specified as 40%. This study investigates the weighed combination of moments in the y and z directions, specifically M_y and M_z. The resultant topology is plotted in Figure 15.

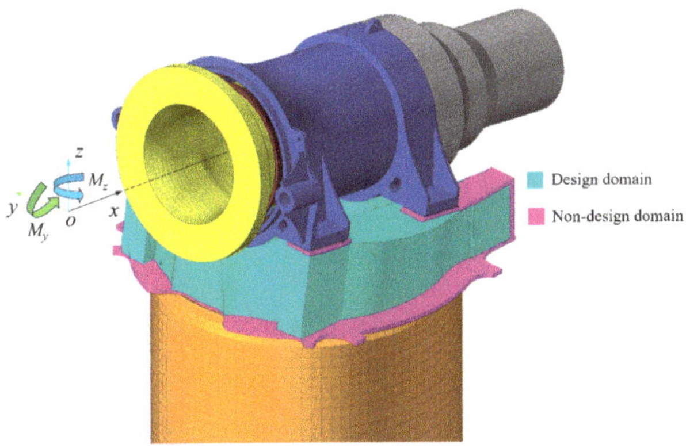

Figure 14. The finite element model of the assembly.

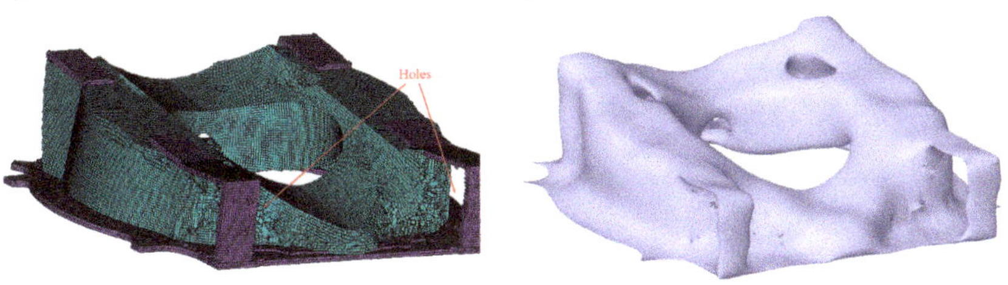

Figure 15. The optimized front framework (**a**) finite element model and (**b**) STL model after smoothing process.

Figure 15 illustrates that, under the loading conditions influenced by moments M_y and Mz, the material distribution from the apex of the tower via the rear bearing seat establishes a clear force transmission channel at the rear end of the front structure. The apparent holes in the rear area suggest that these regions are ineffective or erroneous. The implementation of the k-d tree algorithm to compute the aforementioned model on a standard office computer (Intel i7 2.93 GHz CPU, 64 GB RAM) required approximately 2.5 h for completion, whereas previously, complex models of this magnitude typically necessitated cloud computing platforms or supercomputers, where more time is required for processing. This engineering application demonstrates that the *k*-d tree technique can swiftly and effectively handle complex geometric shapes and extensive datasets, a task that was difficult in previous topology optimization studies.

4. Conclusions

This study has presented an efficient filtering method for structural TO utilizing the *k*-d tree data structure, applicable for addressing practical manufacturability restrictions. The use of the *k*-d tree algorithm obviates the necessity for laborious repetitive examinations and offers a scalable solution for large-scale optimization challenges, where conventional methods would falter under computing demands.

Numerical examples demonstrate that the proposed filtering approach successfully eradicates checkerboard patterns while preserving robust performance across diverse mesh densities. The *k*-d tree algorithm demonstrates remarkable advantages over traditional brute-force techniques, particularly for large-scale problems. Furthermore, the approach precisely enforces constraints even with irregular elements through adaptive tolerance adjustment. The algorithm addresses symmetry constraints using coordinate transformation and satisfies local volume constraints through multiple neighborhood searches. Although this study exemplifies only these two types of constraints, the proposed framework can be readily extended to other manufacturability constraints via the same efficient spatial query mechanism. The industrial case study further confirms the method's practical value. It reduces the optimization runtime of large structural components such as wind turbine frameworks from over 8 h to around 2.5 h and enables optimized structures to achieve 20 percent weight reduction while maintaining 7.7 percent higher stiffness. This directly lowers manufacturing hardware costs for enterprises and supports lightweight high-performance design goals in engineering practice.

Future works will focus on three key points. First, optimize the *k*-d tree's recursive partitioning logic to adapt to 3D models with irregular curved boundaries common in large wind turbine components. Second, integrate the method with additive manufacturing constraints such as overhang angle limits to expand its application scope in wind turbine part manufacturing. Third develop a lightweight version of the algorithm compatible with edge computing devices for on-site real time optimization in wind turbine component production workshops.

Author Contributions: J.H.: validation and software, methodology; A.S.: validation and software, methodology, revision; K.L.: conceptualization, methodology, writing—original draft preparation and revision; Y.C.: writing and editing; R.G.: writing and editing; J.J.: writing—reviewing and editing; T.T.: writing—reviewing and editing. All authors have read and agreed to the published version of the manuscript.

Funding: This work was financially supported by the National Key Research and Development Program of China (No. 2024YFE0208600), the National Natural Science Foundation of China (No. U24B2090), the Fundamental Research Funds for the Central Universities (No. 2024JC006).

Data Availability Statement: The data presented in this study are available on request from the corresponding author.

Conflicts of Interest: Author Tao Tao was employed by China Southern Power Grid Technology Co., Ltd. The remaining authors declare that the research was conducted in the absence of any commercial or financial relationships that could be construed as a potential conflict of interest.

References

1. Bendsøe, M.P.; Kikuchi, N. Generating optimal topologies in structural design using a homogenization method. *Comput. Methods Appl. Mech. Eng.* **1988**, *71*, 197–224. [CrossRef]
2. Bendsøe, M.P. Optimal shape design as a material distribution problem. *Struct. Optim.* **1989**, *1*, 193–202. [CrossRef]
3. Bendsøe, M.P.; Sigmund, O. Material interpolation schemes in topology optimization. *Arch. Appl. Mech.* **1999**, *69*, 635–654. [CrossRef]
4. Zhou, M.; Rozvany, G.I.N. The COC algorithm, part II: Topological, geometrical and generalized shape optimization. *Comput. Methods Appl. Mech. Eng.* **1991**, *89*, 309–336. [CrossRef]
5. Long, K.; Wang, X.; Gu, X. Local optimum in multi-material topology optimization and solution by reciprocal variables. *Struct. Multidiscip. Optim.* **2018**, *57*, 1283–1295. [CrossRef]
6. Xie, Y.M.; Steven, G.P. A simple evolutionary procedure for structural optimization. *Comput. Struct.* **1993**, *49*, 885–896. [CrossRef]
7. Allaire, G.; Jouve, F.; Toader, A.M. Structural optimization using sensitivity analysis and a level-set method. *J. Comput. Phys.* **2004**, *194*, 363–393. [CrossRef]
8. Wang, M.Y.; Wang, X.; Guo, D. A level set method for structural topology optimization. *Comput. Methods Appl. Mech. Eng.* **2003**, *192*, 227–246. [CrossRef]
9. Guo, X.; Zhang, W.; Zhong, W. Doing topology optimization explicitly and geometrically—A new moving morphable components based framework. *J. Appl. Mech.* **2014**, *81*, 081009. [CrossRef]
10. Fu, Y.F.; Rolfe, B.; Chiu, L.N.S.; Wang, Y.; Huang, X.; Ghabraie, K. SEMDOT: Smooth-edged material distribution for optimizing topology algorithm. *Adv. Eng. Softw.* **2020**, *150*, 102921. [CrossRef]
11. Fu, Y.F.; Rolfe, B.; Chiu, L.N.S.; Wang, Y.; Huang, X.; Ghabraie, K. Smooth topological design of 3D continuum structures using elemental volume fractions. *Comput. Struct.* **2020**, *231*, 106213. [CrossRef]
12. Fu, Y.F.; Long, K.; Rolfe, B. On non-penalization SEMDOT using discrete variable sensitivities. *J. Optim. Theory Appl.* **2023**, *198*, 644–677. [CrossRef]
13. Wei, P. Level set band method: A combination of density-based and level set methods for the topology optimization of continuums. *Front. Mech. Eng.* **2020**, *15*, 390–405. [CrossRef]
14. Sigmund, O.; Petersson, J. Numerical instabilities in topology optimization: A survey on procedures dealing with checkerboards, mesh-dependencies and local minima. *Struct. Optim.* **1998**, *16*, 68–75. [CrossRef]
15. Zhou, M.; Shyy, Y.K.; Thomas, H.L. Checkerboard and minimum member size control in topology optimization. *Struct. Multidiscip. Optim.* **2001**, *21*, 152–158. [CrossRef]
16. Diaz, A.; Sigmund, O. Checkerboard patterns in layout optimization. *Struct. Optim.* **1995**, *10*, 40–45. [CrossRef]
17. Poulsen, T.A. A simple scheme to prevent checkerboard patterns and one-node connected hinges in topology optimization. *Struct. Multidiscip. Optim.* **2002**, *24*, 396–399. [CrossRef]
18. Haber, R.B.; Jog, C.S.; Bendsøe, M.P. A new approach to variable-topology shape design using a constraint on perimeter. *Struct. Optim.* **1996**, *11*, 1–2. [CrossRef]
19. Petersson, J.; Sigmund, O. Slope constrained topology optimization. *Int. J. Numer. Methods Eng.* **1998**, *41*, 1417–1434. [CrossRef]
20. Sigmund, O. Morthology-based black and white filters for topology optimization. *Struct. Multidiscip. Optim.* **2007**, *33*, 401–424. [CrossRef]
21. Bourdin, B. Filters in topology optimization. *Int. J. Numer. Methods Eng.* **2001**, *50*, 2143–2158. [CrossRef]
22. Groenwold, A.A.; Etman, L.F. A simple heuristic for gray-scale suppression in optimality criterion-based topology optimization. *Struct. Multidiscip. Optim.* **2009**, *39*, 217–225. [CrossRef]
23. Wang, M.Y.; Wang, S. Bilateral filtering for structural topology optimization. *Int. J. Numer. Methods Eng.* **2005**, *63*, 1911–1938. [CrossRef]
24. Sigmund, O.; Maute, K. Sensitivity filtering from a continuum mechanics perspective. *Struct. Multidiscip. Optim.* **2012**, *46*, 471–475. [CrossRef]
25. Bruns, T.E.; Tortorelli, D.A. Topology optimization of non-linear elastic structures and compliant mechanisms. *Comput. Methods Appl. Mech. Eng.* **2001**, *190*, 3443–3459. [CrossRef]
26. Guest, J.K.; Prévost, J.H.; Belytschko, T. Achieving minimum length scale in topology optimization using nodal design variables and projection functions. *Int. J. Numer. Methods Eng.* **2004**, *61*, 238–254. [CrossRef]
27. Wang, F.; Lazarov, B.S.; Sigmund, O. On projection methods, convergence and robust formulations in topology optimization. *Struct. Multidiscip. Optim.* **2011**, *43*, 767–784. [CrossRef]
28. Sigmund, O. A 99 line topology optimization code written in Matlab. *Struct. Multidiscip. Optim.* **2001**, *21*, 120–127. [CrossRef]
29. Lazarov, B.S.; Sigmund, O. Filters in topology optimization based on Helmholtz-type differential equations. *Int. J. Numer. Methods Eng.* **2011**, *86*, 765–781. [CrossRef]
30. Andreassen, E.; Clausen, A.; Schevenels, M.; Lazarov, B.S.; Sigmund, O. Efficient topology optimization in MATLAB using 88 lines of code. *Struct. Multidiscip. Optim.* **2011**, *43*, 1–6. [CrossRef]

31. Zhao, Z.L.; Rong, Y.; Yan, Y.; Feng, X.Q.; Xie, Y.M. A subdomain-based parallel strategy for structural topology optimization. *Acta Mech. Sin.* **2023**, *39*, 422357. [CrossRef]
32. Foley, T.; Sugerman, J. KD-tree acceleration structures for a GPU raytracer. In Proceedings of the ACM SIGGRAPH/EUROGRAPHICS Conference on Graphics Hardware, Los Angeles, CA, USA, 30–31 July 2005; pp. 15–22.
33. Narasimhulu, Y.; Suthar, A.; Pasunuri, R.; Vadlamudi, C.V. CKD-Tree: An Improved KD-Tree Construction Algorithm. In Proceedings of the ISIC2021: International Semantic Intelligence Conference, New Delhi, India, 25–27 February 2021; pp. 211–218. Available online: https://ceur-ws.org/Vol-2786/Paper28.pdf (accessed on 15 March 2024).
34. Rozvany, G.I. A critical review of established methods of structural topology optimization. *Struct. Multidiscip. Optim.* **2009**, *37*, 217–237. [CrossRef]
35. Li, Q.; Liang, G.; Luo, Y.; Zhang, F.; Liu, S. An explicit formulation for minimum length scale control in density-based topology optimization. *Comput. Methods Appl. Mech. Eng.* **2023**, *404*, 115761. [CrossRef]
36. Liu, Y.; Li, Z.; Wei, P.; Wang, W. Parameterized level-set based topology optimization method considering symmetry and pattern repetition constraints. *Comput. Methods Appl. Mech. Eng.* **2018**, *340*, 1079–1101. [CrossRef]
37. Zuo, Z.H.; Xie, Y.M.; Huang, X. Optimal topological design of periodic structures for natural frequencies. *J. Struct. Eng.* **2011**, *137*, 1229–1240. [CrossRef]
38. Dou, S. A projection approach for topology optimization of porous structures through implicit local volume control. *Struct. Multidiscip. Optim.* **2020**, *62*, 835–850. [CrossRef]
39. Zuo, Z.H.; Huang, X.; Yang, X.; Rong, J.H.; Xie, Y.M. Comparing optimal material microstructures with optimal periodic structures. *Comput. Mater. Sci.* **2013**, *69*, 137–147. [CrossRef]
40. Huang, X.; Xie, Y.M. Optimal design of periodic structures using evolutionary topology optimization. *Struct. Multidiscip. Optim.* **2008**, *36*, 597–606. [CrossRef]
41. Svanberg, K. The method of moving asymptotes—A new method for structural optimization. *Int. J. Numer. Methods Eng.* **1987**, *24*, 359–373. [CrossRef]
42. Wu, J.; Aage, N.; Westermann, R.; Sigmund, O. Infill optimization for additive manufacturing—Approaching bone-like porous structures. *IEEE Trans. Vis. Comput. Graph.* **2017**, *24*, 1127–1140. [CrossRef]
43. Alkebsi, E.A.; Ameddah, H.; Outtas, T.; Almutawakel, A. Design of graded lattice structures in turbine blades using topology optimization. *Int. J. Comput. Integr. Manuf.* **2021**, *34*, 370–384. [CrossRef]
44. Stanford, B.; Beran, P.; Bhatia, M. Aeroelastic topology optimization of blade-stiffened panels. *J. Aircr.* **2014**, *51*, 938–944. [CrossRef]
45. Zhang, C.; Long, K.; Zhang, J.; Lu, F.; Bai, X.; Jia, J. A topology optimization methodology for the offshore wind turbine jacket structure in the concept phase. *Ocean Eng.* **2022**, *266*, 112974. [CrossRef]
46. Lan, R.; Long, K.; Saeed, A.; Geng, R.; Chen, Y.; Zhang, J.; Tao, T.; Liu, J. Fail-safe topology optimization for a four-leg jacket structure of offshore wind turbines. *Structures* **2024**, *62*, 106183. [CrossRef]
47. Zhou, Y.; Zhang, J.; Long, K.; Saeed, A.; Tao, T.; Chen, J. Topology optimization on a jacket structure for offshore wind turbines by altering structural design domain. *Appl. Ocean Res.* **2025**, *154*, 104421. [CrossRef]
48. Lu, F.; Long, K.; Zhang, C.; Zhang, J.; Tao, T. A novel design of the offshore wind turbine tripod structure using topology optimization methodology. *Ocean Eng.* **2023**, *280*, 114607. [CrossRef]

computation

MDPI

Article

Mechanical Evaluation of Topologically Optimized Shin Pads with Advanced Composite Materials: Assessment of the Impact Properties Utilizing Finite Element Analysis

Ioannis Filippos Kyriakidis [1,2], Nikolaos Kladovasilakis [2,*], Eleftheria Maria Pechlivani [2,*] and Konstantinos Tsongas [1,*]

[1] Advanced Materials and Manufacturing Technologies Laboratory, Department of Industrial Engineering and Management, School of Engineering, International Hellenic University, 57001 Thessaloniki, Greece; gkyriakidis@iti.gr

[2] Information Technologies Institute, Centre for Research and Technology Hellas, 57001 Thessaloniki, Greece

* Correspondence: nikoklad@iti.gr (N.K.); riapechl@iti.gr (E.M.P.); ktsongas@ihu.gr (K.T.)

Abstract: In this paper, the evaluation of the mechanical performance of novel, designed topologically optimized shin pads with advanced materials will be conducted with the aid of Finite Element Analysis (FEA) to assess the endurance of the final structure on impact phenomena extracted from actual real-life data acquired from contact sports. The main focus of the developed prototype is to have high-enough energy absorption capabilities and vibration isolation properties, crucial for the development of trustworthy protective equipment. The insertion of advanced materials with controlled weight fractions and lattice geometries aims to strategically improve those properties and provide tailored characteristics similar to the actual human skeleton. The final design is expected to be used as standalone protective equipment for athletes or as a protective shield for the development of human lower limb prosthetics. In this context, computational investigation of the dynamic mechanical response was conducted by replicating a real-life phenomenon of the impact during a contact sport in a median condition of a stud kick impact and an extreme case scenario to assess the dynamic response under shock-absorption conditions and the final design's structural integrity by taking into consideration the injury prevention capabilities. The results demonstrate that the proposed lattice geometries positively influence the injury prevention capabilities by converting a severe injury to light one, especially in the gyroid structure where the prototype presented a unified pattern of stress distribution and a higher reduction in the transmitted force. The incorporation of the PA-12 matrix reinforced with the reused ground tire rubber results in a structure with high enough overall strength and crucial modifications on the absorption and damping capabilities vital for the integrity under dynamic conditions.

Keywords: topology optimization; dynamic mechanical properties; protective equipment; computational mechanics; finite element analysis

1. Introduction

Injury prevention in the sports industry is a very important aspect of research with emotional, health, and financial contributions to the sports organizations and the players. The football industry is rapidly evolving with a revenue growth rate of approximately 8–10% on a yearly basis and total produced revenue of around 40 billion euros, especially in the most prestigious European Football Leagues Associations. The total number of professional, amateur, and youth league football players is constantly on the rise, and the need for assessing and minimizing the injury risks is evident not only in the big market teams but also in the lower divisions where funding is limited [1,2]. Based on the fast-paced philosophy of modern football, the majority of those injuries (70–80% of the total injuries) refer to the lower limb region and are mainly contact injuries, varying from bruises and contusions to more serious injuries that can be caused by ligament tears and bone and tendon fractures. Roughly 60% of the aforementioned leg injuries involve below-knee injuries, mainly in the ankle region and the tibia/fibula bones [3–5]. Fractures in the fibula and tibia are mainly evident in football, and along with them, the danger of permanent damage to the bones, tendons, or neighboring ligaments may occur based on the severity of the injury. The injury severity is mainly split into four basic categories depending on the recovery time and complexity. In an effort to minimize contact injuries and enhance safety, the insertion of shin guards as protective equipment was included in the game of football and in other contact sports, and this equipment stands as a mandatory part of the overall athletic gear, according to the recent regulations [6–9]. In Table 1, a brief overview of the possible leg injuries in football is presented, along with their severity based on the estimated recovery timeline.

Table 1. Different types of injuries on the tibia/fibula area and the severity of them based on the estimated recovery span on days [3–6].

Injury Severity (Recovery Time)	Injury Type	Possible Incident That Causes the Injury
Slight (1–3 days)	Irritations–Microtrauma Shin Splints	Repetitive number of tackles Overuse or overstressed (Design Related)
Mild (4–7 days)	Bone Bruise/Contusion	Severe Impact
Moderate (8–28 days)	Vascular Injury/Hematoma Bone Bruise/Contusion Tibial Compartment Syndrome	Severe Impact Severe Impact Heavy shock blow to the tibia/fibula region
Severe (over 28 days)	Tibial Compartment Syndrome Bone Fracture	Heavy shock blow to the tibia/fibula region Happens in heavy shock blow, especially if it is a stud kick

Conventionally developed injection-molded shin guards tended to minimize light to moderate contact injuries, but the bulky, heavy design did not provide enough shock absorption to mitigate the active stresses and lower the risk of more severe injuries such as bone fractures. This inability could lead to higher stress distribution and allocation to other articulations, such as the knee or the ankle, and lead to long-term permanent damage due to cumulative fatigue. As is visible from Table 1, the existing designs do not resolve the injury issue at a satisfying rate and are also responsible for the development of some minor injuries related to the wearable that could be minimized with an improved, optimized design. In Figure 1, an overview of the different injuries' severity allocation is presented based on the estimated recovery time according to recent metrics for the calendar year of 2023.

As is visible from Figure 1, especially in amateur-level athletes, where the emphasis on the recovery process after the activities is not the proposed one and the conditioning of the athletes is worse compared to the professional athletes, the injury risk and severity are elevated. A slight elevation in the more severe injuries is also observed in the youth-level leagues. The reevaluation and optimization of the conventionally designed shin guards could lead to a decreased number of serious injuries with results on the physical and social life of the athletes while simultaneously allowing the better development of their skill level, especially for youth players where the projected growth and potential is still higher and based mainly on the availability factor (fit for football activities) and the frequent efficient training [10–13].

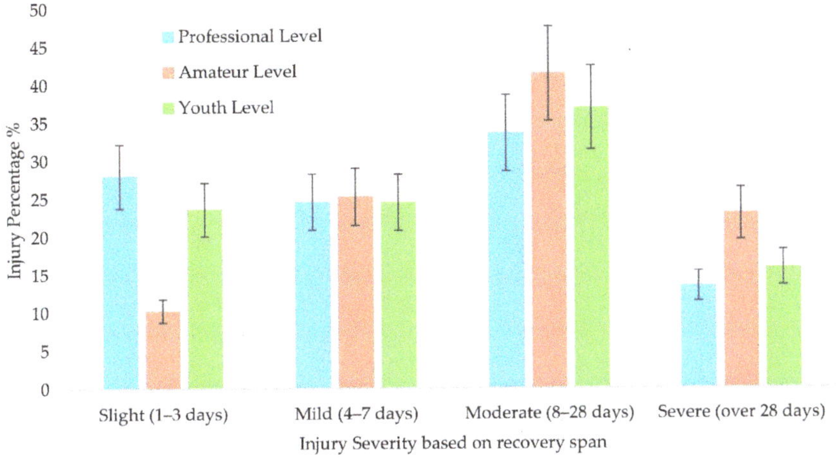

Figure 1. Injury severity level per 100 reported injury cases regarding the tibia–fibula area [3–6].

In this context, many optimization strategies based on design, material selection, and manufacturing processes have been studied with the aim of providing tailored mechanical properties, shape, size, and weight for each unique athlete. Additive manufactured shin guards have been studied at the prototype level, utilizing different composite materials, with the reinforcement being mainly in fiber form (carbon, glass). The results indicated the final structure presented slightly more suitable mechanical properties regarding the overall stiffness and the impact capabilities and overall improved strength-to-weight ratio [14–17]. Besides the non-eco-friendly conventional fibers, alternatives such as the reused tire rubbers could enhance the damping and the energy absorption capabilities, leading to structures that ensure maximum comfort and reduce the cases of mild injuries due to poor manufacturing while simultaneously helping address the more severe ones with effective stress distribution, as it was shown in the previous literature [18–21].

It was also observed that in all cases, the initial bulk solid design was inadequate for constant use, and therefore strategic material removal processes (density-based removal or truss-based removal) for the development of repetitive geometric patterns were analyzed, with the ultimate goal of achieving a lightweight structure with maximized performance metrics compatible and tailored for the demands of the high-strength shock impacts. This process is widely known as topology optimization, with many applications in industrial processes and products in the automotive and aerospace industries. Lattice geometries have proved to enhance the structure's elasticity and result in more unified stress distribution and energy absorption efficiency, especially in the case of the Triply Periodic Minimal Surface (TPMS) structures. Combined with high-precision manufacturing techniques that allow the rapid transformation of a design to a prototype, could help enhance the compatibility of this structure to the human leg, allowing maximum comfort due to light bumps and high crashworthiness in the more extreme cases of hits, such as the stud kicks incidents in competitive games [22–24].

In this paper, a computational investigation of topologically optimized shin guards is conducted to assess the optimal lattice geometry with a focus on efficient impact absorption and damping capabilities, ensuring maximum comfort and minimization of severe tibia-fibula injuries due to hard kicks on the regions during sports activities. In this context, an initial draft bulk design was designed aligned with the shape of an average male athlete's leg, and with the aid of 3D scanning, three different lattice geometries, (2.5D Voronoi, Strut Octet, and TPMS gyroid) were utilized for the customized prototypes on the same relative density (40%), which was confirmed in previous cases as the solution for optimal energy absorption combined with adequate enough overall strength. For the material selection, a PA-12-based composite was selected with ground tire rubber (GTR) insertion of 10 wt.%. The GTR insertion was proved in a different study that improved crucial elasticity properties, and the matrix material presented similar mechanical properties to other thermoplastics that were already studied in the literature [14,15,19,21,22,24]. The three aforementioned prototypes underwent impact testing with the aid of Finite Element Analysis (FEA) to assess the dynamic mechanical response in real-life based scenarios in the extreme case of a stud kick to the shin area, which was described as the condition where the maximum forces were generated. An assessment of the overall stresses and the distribution of those was conducted, providing valuable insights regarding the structures' elasticity, force tolerance, energy dissipation, and shock absorption properties. The results indicated that the gyroid structure shin guard presented the most unified stress distributions and ensured the maximum comfort and safety and was proposed as the go-to solution in this use case. The novelty in this paper lies in the proper material selection that can promote environmental sustainability, the utilization of complex lattice geometries for the provision of tailored dynamic properties, and the real-life simulation of the stud's kick impact testing, providing results that can be used directly for possible upcycling with rapid manufacturing technologies such as 3D printing. An indicative flowchart of this current study is presented in Figure 2.

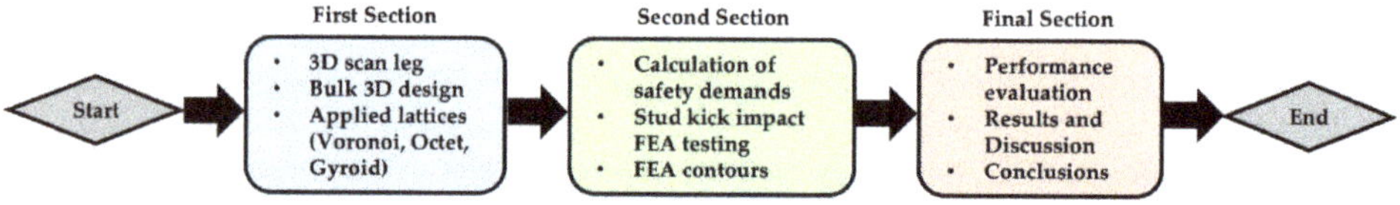

Figure 2. Workflow of the scientific paper.

2. Materials and Methods

2.1. Design Conceptualization

To study the effect of the different lattice geometries, an initial draft solid prototype was developed. To accurately replicate the angles on the tibial region and design a draft with an exact fit, a 3D scan of an amateur football player's leg was conducted with the aid of an Artec Eva™ 3D scanner (Artec 3D, Luxembourg, Luxembourg), and the raw data were converted to a compatible 3D CAD design file (3D Slicer, Version 5.6.2.). The Artec Eva™ has an accuracy of 0.1 mm for small to medium-sized objects. To achieve the maximum precision and the accurate illustration of the leg's morphology, the high-definition data acquisition mode was utilized, capturing 18 million points per second at a scanning speed of 16 frames per second. The metrics were then compared to benchmarks regarding the dimensions and the morphology of the average shin regions in male athletes in order to assess the size of the proposed shin guards based on the existing market. In this case, a medium-sized shin guard was selected and designed with the aid of Solidworks ™ Version PDM 2023 (Dassault Systemes SE, Vélizy-Villacoublay, France) as a preliminary design. Players in the wide attacking positions have to face the maximum number of challenges. The average winger in today's game has a median height of 1.71–1.75 m, and his weight varies between 65 and 70 kg. The shin guard's height was measured at 16.5 cm, and the maximum length was 10 cm, narrowed down to 6.5 cm in the calf region below. According to the analytics, the optimal way to wear shin guards is inside the sock and at a placement around 5–7 cm above the ankle in the interface between the talus area and the tibial-fibula area [25–27]. In Figure 3, the expected fit of the proposed shin guard models on the tibial region is illustrated; as a reference point, the model with the Voronoi lattice geometries is presented. The metrics of the human leg were taken from an amateur football player and are presented in Table A1 in Appendix A.

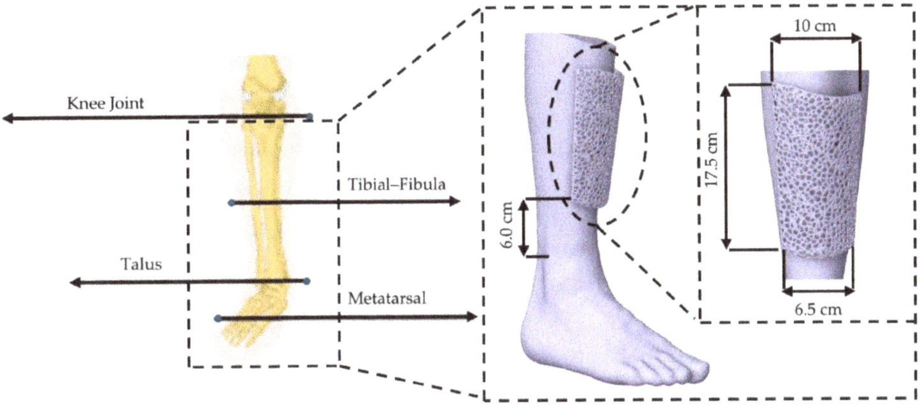

Figure 3. Indicative shin guard's fit.

2.2. Materials

To develop an appropriate material model, an experimental analysis of the filler effect was conducted in a previous study. The selected reinforcement is an acquired waste ground tire rubber (RETIRE ABEE, Drama, Greece), which presented positive effects as a filler material regarding the energy absorption and the damping capabilities. Since the rubber's effect is not studied in this case study, the weight fraction of 10 wt.% was selected as it was proven as optimal in previous cases where energy dissipation capabilities were demanded. The process consisted of shredding, removing inadequate additives, such as steel wires, and milling the remaining rubber into appropriate shape and size particles for further exploitation with advanced manufacturing technologies. In Figure 4, a preliminary analysis of the filler was conducted with the aid of the Phenom ProX (Thermo Fisher Scientific, Waltham, MA, USA) scanning electron microscope (SEM).

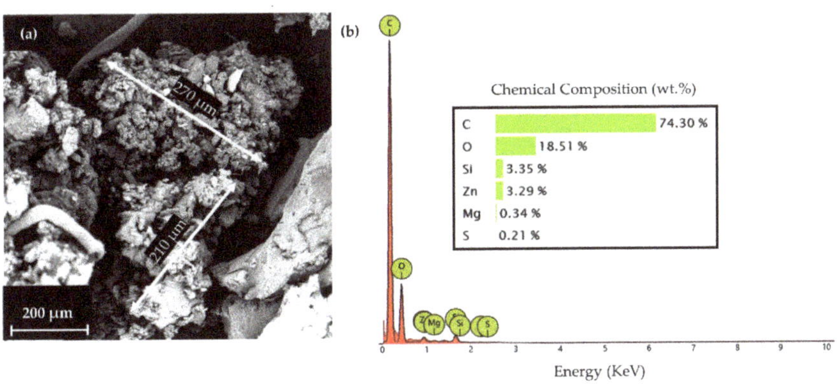

Figure 4. GTR characterization: (**a**) Particle's morphology; (**b**) EDX analysis [19].

2.3. Topological Optimization

The insertion of the proposed lattice geometries was performed with the aid of nTopology™ Version 5.9.2 (nTopology Inc., New York, NY, USA). A 2.5D lattice geometry (Voronoi), a strut-based (octet) structure, and a triply periodic mimical surface (TPMS) (gyroid) structure were selected in this use case. Generally, in the development of architected materials, the ideal relative densities vary based on the different types of lattice structures. Densities above 60% tend to present minimal changes in the properties of the final structure compared to a 100% solid one, while relative densities below 20% tend to present foam-like behavior [24,28]. The optimization process's objective function was to minimize the transmitted force and achieve the maximum energy absorption (EA) per unit cell. The optimization constraints were the material's failure limits and the design constraints according to the European standard for protective equipment regarding performance and safety [29]. A generic algorithm (GA) with the following objective functions was developed as follows:

$$\mathrm{maxf(r.d.)} = \mathrm{EA_{cell}(r.d.)} \tag{1}$$

$$\mathrm{minf(r.d.)} = \mathrm{F_{transmited}(r.d.)} \tag{2}$$

where r.d. is applied relative density of each lattice geometry and the following constraints:

$$\sigma(\mathrm{r.d.}) < \sigma_{\mathrm{ultimate}}, \mathrm{V(r.d.)} < \mathrm{V_{total}}$$

where σ(r.d.) is the projected unit cells developed stress and V(r.d.) the projected volume of the optimized design. Based on the GA, an average of 40–45% relative density was selected for all cases in order to efficiently observe the effects of each type of architected material with conformal design in order not to modify the angularity of the bulk prototype, which was designed based on the curvature of the shin region. In Table 2, the main critical metrics regarding the wall thickness and the length of the unit cell for each structure are presented, and in Figure 5, an illustration of the overall final prototypes is provided.

Table 2. Final metrics of the proposed prototypes.

Prototype	Bulk Mass/Final Mass (g)	Relative Density (%)	Unit Cell Length (mm)	Strut/Wall Thickness (mm)
Voronoi Shin Guard	111/50	41	20	2.20
Octet Shin Guard	111/55	44	20	2.90
Gyroid Shin Guard	111/56	45	5	2.35

2.4. Finite Element Analysis

The final optimized design was evaluated with the aid of ANSYS™ Version 2024 R2 (ANSYS, Inc., Canonsburg, PA, USA) in loads reflecting those of a stud kick in a football match, which was proved to be the ultimate integrity test regarding this specific use case. The optimized prototypes were inserted and attached to the scanned leg, and with the aid of the explicit dynamics model, the impact process of the kick was accurately simulated. Regarding the material model, an equivalent unit cell was produced, and the material properties were calculated with the aid of the Material Designer tool in ANSYS ™ Version 2024 R2, and a Representative Volume Element (RVE) of the proposed composite (PA-12/GTR 10 wt.%) was constructed. The proposed material presented similar properties in all 3 axes (x, y, and z), and therefore, the isotropic elasticity model was utilized in this case. The developed models were inserted into an explicit dynamics model that accurately simulated the process of the kick in the shin guard area. For the material model, experimental identification of the mechanical response and the properties of the microstructure was already conducted [24,28].

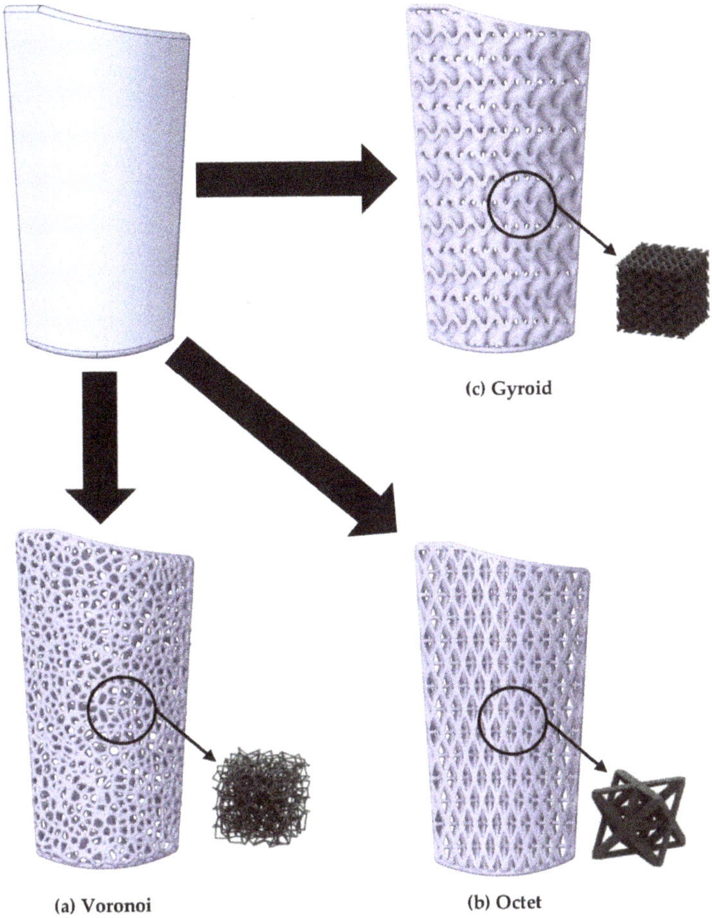

Figure 5. Topologically optimized prototypes: (**a**) Voronoi-based shin guard; (**b**) octet-based shin guard; (**c**) gyroid-based shin guard.

2.5. Evaluation of the Boundary Conditions and the Prototype's Performance

For the development of the impact study, an explicit dynamics model was developed with the aid of ANSYS™ Version 2024 R2 (ANSYS, Inc., Canonsburg, PA, USA). Regarding the boundary conditions, the leg was considered the fixed area since, during the impact, the leg is, in most cases, on the ground. Also, this situation is the one where the leg and the shin guard have to tolerate the whole impact energy compared to cases where the foot is off the ground. To recreate the kicking motion, an impactor with studs was created. The average metallic stud diameter is around 3 mm, and the average impactor's speed is around 3 m/s in the case of a football kick, according to the European standard for protective equipment (EN 13601:2009) [29]. The translated contact speed was calculated with the aid of the following equation:

$$V_{contact} = \frac{m_{impactor} \cdot V_{impactor} + m_{shin} \cdot V_{shin}}{m_{impactor} + m_{shin}} m/s \quad (3)$$

In this equation, the leg's velocity (V_{shin}) is considered 0 since the leg in this case is considered stable on the ground. The impactor's velocity ($V_{impactor}$) and the effective mass ($m_{impactor}$) have been considered to be the whole leg area since the impactor is on the move in a motion replicating a tackle towards the ball that ended by hitting the shin instead. The overall energy that was transmitted to the leg and not absorbed by the pad is translated into the equivalent forces on the tibial area with the aid of the following equation:

$$F_{transmitted} = \frac{E_{transmitted}}{d_{soft\text{-}tissue}} = \frac{E_{internal} - E_{pad}}{d_{soft\text{-}tissue}} N \quad (4)$$

where $E_{internal}$ is the overall energy generated by the system during the impact process and E_{pad} is the energy that was absorbed by the shin guard. For the soft-tissue deformation, according to the literature, this value ranges between 3.5 and 6 mm, and it presents minimal variation regardless of the impact's intensity; therefore, a median value of 4 mm was taken into consideration for this use case. Accurate modeling of the soft tissue would result in excessive computational cost due to the high number of required elements. Therefore, some key bone and tissue properties were incorporated to develop the simplified leg model for the shin-guard fit, as illustrated previously in Figure 3. In general, the average bone consists of the solid outer part and the inner bone marrow, but for the development of the material model, an average unified bone was selected, in accordance with relevant studies regarding the mechanical response of the tibial and fibula bones [30–32]. In Table 3, some key metrics regarding the leg properties and the soft tissue properties that were utilized for the material model are presented.

Table 3. Shin regions components crucial properties [30–32].

Component	Young's Modulus (MPa)	Yield Strength (MPa)	Fracture Stress (MPa)
Tibial Bone	1393 ± 123	95 ± 8	155 ± 12
Fibula Bone	1287 ± 116	69 ± 6	127 ± 11
Soft Skin Tissue	0.2 ± 0.04	-	7.6 ± 0.8

The transmitted force is compared to the tibia's tolerance to compare the possible injuries after the impact and evaluate the performance of the guard based on the provided safety for the user. According to the literature, the maximum tolerated force of the tibial bone is around 3000 N [33–36]. In Table 4, a benchmark of the possible injuries after the impact is presented based on the equivalent transmitted forces on the shin region.

Table 4. Injury aggravation based on calculated transmitted forces [6,10,11,32].

Transmitted Force (N)	Injury Severity	Possible Injury
0–400	Slight	Mild Pain
401–1000	Mild	Contusion
1001–3000	Moderate	Tissue Damage
3001+	Severe	Fracture

3. Results

3.1. Material Model and Mesh Generation Process

To identify the material model, a study on the microstructure with the aid of the material designer was conducted. For the precise description of the rubber particles' distribution, the short fibers model was utilized after taking into consideration the SEM analysis of Figure 4 with a particle range deviation of 200–300 μm and a weight fraction of 10 wt.%. In Table 5, the results of the material model development are presented regarding the Young's modulus, the shear modulus, and the Poisson ratio to assess the final material behavior of the proposed composite. Based on the provided info regarding the material properties, the matrix and reinforcements morphology, and the distribution of the reinforcement inside the unit cell, the material designer automatically generated those estimated properties in all three dimensions (x, y, and z). The z-axis was considered to be the anterior–posterior direction (impact direction), the x-axis is the longitudinal direction of the shin, and the y-axis was considered to be the lateral direction across the leg. The comparison of those properties in all three dimensions could provide feedback regarding the degree of homogeneity and the isotropic or anisotropic nature of the final composite.

Table 5. Main mechanical properties of the PA-12/GTR 10 wt.% representative volume element unit cell.

Property Direction	Young's Modulus (E), MPa	Shear Modulus (G), MPa	Poisson's Ratio	Yield Strength (σ), MPa
X-axis	1224.1	440.62	0.389	29.9
Y-axis	1218.0	440.69	0.381	30.3
Z-axis	1224.9	442.78	0.383	30.2

The results from Table 5 indicate that the composites' behavior approaches isotropic standards with minimal deviations due to anisotropies (less than 10%). Therefore, the isotropic elasticity model was utilized in this use case. For the extraction of mesh-independent results, an evaluation of the equivalent von Mises stresses compared to the total number of elements was conducted in order to achieve the optimal mesh to eliminate stress singularities. An indicative example of the mesh convergence process for the Voronoi Shin Guards is presented in Figure 6.

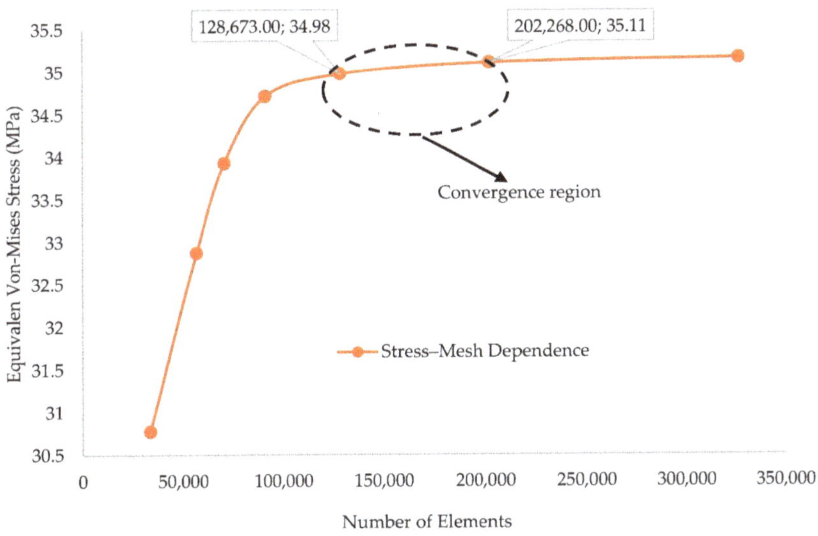

Figure 6. Mesh convergence results for the stud kick impact FEA simulation for the Voronoi shin guard.

From Figure 6, it is hinted that the convergence region is around the mark of 130,000 to 200,000 total elements. The deviation of the developed von Mises stress value was below 5%, and a plateau is observed in this region. Therefore, a median value of 150,000 was selected in this case. A similar procedure was followed in all cases. Regarding the mesh concentration, the main Region of Interest (ROI) was selected to be the triple point between the impactor, the shin guard, and the outer skin of the leg in the shin region. To ensure that in all cases the worst-case scenario is taken into consideration, the whole leg was set as fixed to the ground, replicating a challenge on the standing leg, therefore ensuring that all generated forces would be present in the ROI. Finer mesh was selected on the shin guard since complex lattice geometries were applied, and the contact area between the guard and the leg was used to determine the developed forces in the structure and the human leg. The mesh for the impactor was rougher in order to replicate the geometry of the football shoe studs, which are designed to make micro-punctures to the pitch's surface and provide stability during the player's movement, especially in rainy conditions. In Figure 7, an illustration of the different ROIs is presented, and the mesh size for each region for the reference prototype of the Voronoi shin guard.

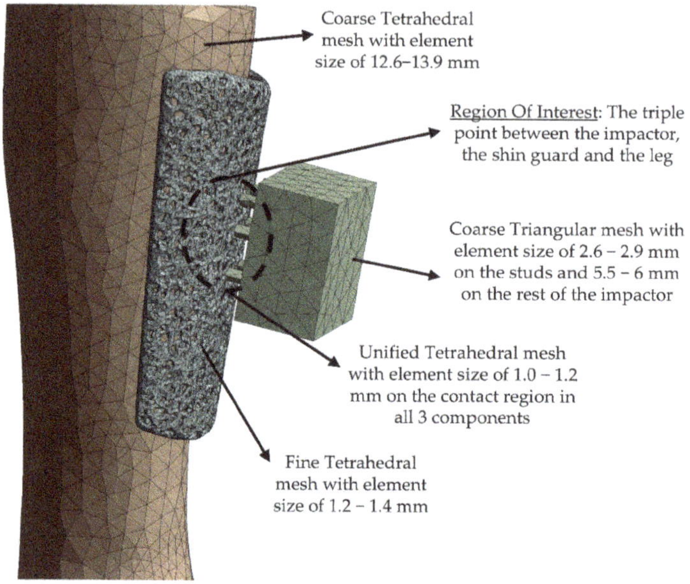

Figure 7. Final generated mesh with the equivalent regions of interest.

3.2. Finite Element Analysis Dynamic Results

3.2.1. Evaluation of the Structural Integrity According to the European Standards

For the evaluation of the structural integrity of the proposed shin guards, the boundary conditions regarding the impact velocity at the contact point and the duration of the stud kick were assessed with the aid of the European standard for protective equipment (EN 13601:2009) [29]. The impact velocity for the shin guard testing was set at 3 m/s, and the impact duration was set at 2 milliseconds (0.002 s). Those values present a moderate ferocity impact, describing the average conditions of a stud kick [33]. In Figure 8, the developed von Mises stresses are presented based on the equivalent elastic strain for all structures along with the equivalent finite element analysis contours.

The results of Figure 8 indicate that in all cases, a similar response is observed with mild deviations regarding mainly the elastic strain. This result was expected since similar relative density and the same basic composite were applied in all cases. The observed deviations occurred based on the different behavior of each architected material. The elastic strain at the retraction point is higher in the case of the gyroid shin guard, which was expected since TPMS structures tend to present greater elasticity due to their mild bending-dominated behavior. On the contrary, the strut octet structure presents a brittle-like and stretching-dominated behavior. This is also translated in Figure 8 by the higher overall stress at the retraction point; this value indicates that, in terms of absolute strength, the octet shin guard presents the better response. Regarding the Voronoi structure, it seems that the structure presents less overall strength and approaches a mild stretching-dominated behavior similar to the strut-type octet shin guard. Since Voronoi is a stochastic structure without a regular pattern, the behavior of the prototype could vary based on the unit cell properties (length, thickness) and the impact angle or region [28,37–39]. In Figure 9, the stress contours at the retraction point are presented for all three prototypes.

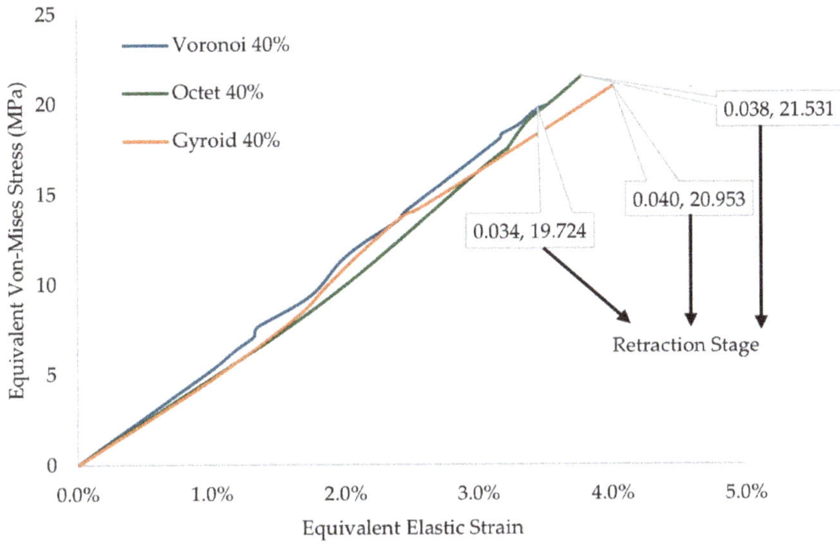

Figure 8. Stress–strain curve during the kicking motion.

The contours of Figure 9 confirm the indication of a brittle-like behavior in the octet structure. This is visible from the localized stress concentrations on the impact region only. The octet structures seem to present better absolute strength, but the narrow stress distribution indicates less energy-absorbing capabilities, which could result in negative effects in terms of force mitigation and result in chronic discomfort. This inadequate absorption could lead to issues in other articulations, resulting in possible knee chondromalacia or other generic knee injuries after long-term use. In the cases of the Voronoi and the gyroid designed shin guards, a wider stress distribution is observed, meaning more unified absorption and less shock discomfort to the user due to the equivalent force reaction. In the case of the gyroid structure, the distribution is approaching a specific pattern, while in the case of the Voronoi structure, the contours tend to be more randomized. This difference is present mainly because of the different geometry type, since Voronoi does not present a specific pattern. The fact that important stress concentrations are presented at the edges of the guard indicates that the applied forces are approaching the structure's maximum strength. In Table 6, the overall forces generated during the impact and the internal energy of the system are presented.

The metrics of Table 6 confirm the minimal absorption of the Octet Shin Guard due to the structures' stretching-dominated behavior. The energy dissipation of the Voronoi and the Octet Shin Guards is proportional to the overall energy that was generated during the impact. The gyroid shin guard seems to present higher absorption efficiency. The overall reaction force presents the generative force of the kick. Compared to the metrics of Table 4 regarding the possible injury severity, the overall forces generated could result in mild pain or bruising. This was expected since the majority of the tackles do not result in moderate or severe injuries where the player is unable to continue. Overall, all structures present suitable integrity for long-term use regarding the overall stress tolerance, something that is also indicated by the linear behavior on the stress–strain curve in Figure 8, which hints at elastic deformation.

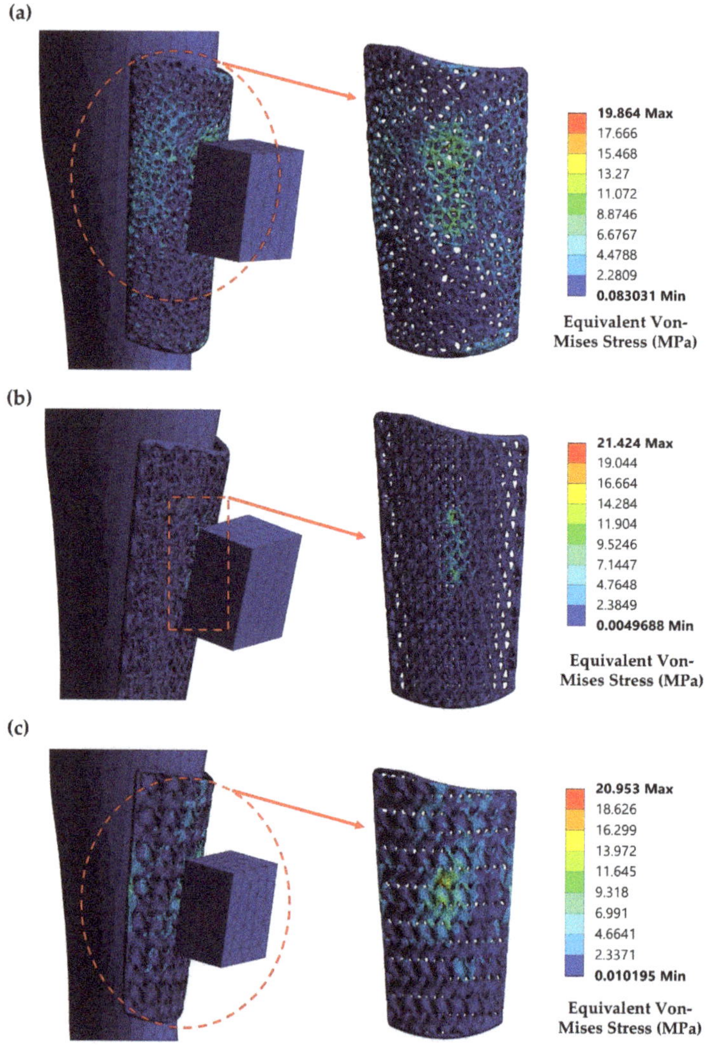

Figure 9. Stress contours for the proposed shin guards' prototypes: (**a**) Voronoi structure; (**b**) octet structure; (**c**) gyroid structure.

Table 6. Overall force and work production on the system.

Shin Guard Type	Internal Energy (mJ)	Energy Absorbed (mJ)	Force Reaction (N)
Voronoi	477.68	6.13	206.23
Octet	519.56	9.69	260.81
Gyroid	600.72	67.61	217.38

3.2.2. Evaluation of Energy Dispersion on the Extreme Case Scenario

Besides the structural integrity of the shin guard in moderate cases, another crucial value to describe the efficacy of the prototype is the ability to reduce the number of forces transmitted to the leg by a fair amount to prevent serious injuries. Commercial shin guards present a fair force transmission reduction rate between 68 and 77% in leg breaking forces (2500–4000 N), resulting in protection from severe injuries and a reduction in those by 15–20% [2,10,12,33]. To assess the force reduction capabilities of the shin guard, an extreme case of a leg-breaking kick was conceptualized. According to sports analytics, high-intensity kicks in combat sports can reach impact velocities in the range of 7–9 m/s, with the high end mainly present in martial arts sports. For the case of the football shin guards' efficiency, an average leg velocity of 7 m/s was utilized. To calculate the impact velocity on the shin region, Equation (3) was utilized. For the impactor's mass, all body areas that contribute to the human motion are taken into consideration. The average lower body mass from the hip and below is equivalent to 15% of the overall body mass. Therefore, the mass of the leg region from the hip to the foot is considered as 7.5% of the total impactor's mass. To calculate the mass on the recipient area, the overall shin region plus the shin guard's mass were considered, and since the foot is fixed on the ground, the recipient's velocity was set to 0 m/s. In Table 7, the main metrics are presented and the final impact velocity is based on Equation (3) for each specific use case scenario. The overall body mass was considered 67 kg for an average-height winger or full-back since most sliding tackle challenges tend to happen in these positions, as it was previously discussed in Section 2.1.

Table 7. Main metrics to conceptualize the extreme case scenario.

Shin Guard Type	Impactors Mass (kg)	Recipient Mass (kg)	Offenders' Velocity (m/s)	Impact Velocity on the Shin Region (m/s)
Voronoi		1.250		5.63
Octet	5.1	1.255	7	5.61
Gyroid		1.256		5.60

Since the results of Table 7 indicate that the deviation of the impact velocity for each case is minimal (less than 1%), an average impact velocity of 5.6 m/s was used in all cases for an impact duration time of 0.02 s, similar to the European Standard for protective equipment testing [29]. The results of the stress contours for the extreme case scenario are presented in Figure 10.

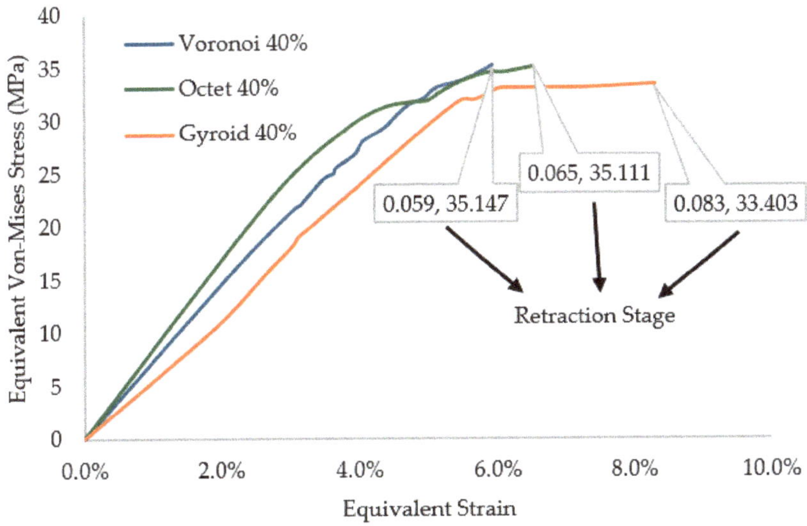

Figure 10. Stress–Strain curve during the kicking motion in the extreme case scenario.

The results of Figure 10 indicate that in all cases, the ferocity of the impact results in permanent deformation of the structure, which is visible by the plateau in all three curves in the elastic strain of 3.5–4.5% based on each case. As expected, the gyroid structure seems to present higher plastic deformation and slightly less stress tolerance due to its bending-dominated nature. The Voronoi structure seems to present minimal plastic deformation, and the octet structure presents a moderate plastic region. The overall stress tolerance is higher in the octet and the Voronoi structure. In Figure 11, the stress contours at the retraction point are presented for all three prototypes.

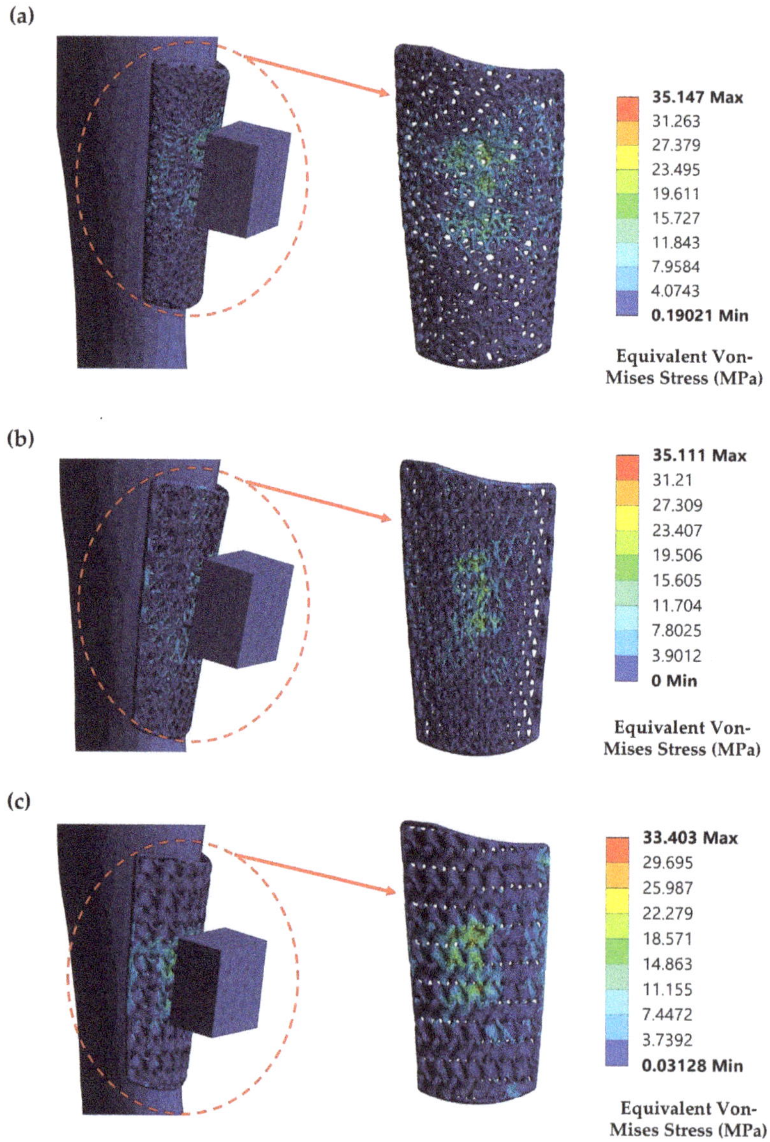

Figure 11. Stress contours at the retraction point in the extreme case scenario for: (**a**) Voronoi Structure; (**b**) octet structure; (**c**) gyroid structure.

From the contours of Figure 11, it is visible that the stresses in this case have been distributed to wider shin guard areas, indicating a plastic deformation in all cases. The octet structure still presents higher localized stresses in the impact region, while in the other two cases, a more uniform stress distribution is observed. In the gyroid structure, the widespread distribution seems to follow a specific pattern, while in the Voronoi structure, the stress concentrations are widespread in random areas of the shin guard and especially on the edges of the prototype, hinting that the failure point is closer than in the other two cases. A representation of the generated internal energy and forces is briefly presented in Table 8.

Table 8. Overall force and work production on the system in the extreme case scenario.

Shin Guard Type	Internal Energy (mJ)	Energy Absorbed (mJ)	Force Reaction (N)
Voronoi	3458.4	1359.1	3219.2
Octet	3662.3	1715.4	3132.8
Gyroid	3275.3	2189.9	3408.3

From the metrics of Table 8, it is visible that all structures have inserted a plastic deformation range, visible by the increased absorption rate in all three cases. The developed forces in all cases are above 2500–3000 N, meaning that the impact would result in a leg break in all cases. The absorption rate is again better in the gyroid structure, which is confirmed by the absolute number and the extended plastic region of Figure 10.

3.3. *Performance Evaluation Overview and Comparison to the Commercial Shin Guards*

To assess the overall performance of the three proposed prototypes, a calculation of injury prevention was conducted. The difference between the absorbed energy and the overall internal energy of the system from Table 8 is the energy that the shin region handled during the impact. This difference was converted to the equivalent transmitted force with the aid of Equation (4). For soft tissue deformation, a median value of 4 mm was utilized in all cases, as it was described in Section 2.5. The final transmitted forces were also compared to the overall generated forces to assess the efficiency and compare it to the commercial shin guards. The overall performance evaluation regarding injury prevention and the force reduction efficiency is presented in Table 9.

Table 9. Performance overview of the proposed prototypes in leg-breaking forces.

Shin Guard Type	Unabsorbed Energy (mJ)	Transmitted Force (N)	Force Transmission Reduction (%)
Voronoi	2099.3	524.8	83.6
Octet	1946.9	486.7	84.4
Gyroid	1085.4	271.4	91.9

From Table 9, it is visible that all the structures present adequate force transmission reduction to the leg compared to commercial shin guards. It is also worth mentioning that the application of each prototype could lower the injury severity from a possible fracture to a less severe injury (compared with the metrics of Table 4), with significantly less recovery time and long-term effect on the athlete's health. With a direct comparison of the final transmitted forces with Table 1, in the cases of the Voronoi and octet structure, it indicates that a potential fracture with a possible recovery time of multiple months and maybe permanent long-term effects on the health of the athlete could be converted to a mild injury such as a bone bruise or contusion with no permanent effects and an estimated recovery time of 1–2 weeks, and in the case of the gyroid structure this potential fracture could be converted to a microtrauma with an estimated recovery of several days or just some discomfort that is not ruling out the athlete from football activities completely. The influence of the lattice geometries on elasticity and absorption properties was known and also aligned with results from previous research studies. Especially for TPMS-based structures, the natural curvature in their shape leads to smooth stress reduction and fewer stress concentrations [17,28,37]. The results indicate that the application of architected materials in the case of protective sports equipment can improve the product's efficiency and the user's safety.

4. Conclusions

In this paper, an investigation of the dynamic behavior of topologically optimized shin guards through a computational impact response assessment was conducted. From the investigation process, the stress tolerance, the energy absorption efficiency, and the transmitted force reduction (in absolute numbers and their rate) were extracted to assess the effect of the different lattice geometries on the structural integrity of the developed prototypes, the injury prevention capabilities, and the overall efficacy regarding safety and comfort. The relative density of the prototypes was kept at 40% to ensure the influence of each different type of architected material on the overall response of the developed prototype, and for the base material, a composite of PA-12 with 10 wt.% of reused GTR was utilized. The GTR efficacy on the absorption properties was already assessed in previous research. The final prototypes presented better force reduction efficacy compared to commercial shin guards, 80–90% compared to 70–80% of the already existing ones, according to the literature around shin guard efficacy [2,33,40], and aided in the reduction in potential leg-breaking transmitted forces to forces that could result in a mild injury or some discomfort with minimal or no recovery time demand. All prototypes presented adequate stress tolerance when tested according to the European standard for football shin guards (EN 13601:2009). Overall, the results of this computational study indicate that there is potential room for further upcycling. In later stages, the development of an actual prototype to test in a lab-scale environment with the aid of impact testing (e.g., drop impact) or fatigue analysis to assess the long-term durability is an adequate intermediate step before the development of an actual pair designed for youth-level players to assess it in milder physical conditions before the final developed models for professional or amateur adult athletes. Also, possible fracture analysis on conditions beyond the failure point could provide valuable information for different use cases or for analyzing the long-term efficacy and expected life cycle of the proposed designs.

Author Contributions: Conceptualization, I.F.K., N.K. and K.T.; methodology, I.F.K. and N.K.; software, I.F.K. and N.K.; validation, I.F.K., N.K. and K.T.; formal analysis, I.F.K.; investigation, I.F.K.; resources, E.M.P.; data curation, I.F.K.; writing—original draft preparation, I.F.K.; writing—review and editing, I.F.K., N.K., E.M.P. and K.T.; visualization, I.F.K.; supervision, E.M.P. and K.T.; project administration, E.M.P. and K.T.; funding acquisition, E.M.P. All authors have read and agreed to the published version of the manuscript.

Funding: This research received no external funding.

Data Availability Statement: The original contributions presented in this study are included in the article material. Further inquiries can be directed to the corresponding authors.

Conflicts of Interest: The authors declare no conflicts of interest.

Appendix A

In this section the athlete's metrics after the scanning and the combine measurements are presented in Table A1. The consent form was applied as an attachment and is available upon request.

Table A1. Athlete's main metrics.

Position	Left Winger (LW)
Height (cm)	173
Weight (kg)	67
Knee-Ground Height (cm)	52
Ankle Height (cm)	10
Shin Height (cm)	29
Calve Perimeter (cm)	37
Below Calve Perimeter (cm)	22

References

1. Buckingham, P.; European Football Revenue Hit Record €38bn in 2023–24 Season. The Athletic, Jun 12 2025. Available online: https://www.nytimes.com/athletic/6419926/2025/06/11/european-football-revenue-premier-league/ (accessed on 10 July 2025).
2. Tatar, Y.; Ramazanoglu, N.; Camliguney, A.F.; Saygi, E.K.; Cotuk, H.B. The Effectiveness of Shin Guards Used by Football Players. *PubMed* **2014**, *13*, 120–127.
3. Fuller, C.W.; Ekstrand, J.; Junge, A.; Andersen, T.E.; Bahr, R.; Dvorak, J.; Hägglund, M.; McCrory, P.; Meeuwisse, W.H. Consensus Statement on Injury Definitions and Data Collection Procedures in Studies of Football (Soccer) Injuries. *Br. J. Sports Med.* **2006**, *40*, 193–201. [CrossRef]
4. Jones, S.; Almousa, S.; Gibb, A.; Allamby, N.; Mullen, R.; Andersen, T.E.; Williams, M. Injury Incidence, Prevalence and Severity in High-Level Male Youth Football: A Systematic Review. *Sports Med.* **2019**, *49*, 1879–1899. [CrossRef]
5. Robertson, G.A.J.; Ang, K.K.; Jamal, B. Fractures in Soccer: The Current Evidence, and How This Can Guide Practice. *J. Orthop.* **2022**, *33*, 25–30. [CrossRef]
6. Gurau, T.V.; Gurau, G.; Musat, C.L.; Voinescu, D.C.; Anghel, L.; Onose, G.; Munteanu, C.; Onu, I.; Iordan, D.A. Epidemiology of Injuries in Professional and Amateur Football Men (Part II). *J. Clin. Med.* **2023**, *12*, 6293. [CrossRef]
7. Nwosu, C. Tibial Fractures Following Participation in Recreational Football: Incidence and Outcome. *Niger. J. Clin. Pract.* **2019**, *22*, 492. [CrossRef] [PubMed]
8. Ruznan, W.S.; Laing, R.M.; Lowe, B.J.; Wilson, C.A. Impact Attenuation Provided by Shin Guards for Field Hockey. *Sports Eng.* **2017**, *21*, 161–175. [CrossRef]
9. Jeong, H.S.; O'sullivan, D.M.; Lee, S.C.; Lee, S.Y. Safety Evaluation of Protective Equipment for the Forearm, Shin, Hand and Foot in Taekwondo. *PubMed* **2019**, *18*, 376–383.
10. Vriend, I.; Valkenberg, H.; Schoots, W.; Goudswaard, G.J.; Van Der Meulen, W.J.; Backx, F.J.G. Shinguards Effective in Preventing Lower Leg Injuries in Football: Population-Based Trend Analyses over 25 Years. *J. Sci. Med. Sport* **2014**, *18*, 518–522. [CrossRef]
11. Shakib, A.; Lazar, E.; Cohen, T.; Quenneville, C.E. Investigation of Tibia and Fibula Fracture Risk during Football Impacts Using Finite Element Human Body Models. *Proc. Inst. Mech. Eng. Part P J. Sports Eng. Technol.* **2025**. [CrossRef]
12. Cazón-Martín, A.; Iturrizaga-Campelo, M.; Matey-Muñoz, L.; Rodríguez-Ferradas, M.I.; Morer-Camo, P.; Ausejo-Muñoz, S. Design and Manufacturing of Shin Pads with Multi-Material Additive Manufactured Features for Football Players: A Comparison with Commercial Shin Pads. *Proc. Inst. Mech. Eng. Part P J. Sports Eng. Technol.* **2018**, *233*, 160–169. [CrossRef]
13. Moghaddam, E.; Afsharfard, A. Developing a Structurally Modified Mechanical Lumped Model of the Human Tibia and Shin Guard Using Modal Analysis. *Ann. Biomed. Eng.* **2024**, *53*, 845–854. [CrossRef]
14. Alarifi, I.M. Simulation and Mechanical Testing of 3D Printing Shin Guard Composite Materials. *Virtual Phys. Prototyp.* **2024**, *19*, e2411022. [CrossRef]
15. Alarifi, M.I.; Alarifi, I.M. Comprehensive Structural Evaluation of Composite Materials in 3D-Printed Shin Guards. *J. Mater. Res. Technol.* **2023**, *27*, 6912–6923. [CrossRef]
16. Putro, A.J.N.; Bagaskara, G.; Prasetya, I.A.; Jamasri, N.; Wiranata, A.; Wu, Y.-C.; Muflikhun, M.A. Optimization of Innovative Hybrid Polylactic Acid+ and Glass Fiber Composites: Mechanical, Physical, and Thermal Evaluation of Woven Glass Fiber Reinforcement in Fused Filament Fabrication 3D Printing. *J. Compos. Sci.* **2025**, *9*, 164. [CrossRef]
17. Kyriakidis, I.F.; Kladovasilakis, N.; Pechlivani, E.M.; Tsongas, K. Mechanical Performance of Recycled 3D Printed Sustainable Polymer-Based Composites: A Literature Review. *J. Compos. Sci.* **2024**, *8*, 215. [CrossRef]
18. Alami, A.H.; Olabi, A.G.; Alashkar, A.; Alasad, S.; Aljaghoub, H.; Rezk, H.; Abdelkareem, M.A. Additive Manufacturing in the Aerospace and Automotive Industries: Recent Trends and Role in Achieving Sustainable Development Goals. *Ain Shams Eng. J.* **2023**, *14*, 102516. [CrossRef]

19. Kyriakidis, I.F.; Kladovasilakis, N.; Gavriilopoulos, M.; Tzetzis, D.; Pechlivani, E.M.; Tsongas, K. Topologically Optimized Anthropomorphic Prosthetic Limb: Finite Element Analysis and Mechanical Evaluation Using Plantogram-Derived Foot Pressure Data. *Biomimetics* **2025**, *10*, 261. [CrossRef]
20. Kohári, A.; Bárány, T. Sustainable Thermoplastic Elastomers Based on Thermoplastic Polyurethane and Ground Tire Rubber. *J. Appl. Polym. Sci.* **2024**, *141*, e56157. [CrossRef]
21. Rahmani, M.; Adamian, A.; Hosseini-Sianaki, A. Effect of Waste Ground Rubber Tire Powder on Vibrational Damping Behavior and Static Mechanical Properties of Polypropylene Composite Plates: An Experimental Investigation. *J. Mater. Eng. Perform.* **2021**, *30*, 8529–8537. [CrossRef]
22. Ghorbani, F.; Gharehbaghi, H.; Farrokhabadi, A.; Bolouri, A. Evaluation of the Mechanical Properties and Energy Absorption in a Novel Hybrid Cellular Structure. *Aerosp. Sci. Technol.* **2024**, *148*, 109105. [CrossRef]
23. Babamiri, B.B.; Barnes, B.; Soltani-Tehrani, A.; Shamsaei, N.; Hazeli, K. Designing Additively Manufactured Lattice Structures Based on Deformation Mechanisms. *Addit. Manuf.* **2021**, *46*, 102143. [CrossRef]
24. Kladovasilakis, N.; Tsongas, K.; Tzetzis, D. Development of Novel Additive Manufactured Hybrid Architected Materials and Investigation of Their Mechanical Behavior. *Mech. Mater.* **2022**, *176*, 104525. [CrossRef]
25. Aitken, S.A. Normative Values for Femoral Length, Tibial Length, and the Femorotibial Ratio in Adults Using Standing Full-Length Radiography. *Osteology* **2021**, *1*, 86–91. [CrossRef]
26. Engage Shin Guards-Size Guide. Available online: https://engageind.com/pages/size-guide-shin-guards (accessed on 16 July 2025).
27. Shin Guards Size Chart. Available online: https://www.flaxta.com/pages/shin-guards-size-chart?srsltid=AfmBOooSdeQ62WqTjHBzupy44074BHAIVXvQQFriYeg-FDTRQavSkOYs (accessed on 16 July 2025).
28. Kyriakidis, I.F.; Kladovasilakis, N.; Pechlivani, E.M.; Korlos, A.; David, C.; Tsongas, K. In Situ Investigation of Tensile Response for Inconel 718 Micro-Architected Materials Fabricated by Selective Laser Melting. *Materials* **2024**, *17*, 4433. [CrossRef]
29. ITEH Standards. Available online: https://standards.iteh.ai/catalog/standards/cen/dfbb7999-4a71-4381-beae-065939aa1a09/en-13061-2009 (accessed on 16 July 2025).
30. Hernández-Irizarry, R.; Quinnan, S.M.; Reid, J.S.; Toney, C.B.; Rozbruch, S.R.; Lezak, B.; Fragomen, A.T. Intentional Temporary Limb Deformation for Closure of Soft-Tissue Defects in Open Tibial Fractures. *J. Orthop. Trauma* **2020**, *35*, e189–e194. [CrossRef]
31. Khogalia, E.H.; Choo, H.L.; Yap, W.H. Performance of Triply Periodic Minimal Surface Lattice Structures under Compressive Loading for Tissue Engineering Applications. *AIP Conf. Proc.* **2020**, *2233*, 020012. [CrossRef]
32. Sudneva, A.I.; Smirnov, A.V.; Stepanov, M.D.; Kharaldin, N.A.; Stepanov, A.V.; Borovkov, A.I. Tibia and Fibula Stress Strain Research. *IOP Conf. Ser. Mater. Sci. Eng.* **2020**, *986*, 012036. [CrossRef]
33. Ankrah, S.; Mills, N.J. Performance of Football Shin Guards for Direct Stud Impacts. *Sports Eng.* **2003**, *6*, 207–219. [CrossRef]
34. Vagner, M.; Cleather, D.J.; Olah, V.; Vacek, J.; Stastny, P. A Systematic Review of Dynamic Forces and Kinematic Indicators of Front and Roundhouse Kicks across Varied Conditions and Participant Experience. *Sports* **2023**, *11*, 141. [CrossRef] [PubMed]
35. Corcoran, D.; Climstein, M.; Whitting, J.; Del Vecchio, L. Impact Force and Velocities for Kicking Strikes in Combat Sports: A Literature Review. *Sports* **2024**, *12*, 74. [CrossRef]
36. Johnson, C.D.; Tenforde, A.S.; Outerleys, J.; Reilly, J.; Davis, I.S. Impact-Related Ground Reaction Forces Are More Strongly Associated with Some Running Injuries than Others. *Am. J. Sports Med.* **2020**, *48*, 3072–3080. [CrossRef]
37. Kladovasilakis, N.; Tsongas, K.; Karalekas, D.; Tzetzis, D. Architected Materials for Additive Manufacturing: A Comprehensive Review. *Materials* **2022**, *15*, 5919. [CrossRef] [PubMed]
38. Bauer, J.; Meza, L.R.; Schaedler, T.A.; Schwaiger, R.; Zheng, X.; Valdevit, L. Nanolattices: An Emerging Class of Mechanical Metamaterials. *Adv. Mater.* **2017**, *29*. [CrossRef] [PubMed]
39. Li, Y.; Jiang, D.; Zhao, R.; Wang, X.; Wang, L.; Zhang, L.-C. High Mechanical Performance of Lattice Structures Fabricated by Additive Manufacturing. *Metals* **2024**, *14*, 1165. [CrossRef]
40. Scott Zeiter. Institute for Preventative Sports Medicine-Press Releases. Copyright © 2002-the Institute for Preventative Sports Medicine. Available online: https://www.ipsm.org/press_releases/shinguard.html (accessed on 15 September 2025).

computation

MDPI

Article

Mining Scraper Conveyors Chain Drive System Lightweight Design: Based on DEM and Topology Optimization

Qiang Zhang [1], Wei Liu [1], Anhao Jia [1,*], Shouji Sun [1], Xin Li [2] and Xiangjun Song [3]

1 College of Mechanical and Electronic Engineering, Shandong University of Science and Technology, Qingdao 266000, China
2 Qingdao Special Equipment Inspection and Testing Institute, Qingdao 266000, China
3 Xi'an Heavy Equipment Tongchuan Coal Mining Machinery Co., Ltd., Loudi 417099, China
* Correspondence: jiaanhao2025@outlook.com

Abstract: For the issue of excessive mass in the chain drive system of long-distance scraper conveyors, this paper proposes a method to optimize the scraper chains by integrating discrete element simulation (DEM) with topological optimization. The aim is to reduce the system's mass while maintaining its transportation capacity and structural integrity. The SGZ1000 model scraper conveyor with a length of 400 m was selected as the research object. Studies have demonstrated that for 56 × 187 mm scraper chains, a non-equally spaced configuration (6p-8p-6p, where p represents the chain link pitch) outperforms an equally spaced configuration (6p). While ensuring the conveying capacity of the scraper chains, the optimized configuration reduces the number of scrapers in chains of equal length by 11.11%. For a 400 m scraper conveyor, adopting the 6p-8p-6p scraper spacing reduces the number of scrapers by 72 and decreases the mass by 6357.6 kg. Additionally, utilizing topologically optimized scrapers further reduces the total mass by 10,131.4 kg. Compared to the original chain drive system, the optimized scraper chains have reduced the mass by 26.2%, significantly lowering the no-load energy consumption of the long-distance scraper conveyor.

Keywords: scraper conveyor; chain drive system; topological optimization; lightweight

1. Introduction

The scraper conveyor, as the core equipment for coal mining [1], has seen its length increase from 200–300 m to over 500 m with the construction of super-long fully-mechanized mining face coal mines [2]. To meet the rapidly growing demand for the transportation capacity of scraper conveyors, the width of the middle trough, the diameter of the chain, and the mass of the scraper of scraper conveyors are continuously increasing. This leads to an increase in the energy consumption of the scraper conveyor when transporting the same volume of coal, as well as an increase in the production cost for enterprises [3].

When the scraper conveyor is in operation, the chain drives a large number of scrapers to move synchronously, and the coal in the middle trough is pushed by the scrapers, thus achieving the continuous transportation of coal [4]. When the width of the middle trough increases, the resistance that the scrapers encounter while pushing the materials will also increase accordingly. To ensure that the scrapers have sufficient strength and prevent them from bending or being damaged during the movement, the thickness of the scrapers is usually increased. This increases the mass of the scraper and results in a rise in the no-load energy consumption of the chain drive system. Currently, the chain diameter of the world's longest 600 m scraper conveyor developed by China National Coal

Zhangjiakou Coal Mining Machinery Co., Ltd. has reached 65 mm, and the mass of a single scraper exceeds 120 kg. The mass of just the scrapers in the chain drive system exceeds 144,000 kg, which seriously affects the no-load energy consumption of the scraper conveyor. Reducing the no-load mass of the scraper conveyor's chain drive system is an effective strategy to reduce the no-load energy consumption of the scraper conveyor [5]. Since 2020, many scholars and scraper conveyor manufacturing enterprises have carried out a great deal of exploration [6–9]. They mainly conduct research from two aspects: reducing the mass of the scraper itself and decreasing the friction coefficient of the scraper. Limited by traditional machining methods and costs, these new technologies have not been widely applied in scraper conveyors. Topology optimization, as the most reliable method for achieving structural light weighting [10,11], has been widely verified and applied in fields such as aerospace [12,13]. In order to better apply topology optimization technology to actual production, how to better combine topology optimization with the actual production process and achieve the integration of design and manufacturing, as well as how to further improve the efficiency and accuracy of multi-objective optimization algorithms and achieve more complex multi-objective trade-offs, and other research, has become a new hotspot in the current field of topology optimization [14,15]. Applying topology optimization technology to scrapers holds the promise of reducing the no-load energy consumption of the chain drive system of scraper conveyors and promoting low-carbon coal mining [16].

To address the issue of excessive mass in the chain drive system of the scraper conveyor, this paper conducts lightweight research from two aspects: first, reducing the number of scrapers by optimizing the scraper spacing; second, lowering the structural mass of the scrapers themselves through topological optimization. While ensuring the conveying capacity and structural strength of the scraper chains, this approach reduces their mass, thereby lowering the no-load energy consumption of the chain drive system. This study provides guidance for the design of long-distance and low-energy-consuming scraper conveyors in the future.

2. Optimization of Scraper Spacing

2.1. Mining Scraper Conveyors Chain Drive System

Figure 1 shows that the chain drive system of the scraper conveyor consists of scrapers, a round-link chain, and sprockets. The scrapers are relatively fixed to the round-link chain and are collectively known as scraper chains. When the scrapers move synchronously with the chains, they provide thrust to the coal on the middle trough, thereby achieving coal transportation [17]. Currently, the distance La between adjacent scrapers is usually an integer multiple of the chain link pitch. To ensure the conveying capacity of the scraper conveyor, the distances between adjacent scrapers are kept equal and relatively small, which results in a large number of scrapers being attached to the chain. This configuration significantly increases the no-load running resistance of the chain drive system of the scraper conveyor [18]. The total mass (M_a) of the scrapers of a scraper conveyor with a length (L) can be calculated as follows:

$$M_a = \frac{2L}{L_a}M \tag{1}$$

where M is the mass of the scraper, kg; L_a is the spacing between adjacent scrapers, m.

Figure 1. Chain drive system of scraper conveyor: (**a**) Physical object of the scraper conveyor; (**b**) scraper chains model.

There are two ways to reduce the total mass of the scrapers in the chain drive system:

(1) Increasing the spacing between adjacent scrapers;

(2) Reducing the mass of the scrapers.

The spacing between the scrapers of a scraper conveyor is typically around 1 m. Changes in this spacing directly affect the conveying capacity of the scraper chains. To address this, we employ the DEM analysis to optimize both the spacing and arrangement of the scrapers. Under the constraint of maintaining the conveying capacity, we aim to alter the combination form of the scraper spacing. This adjustment indirectly increases the average spacing between adjacent scrapers. As a result, the number of scrapers used in the chain drive system is reduced.

2.2. Scraper Spacing Optimization Scheme

The SGZ1000 scraper conveyor with a length of 400 m is taken as an example. The matching round-link chain has a specification of 56 × 187 mm. Each scraper weighs 88.3 kg. There are six chain links pitched between adjacent scrapers, and the scrapers' spacing is 1.122 m. Figure 2a shows that the spacing between adjacent scrapers is evenly distributed, representing the conventional arrangement method of scrapers in current scraper conveyors. This paper proposes increasing the average spacing between scrapers by optimizing the combination form of the scraper spacing. Figure 2b,c demonstrate non-uniform spacing combination schemes that group scrapers into groups of three, thereby increasing the average spacing between scrapers.

A simulation model of the scraper conveyor's material conveying capacity is established using the DEM to analyze changes in conveying capacity under different scraper arrangement schemes. The scraper spacing schemes are detailed in Table 1.

Table 1. Scraper spacing combination schemes.

Combination Scheme	Scraper Spacing 1	Scraper Spacing 2	Scraper Spacing 3
1	4p	6p	10p
2	4p	10p	6p
3	6p	4p	10p
4	6p	10p	4p
5	10p	4p	6p
6	10p	6p	4p
7	6p	8p	6p
8	6p	6p	8p
9	8p	6p	6p
10	4p	8p	8p
11	8p	4p	8p
12	8p	8p	4p

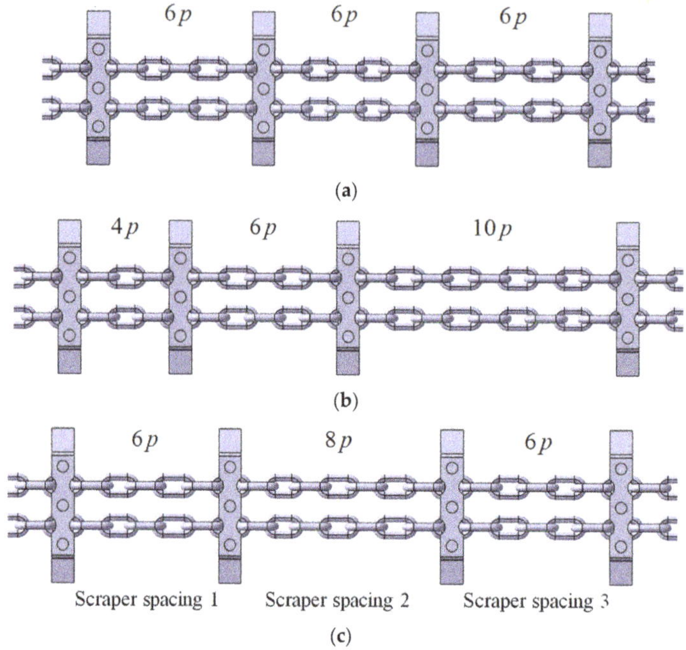

Figure 2. Different scraper spacing combination schemes: (**a**) Uniform scraper spacing; (**b**) scraper spacing combination scheme: 4p-6p-10p; (**c**) scraper spacing combination scheme: 6p-8p-6p.

2.3. *Conveying Capacity Under Different Schemes*

Figure 3 shows the simulation model, which consists of a middle trough, scraper chains, a coal guard plate, and piled bulk coal. The coal guard plate is designed to provide support for the piled bulk coal, preventing it from spilling beyond the middle trough. First, a large volume of coal is piled in the middle trough. Then, different scraper spacing combination schemes are selected to simulate the transportation of coal materials. To ensure consistency across different simulation schemes, the following parameters are controlled to be the same: the number of chain links, the number of scrapers, the initial position of the scraper chains, the moving speed of the scraper chains, and the moving distance. The parameter settings of the simulation model are listed in Table 2.

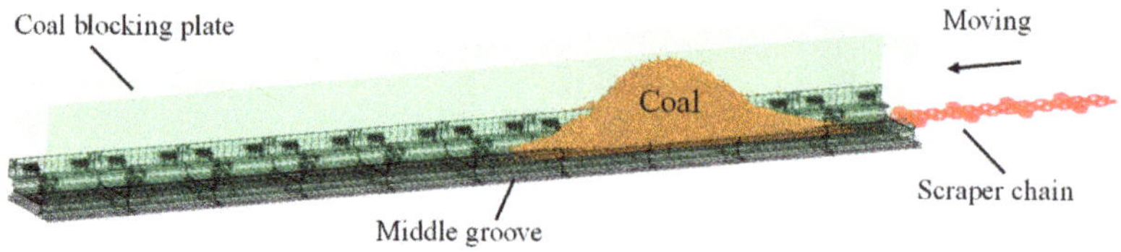

Figure 3. Simulation model of the conveying capacities of scraper chains.

The coal particle density in the simulation model is 1340 kg/m^3, the coal particle radius R = 10 mm, the elastic modulus is taken as 1.6 GPa, and the Poisson's ratio is 0.25 [19]. The contact effect between coal particles uses the Hertz–Mindlin model. The discrete element simulation mesh size is taken as 2R, with a total of 305,613 grids.

The scraper chains with equal scraper spacing (6p-6p-6p) were taken as the control group. According to the simulation model in Figure 3, the movement speed and state distribution of coal particles at different times during the process of the scraper chain moving from one end of the middle trough to the other are simulated.

Table 2. Parameter settings of the simulation model.

Parameter Settings of the Simulation Model	Value
The width of the middle trough	1000
The length of the middle trough (mm)	12,000
The speed of the scraper chain (m/s)	1.5
Chain specification (mm)	56 × 187
Coal particle diameter (mm)	20
Total mass of piled bulk coal (kg)	1767
Static friction coefficient between coal and coal	0.42
Coefficient of kinetic friction between coal and coal	0.11
Static friction coefficient between coal and metal	0.53
Coefficient of kinetic friction between coal and metal	0.31

Their simulation results are shown in Figure 4a–d, which correspond to the 5th, 7th, 9th, and 13th seconds of the simulation model, respectively. At the 5th second, the scraper chains traversed the piled bulk coal and propelled the coal particles forward using the scrapers. When the amount of coal particles exceeded the conveying capacity of the scraper chains, some coal particles slid to both sides of the middle trough as the scraper chains moved. At the 13th second, the scraper chains completely disengaged from the middle trough, leaving the remaining coal particles, which exceeded the maximum conveying capacity of the scraper chains, on the middle trough. Based on this simulation process, simulation calculations were conducted for 12 groups of scraper chain schemes.

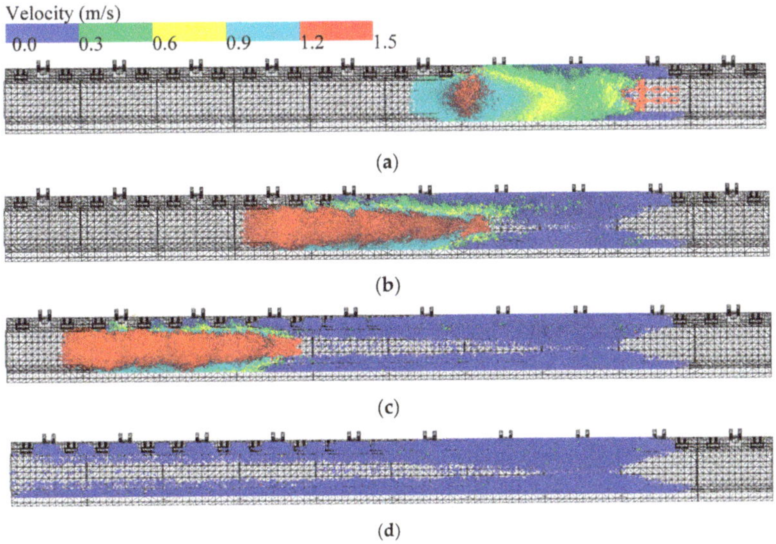

Figure 4. Cloud maps of coal particle velocity distribution at different times with evenly spaced scraper arrangements: (**a**) Simulation result at 5 s; (**b**) simulation result at 7 s; (**c**) simulation result at 9 s; (**d**) simulation result at 13 s.

Following the completion of the simulation, the mass variation curves of the coal particles were compared across different conveying schemes. The conveying capacity of the different scraper chain schemes was evaluated based on the final residual mass of the piled bulk coal within the same conveying time.

The simulation results for different scraper chain schemes are shown in Figure 5. During the period from the 9th to the 13th second, the scraper chains gradually disengaged from the middle trough, and the mass of the remaining coal particles on the middle trough declined steadily. Once the scraper chains had completely left the middle trough, the mass of the remaining coal particles remained constant. Based on the initial and final coal particle masses in the trough, the conveyor efficiency ratios (K) for the different scraper chain schemes were calculated.

$$K = (m_1 - m_2)/m_1 \tag{2}$$

where m_1 is the mass of the initial coal, kg; m_2 is the mass of the end coal, kg.

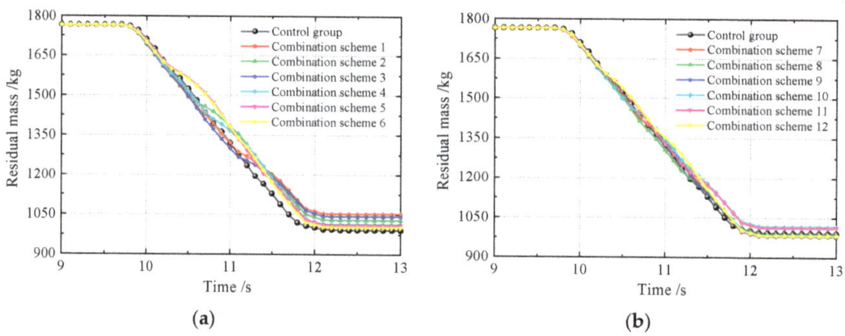

Figure 5. Variation curves of remaining coal particle mass in the middle trough under different schemes: (**a**) Comparison of results for schemes 1–6; (**b**) comparison of results for schemes 7–12.

Material conveying simulation was conducted for different scraper spacing combination schemes in Table 1, and the variation law of material mass with time under different scraper spacing combination schemes was compared. When the scraper chain in the simulation model detaches from the middle trough, the coal particles pushed by the scraper chain fall off the middle trough, and the mass of the coal particles in the simulation model decreases. Initially, the total mass of coal particles in different models is equal. After being conveyed by different combinations of scraper chains, the remaining mass of coal particles varies. The conveying capacity of the scraper is analyzed based on the remaining mass of coal particles. In Figure 5a, the combination scheme 1–6 corresponds to the simulation results of different scraper combination spacings from groups 1 to 6 in Table 1. In Figure 5b, combination scheme 7–12 corresponds to the simulation results of different scraper combination spacings from groups 7 to 12 in Table 1.

The overall coal conveying capacity of these scraper chain schemes is lower than that of the control group. Schemes 7 and 8, arranged with different combination spacings of 6p, 6p, and 8p, show stable fluctuations in coal conveying capacity between 10 and 12 s, with an overall capacity higher than that of the control group. Schemes 9–12, arranged with different combination spacings of 4p, 8p, and 8p, demonstrate relatively stable fluctuations in coal conveying capacity between 10 and 12 s. Some of these schemes performed better than the control group, while others performed worse.

The simulation results, which were statistically analyzed, are shown in Table 3. Initially, the mass of coal particles in the middle trough was 1767 kg. At the end of the simulation for the control group, the mass of the remaining coal particles was 991.58 kg. After being conveyed by the scraper chains, its mass was reduced by 43.9%. The comparison results show that the scraper chains of Scheme 7 are the optimal scheme. The comparison results of the conveying capacity with the control group are shown in Figure 6a,b. At the end, the mass of the remaining coal particles was 980.58 kg, and their mass was reduced by 44.5%, which demonstrates better performance than the control group.

Table 3. Analysis of simulation results.

Combination Scheme	Residual Mass (kg)	Conveying Ratio (%)
1	1053.32	40.4
2	1030.17	41.7
3	1044.17	40.9
4	1014.13	42.6
5	1011.44	42.8
6	1002.82	43.3
7	980.58	44.5
8	987.19	44.1
9	982.03	44.4
10	1016.60	42.5
11	1012.22	42.7
12	983.38	44.3

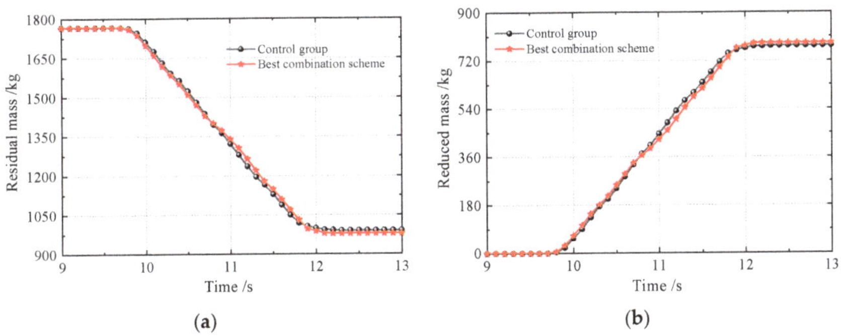

Figure 6. Comparison of conveying capacity curves between the optimal scheme and control group: (**a**) Comparison of remaining coal mass; (**b**) comparison of coal mass reduction.

This scheme improves the average spacing of the scrapers while ensuring the conveying capacity of the scraper chains. The scraper spacing of the scraper chains in Scheme 7 is 6p-8p-6p. Compared with the original scraper chains with an equal spacing of 6p, the average scraper spacing is increased by 11.11%. The total mass of the scrapers in the original scraper conveyor was 62,959.0 kg. After changing the scraper spacing, the total mass of the scrapers was reduced by 6995.4 kg. The effect of reducing the mass of the chain drive system by optimizing the spacing of the scrapers is obvious.

On the other hand, the chain of the scraper conveyor is of a large mass. When installing the chain underground, hundreds of meters of chain are composed of numerous small sections of chain joined together through connecting links. Now, the small sections of the scraper chain before leaving the factory have been changed to a non-uniform arrangement and are still connected through connecting links, which will not cause problems in the installation and maintenance of the scraper chain. The tensioning of the chain is achieved by the tensioning cylinder pushing the tail sprocket. The meshing transmission form between the sprocket and the chain link remains unchanged, and the tensioning adjustment method of the chain remains the same. The non-equal spacing arrangement of the scrapers will not affect the meshing transmission process of the chain or the tensioning adjustment of the chain drive system.

3. Topological Optimization

3.1. Determine the Scraper Load

By optimizing the scraper spacing, the number of scrapers in the chain drive system of the scraper conveyor is indirectly reduced, while the mass of each individual scraper remains unchanged. To further reduce the no-load mass of the chain drive system, a topological optimization method is proposed to improve the scraper structure and reduce the self-mass of the scrapers. To determine the load and constraint conditions during the topological optimization of the scraper, a scraper conveying load model was established. Figure 7 shows that the scraper mainly bears the coal-pushing resistance along the movement direction and the pressure of a part of the coal material falling above the scraper. The magnitudes of both loads are related to the height of the piled bulk coal [20].

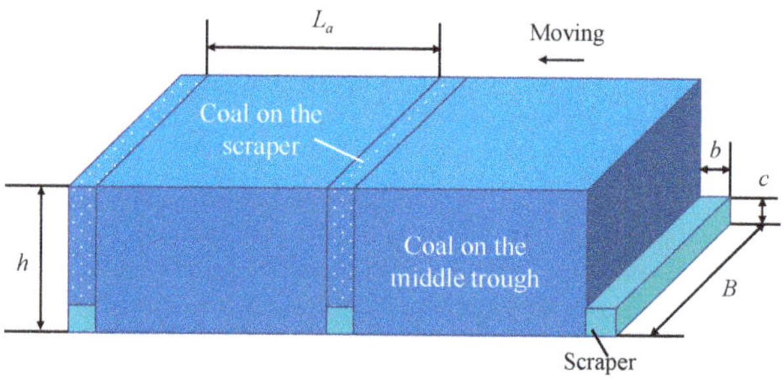

Figure 7. Scraper load model of scraper conveyor.

Determine the maximum average height (h) of the piled bulk coal on the middle trough based on the maximum conveying capacity (Q) of the scraper conveyor:

$$Q = 3.6Bhv\gamma \tag{3}$$

where B is the length of the scraper, m; v is the running speed of the scraper chains, m/s; and γ is the density of the piled bulk coal, kg/m^3.

According to the spacing between adjacent scrapers, the coal-pushing mass (M_c) of a single scraper can be calculated as follows:

$$M_c = BL_a h\gamma \tag{4}$$

Correspondingly, the coal-pushing resistance (F_c) and the pressure (F_s) of the piled bulk coal on the scraper are respectively:

$$F_c = \mu M_c g \tag{5}$$

$$F_s = \gamma B(h - c)bg \tag{6}$$

where μ is the friction coefficient between the coal and the middle trough; c is the height of the scraper, m; b is the width of the scraper, m; and g is the acceleration due to gravity, m/s^2.

Figure 8 illustrates that the scraper in the scraper conveyor consists of an upper scraper and a lower scraper. The upper scraper serves as the primary load-bearing component, primarily responsible for coal-pushing resistance, while the lower scraper is mainly used for nut installation. Both the upper and lower scrapers are mounted onto the flat ring through bolt connections. Typically, the mass of the upper scraper is significantly greater than that of the lower scraper; therefore, the upper scraper is selected for topological optimization.

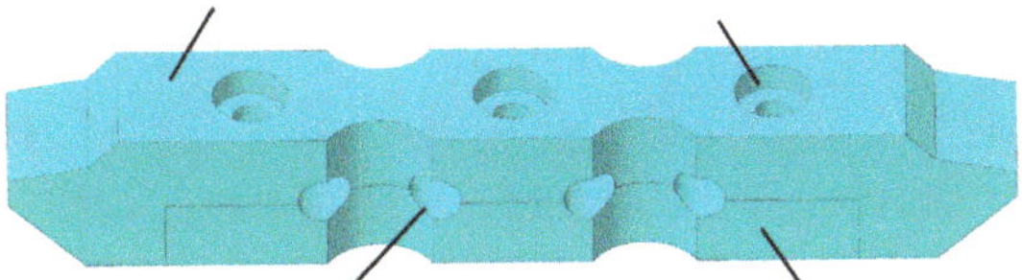

Figure 8. Composition of the scraper.

The SGZ1000 scraper conveyor has a conveying capacity of 3000 t/h, featuring a round link chain with a specification of 56 × 187 mm and a scraper with a specification of 985.8 × 116.0 × 180.6 mm. Calculations revealed that when the pitch of a single scraper is set to 8p, the corresponding coal-pushing resistance is 4293.7 N, and the pressure exerted by the coal on the scraper is 456.9 N. These values are utilized as the load constraint conditions for the scraper, and structural topological optimization is conducted to minimize the overall mass of the scraper.

3.2. *Scraper Topological Analysis*

Topology optimization is an advanced structural optimization design method that primarily determines the optimal material distribution within a given design space under constraints such as loads and boundary conditions, using mathematical algorithms. The basic principle of topology optimization involves discretizing the structure into a finite number of elements and employing optimization algorithms to continuously remove material units that contribute less to structural performance while retaining those that are critical to performance. This ensures that the structure achieves its target performance while satisfying various constraints. Applying topology optimization technology to the scraper of a mining scraper conveyor can help improve the scraper structure and reduce its mass.

The commonly used topological optimization methods at present include the homogenization method, variable density method, level set method, etc. Among them, the homogenization method is one of the earliest proposed topological optimization methods, which was born in the 1980s. Both the variable density method and the level set method are improvements based on this method. The variable density method has a mature algorithm and is widely used in industry, supported by rich cases and experience. This paper selects the variable density method to conduct topological optimization analysis on the scraper structure. Different lightweight targets are selected to perform topological analysis on the upper scraper. The topological results are presented in Figure 9. The finite element analysis of the scraper was carried out by using ANSYS 2019 simulation analysis software, and the structural topology of the target scraper was optimized according to the simulation structure. The finite element model of the scraper used tetrahedral mesh elements with a mesh size of 5 mm, totaling 484,169 nodes. The mesh model of the scraper is shown in Figure 9. Figure 10 shows the load constraint model of the scraper. The chain link is in coordination with the chain link hole of the scraper and is relatively fixed to the chain link through the pre-tightening force of the bolts. The arc surface of the chain link hole of the scraper is set with a fixed constraint, and the coal pushing side of the scraper is set with a load constraint.

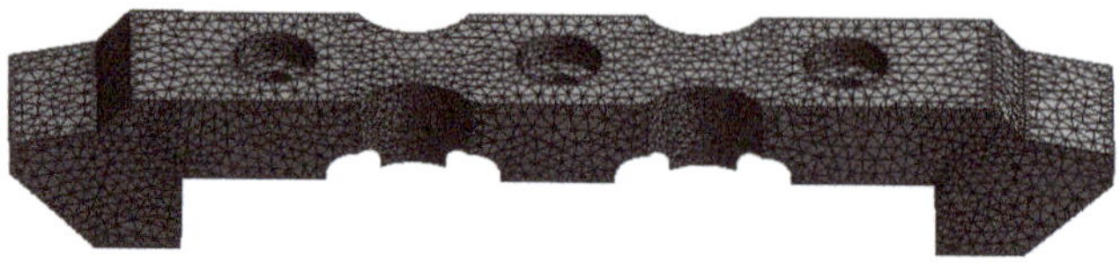

Figure 9. Upper scraper grid model.

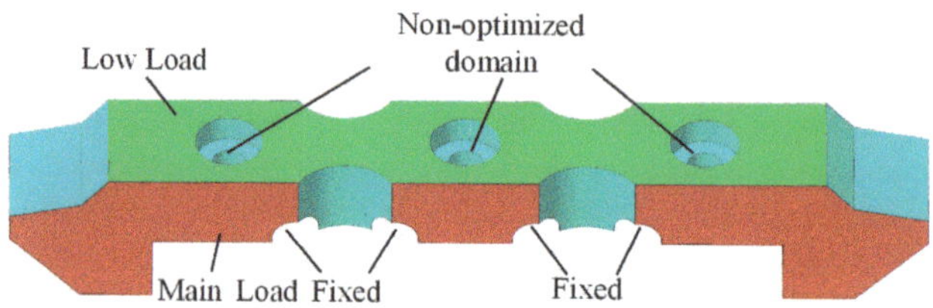

Figure 10. Load constraint on the upper scraper.

Different lightweight targets were selected to conduct topological analysis on the upper scraper. The topological results are shown in Figure 11a–f. As the mass ratio of the topological structure to the original structure decreases, the difference between the topological scraper and the original structure gradually increases. Compared with the original structure, the topological scraper has significantly removed the non-contact surface of the scraper while retaining the main load-bearing surface and installation position. It still maintains the ability to push coal with the scraper.

3.3. Optimization of the Scraper's Topological Structure

Considering the dynamic load effect of the scraper conveyor, the lightweight design of the scraper is not suitable for being too extreme. Generally, topology optimization can achieve a weight reduction of 20% to 30% in the initial design stage without significantly sacrificing structural performance [21]. Therefore, for the scraper's topological optimization, a conservative approach is adopted, aiming to reduce its mass by 25%. The corresponding topologically optimized structure of the scraper is shown in Figure 12.

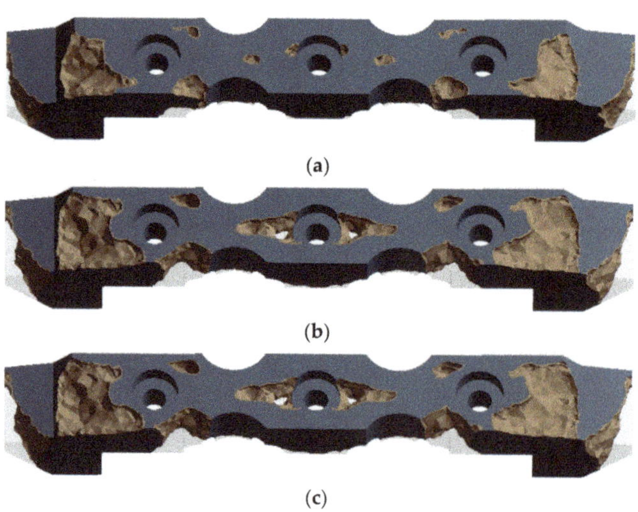

Figure 11. *Cont.*

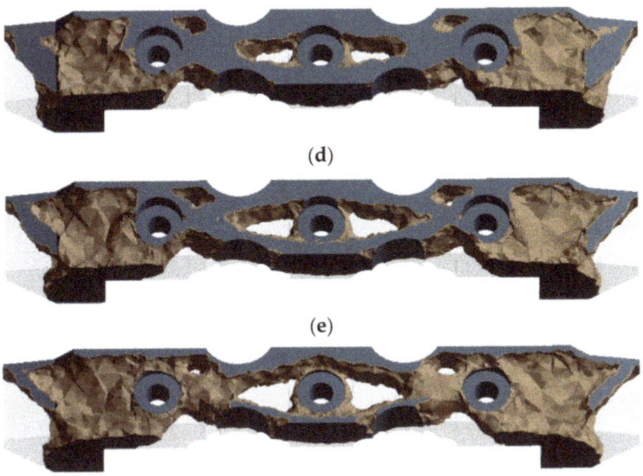

(**d**)

(**e**)

(**f**)

Figure 11. Topological structures of the upper scraper: (**a**) 92.6% of original mass; (**b**) 84.1% of original mass; (**c**) 75.6% of original mass; (**d**) 66.2% of original mass; (**e**) 57.3% of original mass; (**f**) 48.6% of original mass.

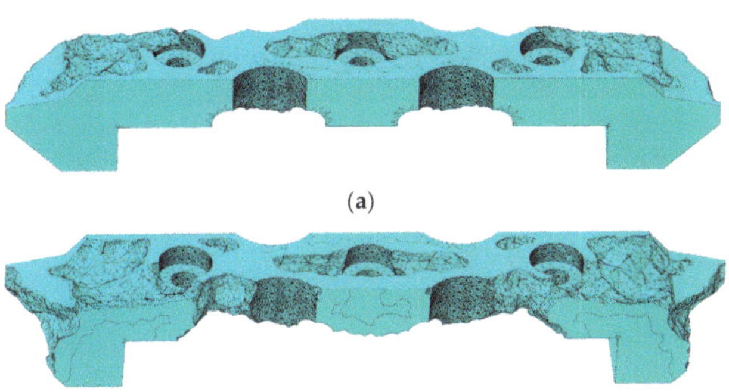

(**a**)

(**b**)

Figure 12. Topological structure of the target scraper: (**a**) Front side of the scraper's topological structure; (**b**) reverse side of the scraper's topological structure.

The structure obtained from topological optimization features a large number of irregular surfaces, which cannot be directly utilized due to the limitations of traditional processing methods and the high costs associated with mass production. Consequently, further optimization of the scraper after topological optimization is necessary. Using 3D software, the structure is optimized based on the original design and the results of topological analysis. Non-essential structures are removed, and the geometry in different regions is adjusted. The optimized topological structure of the scraper is shown in Figure 13. Compared to the structure from topological analysis, the optimized scraper has a flatter overall design while retaining all key features of the topological structure and improving machinability.

Compared to the original scraper before optimization, the mass is reduced by 23.5%. The total mass of a single scraper decreases from 78 kg to 64 kg, resulting in a 17.9% reduction in mass. This light-weighting demonstrates significant effectiveness.

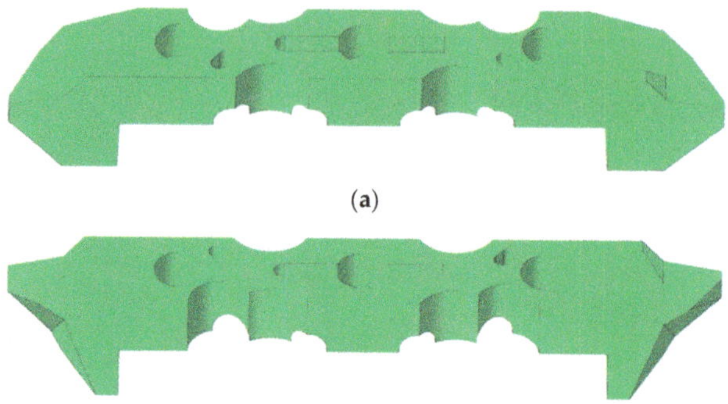

(a)

(b)

Figure 13. Optimization of the scraper's topological structure: (**a**) Front view of the scraper's topological structure; (**b**) back view of the scraper's topological structure.

At present, scrapers are mainly produced by casting. This paper analyzes the areas where materials can be removed through topological optimization and optimizes the structure of the scraper. The optimized scraper has a simple structure and can be processed and manufactured by existing CNC machines or by casting. Compared with the mechanical processing cost of the scraper, the electricity cost of the no-load energy consumption of the chain drive far exceeds the production cost of the scraper. The optimized scraper has extremely strong feasibility for process implementation. The optimized scraper does not affect the meshing transmission process of the chain drive system. During the actual operation of the scraper, the upper part mainly bears the coal pushing load, which is far less than the load-bearing capacity of the scraper. The lower scraper comes into contact with the middle trough and wears out. This paper conducts topological optimization on the upper scraper, which has a minimal impact on the wear life of the scraper.

3.4. Strength Analysis of the Topological Scraper Structure

Mechanical response analyses were conducted on the scrapers before and after topological optimization. Figure 14 shows that under the same load and constraint conditions, the deformations of the original scraper and the topologically optimized scraper were 0.0052 mm and 0.0075 mm, respectively. The relatively small deformation values indicate sufficient rigidity and resistance to external forces, ensuring structural stability. Typically, topological optimization removes materials that contribute less to the structural mechanical properties to achieve weight reduction. However, this process may decrease the local stiffness of the structure, leading to increased deformation under the same load [22]. The primary function of the scraper is to push materials, and the requirement for deformation accuracy of the scraper itself is not stringent. In this case, the difference in deformation of the topologically optimized scraper has minimal impact on the normal operation of the entire system and can be considered negligible.

Figure 15 shows that the maximum equivalent stresses of the original scraper and the topologically optimized scraper were 5.39 MPa and 12.19 MPa, respectively. The equivalent application comparison of the two scrapers under the same boundary constraints and the same action load. Both values were significantly lower than the material's yield stress of 236 MPa. Although the maximum equivalent stress of the topologically optimized scraper increased, it remained within the safe range relative to the material's bearing capacity. The structural performance of the topologically optimized scraper satisfies the actual requirements.

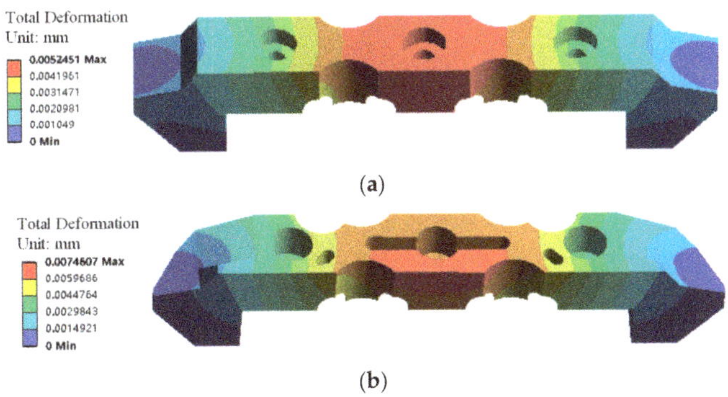

Figure 14. Comparative analysis of deformation displacement of topological scrapers: (**a**) Original scraper; (**b**) topologically optimized scraper.

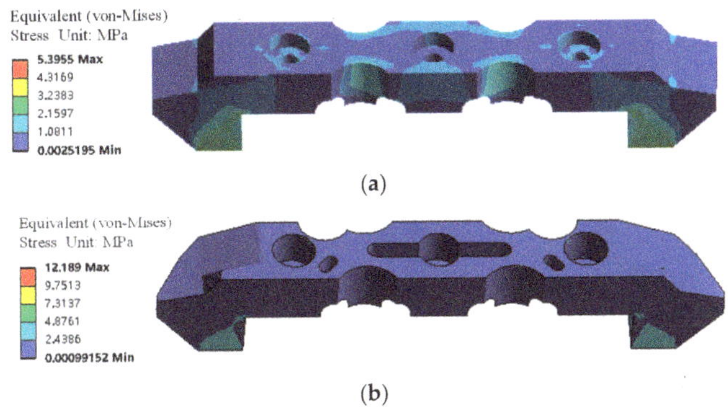

Figure 15. Comparative analysis of equivalent stress of topological scrapers: (**a**) Original scraper; (**b**) topologically optimized scraper.

4. Discussion

For a 400 m scraper conveyor, arranging scrapers at an equal spacing of 6p requires 713 scrapers. When using topologically optimized scrapers, the no-load mass of the chain drive system can be reduced by 11,269.5 kg.

If scrapers are arranged at an uneven spacing of 6p-8p-6p, only 641 scrapers are needed, which is 72 fewer than the equal-spacing arrangement. This reduction in the number of scrapers results in a mass reduction of 6357.6 kg. When using topologically optimized scrapers, the mass of the scrapers can be further reduced by 10,131.4 kg. Compared to the pre-optimization state, the no-load mass of the chain drive system is reduced by a total of 26.2%, thereby significantly lowering the no-load energy consumption of the long-distance scraper conveyor.

5. Conclusions

(1) Through DEM analysis, the conveying capacities of scraper chains under different scraper spacing combination schemes were compared. It was found that for the chain of the 56 $\times$ 187 mm specification, the non-equal spacing arrangement of 6p-8p-6p for scrapers is superior to the equal spacing arrangement of 6p. This arrangement increases the average spacing of scrapers while ensuring the conveying capacity of the scraper chains, and reduces the number of scrapers by 11.11% for scraper chains of the same length.

(2) Through topological optimization of the scraper structure, the total mass of a single scraper is reduced by 17.9%. Compared with the original scraper, under the same load and constraint conditions, the deformation displacement and equivalent stress of the topologically optimized scraper will increase. However, relative to the bearing capacity of the material, they are still within the safe range, and the structural performance of the topologically optimized scraper can meet the actual requirements.
(3) By adopting a non-equal spacing scraper arrangement and topologically optimized scrapers, the no-load mass of the chain drive system of a 400 m scraper conveyor can be reduced by 26.2%. This significantly reduces the no-load energy consumption of the long scraper conveyor, providing guidance for the future design of long-distance and low-energy-consumption scraper conveyors.

Author Contributions: Conceptualization, Q.Z.; methodology, Q.Z. and W.L.; software, A.J.; validation, A.J. and X.L.; formal analysis, X.S.; investigation, X.S.; resources, X.S., A.J., and X.L.; data curation, W.L.; writing—original draft preparation, W.L.; writing—review and editing, Q.Z. and X.L.; visualization, S.S.; supervision, X.L.; project administration, Q.Z.; funding acquisition, Q.Z. All authors have read and agreed to the published version of the manuscript.

Funding: This work was supported by the National Natural Science Foundation of China under Grant. Funding number 52234005.

Data Availability Statement: Data is contained within the article. Further inquiries can be directed to the authors.

Acknowledgments: All individuals mentioned in this section have given their consent to be acknowledged.

Conflicts of Interest: Author Xiangjun Song was employed by the company Xi'an Heavy Equipment Tongchuan Coal Mining Machinery Co., Ltd. Author Xin Li was employed by the Qingdao Special Equipment Inspection and Testing Institute. The remaining authors declare that the research was conducted in the absence of any commercial or financial relationships that could be construed as a potential conflict of interest.

Abbreviations

The following abbreviations are used in this manuscript:

DEM discrete element simulation

References

1. Wang, X.W.; Li, B.; Yang, Z.J. Analysis of the Bulk Coal Transport State of a Scraper Conveyor Using the Discrete Element Method. *J. Mech. Eng.* **2018**, *64*, 37–46.
2. Li, S.; Zhu, Z.C.; Lu, H.; Xue, Y.; Weng, L. Tension Characteristics Analysis of Scraper chains of Heavy-Duty Scraper Conveyor with Time-Varying Loads. *Shock Vib.* **2024**, *2004*, 5589346. [CrossRef]
3. Zhang, Q.; Liu, W.; Wang, Y.; Ma, S.; Su, J.; Zhang, R. Research on postural behavior and structural response prediction of scraper conveyor based on digital twin. *J. China Coal Soc.* **2025**, *50*, 3210–3223.
4. Li, B.; Dong, Y.W.; Xia, R.; Wang, X.; Ma, H.; Jiao, H. Dynamic characteristics of chain drive system under blocking condition of scraper conveyor based on DEM-MBD. *Proc. Inst. Mech. Eng. Part E-J. Process Mech. Eng.* **2025**, 09544089251324580. [CrossRef]
5. Xiong, Y.; Kong, D.Z.; Song, G.F. Research hotspots and development trends of green coal mining: Exploring the path to sustainable development of coal mines. *Resour. Policy* **2024**, *92*, 105039. [CrossRef]
6. Hao, J.; Song, Y.C.; Zhang, P.Z.; Liu, H.; Jia, S.; Zheng, Y.; Zhang, X. Failure analysis of scraper conveyor based on fault tree and optimal design of new scraper with polyurethane material. *J. Mater. Res. Technol.—JMRT* **2022**, *18*, 4533–4548. [CrossRef]
7. Xia, R.; Liang, C.; Wang, X.W. Study on dynamic characteristics of scraper conveyor under various scraper configurations. *Proc. Inst. Mech. Eng. Part E-J. Process Mech. Eng.* **2024**, 09544089231224903. [CrossRef]
8. Hao, J.; Song, Y.C.; Liu, H.J.; Zhang, P.; Chen, L.; Zhang, N.; Jia, S.; Liu, Y. The Optimal Design Model for a New Type of Scraper and Research on Its Material Properties. *Lubricants* **2023**, *11*, 171. [CrossRef]
9. Li, S.; Zhu, Z.C.; Lu, H.; Sheng, H. A system reliability-based design optimization for the scraper chains of scraper conveyors with dependent failure modes. *Maint. Reliab.* **2019**, *21*, 392–402.

10. Noda, M.; Matsushima, K.; Yamada, T. Orientation optimization via topological derivatives in combination with multi-material topology optimization based on extended level set method. *Comput. Methods Appl. Mech. Eng.* **2024**, *418*, 116585. [CrossRef]
11. Sivakumar, K.; Timmaraju, M.V.; Gnanamoorthy, R. Lightweight design of steel sprocket for roller chain drive using explicit dynamic simulation. *Proc. Inst. Mech. Eng. Part C J. Mech. Eng. Sci.* **2024**, *238*, 8809–8818. [CrossRef]
12. Huang, D.F.; Zhou, S.S.; Yan, X.L. Multi-objective topology optimization design of thermal-mechanical coupling structure based on FPTO method. *Optim. Eng.* **2025**, *1*, 53–81. [CrossRef]
13. Hruzík, L.; Struz, J.; Trochta, M.; Klapetek, L.; Pišťáček, D. Modern Design of Carrier for Overhead Conveyor. *Appl. Sci.* **2024**, *14*, 5352. [CrossRef]
14. Rostami, S.A.L.; Kolahdooz, A.; Chung, H.; Shi, M.; Zhang, J. Robust topology optimization of continuum structures with smooth boundaries using moving morphable components. *Struct. Multidiscip. Optim.* **2023**, *66*, 121. [CrossRef]
15. Rostami, S.A.L.; Chung, H.; Lim, H.J. Efficient reliability-based topology optimization for enhanced resilience of piezoelectric actuators under material uncertainties. *Mech. Based Des. Struct. Mach.* **2025**. [CrossRef]
16. Yuan, L.; Zhang, T.; Wang, Y.H.; Wang, X.; Wang, Y.; Hao, X. Scientific problems and key technologies for safe and efficient mining of deep coal resources. *J. China Coal Soc.* **2025**, *50*, 1–12.
17. Lu, Q.; Chen, Y.H.; Cao, X.; Xie, T.; Mao, Q.; Leng, J. Dynamic Coal Flow-Based Energy Consumption Optimization of Scraper Conveyor. *Appl. Sci.* **2025**, *15*, 7366. [CrossRef]
18. But, H.Z.; Zhang, P.; Dong, Y.W.; Wang, X.; Xia, R.; Li, B. Study on the rigid-discrete coupling effect of scraper conveyor under different chain speed-load conditions. *Simul. Model. Pract. Theory* **2024**, *134*, 102943.
19. Wang, Y.D.; Lin, G.C.; Liu, X.A.; Zhao, L.; Jia, B.; Wang, Y.; He, J. Research on coal rock parameter calibration based on discrete element method. *Sci. Rep.* **2024**, *14*, 26507. [CrossRef]
20. Zhang, Q.; Zhang, R.X.; Tian, Y. Scraper Conveyor Structure Improvement and Performance Comparative Analysis. *Strength Mater.* **2020**, *52*, 683–690. [CrossRef]
21. Huang, J.; Long, K.; Chen, Y.; Geng, R.; Saeed, A.; Zhang, H.; Tao, T. A Framework of the Meshless Method for Topology Optimization Using the Smooth-Edged Material Distribution for Optimizing Topology Method. *Computation* **2025**, *13*, 6. [CrossRef]
22. Miler, D.; Hoić, M.; Tomić, R.; Jokić, A.; Mašović, R. Simultaneous Multi-Objective and Topology Optimization: Effect of Mesh Refinement and Number of Iterations on Computational Cost. *Computation* **2025**, *13*, 168. [CrossRef]

computation

MDPI

Article

Topology Optimization for Rudder Structures Considering Additive Manufacturing and Flutter Effects

Heng Zhang *, Shuaijie Shi, Xiaohong Ding *, Jiandong Yang and Min Xiong

School of Mechanical Engineering, University of Shanghai for Science and Technology, Shanghai 200093, China; 15664223539@163.com (S.S.); yjd182318@163.com (J.Y.)
* Correspondence: zhanghengsh@usst.edu.cn (H.Z.); dingxhsh021@126.com (X.D.)

Abstract: This paper presents a multi-constraint topology optimization strategy for rudder structures, integrating additive manufacturing (AM)-related overhang angle and flutter-performance considerations. To the best of our knowledge, this is the first study to couple AM overhang control with mass center (flutter) steering in a single density-based formulation for flight control rudder structures. The approach incorporates constraints on structural volume fraction, overhang angle for AM, and mass center positioning to address multi-function design objectives—structural lightweighting, stiffness, aerodynamic stability, and manufacturability. A build-direction-aware projection filter and a smooth Heaviside mass center constraint are introduced to enforce these requirements during every optimization iteration. The resulting layout converges to a sandwich-type rudder with balanced mechanical performance and AM feasibility. Simulation results show that enforcing overhang constraints reduces support material usage by 46.9% and residual deformation by 14.2%, significantly enhancing AM feasibility. Additionally, introducing center-of-mass constraints improves flutter velocity from 3327 m s^{-1} to 3759 m s^{-1}, indicating a 6.84% increase over conventional optimization and demonstrating improved dynamic stability. These simultaneous gains in manufacturability and aeroelastic safety, achieved without post-processing, underline the novelty and practical value of the proposed constraint set. The strategy thus offers a practical and efficient design method for high-performance, AM-friendly rudder structures with superior mechanical and aerodynamic characteristics, and it can be readily extended to other mission-critical AM components.

Keywords: topology optimization; additive manufacturing; overhang constraints; center of mass constraints; flutter performance

1. Introduction

Rudder structures are essential components in systems requiring high-speed flight and precise control. Their design demands a balance between lightweight construction, high load-bearing capacity, and good flutter performance. Structural optimization provides an effective approach for tailoring material distribution to meet these performance objectives, enhancing stiffness while adhering to mass constraints. As typical thin-walled configurations, stiffened structures offer the combined benefits of low weight and high rigidity, making them ideal for aerospace, marine, and other high-performance engineering applications where structural efficiency is of critical importance.

Topology optimization has been widely applied in various engineering fields, particularly in the aerospace industry. Alain Remouchamps [1] proposed a two-level optimization method that combines topology optimization with geometric parameter adjustment to enhance the structural performance and design flexibility of aircraft pylon structures. Zhu [2] explored the integration of compliance-based topology optimization with detailed size and shape optimization in the design of aircraft components. Kang [3] investigated the reformulation of the topology optimization problem for microsatellite structures into a compliance minimization design under mass moment of inertia constraints, aiming to improve attitude control efficiency while maintaining structural performance. Hansen [4] proposed a multilevel optimization method that integrates evolutionary strategies with finite element-based gradient optimization to achieve concurrent optimization of size and topology for complex aerospace structures. Wang [5] proposed a two-stage optimization framework, in which the stiffened panel is partitioned into characteristic deformation subregions and the stiffener layout is optimized, significantly enhancing the load-bearing capacity of the structure under compressive loading. Zhu [2] summarized the latest developments in topology optimization technologies applied to the design of aircraft and aerospace structures. Due to the highly complex structural forms typically generated by topology optimization, conventional manufacturing methods often struggle to realize such designs or are unable to manufacture them. As a layer-by-layer fabrication method, additive manufacturing (3D printing) offers significant advantages for producing complex geometries with high precision and design flexibility.

Although additive manufacturing (3D printing) eliminates the need for molds or fixtures, which greatly simplifies the fabrication process and enables efficient production of complex, non-standard geometries, it also introduces specific process-related constraints. For example, during the printing process, there is a maximum allowable overhang angle for the bottom surfaces of components (typically between 40° and 50°). When the underside surface angle falls below this threshold, support structures are required to prevent collapse or warping during fabrication [6]. In addition, the removal of support structures not only results in material waste but also reduces production efficiency, particularly when dealing with enclosed structures, where support removal becomes even more challenging. Therefore, it is essential to incorporate manufacturing constraints into the early stages of structural design to achieve seamless integration between design and fabrication. Driven by this approach, an increasing number of studies have integrated additive manufacturing constraints (such as the overhang constraint) with topology optimization to enhance the manufacturability of optimized structures. He [7] proposed a method that incorporates overhang constraints into both layout and geometry optimization processes, achieving self-supporting designs while further improving computational efficiency. Vanek [8] performed topology optimization of the length and size of support structures based on adjusted printing orientations, achieving further reduction in branched support structures. Langelaar [9] developed a self-supporting mathematical model based on the maximum density of support regions. However, this method is limited by the type of mesh elements and can only enforce an overhang constraint of 45 degrees. Luo [10] proposed a self-supporting topology optimization method based on the density-based approach, aiming to control the minimum overhang angle of enclosed cavities and address the issue of enclosed voids that may arise after optimization. Gaynor [11] achieved self-supporting topology design based on the SIMP method by employing a density projection approach, where only elements satisfying the overhang angle constraint are projected as solid elements. Han [12] conducted topology optimization using the BESO method based on hybrid additive–subtractive manufacturing technology, comprehensively considering self-supporting constraints from additive manufacturing and milling constraints from subtractive manufacturing, thereby achieving self-supporting structural designs with higher dimensional accuracy.

On the other hand, the rational control of the center of mass is also of critical importance in engineering practice. Zhou [13] established a mathematical model for the topology optimization of continua considering mass and inertia properties, and applied it to both static and eigenfrequency problems. In addition, center of mass control is also regarded as an effective method for flutter suppression in aircraft design. Li [14] analyzed the effects of slider structural parameters, such as axial position, lateral offset, and mass ratio, on the trim angle of attack for aircraft. The results indicated that aerodynamic drag and the offset of the center of mass from the longitudinal axis of the body are the two necessary factors for generating the trim angle of attack. Tang [15] studied the influence of center of mass position on the dynamic characteristics of stratospheric airships. The results showed that slight perturbations of the center of mass not only alter the damping characteristics of the pitching motion but also affect the frequency response of the yaw attitude. Flutter, as a form of self-excited vibration that may be triggered under high-altitude and high-speed conditions, exhibits non-decaying amplitude over time and, in extreme cases, can lead to structural failure. Mu [16] investigated active control methods to modify the structural stiffness, while Zhang [17] utilized the unique mechanical properties of metamaterials to alleviate flutter issues partially; however, such approaches often suffer from high costs and implementation complexity. Cao [18] proposed an improved level set method incorporating center of mass constraints to achieve structural lightweighting, and applied this method to the optimization of a trapezoidal rudder. Numerical analysis demonstrated that adjusting the center of mass position can have a positive impact on flutter suppression performance. Phongkumsing [19] improved the flutter resistance of bridge structures by placing specific counterweights to adjust the center of mass position, thereby reducing aerodynamic moments. Overall, center of mass control not only helps optimize the spatial distribution of structural mass but also effectively adjusts the inertial properties of the system.

This study focuses on the design of the rudder structure and performs topology optimization using the density-based method. Through structural analysis, key additive manufacturing constraints, including build direction, maximum overhang angle limitation, and mass center control, are incorporated while ensuring structural stiffness. The optimized rudder sandwich structure simultaneously achieves high structural performance and manufacturability. This reduces the reliance on support structures during printing and improves both manufacturing efficiency and the structural engineering applicability.

2. Optimization Method

The skin surface of the rudder structure exhibits noticeable curvature and deviation from a single horizontal plane. As a result, using a standard build direction shown in Figure 1a would lead to extensive overhangs that are difficult to support effectively. Additionally, the internal stiffeners in traditional sandwich-type rudder designs typically extend radially from the rudder control shaft toward the outer surface in a branched pattern, further complicating support requirements when printing in the vertical direction. To address these challenges, this study adopts the build direction shown in Figure 1b as the principal printing orientation. This orientation aligns better with the geometry of the rudder structure, minimizes the warp deformation, improves skin surface quality, and significantly reduces the need for supporting materials, thereby enhancing overall manufacturing efficiency.

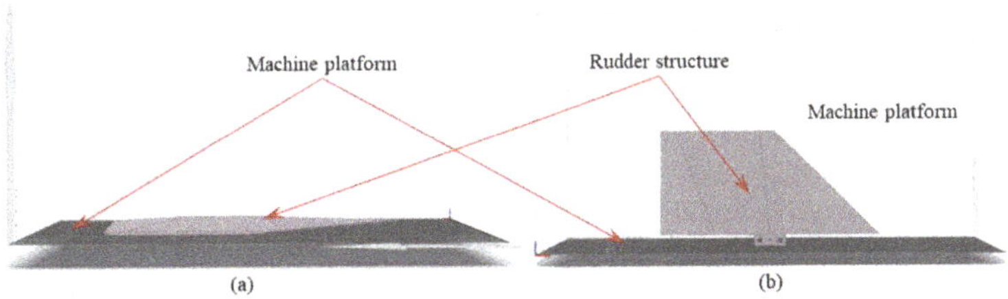

Figure 1. Build direction for the rudder structure: (**a**) build direction 1 for the rudder, (**b**) build direction 2 for the rudder.

2.1. Additive Manufacturing-Related Overhang Constraints

During the additive manufacturing process, components are fabricated layer by layer along the build direction, typically perpendicular to the machine platform. The overhang angle refers to the angle formed between an overhanging surface and the plane of the machine platform. According to current additive manufacturing process standards, when the overhang angle is greater than a critical range of approximately 40° to 50°, the structure can be printed without the need for support. However, if the overhang angle is smaller than this threshold, additional support structures are required to prevent geometric instability, such as sagging or warping. As shown in Figure 2, when the overhang angle a_1 exceeds the critical overhang angle, the component can be printed directly without supports. Conversely, when the overhang angle a_2 is smaller than the critical angle, support structures are necessary to ensure the part quality and the stability of the printing process [20]. In the layer-by-layer additive manufacturing process, the printability of a material point largely depends on whether adequate support exists beneath it. Within the finite element framework, each material point corresponds to a finite element. In this work, the projection function-based overhang constraint [21] is used.

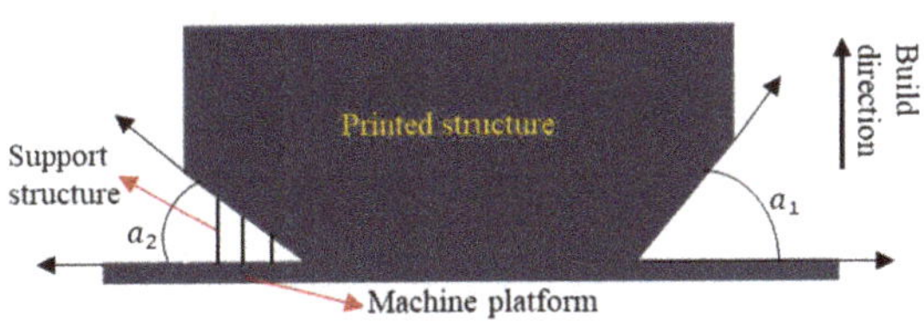

Figure 2. Schematic illustration of overhang angles and support structures.

In this method, three variables are used, which are ψ, ϕ, and S_i. ψ indicates whether material is retained at a given location, and ϕ represents "material placement variable", which determines whether material will be projected to the density design variable space, which is defined as

$$\phi_i = \psi_i S_i \tag{1}$$

To quantitatively evaluate whether a finite element is adequately supported during the layer-by-layer manufacturing process, the equivalent support indicator S_i is calculated as follows:

$$S_i = \frac{tanh(\beta_T T) + tanh\left[\beta_T\left(\mu_s^i(\phi^{\eta_T}) - T\right)\right]}{tanh(\beta_T T) + tanh\left[\beta_T(1-T)\right]} \tag{2}$$

where T is the threshold value, which varies between 0 and 1. β_T is a projection parameter. η_T is a penalization parameter. μ_s^i is the average of the material placement variables, ϕ, for a particular point, i, and is defined in the following equation:

$$\mu_s^i = \frac{\sum_{j\in N_s^i} \varnothing^j w_S}{\sum_{j\in N_s^i} w_s} \tag{3}$$

where w_s is the support region weighting function, and j is a counter of ϕ in the support neighborhood set, N_s^i.

2.2. Mass Center Constraint

For the rudder structure, the mass center position has a significant effect on the flutter performance. Appropriately adjusting the structural mass distribution can enhance the overall stability and vibration resistance. For the topology optimization problem based on the density method, a class of smooth characteristic functions $H(\phi)$ is usually introduced over the design region Ω to represent the existence of the material (ϕ is a design variable), and then the expression for the mass center in the continuous domain is constructed.

For this purpose, the structural mass center can be defined as the mass-weighted average of the material distribution, which is mathematically expressed as follows:

$$R_c = \frac{\int_\Omega H(\phi) r d\Omega}{\int_\Omega H(\phi) d\Omega} \tag{4}$$

where **r** is the position vector.

To avoid the numerical discontinuities inherent to a step function, $H(\varphi)$ is approximated by the following smoothed Heaviside projection:

$$H(\varphi) = \widetilde{H}(\varphi) = \frac{tanh(\beta\eta) + tanh[\beta(\varphi - \eta)]}{tanh(\beta\eta) + tanh[\beta(1 - \eta)]} \tag{5}$$

Here, $\beta > 0$ is the projection steepness controlling the smoothness of the transition, and $\eta \in (0, 1)$ is the threshold parameter (typically $\eta = 0.5$). In the numerical implementation, a continuation scheme gradually increases β (e.g., from 1 to 24) during the optimization so that $\widetilde{H}(\varphi)$ evolves from a smooth approximation to a near-binary indicator, thus ensuring both numerical stability and crisp final boundaries.

When $\varphi \geq 0$, the value of $\widetilde{H}(\varphi)$ approaches 1, indicating the presence of solid material; otherwise, it approaches 0, corresponding to a void region.

In the practical finite element implementation, the above integral relations can be transformed into a discrete weighted average form for numerical evaluation.

$$R_c = \sum_{i=1}^{n} \omega_i x_i^c, \quad \omega_i = \frac{\rho_i V_i}{\sum_{j=1}^{n} \rho_j V_j} \tag{6}$$

In the above equation, ρ_i, V_i, and $\mathbf{x}_i^c$ represent the density, volume, and mass center coordinate of the i element, respectively ; ω_i is the normalized weight; and n is the total number of elements. To control the position of the mass center during optimization, the following inequality is used:

$$\| \int_\Omega H(\phi)(r - R_c) d\Omega \| \leq \epsilon \tag{7}$$

This constraint characterizes the distance between the computed mass center and the target position in terms of global integral deviation and ensures that it remains within an acceptable tolerance ϵ. This helps maintain structural stability during the topology evolution process.

2.3. Mathematical Optimization Model

According to practical requirements, the topology optimization mathematical model for the rudder structure, based on minimum compliance under a volume constraint, can be formulated as follows:

$$\begin{cases} \text{find } \mathbf{X} = (x_1, x_2, x_3, \cdots, x_n) \\ \min C(\mathbf{X}) = \mathbf{F}^T\mathbf{U} = \mathbf{U}^T\mathbf{K}\mathbf{U} = \sum\limits_{i=1}^{n} (x_i)^p \mathbf{u}_i^T \mathbf{k}_0 \mathbf{u}_i \\ \text{s.t. } \mathbf{K}\mathbf{U} = \mathbf{F} \\ \quad V = \sum\limits_{i=1}^{n} v_i \le fV_0 = V^* \\ \quad 0 < x_{min} < x_i \le x_{max} \le 1 \\ \quad \alpha_e \ge \alpha_{\text{thresh}} \\ \quad R_{c_{min}} \le R_c \le R_{c_{max}} \end{cases} \tag{8}$$

where $\boldsymbol{X}$ is the design variable; C is the structural compliance; $\boldsymbol{F}$ is the load vector; $\boldsymbol{U}$ is the nodal displacement vector; $\mathbf{K}$ is the global stiffness matrix; $\mathbf{u}_i$ is the element displacement vector for the i-th element; $\mathbf{k}_0$ is the element stiffness matrix; p is the penalty function; V is the volume in optimization process; V_0 is the Initial structural volume; V^* is the Volume upper limit; v_i is the volume of i-th element; f is the volume fraction; x_{min} is the lower bound of the design variable; x_{max} is the upper bound of the design variable; α_e is the overhang surface angle of element e; a_{thresh} is the threshold corresponding to the overhang critical angle, here set as 45°; R_c is the mass center position of the optimized structures; $R_{c_{min}}$ is the lower bound of the mass center position; and $R_{c_{max}}$ is the upper bound of the mass center position.

In this work, the density-based method is used to identify the structural configuration. The SIMP-based material interpolation scheme is used to obtain the material layout; thus, Young's modulus can be expressed as

$$E(x_i) = E_0 + (x_i)^p (E_1 - E_0) \tag{9}$$

where E_0 is a small value to avoid numerical instabilities; E_1 is the elastic modulus of the solid material; x_i is the design variable, which is the density of the i-th element; when x_i = 1, it indicates that the element is solid; when x_i = 0, it represents the absence of material, corresponding to a void element. p is the penalty factor.

To avoid mesh dependency in the topology optimization problem, the Helmholtz-type partial differential equation (PDE) filter is utilized [22]:

$$-r^2 \nabla^2 \gamma_p + \gamma_p = \gamma \tag{10}$$

where γ_p is the filtered design variable and r is the filter radius. To reduce the gray area (intermediate density) between solids and fluids, the hyperbolic tangent projection method is applied to the filter design field [23]:

$$\gamma_h = \frac{\tanh(\beta\eta) + \tanh\left[\beta\left(\gamma_p - \eta\right)\right]}{\tanh(\beta\eta) + \tanh[\beta(1-\eta)]} \tag{11}$$

where γ_h is the output design variable. η is the projection threshold parameter, here $\eta = 0.5$. And β is a parameter controlling the projection steepness, set $\beta = 8.0$.

Firstly, the design domain is given an initial guess. In this study, a uniform density field with a density value of 0.45 is used as an initial guess. Secondly, based on the initial guess, the finite element analysis is used to solve the governing equations. Thirdly, the objective function and constraints are computed. Finally, a sensitivity analysis is conducted, and design variables are updated. The optimization iteration stops when the following condition is satisfied:

$$\left|\frac{\psi_k - \psi_{k-1}}{\psi_k}\right| < 1.0 \times 10^{-6} \quad (12)$$

Figure 3 is the workflow of the topology optimization design procedure. First, the design model is discretized into a finite element model, and a design variable is assigned to each element. Next, the structural compliance of the component is computed by solving the governing equations. The sensitivities of the objective and constraint functions are then evaluated, and the design variables are updated until convergence is achieved. The convergence criterion is that the change in the objective function between two successive iterations is smaller than the prescribed tolerance.

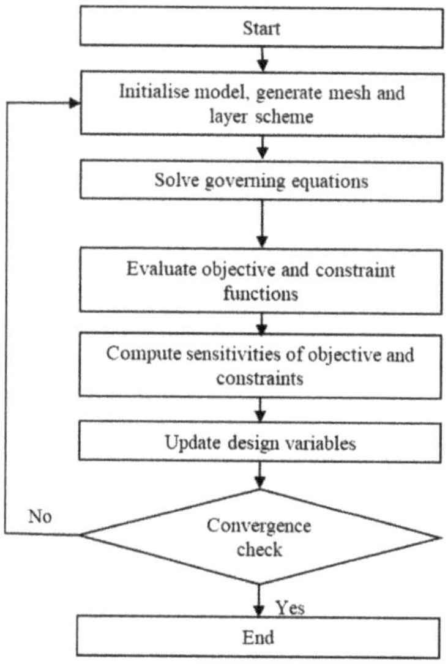

Figure 3. Topology optimization design flowchart.

2.4. Design Procedure

The optimal material layout can be obtained by solving the mathematical optimization model expressed in Equation (5). The proposed topology optimization process for the rudder structure is illustrated in Figure 4, which contains the following steps:

(1) Define the design domain for the rudder structure and the design variables, then set the boundary and load conditions.

(2) Define an overhang constraint based on the additive manufacturing build direction to ensure both manufacturing feasibility and set the allowable range for the mass center position to improve the flutter performance.

(3) A topology optimization model is then formulated, incorporating constraints on volume, stiffness, manufacturing adaptability, and center of mass regulation. The model is solved using the SIMP method, with design variables iteratively updated until the performance objectives are satisfied and convergence is achieved.

(4) Upon completion of the optimization process, engineering modeling is performed. Practical manufacturing requirements, including additive manufacturing constraints, are fully considered to generate a final sandwich-type rudder structure that achieves both high structural performance and manufacturability.

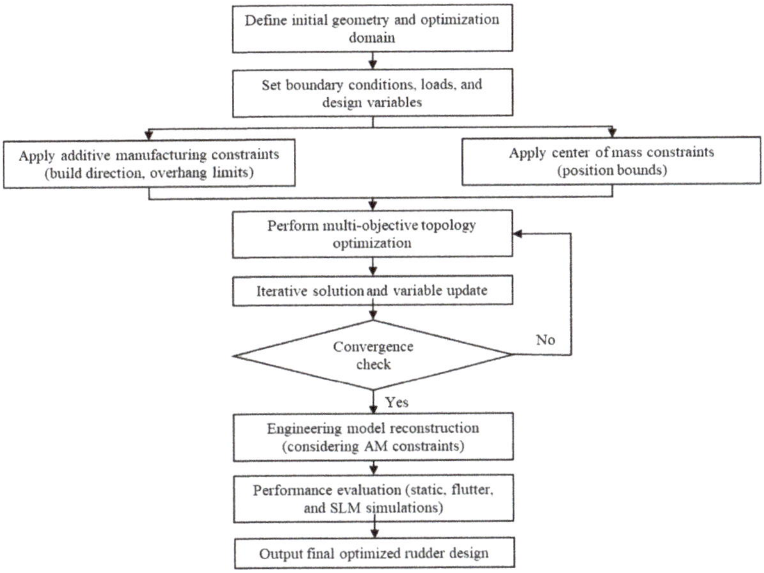

Figure 4. Design flowchart of proposed topology optimization method considering additive manufacturing-related overhang and mass center constraints.

3. Design Verification

3.1. Design of the Rudder Based on the Proposed Method

The cross-section of the solid-core rudder structure is shown in Figure 5a. The rudder structure is divided into three parts, which are the surface skin, the internal solid-core region, and the rudder shaft. Among these, the internal solid region serves as the design domain for topology optimization, while the skin and the shaft are non-design domains. The total weight of the solid-core rudder structure is 1.514 kg. Titanium alloy is used as the structural material, and its properties are listed in Table 1. The applied aerodynamic-and-inertial-load case corresponds to the worst-case operating condition (maximum dynamic pressure) within the flight envelope. The loads are applied on the surface of the rudder, the load direction is perpendicular to the surface, and the magnitude of the load gradually decreases from the leading edge to the trailing edge [24]. All six degrees of freedom of the cylindrical holes at the rudder shaft are constrained, as shown in Figure 5b.

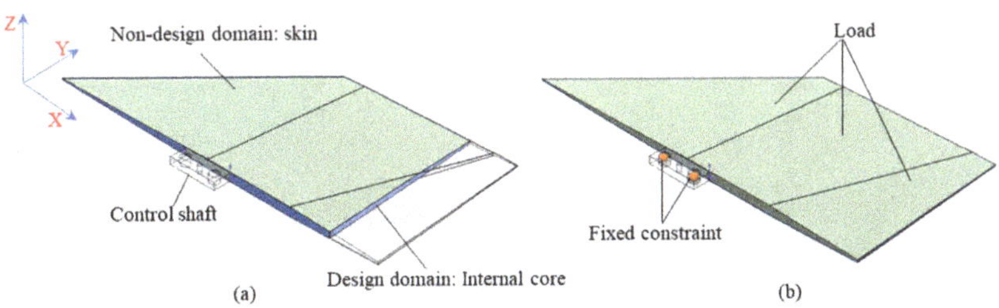

Figure 5. The rudder structure: (**a**) cross-sectional view, (**b**) boundary condition.

Based on the mathematical model shown in Equation 5, the optimization model for the design of rudder structures with high flutter performance is created. In order to minimize the usage of supporting materials, the overhang constraint is typically set to 45° relative to the x-axis to enhance self-supporting capability. To improve the flutter performance, the mass center is constrained in the X-axis direction during the optimization process, with values ranging from −250 mm to 12.5 mm (based on the center of mass coordinate x_c from the empirical design). In addition, the minimum feature size is set to 15 mm.

Table 1. Material properties of the control surface structure.

Material	Titanium Alloy
Elasticity Modulus(GPa)	110
Poisson's ratio	0.33
Density (kg/m^3)	4400

Based on the above optimization mathematical model and parameters, topology optimization for the rudder structure is performed, with its iteration histories shown in Figure 6. The left vertical axis is the objective function, and the horizontal axis indicates the iteration steps. In addition, the figure also shows intermediate results corresponding to the 40th, 80th, 120th, and the final convergence iteration steps. In the optimization process, the internal material layout grows towards the leading and trailing edge, and finally, a tree-like structural configuration is obtained. Based on the optimized material layout shown in Figure 7a, the engineering-designed rudder structure is shown in Figure 7b, and the angle of the stiffener meets the 45° overhang angle constraint relative to the horizontal machine platform. The mass of the optimized rudder structure is 0.875 kg. The structural features shown in Figure 7b, which feature a tree-like high-stiffness and manufacturable stiffener layout, demonstrate the advantages of the proposed topology optimization method.

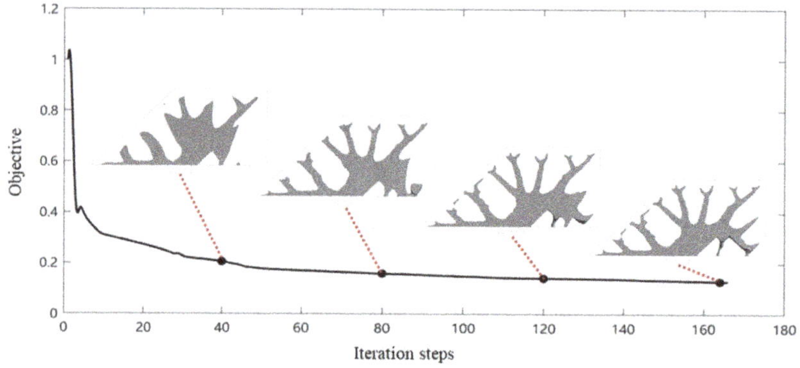

Figure 6. The iteration histories of the topology optimization.

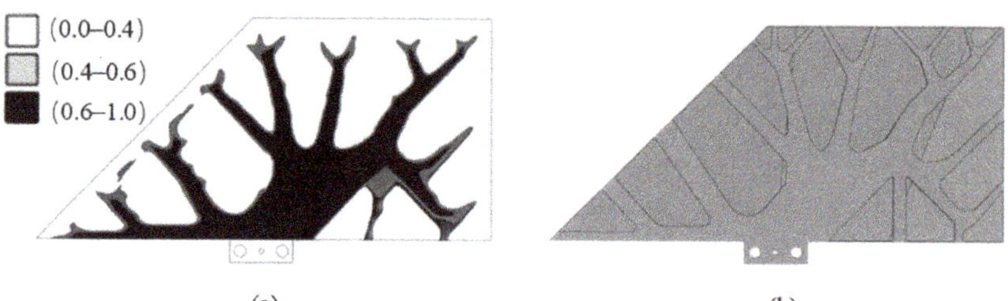

Figure 7. The optimization result: (**a**) the material layout, (**b**) post-processed geometry model.

3.2. *Comparative Case Studies*

To demonstrate the advantages and effectiveness of the proposed optimization model for rudder structures design, two benchmark cases are conducted, and the results are compared with state-of-the-art methods. For the two comparative examples, one is topology optimization without considering both the overhang and location of center of mass constraints, which is denoted as Comparative case study 1. The mathematical model for the optimization is as follows:

$$\begin{cases} \text{find } \mathbf{X} = (x_1, x_2, x_3, \cdots, x_n) \\ \min C(\mathbf{X}) = \mathbf{F}^T\mathbf{U} = \mathbf{U}^T\mathbf{K}\mathbf{U} = \sum\limits_{i=1}^{n} (x_i)^p \mathbf{u}_i^T \mathbf{k}_0 \mathbf{u}_i \\ \text{s.t. } \mathbf{K}\mathbf{U} = \mathbf{F} \\ \quad V = \sum\limits_{i=1}^{n} v_i \leq f V_0 = V^* \\ \quad 0 < x_{min} < x_i \leq x_{max} \leq 1 \end{cases} \tag{13}$$

The other comparative example is topology optimization considering only the overhang constraint, which is denoted as Comparative case study 2. The mathematical model for the optimization is as follows:

$$\begin{cases} \text{find } \mathbf{X} = (x_1, x_2, x_3, \cdots, x_n) \\ \min C(\mathbf{X}) = \mathbf{F}^T\mathbf{U} = \mathbf{U}^T\mathbf{K}\mathbf{U} = \sum\limits_{i=1}^{n} (x_i)^p \mathbf{u}_i^T \mathbf{k}_0 \mathbf{u}_i \\ \text{s.t. } \mathbf{K}\mathbf{U} = \mathbf{F} \\ \quad V = \sum\limits_{i=1}^{n} v_i \leq f V_0 = V^* \\ \quad 0 < x_{min} < x_i \leq x_{max} \leq 1 \\ \quad \alpha \geq \alpha_{\text{thresh}} \end{cases} \tag{14}$$

Both of the examples are based on the same design parameters except for the optimization model. The optimized results are shown in Figures 8a and 8b, respectively. The result of Comparative case study 1, shown in Figure 8a, has a mass of 0.857 kg, while the result of Comparative case study 2, shown in Figure 8b, has a mass of 0.887 kg. From the material layout, it can be found that the Comparative case study 2, which considers the overhang constraint, has enhanced self-supporting capability, reduces the need for additional support material, and improves manufacturability of the rudder.

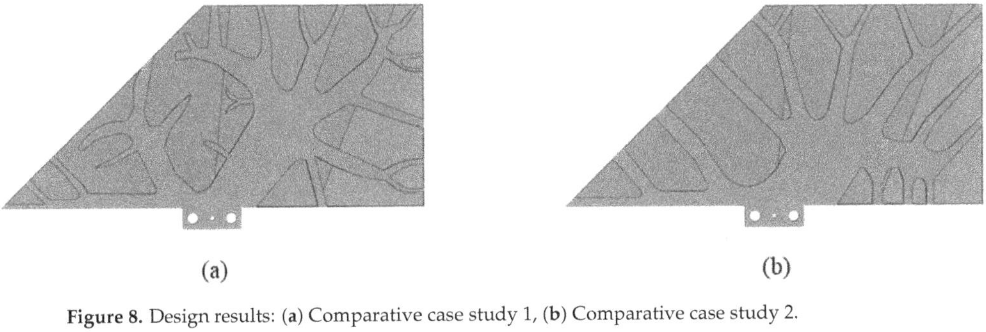

Figure 8. Design results: (**a**) Comparative case study 1, (**b**) Comparative case study 2.

3.3. Performance Comparison

3.3.1. Comparison of Mass Center

The mass centers of each optimized rudder structure are shown in Figure 9. The distance from the mass center to the rotation axis is $x_C = 12.49$ for the Comparative case study 1, and the distance is $x_C = 15.17$ for the Comparative case study 2, which considers the overhang constraint. It should be noted that these designs do not account for mass center constraints. The mass center is changed to $x_C = 12.52$ when considering both of overhang and mass center constraints. Compared with the result of Comparative case study 2, the mass center moves forward by 17.49% after introducing mass center constraints. When comparing with the result of Comparative case study 1, the mass center moves backward by 0.24%, but shows better manufacturability performance. These comparison results demonstrate the effectiveness of the consideration of the mass center constraint to control the mass center of the optimized structure. This also highlights the necessity of integrating mass center constraints alongside manufacturing constraints to achieve a more balanced and effective design.

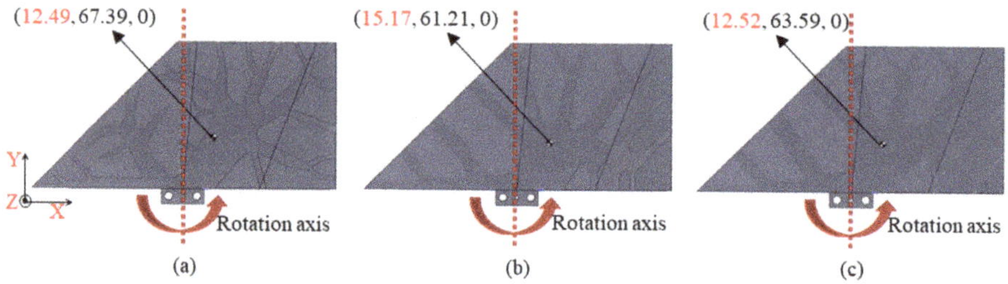

Figure 9. Mass center of different design results: (**a**) mass center of Comparative case study 1, (**b**) Mass center of Comparative case study 2, (**c**) mass center of result obtained by proposed optimization model.

3.3.2. Comparison of Static Performance

Under the same boundary conditions, static analysis for the three different design results is conducted. The simulation results are shown in Figure 10, in which the maximum displacement of the Comparative case study 1 is 16.368 mm, that of the Comparative case study 2 with the overhang constraint is 16.399 mm, and that of the one with the overhang and mass center constraints is 16.547 mm. Compared with the Comparative case study 1, the maximum displacement of Comparative case study 2 increases about 0.19%, while the maximum displacement of the rudder structure obtained by the proposed optimization model increases by 1.08%. The results show that the proposed optimization model integrates the design of other functions while maintaining structural stiffness and achieves the design of a multifunctional structure.

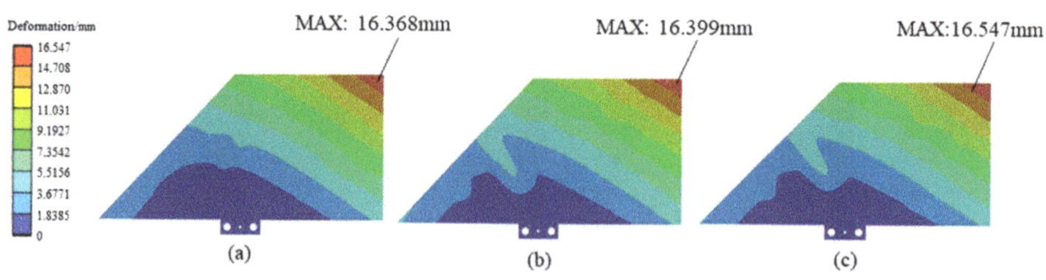

Figure 10. Displacement nephogram of different design results: (**a**) displacement nephogram of Comparative case study 1, (**b**) displacement nephogram of Comparative case study 2, (**c**) displacement nephogram of result obtained by proposed optimization model.

3.3.3. Comparison of Flutter Performance

The flutter analysis of the three different rudder structures is performed using the *p–k* method. The boundary condition constrains the six degrees of freedom of the circular holes shown in Figure 5b, and the flight speed is 6 Mach. In the *p–k* root-locus calculation, we track the eigen-pairs at every speed; the first bending (B1) and second torsional (T2) mode shapes are identified from their modal strain-energy content and used to interpret the instability mechanism. The analysis results are shown in Figure 11, and the critical flutter speed can be determined by evaluating the intersection point in the *v*-*g* (velocity-damping) and *v*-*f* (velocity-frequency) diagram. At the critical velocity, the B1 and T2 curves in Figure 11 coalesce in frequency, and their damping simultaneously changes sign, confirming a classical bending—torsion coupled flutter rather than a single-mode divergence. This explicit consideration of mode shapes and natural frequencies ensures that the chosen V_F is physically meaningful, not a mere velocity bound. From Figure 11, the flutter speed of the Comparative case study 1 is 3518 m/s, and that of Comparative case study 2 is 3327 m/s. Compared with Comparative case study 1, the flutter speed of Comparative case study 2 decreases by 5.42%. When both the overhang and mass center constraints are considered, the flutter speed increases significantly to 3759 m/s, and has a 6.84% improvement over the Comparative case study 1. These results indicate that the Comparative case study 2, which only considers the overhang constraint, has the worst flutter performance; this is because its mass is far from the rotation axis. By relocating the mass centroid closer to the torsional axis, the combined-constraint design shifts the B1–T2 coupling to a higher speed and thereby enhances aeroelastic stability. The consideration of mass center constraints can effectively affect the flutter performance of the rudder and enhance the aerodynamic stability of the structure.

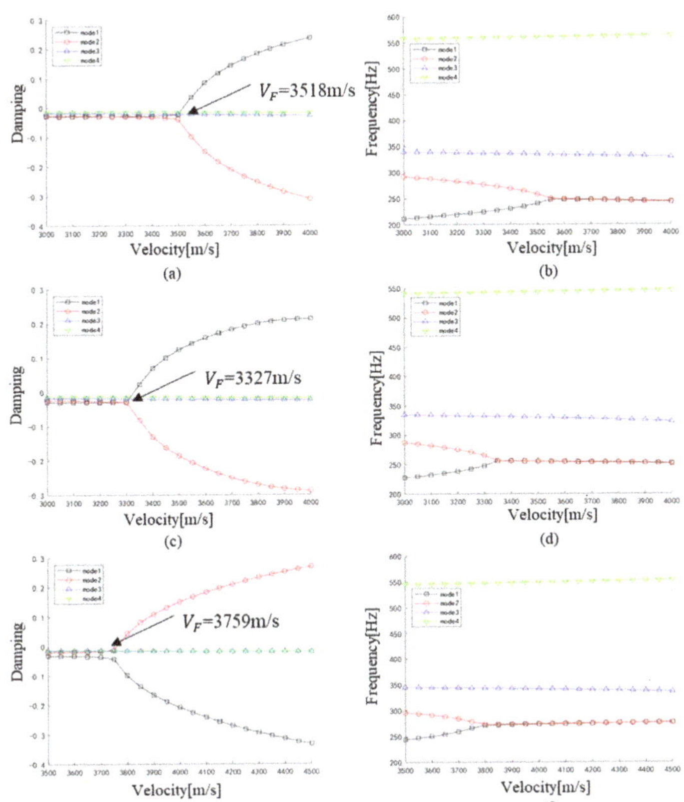

Figure 11. Flutter analysis results: (**a**,**b**) are the *v*-*g* and *v*-*f* diagrams for the Comparative case study 1, (**c**,**d**) are the *v*-*g* and *v*-*f* diagrams for the Comparative case study 2, and (**e**,**f**) are the *v*-*g* and *v*-*f* diagrams for the optimal result obtained by the proposed method.

3.3.4. Comparison of Manufacturing Process Simulation

The additive manufacturing process simulation of Selective Laser Melting (SLM) was conducted for the three different rudder structures to verify the manufacturability. Ti-6Al-4V was used as the material, and inherent strains (−0.0131, −0.0102, 0.0165) were applied to each element layer by layer using the element birth–death technique [25]. As illustrated in Figure 12, the left column of subfigures shows the rudder structures and their supports, while the right column of subfigures displays the results of residual deformation. For Comparative case study 1, about 0.32 kg of internal support material should be added to manufacture this optimized rudder structure, and the maximum residual deformation is 1.20 mm. For Comparative case study 2, the maximum residual deformation decreases to 1.19 mm, and the support material is significantly reduced to 0.17 kg because of the overhang constraint. When both the overhang and mass center constraints are applied, the residual deformation is further reduced to 1.03 mm, while the support material remains at 0.17 kg. It can be concluded that compared with Comparative case study 1, the consideration of overhang and mass center constraints leads to a 14.2% reduction in maximum residual deformation and a 46.9% reduction in support material usage, thereby improving manufacturing efficiency.

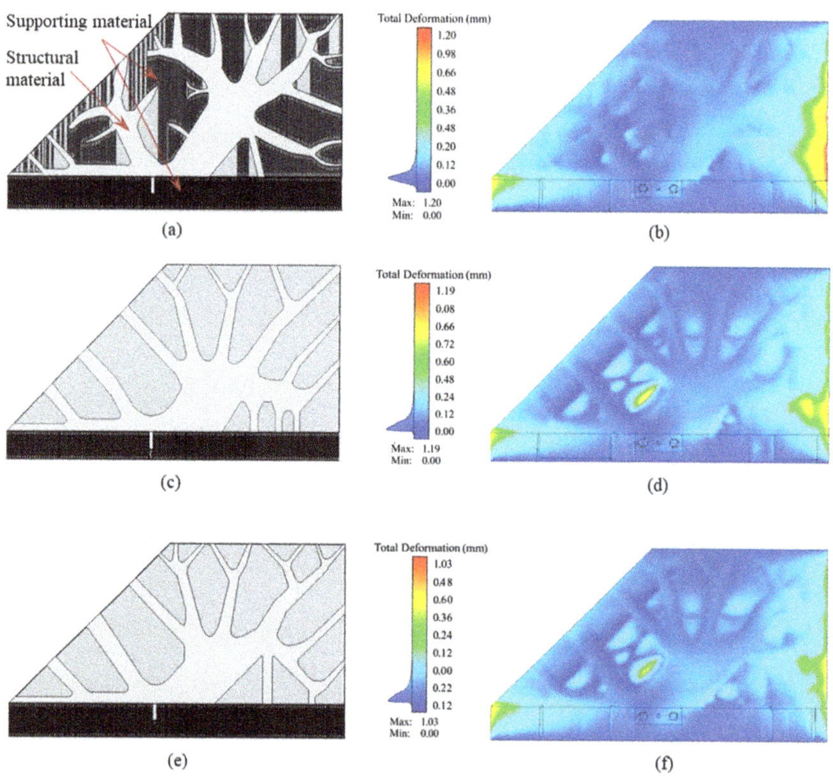

Figure 12. Schematic of sandwich rudder support structure with SLM simulated residual displacement cloud: (**a**,**b**) are optimized rudder structure with supporting and residual deformation nephogram for the Comparative case study 1, (**c**,**d**) are optimized rudder structure with supporting and residual deformation nephogram for the Comparative case study 1, and (**e**,**f**) are optimized rudder structure with supporting and residual deformation nephogram for the optimal result obtained by proposed method.

3.3.5. Discussion

According to the performance comparison in Table 2, the rudder structure of Comparative case study 1 exhibits the minimum maximum displacement of 16.368 mm, indicating superior stiffness compared with other design cases. The consideration of additive manufacturing-related overhang constraints results in a slight reduction in stiffness, but the optimized structures still show high stiffness performance for practical engineering applications.

Table 2. Analysis of comparative performance metrics for different constrained sandwich rudders.

Performance	Comparative Case Study 1	Comparative Case Study 1	Result Obtained by Proposed Method	Rate
Maximum deformation (mm)	16.368	16.399	16.547	1.08% ↑
Flutter speed (m/s)	3518	3327	3759	6.84% ↑
Mass (kg)	0.857	0.887	0.875	2.05% ↑
Residual deformation (mm)	1.20	1.19	1.03	14.2% ↓
Support weight (kg)	0.32	0.17	0.17	46.9% ↓
Mass Center of x_c	12.49	15.17	12.52	0.24% ↑

In terms of flutter performance, the Comparative case study 1 has a critical flutter speed of 3518 m/s. The flutter speed of Comparative case study 2, which considers the overhang constraint, decreases to 3327 m/s due to the rearward shift in the mass center. When both overhang and mass center constraints are considered, the mass distribution is optimized, and the center of mass shifts forward, the flutter speed increases to 3759 m/s, and shows an improvement of 6.85% over the Comparative case study 1. This demonstrates that the mass center constraint can effectively improve the flutter performance.

From a manufacturing perspective, the consideration of additive manufacturing-related overhang constraints improves self-supporting capability. As a result, support material usage is reduced by 46.9%, and manufacturing efficiency is significantly improved. Additionally, SLM simulation shows that the maximum residual deformation is reduced by 14.2% when both the overhang and mass center constraints are applied, further verifying the effectiveness of the proposed method.

In summary, the proposed topology optimization approach—integrating overhang and mass center constraints—improves the manufacturability and dynamic performance of the rudder structure while preserving fundamental structural stiffness. This approach provides a practical and effective solution for the engineering design of high-performance, additively manufacturable rudder components.

4. Conclusions

In this study, a topology optimization approach for multifunctional rudder structure design is proposed based on the density-based method. Both overhang angle and mass center constraints were simultaneously integrated into the optimization mathematical model to achieve optimized rudder structures with lightweight, enhanced additive manufacturing adaptability and high flutter performance. The main conclusions are as follows:

(1) This study incorporates additive manufacturing overhang constraints into the density-based topology optimization formulation. Self-supporting rudder structures with high stiffness are obtained. The simulation results indicate that the maximum displacement increases by only 1.08% compared to the result of conventional design without overhang constraint, whereas the maximum residual deformation is reduced by 14.2%, and support material usage is decreased by 46.9%. These improvements greatly enhance printing stability and material utilization.

(2) The synergistic integration of mass center constraints with AM-oriented overhang constraints achieves dual optimization: (1) controlled mass redistribution—the mass center deviation is limited to 0.24%; (2) significant improvements in rudder flutter performance, demonstrating 6.85% improvement in flutter analysis, and the critical flutter speed increases from 3327 m/s to 3759 m/s, thereby enhancing aerodynamic stability.

In summary, the developed optimization framework effectively improves additive manufacturing compatibility and flutter performance of rudder structures while maintaining structural stiffness. It provides a practical and implementable strategy for the design of high-performance rudder structures and demonstrates strong potential for engineering applications.

Author Contributions: Conceptualization, H.Z. and X.D.; methodology, H.Z., S.S. and X.D.; software, S.S.; validation, S.S., J.Y. and M.X.; formal analysis, S.S. and M.X.; investigation, H.Z. and S.S.; resources, H.Z. and X.D.; data curation, S.S.; writing—original draft preparation, H.Z. and S.S.; writing—review and editing, H.Z. and S.S.; visualization, S.S. and J.Y.; supervision, H.Z. and X.D.; project administration, H.Z. and X.D.; funding acquisition, H.Z. All authors have read and agreed to the published version of the manuscript.

Funding: This research was funded by National Natural Science Foundation of China grant number 52375257, Shanghai Pujiang Program grant number 24PJD073.

Data Availability Statement: The paper contains an adequate amount of details on the methodology and implementation. All the data generated or analyzed during this study are included in this paper. The data that support the findings of this study are available from the corresponding author upon reasonable request.

Conflicts of Interest: The authors declare that they have no known competing financial interests or personal relationships that could have appeared to influence the work reported in this paper.

References

1. Remouchamps, A.; Bruyneel, M.; Fleury, C.; Grihon, S. Application of a bi-level scheme including topology optimization to the design of an aircraft pylon. *Struct. Multidiscip. Optim.* **2011**, *44*, 739–750. [CrossRef]
2. Zhu, J.H.; Zhang, W.H.; Xia, L. Topology Optimization in Aircraft and Aerospace Structures Design. *Arch. Comput. Methods Eng.* **2016**, *23*, 595–622. [CrossRef]
3. Kang, Z.; Wang, X.; Wang, R. Topology optimization of space vehicle structures considering attitude control effort. *Finite Elem. Anal. Des.* **2009**, *45*, 431–438. [CrossRef]
4. Hansen, L.U.; Horst, P. Multilevel optimization in aircraft structural design evaluation. *Comput. Struct.* **2007**, *86*, 104–118. [CrossRef]
5. Wang, B.; Hao, P.; Li, G.; Tian, K.; Du, K.; Wang, X.; Zhang, X.; Tang, X. Two-stage size-layout optimization of axially compressed stiffened panels. *Struct. Multidiscip. Optim.* **2014**, *50*, 313–327. [CrossRef]
6. Kranz, J.; Herzog, D.; Emmelmann, C. Design guidelines for laser additive manufacturing of lightweight structures in TiAl6V4. *J. Laser Appl.* **2014**, *27*, S14001. [CrossRef]
7. He, L.; Gilbert, M.; Johnson, T.; Pritchard, T. Conceptual design of AM components using layout and geometry optimization. *Comput. Math. Appl.* **2019**, *78*, 2308–2324. [CrossRef]
8. Vanek, J.; Galicia, J.A.G.; Benes, B. Clever support: Efficient support structure generation for digital fabrication. *Comput. Graph. Forum* **2014**, *33*, 117–125. [CrossRef]
9. Langelaar, M. An additive manufacturing filter for topology optimization of print-ready designs. *Struct. Multidiscip. Optim.* **2017**, *55*, 871–883. [CrossRef]
10. Luo, Y.; Sigmund, O.; Li, Q.; Liu, S. Additive manufacturing oriented topology optimization of structures with self-supported enclosed voids. *Comput. Methods Appl. Mech. Eng.* **2020**, *372*, 113385. [CrossRef]
11. Gaynor, A.T.; Guest, J.K. Topology optimization considering overhang constraints: Eliminating sacrificial support material in additive manufacturing through design. *Struct. Multidiscip. Optim.* **2016**, *54*, 1157–1172. [CrossRef]
12. Han, S.Y.; Xu, B.; Zhao, L.; Xie, Y.M. Topology optimization of continuum structures under hybrid additive-subtractive manufacturing constraints. *Struct. Multidiscip. Optim.* **2019**, *60*, 2571–2595. [CrossRef]
13. Zhou, P.; Ou, G.; Du, J. Topology optimization of continua considering mass and inertia characteristics. *Struct. Multidiscip. Optim.* **2019**, *60*, 429–442. [CrossRef]

14. Li, R.; Gao, C.; Jing, W.; Qian, Y. Moving mass control and performance analysis for aerospace vehicle. *J. Astronaut.* **2010**, *31*, 2165–2171.
15. Tang, J.; Bai, S.; Xie, W.; Wu, J.; Jiang, H.; Sun, Y. Analysis of Influence of Stratospheric Airship's Key Parameter Perturbation on Motion Mode. *Aerospace* **2023**, *10*, 329. [CrossRef]
16. Xusheng, M.; Rui, H.; Qitong, Z.; Haiyan, H. Machine learning-based active flutter suppression for a flexible flying-wing aircraft. *J. Sound Vib.* **2022**, *529*, 116916. [CrossRef]
17. Xiaopeng, Z.; Yuewu, W.; Wei, Z. Vibration and flutter characteristics of GPL-reinforced functionally graded porous cylindrical panels subjected to supersonic flow. *Acta Astronaut.* **2021**, *183*, 89–100. [CrossRef]
18. Cao, Q.; Dai, N.; Bai, J.; Dai, H. A dimensionality reduction optimization method for thin-walled parts to realize mass center control and lightweight design. *Eng. Optim.* **2024**, *57*, 1291–1307. [CrossRef]
19. Phongkumsing, S.; Wilde, K.; Fujino, Y. Analytical study on flutter suppression by eccentric mass method on FEM model of long-span suspension bridge. *J. Wind Eng. Ind. Aerodyn.* **2001**, *89*, 515–534. [CrossRef]
20. Wang, D.; Yang, Y.; Yi, Z.; Su, X. Research on the fabricating quality optimization of the overhanging surface in SLM process. *Int. J. Adv. Manuf. Technol.* **2013**, *65*, 1471–1484. [CrossRef]
21. Andrew, T.G.; Johnson, T.E. Eliminating occluded voids in additive manufacturing design via a projection-based topology optimization scheme. *Addit. Manuf.* **2020**, *33*, 101149. [CrossRef]
22. Lazarov, S.B.; Sigmund, O. Filters in topology optimization based on Helmholtz-type differential equations. *Int. J. Numer. Methods Eng.* **2011**, *86*, 765–781. [CrossRef]
23. Wang, F.; Lazarov, S.B.; Sigmund, O. On projection methods, convergence and robust formulations in topology optimization. *Struct. Multidiscip. Optim.* **2011**, *43*, 767–784. [CrossRef]
24. Wang, Q.; Ding, X.; Shi, X.; Li, H.; Zhang, H. Concurrent topology optimization for double-skin stiffened structures considering external shape and modal characteristics. *Struct. Multidiscip. Optim.* **2025**, *68*, 49. [CrossRef]
25. Yan, X.; Yang, R.; Lian, G.; Jie, Y. Residual deformation prediction in metal 3D printing process based on modified inherent strain theory. *Appl. Laser* **2023**, *43*, 29–36.

computation

MDPI

Article

Simultaneous Multi-Objective and Topology Optimization: Effect of Mesh Refinement and Number of Iterations on Computational Cost

Daniel Miler, Matija Hoić *, Rudolf Tomić, Andrej Jokić and Robert Mašović

University of Zagreb, Faculty of Mechanical Engineering and Naval Architecture, Ivana Lučića 5, 10002 Zagreb, Croatia; daniel.miler@fsb.unizg.hr (D.M.); rudolf.tomic@fsb.unizg.hr (R.T.); andrej.jokic@fsb.unizg.hr (A.J.); robert.masovic@fsb.unizg.hr (R.M.)
* Correspondence: matija.hoic@fsb.unizg.hr

Abstract: In this study, a multi-objective optimization procedure with embedded topology optimization was presented. The procedure simultaneously optimizes the spatial arrangement and topology of bodies in a multi-body system. The multi-objective algorithm determines the locations of supports, joints, active loads, reactions, and load magnitudes, which serve as inputs for the topology optimization of each body. The multi-objective algorithm dynamically adjusts domain size, support locations, and load magnitudes during optimization. Due to repeated topology optimization calls within the genetic algorithm, the computational cost is significant. To address this, two reduction strategies are proposed: (I) using a coarser mesh and (II) reducing the number of iterations during the initial generations. As optimization progresses, Strategy I gradually refines the mesh, while Strategy II increases the maximum allowable iteration count. The effectiveness of both strategies is evaluated against a baseline (Reference) without reductions. By the 25th generation, all approaches achieve similar hypervolume values (Reference: 2.181; I: 2.112; II: 2.133). The computation time is substantially reduced (Reference: 42,226 s; I: 16,814 s; II: 21,674 s), demonstrating that both strategies effectively accelerate optimization without compromising solution quality.

Keywords: mechanism optimization; multi-objective optimization; topology optimization; computational cost reduction

1. Introduction

Topology optimization (TO) is a commonly used technique for designing lightweight load-bearing structures by efficiently distributing available material across a predefined domain [1]. In compliance minimization problem statements, topology optimization has been shown to improve the stiffness of a structure for a given material volume and set of input conditions within a discretized domain. The required inputs typically include domain size, support locations, available material volume fraction, and locations and magnitudes of applied loads [2]. While TO has been extended to dynamic loading scenarios [3], conventional methods generally assume fixed support locations, limiting their applicability in cases where support layouts must also be optimized.

A key limitation of traditional TO approaches is their reliance on predefined boundary conditions, which restricts their use in problems where support positions are unknown or variable. Generally, support locations are assigned on one side of the domain, leading to suboptimal solutions when real-world constraints dictate alternative layouts. To address this issue, researchers have explored methods to incorporate support location optimization within the TO framework. A comprehensive review of topology optimization methods addressing design-dependent loads and supports was conducted by [4]. Early studies provided both analytical and numerical solutions to the problem of support placement optimization [5–7]. Buhl [6] extended TO by treating support locations as additional design variables, adjusting their costs to guide placement selection. Similarly, Lee and Xie [7] introduced element-based support locations, which were included as additional design variables. Further, Panesar et al. [8] integrated the system and structural design aspects to enable the production of multi-functional parts with embedded components. This enabled the production of parts with optimal designs and embedded electrical components. Zhu et al. [9] further advanced this approach by optimizing component placement alongside structural configuration, facilitating the better integration of embedded elements.

However, these TO approaches primarily focus on single-domain structures and do not extend to multi-body systems, where interactions between multiple interconnected components must be considered. Multi-body topology optimization extends traditional topology optimization to systems with multiple interacting components, requiring considerations of contact mechanics, dynamic interactions, and structural constraints. Firstly, Ma et al. [10] developed a multi-domain topology optimization to enable controlled material distribution across subdomains; however, the approach was still limited to one body. Ghandriz et al. [11] optimized multiple interconnected components using the modified Solid Isotropic Material with Penalization (SIMP) method to avoid numerical instabilities, while sensitivities were approximated to reduce computational costs. However, their study did not account for variable support locations. Further, Fernandez et al. [12] aimed to solve the topology optimization problem of 3D deformable bodies in contact, which was performed using mortar segment-to-segment discretization and adjoint sensitivity analysis to improve computational efficiency. Sun and Hu [13] focused on the dynamic topology optimization of flexible multi-body systems, addressing time-varying systems and coupled optimization strategies. Fu et al. [14] integrated trajectory and topology optimization, utilizing the mode-superposition and adjoint sensitivity analysis to optimize both structure and control design variables. All the listed advancements improved the capabilities of multi-body topology optimization, making it more efficient and applicable to robotics, aerospace, and automated machinery fields. All the referenced papers solely utilize gradient-based optimization methods, which are ineffective when design variables include discrete dimensions, support locations, or actuator positions.

While gradient-based methods have been used for actuator placement and TO problems [15], they are limited to continuous design variables, struggle with discrete variables, cannot guarantee global optimality for non-convex problems [16], and are not suitable for multi-objective (MO) problems [17]. This limitation makes them less effective for problems involving multi-body systems (mechanisms in particular) where contact problems (e.g., cams, gears, or robotic grippers) introduce non-smooth forces due to sudden engagement or disengagement. The optimization of parallel mechanisms or robotic arms with complex workspace constraints can lead to highly irregular response surfaces, causing gradients to be misleading [18]. Similarly, problems with backlash, friction, and hysteresis are also difficult to model with smooth functions due to nonlinearities [19,20]. Additional difficulties might arise when designing near the elastic limit of the material due to the possible occurrence of plastic deformations, which might lead to structural buckling or failure events introducing sharp changes in the response. In that case, stochastic search methods offer better adaptability. Although stochastic search methods such as genetic algorithms or particle swarm optimization come with computational cost concerns, their ability to explore complex, non-convex search spaces make them well-suited for this class of optimization problems [20,21].

Real-world engineering problems are regularly solved using stochastic search methods, which also facilitate finding the global minimum. MO optimization is widely used in engineering applications, enabling the simultaneous optimization of objectives such as weight, stiffness, displacement, and cost [20,22,23]. Optimization problems are formulated using objective (fitness) functions supplemented by boundary conditions and design variable ranges [24]. Since structural modifications require computational models to be predefined, MO algorithms optimize dimensions rather than the structural topology. Due to the complexity of engineering problems, stochastic methods such as genetic algorithms, particle swarm optimization, and simulated annealing are often employed [25–28].

For this reason, in this paper we propose a unified approach that simultaneously optimizes (1) multi-body system topology and (2) support and load locations, along with strategies for the reduction in its computational cost. The optimization framework integrates topology and multi-objective optimization to comprehensively optimize multi-body mechanisms. The joints, actuators, and individual component geometries are considered, ensuring that the entire system is optimized rather than treating components in isolation. Two strategies for reducing the computational cost of the approach were proposed and their effects on the costs and quality of results were evaluated. Finally, the presented approach consistently produces near-optimal solutions, effectively avoiding common suboptimal local minima.

Although this study presents a 2D case for proof of concept, the proposed methodology is extendable to 3D structures, making it applicable to robotic systems, compliant mechanisms, and structural assemblies. The remainder of the paper is structured as follows: The optimization method is outlined in Section 2, which also includes the method flowchart and the underlying mathematical model. Next, strategies for reducing the computational cost are proposed in Section 3. Further, an example case is presented in Section 4, covering the mathematical problem formulation. Section 5 contains the results and comparisons between the results obtained using the computational cost reduction strategies proposed earlier. Results are compared visually and using the hypervolume indicator values with the same referent point. Finally, the conclusions and limitations of the paper are given in Section 6.

2. Optimization Method Overview

The optimization procedure for multi-body systems applicable to mechanisms has been developed (as shown in Figure 1). The considered multi-body system consists of bodies connected via hinged joints, with one or more bodies being fixed using supports or encastres. Each body within the system is considered as a separate domain during topology optimization. As an input, a simple analytical mechanical model of the system is created (a set of equilibrium equations), containing loads, boundary conditions, and variable ranges, enabling the calculation of loads in connecting elements, actuators, and supports. Connections between domains are then modelled by abstracting joints with fixed degrees-of-freedom (DoFs) and reaction forces along specific DoFs. The domain sizes used in topology optimization are scaled based on body lengths and the system may additionally include linear actuators, such as hydraulic or pneumatic cylinders, modelled as rigid bodies.

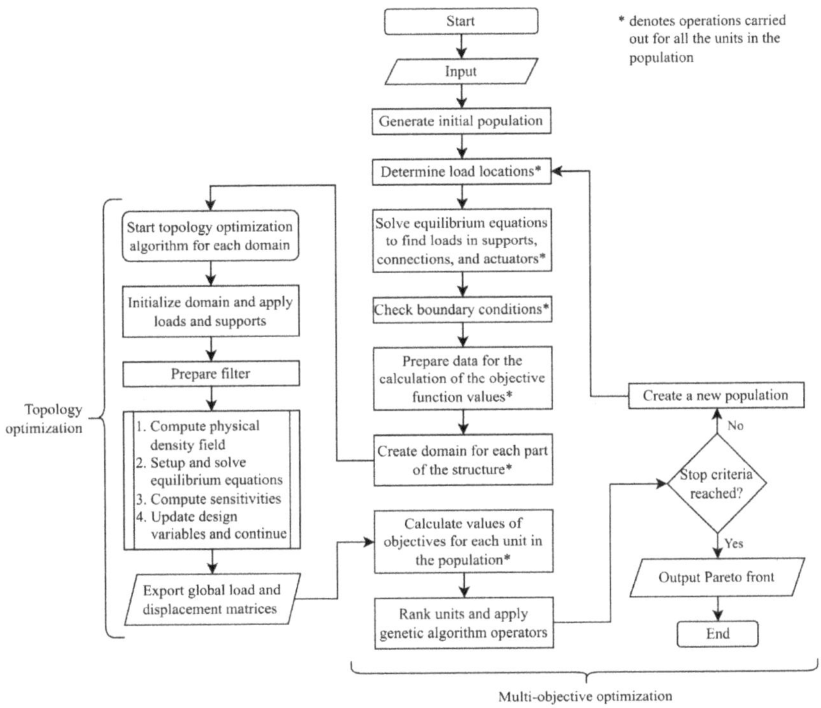

Figure 1. Optimization process diagram.

The procedure simultaneously optimizes the macrogeometry of the system (lever lengths, distances between joints, locations of load points) and the geometry of individual parts to reduce their mass. This is achieved through a two-layer optimization approach, where a multi-objective optimization algorithm determines the multi-body system microgeometry, while a nested topology optimization algorithm refines the structures of individual bodies. The multi-objective algorithm incorporates design variables, boundary conditions, and objective functions to optimize the overall system. It calls on the topology optimization algorithm, which computes the compliance-related objective function values (for more details, see Section 2.2).

The optimization procedure considered in this paper uses two objective functions—the volume ratio of the multi-body system (f1) and the total compliance (f2). Both values were calculated using the topology optimization algorithm (see Section 2.2). The mechanical model deconstructs the system into separate domains, expressing their interactions through loads and supports. Each domain is processed individually, using the loads and support data obtained from the analytical model. Possible domain overlapping was not possible since it was assumed that bodies were not located in the same plane (topology optimization was performed in a 2D space) and were then joined by joints normal to each of the planes, ensuring no physical overlaps occurred between them. Loads in joints were assigned based on the equilibrium equations derived from the mechanical model, with reaction forces depending on joint and support positions defined by the multi-objective optimizer.

The algorithm optimizes the internal structure of each domain within the population of candidate solutions, generating global load vectors (F), global displacement vectors

(U), and the graphical representations of optimal topologies, and were obtained for all the domains of all units. The optimization problem is formulated as:

$$\begin{aligned}
&\min_{\mathbf{x}\in\mathbb{R}^n}(f_1(\mathbf{x}), f_2(\mathbf{x})) \\
&\text{subjected to}: \quad h_j(\mathbf{x}) = 0, \qquad j = 1,\ldots,p \\
&\qquad\qquad\qquad g_k(\mathbf{x}) = 0, \qquad k = 1,\ldots,r \\
&\qquad\qquad\qquad \mathbf{K}_i\mathbf{U}_i - \mathbf{F}_i = 0 \qquad i = 1,\ldots,n \\
&\qquad\qquad\qquad V_i(\mathbf{y}_i) - v_i \cdot V_{\Omega i} = 0 \quad i = 1,\ldots,n \\
&\text{where}: \qquad f_1(\mathbf{x}) = \frac{\sum_{i=1}^{n} v_i \cdot N_i}{\sum_{i=1}^{n} N_i}; f_2(\mathbf{x}) = \sum_{i=1}^{n} c_i(\mathbf{y}_i) = \sum_{i=1}^{n} \mathbf{U}_i^T\mathbf{K}_i\mathbf{U}_i \\
&\qquad\qquad\qquad \mathbf{x} = \begin{bmatrix} v_1 & v_2 & \ldots & v_n & l_1 & l_2 & \ldots & l_m \end{bmatrix}
\end{aligned} \tag{1}$$

where n is the number of domains; p and r are total numbers of equality ($h_\mathrm{i}(\mathbf{x})$) and inequality ($g_\mathrm{k}(\mathbf{x})$) constraints, respectively; $\mathbf{y}_\mathrm{i}$ is the material distribution of the i-th domain; $V_\mathrm{i}(\mathbf{y}_\mathrm{i})$ is the volume of the material in the i-th domain; v_i is the volume fraction of the i-th domain and $V_{\Omega\mathrm{i}}$ is the total volume of the i-th domain; N_i is the total number of elements in the i-th domain; $c_\mathrm{i}(\mathbf{y}_\mathrm{i})$ is the compliance of the i-th domain; and $\mathbf{x}$ is the vector containing the design variables, with l denoting lengths between supports/joints.

The optimization was carried out using MATLAB R2024b running on a Microsoft Windows 10 system with Intel i5-8500 CPU at 3.00 GHz and 32 GB of RAM. It should be noted that the optimization procedures were carried out without the use of parallel computing which could be implemented in future work to further reduce computational costs.

2.1. Multi-Objective Optimization Settings

The optimization problem is non-convex due to the discrete–continuous design variables. Thus, the genetic algorithm was used to solve the above-described multi-objective optimization problem due to its ability to solve non-convex and non-smooth optimization problems [16,21,24]. The following settings were used as default values in this paper: population size n_pop = 100, number of generations n_gen = 25, the crossover distribution index e_tac = 20, and the mutation constant e_tam = 20. While larger n_pop and n_gen would surely yield higher-quality solutions, they would also significantly increase the computational costs of the optimization. The number of design variables depends on the number of bodies n in the multi-body system and its structure, which affects the number of linkages.

Further, the multi-objective optimization algorithm also incorporated the mechanical model of the example case to obtain the data necessary for the calculation of the objective function values. All the necessary values were then input to topology optimization algorithm to obtain the minimum compliance of every domain, which was needed to determine the objective function values of all the units within the population. Given that the proposed procedure was focused on the bi-objective problems, Non-dominated Sorting Genetic Algorithm II (NSGA-II) [28] was used to carry out the multi-objective optimization due to its wide application and good results in solving such problems [29]. The implementation provided in [30] was used. The selected algorithm has a fast non-dominated sorting approach and employs the elitism mechanism to preserve the best solutions across generations. It has a broad application in engineering optimization tasks where maintaining diversity along the Pareto front, as well as ensuring convergence, is vital. Although other evolutionary MO algorithms could also be used, such as SPEA2 or HypE [29,31], NSGA-II was chosen due to its robustness, simplicity, and availability in open-source implementations. It also enables fast non-dominated sorting, maintains the diversity of solutions through crowding distance, and is widely used to optimize mechanical designs.

2.2. Topology Optimization Settings

The topology optimization was carried out as a sub-program of the multi-objective optimization. For each evaluation of the objective function, a topology optimization algorithm was applied to optimize the structure of each body within the multi-body system. The domain sizes were determined based on the lengths of the bodies; each body was considered to be a linkage between either two joints, the joint and the load, or the joint and the support. All the domain heights were set to *nely* = 100 and domain lengths to *nelx* = 100 + l_i, where linkage length l was rounded to the nearest integer. Hence, the domain sizes were changed based on the length of the observed body. The maximum number of iterations was set to *max_iter* = 25.

The SIMP method with density filtering was used to carry out the topology optimization and the relaxed Heaviside projection was used to increase the sharpness of the material distribution. The aim was to obtain the minimum compliance topology and the implementation by Ferrari and Sigmund [2] was used to carry out the calculations. It should be noted that the authors are aware that the selected algorithm is educational and that there are implementations with a lower computational cost. However, it is selected as it is very clear, widely available, and researchers from multiple fields are familiar with it. The default values were used: penalty was *penal* = 3, the zero-Neumann filter was used for boundary conditions, and the minimum radius of the filter was *rmin* = 3. A filter radius was constant throughout the manuscript and was expressed in element lengths. This way, the mesh refinement was limited so that the element size never became too small relative to the filter radius, ensuring the filter remained effective. The Rrelaxed Heaviside projection filtering scheme corresponded to ft = 3 and parameters *eta* and *beta* of 0.5 and 2 were used, respectively. Finally, the move limit was *move* = 0.2.

The code was slightly altered to enable the optimization procedure to be carried out with changes limited to enabling the input of additional variables to facilitate the introduction of cost-reducing strategies. Further, it was necessary to alter the definitions of supports and loads (their positions and magnitudes) to reflect the example case. Finally, segments of the code related to printing the numerical and graphical outputs were removed to reduce the computational cost.

3. Strategies for Reducing the Computational Cost

The computational cost of the proposed algorithm is predominantly affected by the following three factors:

- The number of topology optimization algorithm runs—The multi-objective optimization algorithm starts the topology optimization algorithm when analyzing the values of the objective functions. The total number of runs is equal to the product of the number of bodies in the multi-body system, the number of generations, and the population size. In this paper, its effect on the computational cost was not considered as it was rather linear; hence, all three values were taken as constant.
- Mesh refinement/coarsening—Increasing the number of elements used to discretize the domain increases both the calculation accuracy and the computational cost. The cost increase is mainly caused by the computations needed to solve the linear elasticity equations within the finite element problem [32]. Since domain size increases the size of the global stiffness matrix, it will also increase the computational cost. In this paper, variable mesh refinement was included, aiming to reduce the computational costs (Strategy I).
- The number of topology optimization algorithm iterations—Each additional iteration of the topology optimization algorithm increases the number of times the finite element

problem must be solved. As a decrease in the number of iterations will also decrease the computational cost, its effects were examined further in Strategy II.

Finally, since topology optimization is also an iterative method, increases in population and generation sizes significantly increased the time needed to obtain the solutions [33]. Thus, it should be noted that while being of good quality, the results presented in this paper can be further improved by increasing either the population size, the number of generations, or both. Moreover, iterative optimization also requires repeated sensitivity evaluations and filtering operations, further compounding the computational burden.

3.1. *Strategy I—Variable Mesh Refinement*

The aim of Strategy I was to reduce the computational cost of the proposed optimization procedure through changes in the mesh refinement. The strategy assumed that refined topologies were not necessary in the starting generations of the optimization but were indicative and helped the algorithm to navigate towards high-quality solutions. Furthermore, since topology optimization algorithms are nested within the multi-objective optimization genetic algorithm, such an approach notably decreased the number of calculations in the first operations. It must be added that mesh refinement directly affects the structural fidelity of optimized topologies. Coarser meshes are less computationally demanding, but represent geometric features in less detail, possibly compromising the accuracy of calculations. In contrast, refined meshes will yield higher structural fidelity, precise stress and compliance evaluations, and effective density filtering, while increasing the computational cost.

Hence, mesh density in the first 40% of generations was taken as 20% of the final mesh density. Next, the mesh was refined linearly until reaching the final value at 0.8 of the maximum number of generations (n_{gen}). The fully refined mesh was then used until the maximum number of generations n_{gen} was reached. For example, as shown in this paper, the final number of domain rows was taken as 100 and the maximum number of generations n_{gen} = 25. Changes in mesh refinement are described in Figure 2.

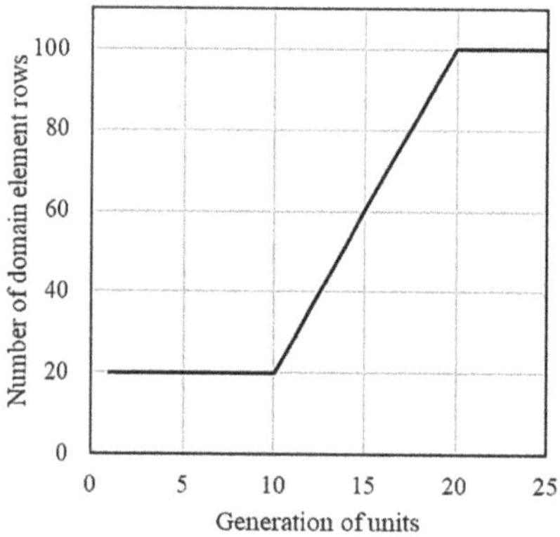

Figure 2. Changes in mesh refinement with the generations.

3.2. *Strategy II—Scalable Number of Topology Optimization Iterations*

The second strategy was based on reducing the number of topology optimization algorithm iterations. Similarly to Strategy I, it was assumed that solutions obtained during the starting generations did not have to be refined; their key role is to guide the algorithm towards the optimal solutions. The domain size was held constant using this strategy.

The number of iterations during the first 40% of generations was taken as 20% of the number of iterations in the final generations. Similarly to Strategy I, it was linearly increased until it reached the final value at 0.8 of the maximum number of generations (n_{gen}). Finally, a maximum number of iterations *max_iter* = 25 was used until reaching the maximum number of generations n_{gen}. The number of domain rows was held constant at 100 and the maximum number of generations was n_{gen} = 25. Changes in the number of iterations of the topology optimization algorithm with generations are given in Figure 3.

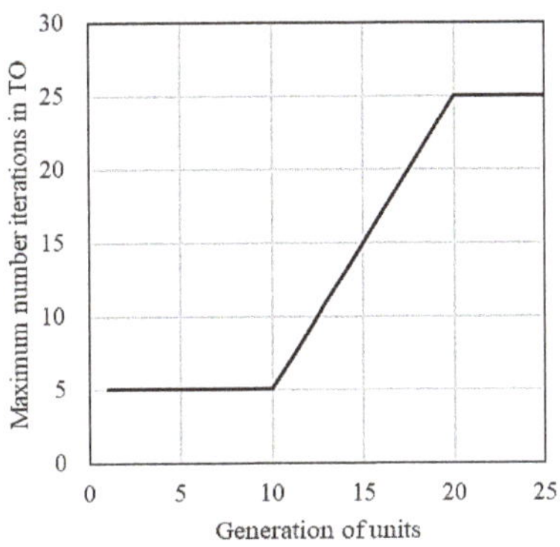

Figure 3. Changes in number of topology optimization algorithm changes with the generations.

4. Example Case

A relatively simple three-body system was selected as an example case to focus on demonstrating the behaviour of the proposed optimization procedure and the impact of cost reduction strategies. Although the system had a limited number of design variables, the coupling between multi-body and topology optimization still introduced significant computational complexity, illustrating the scalability potential of the method for more complex problems. The example multi-body system used for the evaluation of the proposed method and cost reduction strategies is given in Figure 4.

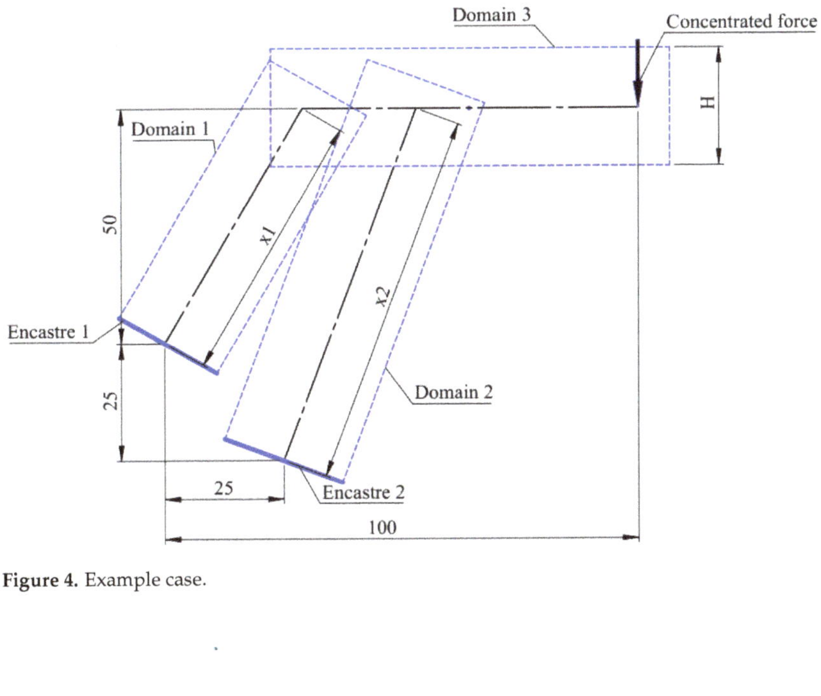

Figure 4. Example case.

The system consists of three bodies, each treated as a separate domain, connected via hinged joints (Domain 1–Domain 3, Domain 2–Domain 3). Domain 1 and Domain 2 are inclined, each anchored at one end through encastre boundary conditions (Encastre 1 and Encastre 2, respectively), while Domain 3 extends horizontally from the upper joint of Domain 1 offset by a vertical distance H and supported by Domain 2. The system is subjected to an external concentrated force applied at the free end of Domain 3. The black dashed lines within each domain represent linkage lengths, while the blue dashed outlines indicate the domain sizes used in the topology optimization. The figure highlights the decomposition of the system into separate domains, allowing for independent yet interconnected optimization, ensuring a globally optimized structural configuration.

The outlined model serves as an input for the multi-objective optimization with nested topology optimization. The macrogeometry of the system, including lever lengths, joint locations, and load positions, is optimized using a multi-objective genetic algorithm, while the microgeometry of each domain is refined using topology optimization to minimize compliance and material usage. The response of the system is computed through equilibrium equations, accounting for the interactions between the domains via reaction forces and degrees of freedom constraints. The complete mathematical model along with all the MATLAB codes used to obtain the results can be found in the Supplementary Materials, with file test_case.m containing all the joint positions and lever lengths.

Equilibrium equations were used to devise the relations between the bodies. Finally, the optimization problem was formulated as follows:

$$
\begin{array}{lll}
\min\limits_{\mathbf{x}\in\mathbb{R}^3}(f_1(\mathbf{x}), f_2(\mathbf{x})) & & \\
\text{subjected to}: & \mathbf{K}_i\mathbf{U}_i - \mathbf{F}_i = 0 & i = 1,\ldots,3 \\
 & V_i(\mathbf{y}_i) - v_i \cdot V_{\Omega i} = 0 & i = 1,\ldots,3 \\
\text{where}: & f_1(\mathbf{x}) = \frac{v_1 \cdot N_1 + v_2 \cdot N_2 + v_3 \cdot N_3}{N_1 + N_2 + N_3} & \\
 & f_2(\mathbf{x}) = c_1(\mathbf{y}_1) + c_2(\mathbf{y}_2) + c_3(\mathbf{y}_3); & \\
 & \mathbf{x} = \left[\begin{array}{ccccc} v_1 & v_2 & v_3 & L_1 & L_2 \end{array}\right] &
\end{array}
\tag{2}
$$

where the variables correspond to those introduced in Equation (1). Moreover, indices 1, 2, and 3 correspond to Domains 1, 2, and 3, respectively.

Finally, the constraints were as follows: the volume fractions v_1, v_2, and v_3 ranged between 0.3 and 0.5; lever L_1 length ranged between 65 and 75; and the lever L_2 length ranged between 85 and 100.

5. Results and Discussion

Computational cost was evaluated using the time needed to carry out the calculations. The optimization was carried out according to the proposed procedure, resulting in Pareto-optimal fronts including all the sets of optimal solutions. The results obtained using Strategies I and II were compared to the results obtained by running the optimization procedure without any mesh coarsening or number of iterations of the topology optimization algorithm. Results obtained in this way are referred to as "reference" in the continuation of this section.

Further, it should be noted that the Pareto fronts obtained in this paper were evaluated using the hypervolume indicator [34,35], a measure that calculates the area between the Pareto-optimal front and a predefined reference point in the objective space. The hypervolume indicator reflects both convergence toward the ideal solutions and the diversity of solutions along the front, with larger values indicating a better Pareto front.

Given the disparity in objective ranges, all Pareto fronts were normalized to a common scale [0, 1] using min–max normalization to enable fair comparison. Finally, the hypervolume was calculated by linearly connecting the discrete Pareto points and measuring the area dominated up to the chosen reference point. A point slightly worse than the nadir point was used as the reference point $R(1.1, 1.1)$ [36].

$$f_1 = \frac{f_1^* - f_{1\min}}{f_{1\max} - f_{1\min}};\ f_2 = \frac{f_2^* - f_{2\min}}{f_{2\max} - f_{2\min}} \tag{3}$$

where f_1^* and f_2^* denote the original values on the Pareto-optimal front, and $f_{1\min}$ and $f_{2\min}$ denote the lowest values of the volume ratio of the multi-body system and the total compliance across all Pareto fronts, respectively. Finally, $f_{1\max}$ and $f_{2\max}$ denote their maximum values and are defined analogously to $f_{1\min}$ and $f_{2\min}$.

5.1. Resulting Pareto Fronts

Figure 5 shows the evolution of Pareto-optimal solutions across four selected generations (5th, 10th, 15th, and 20th generations) for the Reference, Strategy I, and Strategy II optimization approaches. The solutions with rather high compliance were outliers and were not shown in the figure for clarity. In all the figures, the horizontal axis represents the average volume fraction, while the vertical axis is the sum of compliances. The Reference strategy defines a well-developed Pareto front in 5th generation, while Strategy I and Strategy II significantly deviate, particularly for higher compliance values. This is due to both alternative strategies still being in the early exploration phases, as intended, providing a lower number of quality solutions.

As the generations progress, in the 10th and 15th generations, the solutions from Strategy I and Strategy II move closer to the Reference Pareto front, indicating gradual convergence. It should be noted that initial search period (coarsest mesh/lowest number of TO iterations) for both strategies occurs until reaching the 10th generation. Strategy II demonstrates a more structured evolution, aligning better with the Reference front compared to Strategy I, which still shows dispersion at higher compliance values.

Linear mesh refinement and number of TO iterations lasts until reaching generation 20. By the 20th generation, both Strategy I and Strategy II closely approach the Reference set, suggesting that the optimization process has reached a stable state. Strategy II achieves better overall alignment with the Reference front, particularly in the lower compliance region, while Strategy I has more scattered solutions, indicating a slower convergence rate. This trend suggests that Strategy II is more effective in finding high-performance solutions earlier in the optimization process, while Strategy I requires more iterations to achieve similar performance levels.

Overall, the progressive improvement in solution quality for both alternative strategies is evident, with Strategy II demonstrating superior convergence behaviour and Pareto-optimality compared to Strategy I. The final generations indicate that while all three strategies ultimately yield comparable results, their convergence rates and efficiency in identifying optimal solutions differ significantly.

Outputs obtained after running the optimization procedure for $n_{\text{gen}} = 25$ generations using Strategy I and Strategy II were compared to the Reference set in Figure 6. By the final generation, Strategies I and II converged to the Reference Pareto front. Strategy I solutions are more evenly distributed along the Pareto front, aligning well with the Reference solutions, especially in the lower compliance regions. This suggests that Strategy I has effectively found a balanced set of solutions that optimize both stiffness and material usage. Strategy II exhibited slightly more scatter, particularly in the mid-to-high compliance range, indicating minor deviations and possibly a slower convergence rate compared to Strategy II.

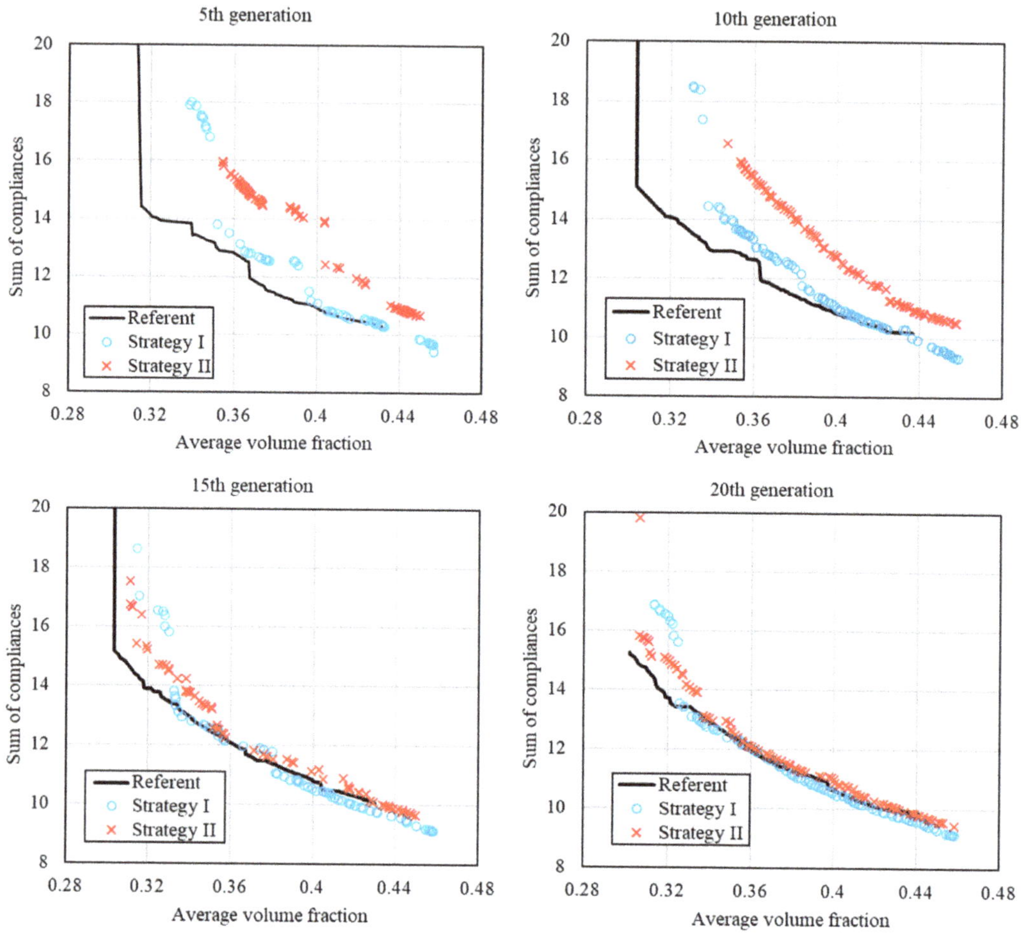

Figure 5. Pareto-optimal fronts obtained after 5, 10, 15, and 20 generations.

Overall, this final generation confirms that all three strategies ultimately achieve comparable Pareto-optimal solutions, albeit through different optimization pathways. The results obtained using Strategy I practically match those obtained using the Reference settings; at some points the Pareto front even provides better solutions. Such behaviour is due to the inherent stochastic nature of the genetic algorithms. The Strategy II results, on the other hand, yielded lower-quality points along the Pareto-optimal front, especially for designs with lower volumes.

For the Reference set, values of objective functions $f_1(\mathbf{x})$ and $f_2(\mathbf{x})$ ranged from 0.3 to 0.438 and 9.685 to 15.27, respectively. For solutions obtained using Strategy I, $f_1(\mathbf{x})$ ranged between 0.3 and 0.458 and $f_2(\mathbf{x})$ between 9.137 and 86.9. Finally, Strategy II solutions had objective function values $f_1(\mathbf{x})$ between 0.3 and 0.465 and $f_2(\mathbf{x})$ between 9.342 and 25.22.

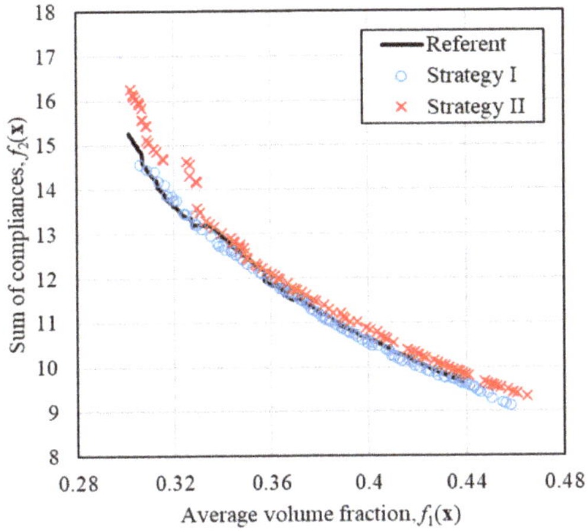

Figure 6. Pareto-optimal fronts obtained after n_{gen} = 25 generations.

5.2. Hypervolume Indicator Values and Computational Time

The HI values for Pareto fronts are given in Table 1. The results of the normalized HI analysis reveal differences in how each optimization strategy behaved across generations. The Reference case consistently achieved the highest hypervolume values, starting at 2.027 (5th generation) and gradually increasing to 2.181 (25th generation). Such a steady improvement indicated that it maintained a strong balance between the objectives. Further, its gradual increase suggests that early-stage decisions strongly influenced the long-term performance, with refinements continuing throughout the optimization process.

Table 1. Hypervolume indicator values and computational times.

Generation No.	Reference	Strategy I	Strategy II
5	2.027	1.221	1.540
10	2.039	1.170	1.688
15	2.074	1.498	1.891
20	2.177	1.605	1.924
25	2.181	2.112	2.133
Computational time	42,226 s	16,814 s (−60.2%)	21,674 s (−48.67%)

In contrast, Strategy I initially performed the worst, with the lowest hypervolume values of 1.221 and 1.170 at the 5th and 10th generation, respectively, indicating poor results in early generations. Such behaviour is due to using coarse mesh during the first 10 generations, which resulted in less-refined results. A significant improvement occurs after 15th generation (1.498), with further increases at the 20th generation (1.605) and 25th generation (2.112). By the final generation, Strategy I nearly matched the Reference solution, demonstrating that it can provide high-performance solutions. Such a rapid increase in the quality of solutions between 20th and 25th generation implied that using the coarse mesh helped to seed units in a quality and useful manner (only generations 20 to 25 were ran in a fully refined mesh) compared to the Reference set, which had a value of 2.027 after five generations of optimization using fully refined mesh.

Strategy II outperformed Strategy I in early generations, achieving higher hypervolume values at the 5th generation (1.540) and 10th generation (1.688). However, its improvement rate slowed in later generations, allowing Strategy I to surpass it by the 25th generation (2.133 vs. 2.112). This suggests that Strategy II provided better results in its early exploration but lacked the refinement needed to sustain its advantage in later iterations. By the 25th generation, all three strategies achieved similar normalized HI values, indicating that despite different optimization approaches, all strategies ultimately converged to solutions of comparable efficiency in the normalized objective space. The Reference solution provided the best results, while Strategy I demonstrated the most improvement, and Strategy II yielded strong early solutions but struggled to refine them.

Computational times were obtained for each case using the tic and toc MATLAB functions. The time elapsed to obtain the Reference set was 42,226 s, which was reduced to 16,814 s and 21,674 s when using Strategy I and Strategy II, respectively. Thus, Strategy I reduced the computational time by 60.2% and Strategy II reduced it by 48.67%, implying significant savings in necessary resources.

After accounting for both the quality of solutions on Pareto fronts and the associated computational costs, it was found that Strategy I provided the most balanced outputs. It provided high-quality solutions, nearly comparable to those found via the Reference strategy, at only a fraction of the computational time.

Finally, the stochastic nature of evolutionary algorithms should be commented on, as it introduces slight variability between optimization runs. The variations caused by the use of random variables during the optimization are mitigated via replications, i.e., repeated tests. The repeated tests indicated stable convergence patterns and minimal variation. However, future work on the subject ought to incorporate formal statistical analyses to comprehensively quantify robustness and repeatability.

5.3. Optimized Structures

To better illustrate the structures obtained for the example case, a total of nine solutions were selected from Pareto-optimal fronts—three for each of the strategies. Among the three, solutions with the lowest compliance, lowest volume fraction, and the balanced solution (50th solution on the Pareto front of the 100 in total) were selected. The selected structures are shown in Figure 7, where Domain 1 has blue borders, Domain 2 has green borders, and Domain 3 has red borders. The solutions with the lowest total compliance were nearly identical, regardless of the applied computational cost reduction strategy. Similar behaviour was observed for balanced solutions (Figure 7, 2nd row). In these, the parts described by Domain 1 and Domain 2 were straight levers; the multi-objective optimization ensured that said parts were positioned to ensure only compressive/tensile loads.

When considering solutions with the lowest volume fraction, the Reference approach followed the same principle, selecting continuous thick beams. On the other hand, a greater variety of solutions was obtained when using Strategy I or Strategy II. The Strategy I low-volume solution comprises a short and thick Domain 3 part, while Domain 1 and Domain 2 had parts with lattice structures. It can also be seen that Domain 2 (green) did not converge, as evidenced by grey areas. The Strategy II solution also included lattice structures for all three domains, with the Domain 3 solution shape being similar to those of higher-volume solutions (rows 1 and 2 of Figure 7).

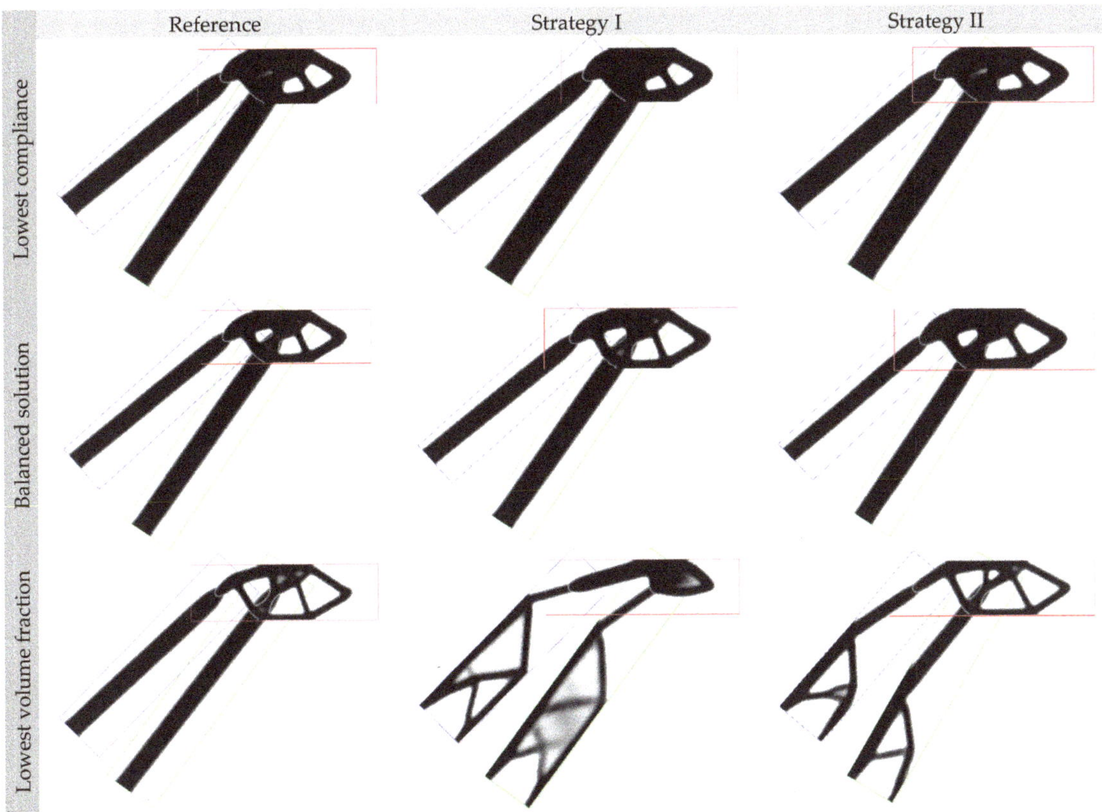

Figure 7. Selected optimal solutions at n_{gen} = 25. Lowest compliance/highest volume fraction solutions (**top**), 50th solution on the Pareto front (**middle**), lowest volume fraction/highest compliance solution (**bottom**). Domain 1 boundaries are shown in blue, Domain 2 boundaries in green, and Domain 3 boundaries in red.

6. Conclusions

In this study we introduced an optimization approach comprising multi-objective and topology optimization. The approach enables the simultaneous optimization of multi-body structures by refining both support and joint locations and internal material distribution. The sum of compliances and the overall material volume fraction were used as objective functions for an example multi-body system. Further, two strategies were developed to address the computational cost challenges associated with running multiple topology optimizations per unit within the multi-objective optimization algorithm. Strategy I uses coarser mesh in early generations, gradually refining it as the multi-objective algorithm converges. Strategy II decreases the number of topology optimization algorithm iterations in early generations, progressively increasing it in later stages of the optimization process.

In the case study addressed, the results demonstrated that both strategies significantly reduced the computational time compared to the Reference set obtained with no reductions, while achieving similar Pareto-optimal solutions. Strategy I reduced the computational time by 60.2%, while Strategy II achieved a 48.67% reduction. Hypervolume indicator (HI) values were calculated for each of the three strategies, showing that all three ultimately converged to comparable HI values, with Strategy I showing the most improvement in later generations. It should be added that Pareto front values were normalized prior to calculating the HI values to prevent one objective from dominating the hypervolume calculation. Among the two strategies, Strategy I demonstrated the most balanced trade-off between efficiency and solution quality, closely matching the performance of the Reference method. Finally, it should be noted that conclusions were made based on the observed case. Hence, additional research is needed to explore whether these observations hold for a generalized case with diverse multi-body systems, and to provide mathematical validation of their applicability across different scenarios.

The primary limitations of this study include the lack of dynamic optimization, as the proposed method is currently limited to static loading conditions. Additionally, the study is confined to 2D structures, and while theoretically extendable to 3D cases, associated challenges are yet to be addressed. The extension of the proposed methodology to 3D problems involves increased computational complexity due to a higher number of DOFs, more complex meshing requirements, and greater computational load per iteration. Future work should address these challenges by employing advanced computational techniques such as parallel processing or surrogate modelling. Finally, the scalability of the genetic-algorithm-based optimization should be further examined for larger, more complex problems, as alternative methods like surrogate models or hybrid metaheuristics may offer better performance. However, it provides an important first step for addressing the aforementioned problems.

The proposed optimization framework is feasible for integration into standard CAD/CAE workflows, primarily for preliminary design optimization. However, as noted earlier, practical applications for complex 3D scenarios may encounter an exponential growth in computational costs.

Supplementary Materials: The following supporting information can be downloaded at: https://www.mdpi.com/article/10.3390/computation13070168/s1, the MATLAB code to carry out the study.

Author Contributions: Conceptualization, D.M., M.H. and A.J.; methodology, D.M., M.H. and A.J.; validation, D.M. and M.H.; formal analysis, D.M., R.M. and R.T.; investigation, D.M., M.H. and A.J.; resources, M.H. and R.T.; data curation, D.M., R.T. and R.M.; writing—original draft preparation, D.M.; writing—review and editing, D.M., M.H., R.T., A.J. and R.M.; visualization, D.M. and R.M.; supervision, M.H. and A.J. All authors have read and agreed to the published version of the manuscript.

Funding: This research received no external funding.

Data Availability Statement: The authors declare that the data supporting the findings of this study are available within the paper and its supplementary information files. Additional data and clarifications can be provided on request from the corresponding author.

Acknowledgments: The authors have reviewed and edited the output and take full responsibility for the content of this publication.

Conflicts of Interest: The authors declare no conflicts of interest.

Abbreviations

The following abbreviations are used in this manuscript:

MO	Multi-objective optimization
NSGA-II	Non-dominated Sorting Genetic Algorithm II
TO	Topology optimization

References

1. Bendsøe, M.P.; Sigmund, O. *Topology Optimization: Theory, Methods and Applications*, 2nd ed.; Springer: Berlin/Heidelberg, Germany, 2003.
2. Ferrari, F.; Sigmund, O. A new generation 99 line Matlab code for compliance topology optimization and its extension to 3D. *Struct. Multidiscip. Optim.* **2020**, *62*, 2211–2228. [CrossRef]
3. Srinivas, G.L.; Javed, A. Topology optimization of rigid-links for industrial manipulator considering dynamic loading conditions. *Mech. Mach. Theory* **2020**, *153*, 103979. [CrossRef]
4. Deaton, J.D.; Grandhi, R.V. A survey of structural and multidisciplinary continuum topology optimization: Post 2000. *Struct. Multidiscip. Optim.* **2014**, *49*, 1–38. [CrossRef]
5. Rozvany, G.I.N.; Sokół, T. Exact truss topology optimization: Allowance for support costs and different permissible stresses in tension and compression—Extensions of a classical solution by Michell. *Struct. Multidiscip. Optim.* **2012**, *45*, 367–376. [CrossRef]
6. Buhl, T. Simultaneous topology optimization of structure and supports. *Struct. Multidiscip. Optim.* **2002**, *23*, 336–346. [CrossRef]
7. Lee, T.U.; Xie, Y.M. Simultaneously optimizing supports and topology in structural design. *Finite Elem. Anal. Des.* **2021**, *197*, 103633. [CrossRef]
8. Panesar, A.; Ashcroft, I.; Brackett, D.; Wildman, R.; Hague, R. Design framework for multifunctional addi-tive manufacturing: Coupled optimization strategy for structures with embedded functional systems. *Addit. Manuf.* **2017**, *16*, 98–106. [CrossRef]
9. Zhu, J.; Zhang, W.; Beckers, P. Integrated layout design of multi-component system. *Int. J. Numer. Methods Eng.* **2009**, *78*, 631–651. [CrossRef]
10. Ma, Z.D.; Kikuchi, N.; Pierre, C.; Raju, B. Multidomain topology optimization for structural and material designs. *J. Appl. Mech. Trans. ASME* **2006**, *73*, 565–573. [CrossRef]
11. Ghandriz, T.; Führer, C.; Elmqvist, H. Structural topology optimization of multibody systems. *Multibody Syst. Dyn.* **2017**, *39*, 135–148. [CrossRef]
12. Fernandez, F.; Puso, M.A.; Solberg, J.; Tortorelli, D.A. Topology optimization of multiple deformable bod-ies in contact with large deformations. *Comput. Methods Appl. Mech. Eng.* **2020**, *371*, 113288. [CrossRef]
13. Sun, J.; Hu, H. Dynamic topology optimization of flexible multibody systems. *Nonlinear Dyn.* **2024**, *112*, 11711–11743. [CrossRef]
14. Fu, Y.; Smith, C.S.; Li, B.; Kennedy, G.J. Simultaneous Trajectory and Topology Optimization of Flexible Multibody Systems. In Proceedings of the AIAA SciTech Forum and Exposition 2024, Orlando, FL, USA, 8–12 January 2024. [CrossRef]
15. Hu, J.; Wallin, M.; Ristinmaa, M.; Liu, Y.; Liu, S. Integrated multi-material and multi-scale optimization of compliant structure with embedded movable piezoelectric actuators. *Comput. Methods Appl. Mech. Eng.* **2024**, *421*, 116786. [CrossRef]
16. Frank, S.; Steponavice, I.; Rebennack, S. Optimal power flow: A bibliographic survey I Formulations and deterministic methods. *Energy Syst.* **2012**, *3*, 221–258. [CrossRef]
17. Papazoglou, G.; Biskas, P. Review and Comparison of Genetic Algorithm and Particle Swarm Optimiza-tion in the Optimal Power Flow Problem. *Energies* **2023**, *16*, 1152. [CrossRef]
18. Aboulissane, B.; El Bakkali, L.; El Bahaoui, J. Workspace analysis and optimization of the parallel robots based on computer-aided design approach. *Facta Univ. Ser. Mech. Eng.* **2020**, *18*, 79–89. [CrossRef]
19. Wu, Y.; Wang, Z.; Li, Y.; Chen, W.; Du, R.; Chen, Q. Characteristic modeling and control of servo systems with backlash and friction. *Math. Probl. Eng.* **2014**, *2014*, 328450. [CrossRef]
20. Miler, D.; Hoić, M. Optimisation of cylindrical gear pairs: A review. *Mech. Mach. Theory* **2021**, *156*, 104156. [CrossRef]
21. Frank, S.; Steponavice, I.; Rebennack, S. Optimal power flow: A bibliographic survey II Non-deterministic and hybrid methods. *Energy Syst.* **2012**, *3*, 259–289. [CrossRef]
22. Miler, D.; Žeželj, D.; Lončar, A.; Vučković, K. Multi-objective spur gear pair optimization focused on vol-ume and efficiency. *Mech. Mach. Theory* **2018**, *125*, 185–195. [CrossRef]
23. Ghaderian, M.; Veysi, F. Multi-objective optimization of energy efficiency and thermal comfort in an existing office building using NSGA-II with fitness approximation: A case study. *J. Build. Eng.* **2021**, *41*, 102440. [CrossRef]
24. Arora, J.S. *Introduction to Optimum Design*, 3rd ed.; Academic Press: Oxford, UK, 2004. [CrossRef]
25. Eberhart; Shi, Y. Particle swarm optimization: Developments, applications and resources. In Proceedings of the 2001 Congress on Evolutionary Computation, Seoul, Republic of Korea, 27–30 May 2001; pp. 81–86. [CrossRef]
26. Deb, K. Introduction to Genetic Algorithms for Engineering Optimization. In *New Optimization Techniques in Engineering*; Onwubolu, G.C., Babu, B.V., Eds.; Springer: Berlin, Germany, 2004; pp. 13–51.
27. van Laarhoven, P.J.M.; Aarts, E.H.L. Simulated annealing. In *Simulated Annealing: Theory and Applications*; Springer: Dordrecht, The Netherlands, 1987; p. 7.
28. Deb, K.; Pratap, A.; Agarwal, S.; Meyarivan, T. A fast and elitist multiobjective genetic algorithm: NSGA-II. *IEEE Trans. Evol. Comput.* **2002**, *6*, 182–197. [CrossRef]
29. Bader, J.; Zitzler, E. HypE: An algorithm for fast hypervolume-based many-objective optimization. *Evol. Comput.* **2011**, *19*, 45–76. [CrossRef] [PubMed]

30. Baskar, S.; Tamilselvi, S.; Varshini, P.R. MATLAB Code for Constrained NSGA II. MATLAB Central File Exchange. Available online: https://www.mathworks.com/matlabcentral/fileexchange/49806-matlab-code-for-constrained-nsga-ii-dr-s-baskar-s-tamilselvi-and-p-r-varshini (accessed on 8 July 2025).
31. Zitzler, E.; Laumanns, M.; Thiele, L. SPEA2: Improving the Strength Pareto Evolutionary Algorithm. In *Evolutionary Methods for Design Optimization and Control with Applications to Industrial Problems*; ETH Zurich, Computer Engineering and Networks Laboratory: Zürich, Switzerland, 2001; pp. 95–100. [CrossRef]
32. Yano, M.; Huang, T.; Zahr, M.J. A globally convergent method to accelerate topology optimization using on-the-fly model reduction. *Comput. Methods Appl. Mech. Eng.* **2021**, *375*, 113635. [CrossRef]
33. Mukherjee, S.; Lu, D.; Raghavan, B.; Breitkopf, P.; Dutta, S.; Xiao, M.; Zhang, W. Accelerating Large-scale Topology Optimization: State-of-the-Art and Challenges. *Arch. Comput. Methods Eng.* **2021**, *28*, 4549–4571. [CrossRef]
34. Zitzler, E.; Thiele, L. Multiobjective evolutionary algorithms: A comparative case study and the strength Pareto approach. *IEEE Trans. Evol. Comput.* **1999**, *3*, 257–271. [CrossRef]
35. Cao, Y.; Smucker, B.J.; Robinson, T.J. On using the hypervolume indicator to compare Pareto fronts: Applications to multi-criteria optimal experimental design. *J. Stat. Plan. Inference* **2015**, *160*, 60–74. [CrossRef]
36. Zitzler, E.; Knowles, J.; Thiele, L. Quality assessment of pareto set approximations. In *Multiobjective Optimization*; Lecture Notes in Computer Science (Including Subseries Lecture Notes in Artificial Intelligence and Lecture Notes in Bio-informatics) 5252 LNCS; Springer: Berlin, Germany, 2008; pp. 373–404. [CrossRef]

computation

MDPI

Article

A New Approach to Topology Optimization with Genetic Algorithm and Parameterization Level Set Function

Igor Pehnec *, Damir Sedlar *, Ivo Marinic-Kragic and Damir Vučina

Faculty of Electrical Engineering, Mechanical Engineering and Naval Architecture, University of Split, Rudjera Boskovica 32, 21000 Split, Croatia; imarinic@fesb.hr (I.M.-K.); vucina@fesb.hr (D.V.)

* Correspondence: ipehnec@fesb.hr (I.P.); dsedlar@fesb.hr (D.S.)

Abstract: In this paper, a new approach to topology optimization using the parameterized level set function and genetic algorithm optimization methods is presented. The impact of a number of parameters describing the level set function in the representation of the model was examined. Using the B-spline interpolation function, the number of variables describing the level set function was decreased, enabling the application of evolutionary methods (genetic algorithms) in the topology optimization process. The traditional level set method is performed by using the Hamilton–Jacobi transport equation, which implies the use of gradient optimization methods that are prone to becoming stuck in local minima. Furthermore, the resulting optimal shapes are strongly dependent on the initial solution. The proposed topology optimization procedure, written in MATLAB R2013b, utilizes a genetic algorithm for global optimization, enabling it to locate the global optimum efficiently. To assess the acceleration and convergence capabilities of the proposed topology optimization method, a new genetic algorithm penalty operator was tested. This operator addresses the slow convergence issue typically encountered when the genetic algorithm optimization procedure nears a solution. By penalizing similar individuals within a population, the method aims to enhance convergence speed and overall performance. In complex examples (3D), the method can also function as a generator of good initial solutions for faster topology optimization methods (e.g., level set) that rely on such initial solutions. Both the proposed method and the traditional methods have their own advantages and limitations. The main advantage is that the proposed method is a global search method. This makes it robust against entrapment in local minima and independent of the initial solution. It is important to note that this evolutionary approach does not necessarily perform better in terms of convergence speed compared to gradient-based or other local optimization methods. However, once the global optimum has been found using the genetic algorithm, convergence can be accelerated using a faster local method such as gradient-based optimization. The application and usefulness of the method were tested on typical 2D cantilever beams and Michell beams.

Keywords: topology optimization; genetic algorithm; level set function; parameterization

1. Introduction

Topology optimization is crucial in engineering because it enables the design of lightweight, strong, and efficient structures by optimally distributing material within a given domain, which is essential for applications such as aerospace, automotive, civil engineering, and additive manufacturing. The topology optimization process in structural mechanics aims to distribute material effectively to optimize load responses (bearing capacity). The literature on level set topology optimization encompasses several areas: geometry domain parameterization (SIMP [1], Level set [2]), interpolation methods (RBF, B-spline, NURBS [3]), equilibrium solving (FEM [1] and meshfree methods [4]), and optimization algorithms (gradient [1], non-gradient [5], evolutionary methods [6]).

Most existing methods rely largely on gradient-based optimization techniques, which tend to become trapped in local minima, especially for complex geometries. Furthermore, many of these approaches do not allow for the creation of new holes or topological features during the optimization process, which limits their ability to effectively explore the entire design space.

The process is primarily conceptual, with numerous papers ([1,3,7]) discussing various approaches and models. Effective shape parameterization is vital for geometry optimization. Traditional methods using FE node coordinates as shape variables led to numerous variables, gradient discontinuities, and challenges with mesh re-initialization. An alternative approach involves employing polynomials and parametric curves or surfaces, yielding a reduction in parameters introduced as optimization variables.

Various papers detail basic parameterization approaches and geometry modifications during optimization [8,9]. B-spline curves were utilized in parameterization and evolutionary methods, particularly genetic algorithms, which proved effective for shape synthesis ([8,9]). The homogenization method, which emphasizes mass distribution, is comprehensively detailed by Cappello and Mancuso [9], wherein genetic algorithms are employed to optimize material density to enhance stiffness while adhering to volume constraints.

However, such methods often require a high number of variables, especially with high geometric complexity, which affects the efficiency of the computation.

The complexity arises from solving displacement and geometry simultaneously, with critical reviews available [10]. The level set method has gained traction for efficiently changing model geometry. Introduced in [11], it allows dynamic adaptation, including 3D curve movement techniques [12].

Numerous studies have applied level set methods for contour description in various fields. The level set method, paired with RBF approximation, effectively describes implicit functions, facilitating geometry model adjustments through gradient optimization ([13–15]). A major limitation of gradient-based level set methods is their dependence on initial shapes and their inability to generate new topological features such as holes, making it difficult to explore more optimal configurations. Test cases, such as a 2D cantilever beam, employed RBF coefficients for surface change, permitting hole creation and merging during optimization based on the Hamilton–Jacobi transport equation.

In the work by Jia et al. [6], the evolutionary structural optimization (ESO) method combined with the level set approach enables novel geometries independent of initial configurations. Topology optimization of 3D structures utilizing genetic algorithms is discussed by Burczyński et al. [16], highlighting two parameterization methods: shape and material distribution. Additionally, the work by Ruiter and Keulen [17] introduces the Topology Description Function (TDF) method, utilizing genetic algorithms but maintaining high computational costs. Implicit TDF combined with level set methods allows for new hole creation during "Nucleation" optimization techniques presented in the paper [18].

While global optimization methods suit problems with fewer variables [5], studies focusing on parameterizing the level set method remain limited [19]. Interest in topology optimization within additive manufacturing has grown due to its ability to create complex geometries difficult for traditional methods. This optimization can enhance mechanical properties like stiffness and buckling resistance for specific manufacturing techniques (FDM, SLM) [20].

In most existing approaches, optimization relies heavily on gradient-based algorithms, which tend to become stuck in local minima and are unable to generate or modify topological features such as new holes or passages in the material on their own. This limitation restricts the search space, especially for complex geometries. Several evolutionary methods, e.g., [9], use homogenization theory in combination with genetic algorithms where the design variables are element densities, resulting in high dimensionality and computational complexity. Similarly, Ref. [6] proposes an evolutionary accelerated level set algorithm that combines ESO with level set methods and enables the automatic generation of new holes. However, such algorithms are often dependent on the initial topology and may have difficulties in finding the global optimum for complex structures.

The Smooth-Edged Material Distribution for Optimizing Topology (SEMDOT) method is developed within the context of meshless approximation in the paper [21].

In recent years, topology optimization has increasingly been applied to enhance additive manufacturing (3D printing) processes, aiming to improve material efficiency, mechanical performance, and design flexibility. Building on the advances in material modeling, paper [22] utilized structural analysis with a linear anisotropic material model within the topology optimization framework. Furthermore, a novel approach combining Rational Approximation of Material Properties (RAMP) and the Finite Element Method (FEM) was proposed in [23] to minimize peak stresses in multi-layer composite joints.

The work by Shin et al. [24] discusses using machine learning (ML) to mitigate conventional topology optimization (TO) computational costs. ML, especially deep learning (DL), accelerates the process and predicts optimal topology from intermediate stages, expediting time-consuming phases. The study by Deng and To [25] proposes a new parametric level set method utilizing deep neural networks (DNNs) to convert PDEs into parameterized ODEs for diverse designs. The integration of neural networks with genetic algorithms may significantly enhance data efficiency and solution quality in high-dimensional problems [26].

Topological optimization also has significant applications in civil engineering. Computer-aided methods have been developed for performance-based structural design, focusing on nonlinear pushover analysis—an inherently complex and iterative process [27]. The method targets 2D-braced steel frames, employing pushover analysis combined with optimization techniques, optimality criteria, and an ant colony metaheuristic algorithm to automate the design process. Its goal is to achieve optimal drift performance while minimizing total structural weight.

Another method applies a similar approach to reinforced concrete (RC) buildings, integrating pushover analysis with numerical optimization, optimality criteria, and an artificial bee colony algorithm [28]. This technique is used for the optimal design of concrete beams, columns, and shear walls.

In the context of civil engineering and structural design, the newly developed method presented in this paper complements existing approaches by introducing a robust topology optimization framework based on parameterized level set functions and genetic algorithms. It enhances the global search capacity and convergence speed (near global optimum), making it suitable for complex structural design problems where traditional gradient-based methods may struggle with local minima and initial solution dependency.

This paper presents an optimization method using a parameterized level set function with B-spline surfaces and genetic algorithms in MATLAB. Our research contributes to topology optimization, with potential acceleration through machine learning. DL, particularly convolutional neural networks (CNNs), could improve shape prediction and parameter optimization, enhancing both efficiency and accuracy.

A new topological optimization method, using genetic algorithms and B-splines, was tested on standard examples, reducing optimization parameters and dimensionality. Numerical efficiency benefits from substitution material formulations, eliminating remeshing.

Maintaining a consistent range for objective functions and constraints is essential, using methods like standardization and logarithmic transformations to calibrate varying values. This paper introduces an extended objective function to enhance convergence with genetic algorithms and presents a novel penalty operator targeting similar individuals within each population generation, facilitating high-quality solutions in 2D topological optimization. The method presented in the chapter 'Mathematical Formulations' provides the detailed mathematical foundation and implementation details of this approach.

Most existing methods rely heavily on gradient-based algorithms, which tend to become trapped in local minima and generally do not facilitate the creation of new topological features such as holes or internal passages during the optimization process. As a result, these approaches often require favorable initial designs and have difficulty exploring the entire design space, especially for complex or highly non-convex structures.

The main contributions of this work can be summarized as follows:

- The proposed method uses a parameterized level set function in combination with genetic algorithms, enabling a global search that reduces the dependence on the initial topology.
- The method overcomes the limitations of local minima and allows topological changes, such as the creation of holes, during the optimization process.
- Although the method tends to have slower convergence rates, this can be mitigated by integrating local refinement techniques, including gradient-based fine-tuning or memetic algorithms, following the approximate identification of the global optimum.

These limitations can be observed in the images presented in the chapter, with the results.

2. Mathematical Formulations

2.1. Structural Topology Optimization

Typically, topology optimization problems involve minimizing compliance while considering displacement constraints and allowable material distribution, expressed using the material stiffness matrix

$$\begin{gathered} \min \; l(v) \\ \mathrm{u} \in \mathrm{U} \\ \mathrm{E} \in \mathrm{E_{ad}} \\ a_B(u,v) = l(v), \quad \textit{for all} \;\; v \in U, \quad E \in E_{ad} \end{gathered} \tag{1}$$

which represents a weak variation equation with U as virtual (kinematic permissible) displacements, where are E—stiffness matrix; E_{ad}—set of admissible stiffness tensors; $a(u,v)$—internal virtual work of an elastic body; $l(v)$—virtual work of external loads; u—equilibrium displacement field; v—virtual displacement (kinematic permissible) field. The index B indicates the bilinear form.

The linear form of the load $l(v)$ is the summation of the external load f_v acting on the volume Ω and the external load f_s on boundary $\Gamma_s \subset \Gamma \equiv \partial\Omega$ (work of external load):

$$l(v) = \int_{\Gamma_s} v \cdot f_s \cdot d\Gamma + \int_{\Omega} v \cdot f_v \cdot d\Omega \tag{2}$$

The internal virtual work of an elastic body can be expressed as follows:

$$a(u,v) = \int_{\Omega} E(X) \cdot \varepsilon(u) \cdot \varepsilon(v) \cdot d\Omega \tag{3}$$

where X is shape and topology variables (representing material distribution).

Linearized strain field are $\varepsilon = L{\cdot}u$, with L as the differential operator.

From virtual works, it becomes evident that by minimizing the bilinear form, we achieve the equilibrium state of the displacement field. This equilibrium of the bilinear form necessitates the optimization of material distribution to maximize stiffness:

$$\max_{E \in E_{ad}} \left(\min_{u \epsilon U,D} \{a_B(u,v) - l(v)\} \right) \tag{4}$$

The objective function is the minimization of compliance to determine the optimal material distribution while ensuring equilibrium (using a nested approach). The formulation for minimum compliance in a discretized domain can be expressed as follows:

$$\min_{\mathrm{u,E_e}} f^T u K(E_e) u = f, \qquad E_e \in E_{ad} \tag{5}$$

where u—displacement, f—load filed, K—stiffness matrix depending on material properties in element e (E_e). For N number of elements, the following applies:

$$K = \sum_{e=1}^{N} K_e(E_e) \tag{6}$$

K_e—element of global stiffness matrix.

The objective function can be expressed as a minimization of volume function with respect to the following stress constraints:

$$\min_{E_e} V K(E_e) u = f, \qquad \sigma_e < \sigma_{ad} \qquad E_e \in E_{ad} \tag{7}$$

We utilize a modified Level Set Method combined with the Topology Description Function (TDF). In dealing with shape-changing during optimization, two common methods for stress and strain calculations using FEM are substitute material method and remeshing. Due to the high computational cost of remeshing, we chose the substitute material method to significantly reduce computation time, applying it throughout all examples in this work.

2.2. B-Spline Parameterization of Level Set Function

The Level Set Method (LSM) relies on an implicit function that describes geometry. The level set function is an n + 1-dimensional function that represents n-dimensional geometry within an n-dimensional space through its isolines.

This characteristic of LSM allows for both geometry and topology changes during the optimization process. For instance, it can facilitate the creation of new holes within the domain without the need for establishing a new geometry parameterization.

Figure 1 illustrates the 3D function Φ (Level set function) used to describe the 2D problem. The level set function Φ intersects the rectangular domain D (hatched area). When the rectangular domain D lies on the x-y surface, the cross-section of the function Φ and the rectangular domain D together define a new domain $\Omega \in \mathrm{D}$. There is a region with material defined as $\Phi(\mathrm{x,t}) < 0\ \forall x \in \Omega\backslash\partial\Omega$, and region without material define as $\Phi(\mathrm{x,t}) > 0\ \forall x \in \Omega\backslash\partial\Omega$. The zero-isoline of the level set function $\Phi(\mathrm{x,t}) = 0$ represent the contour $\partial\Omega$, $\forall \mathrm{x} \in \partial\Omega \cap \mathrm{D}$ on the x-y surface (boundary). Here, x denotes space variables. The change in the shape is numerically considered as a dynamical process, and it depends on the pseudo-time t.

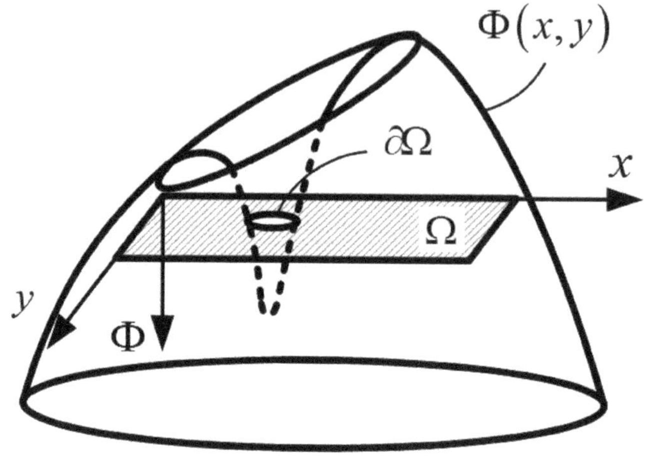

Figure 1. General implicit function Φ.

The weight function H indicates whether the observed point is located inside or outside the following region:

$$H(\Phi(x)) = \begin{cases} 1 & if\ \Phi(x) \le 0, \\ 0 & if\ \Phi(x) > 0, \end{cases} \tag{8}$$

The function Φ is defined in 3D, while the observed shape is in 2D (i.e., in the n − 1 dimension). The isoline function Φ at time t is currently as follows:

$$\Phi(x,t) = 0 \tag{9}$$

All equations derived from expression (9) (such as the Hamilton–Jacobi equation) are only valid for the borders. However, the new approach to topology optimization involves the weight function H applied on a parametrized 3D B-spline surface, whose isoline represents the border of 2D geometry.

The B-curve is defined by Equation (10) through the points P_i:

$$P(t) = \sum_{i=0}^{n} N_{i,n}(t) \cdot P_i, \tag{10}$$

where the basis function of the zero-degree B-curve is defined as follows:

$$N_{i,0}(t) = \begin{cases} 1, & t_i \le t < t_{i+1} \\ 0, & otherwise \end{cases},$$

and, for the other degrees of the B-curve ($0 \le i \le n + d$), as follows:

$$N_{i,j}(t) = \frac{t - t_i}{t_{i+j} - t_i} N_{i,j-1}(t) + \frac{t_{i+j+1} - t}{t_{i+j+1} - t_{i+1}} N_{i+1,j-1}(t)$$

The degree of the curve falls within the range $1 \leq d \leq n$, and each individual node is uniformly represented as follows:

$$t_i = \begin{cases} 0, & 0 \leq i \leq d \\ \frac{i-d}{n+1-d}, & d+1 \leq i \leq n \\ 1 & n+1 \leq i \leq n+d+1 \end{cases}$$

By multiplying two B-curves in x and y direction yields the 3D surface (B-spline):

$$P(u,v) = \sum_{i=0}^{n} \sum_{j=0}^{m} N_{j,d_n}(u) \cdot N_{j,d_m}(v) \cdot P_{ij} \tag{11}$$

Under this assumption B-spline surface (11) for n control nodes of the B-spline (P_{ij}), the interpolation of the implicit function can be written as follows:

$$\Phi = \sum_{i}^{n} \Phi_{\mathrm{i}} \cdot P_{0i} = \Phi^T(x) \cdot P_0(t), \tag{12}$$

Through Equation (11) (B-spline) and Equation (12) (level set function), the parameterized B-spline function is mathematically linked. In this process, the Pij optimization variable is defined, representing the priming variable P0, i.e., the variable that determines the shape of the B-spline surface and, ultimately, the topological structure.

All finite elements within the 2D domain D of the initial bearing structures, for which Equation (12) yields positive values, represent bearing elements with density ρ.

All finite elements within the domain located above the B-spline surface are designated as non-bearing elements, indicating a material density of zero. The number of variables used in traditional level set method optimizations was typically equal to the number of finite elements in the optimized structure.

To assess the ability to describe geometry with a parameterized level set function, a step function with 676 control points is selected as the test function to be represented by a B-spline, as illustrated in Figure 2:

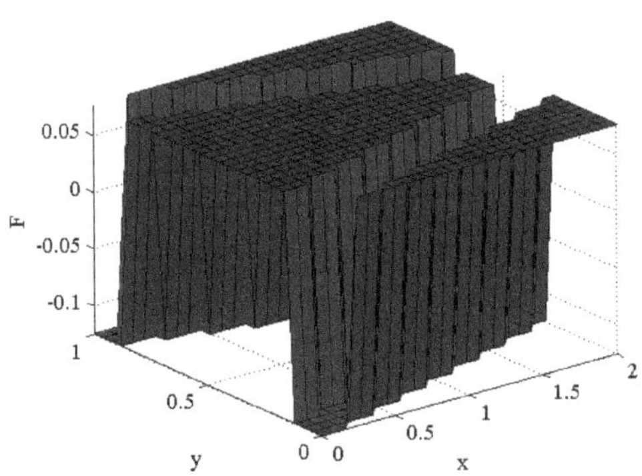

Figure 2. Test step function for B-spline Approximations.

Appropriate parameterization of the level set surface using B-splines can significantly reduce the number of description variables, as illustrated by the results in Table 1, and Figure 3.

Table 1. Table of the influence of the node numbers and the degree of the B-spline.

B-Spline Nodes	2nd Degree	3rd Degree	4th Degree
		Error	
6×6 (36)	1.457	1.504	1.517
12×12 (144)	0.415	0.417	0.429
24×24 (576)	0.0436	0.0405	0.079
48×48 (2304)	7.39×10^{-10}	2.1×10^{-11}	6.03×10^{-10}

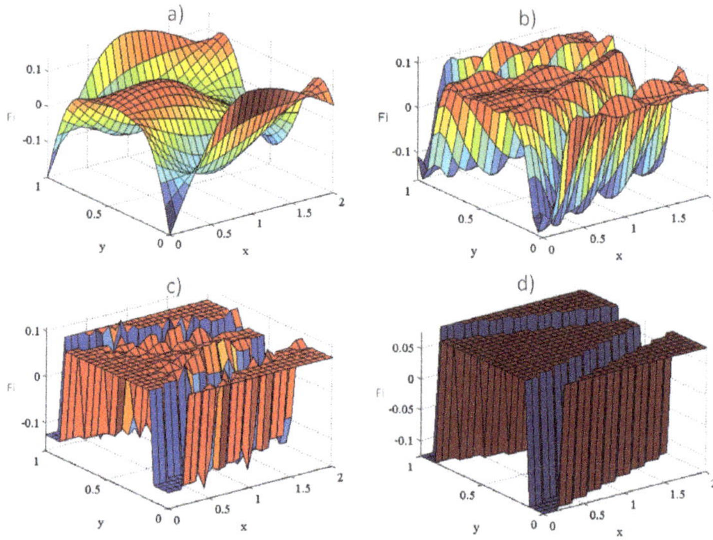

Figure 3. Influence of the B-spline node numbers: (**a**) 36, (**b**)144, (**c**) 576, and (**d**) 2304 nodes.

In the optimization procedure for a beam, we used both 12×12 and 24×24 point grids to define the level set surface, resulting in 144 and 576 optimization variables, respectively. This larger number of variables helps mitigate the issues of local extrema that arise with fewer variables (36), necessitating a global search method like a genetic algorithm.

2.3. New Operators: Objective Function and Constraints

To achieve robust topology optimization results independent of the initial guess, we employed a genetic algorithm, an evolutionary global optimization method well-suited for finding the optimum of a function without becoming stuck in local optima. Our method modifies the traditional level set approach by allowing the creation of new holes, thus addressing its main limitation.

The functionality of this method was tested on cantilevers and Michell beams. We utilized a modified MATLAB finite element code based on Andreassen et al. [29] and Sigmund [30], employing a 2D finite element method for plane stress to analyze physical phenomena such as displacement, stress, and deformation.

Modifications included the incorporation of a B-spline parameterized surface, as described by Christensen [31], Equation (11), allowing the number of control points (P) to correspond to the number of optimization variables. This integration facilitated the use of objective functions and constraints to improve the optimizer's sensitivity.

The objective function was formulated in two steps: minimizing compliance while respecting the volume constraint, Equation (5), and minimizing material volume under stress constraints, Equation (7).

To transform the discrete objective function into a continuous one, we introduced additional terms to enhance the optimizer's sensitivity to variable changes, as shown in Equation (13):

$$F_c = Br_{elem} + \left(\sum |diff(Bspline(z))|\right) \tag{13}$$

where Br_{elem}—number of elements that possess the mechanical characteristics of load-bearing structure materials, and $Bspline(z)$—values of the control points of the level set surface (F in Figure 2).

Furthermore, to improve convergence, we applied logarithmic transformations for stress constraints and utilized the arctangent function for deformation constraints. As stress values can reach magnitudes of 10^7 MPa, a logarithmic transformation, Equation (14) was used to control these values within a range from 8 to 22.

$$Ogr_\sigma = \sum_i^n log(\sigma_i) \tag{14}$$

Excessive deformations were limited using the arctangent function, Equation (15), resulting in values now ranging from 0 to a maximum of 90, instead of very high values:

$$Ogr_\varepsilon = \sum_i^n \arctan(\varepsilon_i) \tag{15}$$

The optimization process began with an arbitrary design, focusing on minimizing the objective function. The findings highlight that the similarity in magnitudes of constraints facilitates their incorporation into a complex objective function, enhancing the optimization procedure's effectiveness.

3. Numerical Examples, Results

To examine the proposed numerical procedure, several test examples were carried out. As described and examined in previous sections, we employed a uniform second-degree B-spline surface to describe the level set function during the topology optimization of a beam subjected to a 10 kN force applied to the right middle end.

The precision of the level set function representation by the B-spline was influenced by the number of control points. The z-coordinates of the B-spline nodes were treated as optimization variables. We selected two mesh sizes, 12 × 12 and 24 × 24 control points, for the B-spline surface. The total number of finite elements for all beam examples was 3200 (80 × 40).

The Young's modulus of elasticity for the structural elements was set as $E = 30\ [GPa]$. In all tested examples, the maximum allowable Von–Mises stress was limited to 20 N/mm^2 to ensure the realism and safety of the structure. In the following figures, the colorbar displays the distribution of Von–Mises stress in N/mm^2. We conducted topological optimization of 2D cantilevers and Michell beams using a genetic algorithm. The number of elite individuals transferred to the next generation was 10. The recombination parameter for individuals was configured so that 80% of individuals from the previous generation (excluding elite individuals) underwent crossover using a random algorithm.

The mutation affected individuals who did not participate in the crossover, with approximately 5% of their chromosomes changed randomly (uniform mutation).

The range within which control points (optimization variables) could vary might influence the genetic algorithm's convergence speed. In this case, the initial population range for optimization variables was selected between −2 and 2. We used real encoding for variables and the objective function during optimization with the genetic algorithm. All calculations were performed on a four-core Intel i5 3.10GH processor-based computer.

3.1. Test Case 1—Cantilever Beam

As a commonly used test case for topology optimization with the level set method, as documented in numerous references such as [4,13,32,33], a cantilever beam with a force acting at its free end was used, as shown in Figure 4:

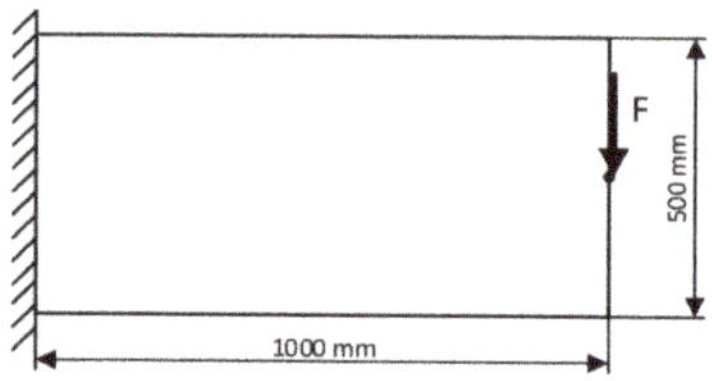

Figure 4. Geometry, load, and boundary conditions of the cantilever beam with a force acting at its free end in the middle.

In this example, the objective function is set to the a minimum compliance, with the volume constraint at 20% of the initial design (640 elements), as shown in Figure 5:

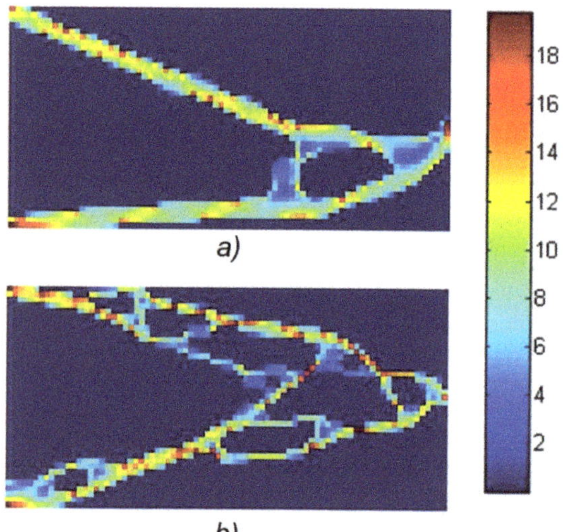

Figure 5. Results of the level set optimization of the cantilever beam (Figure 4) using a genetic algorithm, where the objective function is the minimization of compliance, with (**a**) 144 variables and (**b**) 576 variables.

Figure 5 shows the results of the test case 1 achieved using population of 5184 randomly generated individuals over 500 generations. The maximum Von–Mises stress was 20 [N/mm^2], while the volume constraint was set at 640 elements, corresponding to 20% of the initial design. For 144 variables, the compliance was 6715 [Pa^{-1}], and the calculation time extended to 68 h. Remarkably, only for this case, 1000 generations were required to approach the global optimum (Figure 5a). In the case of 576 optimization variables, the objective function (compliance) amounted to 7776 [Pa^{-1}], with a calculation time of 42 h (Figure 5b). With fewer generations, the procedure yielded results that indicated local extrema, such as the optimum for the L/H ratio of 2.

For comparison, the minimum compliance according to [24], with the same parameters as in the previously described example Test case 1, is 5864 [Pa^{-1}]. We observe that the

Evolutionary Algorithm did not converge to a solution; however, the proposed method came very close to the global optimum, which is the goal of the proposed approach.

In the same test case, the objective function is formulated to minimize volume during topology optimization using the level set function and the genetic algorithm. We achieved the results as shown in Figure 6:

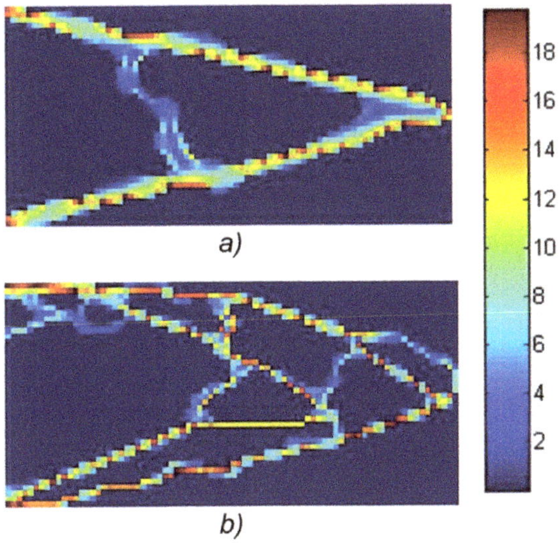

Figure 6. Results of the level set optimized of cantilever beam (Figure 4) using a genetic algorithm where the objective function is minimization of volume, with (**a**) 144 variables and (**b**) 576 variables.

The results shown in Figure 6 represent optimal solutions obtained through the genetic algorithm procedure across 500 generations involving 5184 individuals. The computational process took approximately 35 h for 576 variables (Figure 6b), resulting in an objective function value of 657, corresponding to approximately 20.5% of the full plate volume. In the case of 144 variables, the objective function yielded a value of 663, with a calculation time of around 13 h.

As demonstrated in the preceding figure, achieving convergence was challenging. The genetic algorithm exhibited slow convergence in the vicinity of the solution. Therefore, the obtained results can serve as initial solutions for the gradient method, which offer fast convergence but may converge to local optima. This optimization approach grants the optimizer flexibility in generating the geometry and the capability to discover global optima.

3.2. Test Case 2—Cantilever Beam

The second test example is also a cantilever beam with a force acting on the lower edge at its free end, as shown in Figure 7:

In the provided example, using the same parameters (such as force, material properties, genetic algorithm parameters, allowable stresses, etc.) as in the previous case, we applied the 2D level set method for topology optimization of a cantilever beam subjected to force at its free end, on the bottom side of Figure 8.

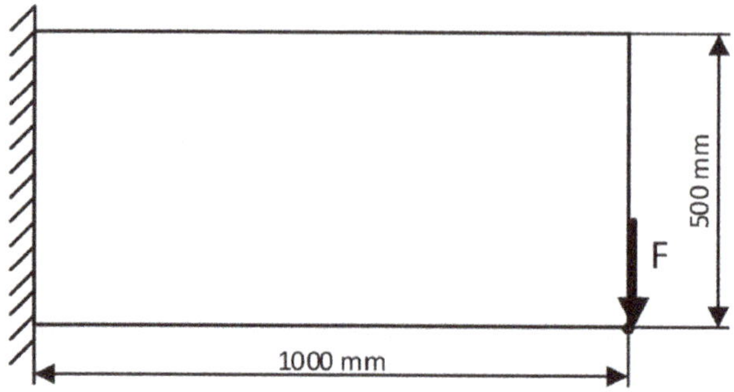

Figure 7. Geometry, load, and boundary conditions of the cantilever beam with a force acting at its free end on the bottom.

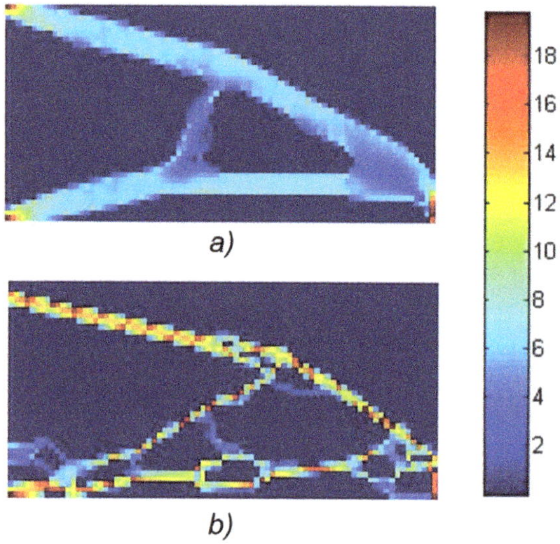

Figure 8. Results of the level set optimized of cantilever beam (Figure 7) using a genetic algorithm where the objective function is minimization of compliance, with (**a**) 144 variables and (**b**) 576 variables.

The proposed method with 144 optimization variables, targeting a volume of 20% of the initial volume (640 elements) with the specified genetic algorithm parameters, failed to converge. However, when targeting a volume of 30% of the initial volume (960 elements), the objective function (compliance) reached 4147 Pa^{-1} Figure 8a). In the case of 576 optimization variables Figure 8b), and a target volume of 20% of the initial volume, the compliance reached 8519 Pa^{-1}.

Again, a comparison with the work of [24] was conducted for Test case 2, where the minimum compliance with the same parameters is 3968 Pa^{-1}. It can be observed that the Evolutionary A more significant deviation from the optimal solution was observed precisely in the example with a higher number of variables. However, the primary goal of this study was to assess whether the proposed method is capable of finding the global minimum, which has been confirmed by the presented results. Future work will focus on developing a comprehensive topological optimization method that reliably identifies the global extremum. In formulating the objective function to minimize the volume of the cantilever beam (Figure 7), the following results were obtained (Figure 9):

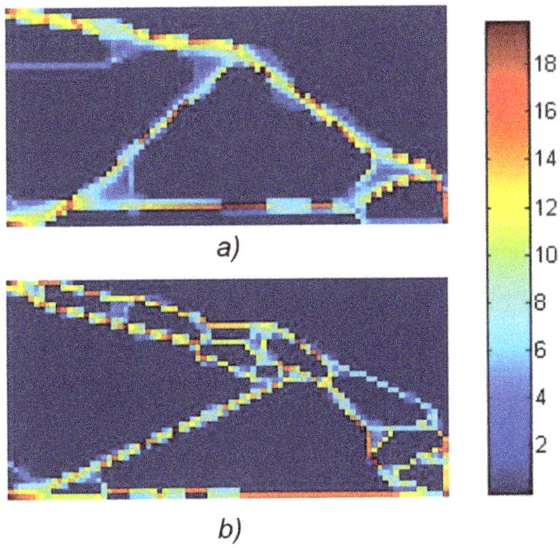

Figure 9. Results of the level set optimized of cantilever beam (Figure 7) using a genetic algorithm where the objective function is minimization of volume, with (**a**) 144 variables and (**b**) 576 variables.

In the second example of optimization using the proposed procedure with 144 optimization variables Figure 9a, the volume was reduced to 22% of the initial volume (707 elements). When increasing the number of optimization variables to 576, the volume was further reduced to 19% of the initial volume (614 elements). The parameters of the genetic algorithm and the allowed stress remained the same as in the previous example.

3.3. Test Case 3—Michell Beam

In the example illustrated in Figure 10—Michell beam, the objective function was set to minimize compliance while maintaining a volume constraint of 15% of the full plate.

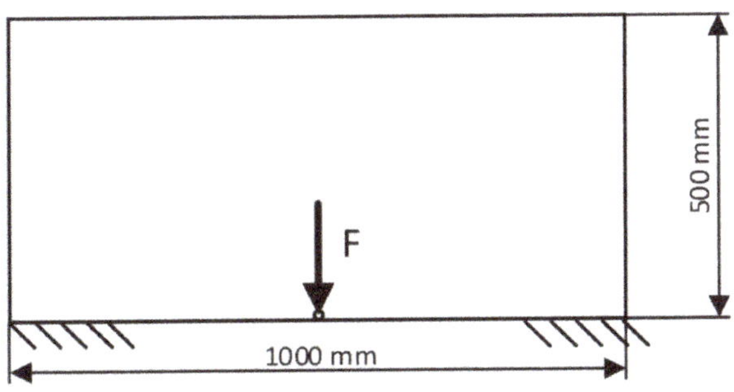

Figure 10. Defining geometry, load, and boundary conditions of the Michell beam for the topology optimization.

The conditions for this optimization remained equal to those in the previous two examples, including parameters of the genetic algorithm and allowed stress. This led to the successful optimization of the Michell beam using the level set method, as demonstrated in Figure 11.

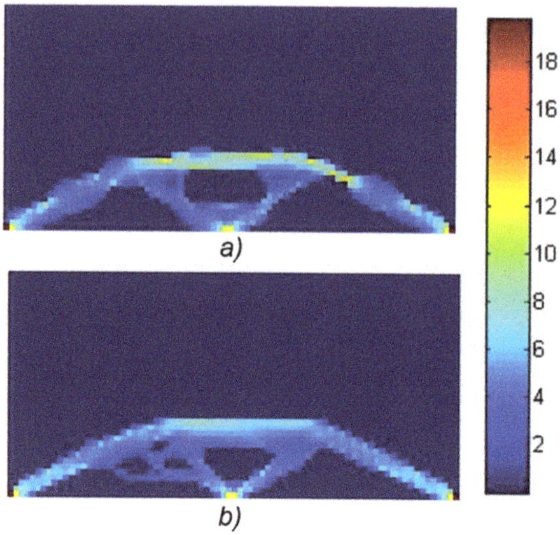

Figure 11. Result of the level set optimization using a genetic algorithm of the Michell beam wher the objective function is minimization of compliance, with (**a**) 144 variables and (**b**) 576 variables.

In the case of 144 optimization variables, for a specified volume of 15% of the initial volume (480 elements), with a population size of 5184 individuals and 200 generations of the genetic algorithm, convergence to a solution was achieved, as shown in Figure 11a, with a compliance objective function value of 1639 Pa^{-1}. When employing 576 optimization variables (as shown in Figure 11b), along with an increased number of generations set to 500, while maintaining the same parameters as in the previous example with 144 variables, a compliance objective function value of 1437 Pa^{-1} was achieved. For test case 3, the minimum compliance according to [24], with the same parameters, is 996 Pa. As with the previous cases, the Evolutionary Algorithm did not fully converge to an exact solution; however, the proposed method achieved a result very close to the global optimum, fulfilling the primary objective of the approach. It is expected that in complex geometries and more challenging problems, the proposed method will be capable of finding the global minimum, since traditional topological optimization methods, such as those in [24], tend to be significantly influenced by the initial solution. In contrast, the proposed approach does not have such dependence, thereby increasing the likelihood of reliably locating the global extreme in complex scenarios. Therefore, the results confirm the method's capability to approximate the global minimum, supporting the ongoing development of a comprehensive topological optimization procedure that can reliably detect the global extreme in future research.

Regarding the formulation of the objective function for minimizing the volume of the Michell beam (Figure 10), the following solutions were obtained (Figure 12):

In the context of minimizing volume for the Michell beam example, optimization with 144 variables reduced the volume to 15% (354 elements) of the full plate, as illustrated in Figure 12a. When employing 576 variables, the volume was further reduced to 8% of the initial design (261 elements), as shown in Figure 12b.

The results demonstrate that a higher number of variables in the optimization process contributes to better convergence towards the global optimum, especially for structures with complex geometries. This is reflected in a finer and more precise material distribution, which allows for more efficient utilization of material resources and a reduction in the overall compliance of the structure. On the other hand, optimization with a smaller number of variables, while potentially enabling a faster identification of the global solution for less complex geometries, often requires the use of alternative methods or numerical techniques to achieve convergence towards a high-quality solution, since it may struggle to accurately represent intricate designs. The uneven stress distribution in the elements is primarily a consequence of the slow convergence towards the optimal solution when employing a global optimization method such as a genetic algorithm. While the addition of a penalty term to the objective function, designed to penalize similar individuals and promote diversity, has certainly improved the method, reaching the ideal optimum as presented in the extensive literature referenced in the introduction [1,3,13], etc., remains challenging. Furthermore, the method's functionality was validated against an analytical solution for a length-to-width ratio of 1:1, where the method successfully identified the optimal solution. It is crucial to emphasize that the proposed method consistently achieves solutions that are very close to the global optimum, regardless of the initial starting solutions. This robustness is a significant advantage.

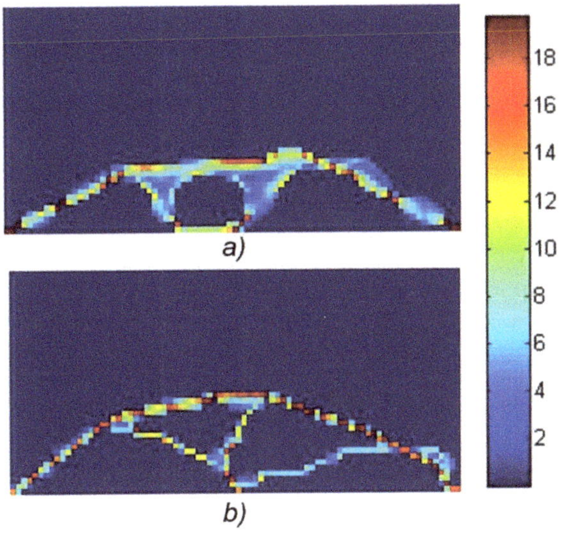

Figure 12. Result of the level set optimization using the genetic algorithm, where the objective function is the minimization of volume, with (**a**) 144 variables and (**b**) 576 variables.

From the obtained results, we can see that the proposed method can be used as a generator of good initial solutions close to the global optimum for conventional methods for topology optimization.

4. Discussion

This study presents a novel approach to topology optimization using a parameterized level set function and genetic algorithms. The method demonstrates promising results in finding global optima, particularly when dealing with complex structures. The use of B-spline surfaces reduces the number of optimization variables, enhancing the efficiency of the genetic algorithm.

This paper also introduces a novel penalty operator designed to enhance convergence and ensure good sensitivity in the optimization process. While the penalty operator alone did not significantly improve convergence, when combined with the extended objective function, it facilitated the generation of high-quality solutions.

The presented method shows potential for accelerating the optimization process and finding more accurate solutions, but faces challenges related to computational cost, particularly when dealing with complex structures and large numbers of variables. Genetic algorithms, while effective for global search, can be computationally expensive. Future research should tackle these limitations by integrating the proposed approach with gradient-based optimization and exploring machine learning techniques for better efficiency and scalability. Additionally, applying the approach to 3D problems is worth investigating.

Topology optimization with the proposed method provides the advantage of finding good initial solutions for other topology optimization procedures, such as SIMP, ESO, and LS, where the selection of suitable initial solutions is crucial for convergence.

It is worth noting that very few papers address the formulation of minimum mass with stress/strain constraints in topology optimization using gradient-based procedures, mainly because achieving satisfactory results often relies heavily on having an excellent initial solution.

In this paper, a novel method for topology optimization, which combines a level set function with a genetic algorithm, is introduced. The developed optimization procedure was implemented using a custom MATLAB code based on the SIMP method for topology optimization, as described in references [29,30]. It is important to note that this code is specifically designed for 2D problems. The results of this study demonstrate the method's capability to discover effective solutions for structural optimization tasks.

The results obtained demonstrate convergence to the global optimum in all examples, even with a smaller number of generations. Consequently, the proposed evolutionary topology optimization method can be employed as a generator of high-quality initial solutions for more computationally efficient gradient-based procedures.

The limitation of this proposed method is the duration of the optimization. However, considering that the method is based on the genetic algorithm, it is amenable to parallelization, which has the potential to significantly reduce the optimization time. In a study by [34], it was demonstrated that geometry optimization could be efficiently carried out using an ad-hoc cluster, resulting in a reduction in processing time proportional to the number of services.

During topology optimization using the proposed method, it was observed that at smaller numbers of individuals per generation, the optimizer identified local optima, leading to premature convergence of the genetic algorithm. Premature convergence can occur due to the following:

- Poor sensitivity of the objective function;
- Instances where multiple individuals produce the same objective function value (resulting in reduced population).

To improve the convergence of the genetic algorithm, an additional penalty operator can be introduced to penalize equivalent individuals during the optimization process. Equivalent individuals receive a specific penalty added to their objective function, promoting greater diversity within the population. In our study, we also conducted tests on penalizing similar individuals to increase diversity; however, this penalty did not contribute to faster convergence of the optimization process.

5. Conclusions

This paper presented a novel approach to topology optimization that integrates a parameterized level set function with genetic algorithms, demonstrating promising capabilities in identifying global optima for complex structures. The use of B-spline surfaces not only reduces the number of optimization variables but also enhances the efficiency of the genetic algorithm, yielding high-quality solutions.

While various penalty operators were investigated to improve convergence and sensitivity, the proposed set of operators proved effective in achieving convergence and generating high-quality solutions. When combined with the extended objective function, this method demonstrated significant potential for enhancing topology optimization processes. However, challenges remain, particularly regarding the computational costs associated with complex structures and large variable sets.

Furthermore, integrating machine learning and deep learning methods could further enhance the optimization process and scalability. Expanding the applicability of the method to 3D problems also represents a significant area for future exploration.

The proposed topology optimization method plays a crucial role in providing effective initial solutions for existing procedures such as SIMP, ESO, and LS, where selecting appropriate initial conditions is vital for achieving convergence.

Author Contributions: Conceptualization, I.P., D.S., I.M.-K. and D.V.; methodology, I.P. and D.S.; software, I.P. and I.M.-K.; validation, I.P., D.S. and I.M.-K.; formal analysis, I.P. and D.S.; investigation, I.P. and D.S.; writing—original draft preparation, I.P. and D.S.; writing—review and editing, D.V. and I.M.-K.; visualization, I.P. and D.S. All authors have read and agreed to the published version of the manuscript.

Funding: This work was funded by the Croatian Science Foundation under the project number HRZZ-IP-2022-10-8856.

Data Availability Statement: The original contributions presented in this study are included in the article, and further inquiries can be directed to the corresponding author.

Conflicts of Interest: The authors declare no conflicts of interest.

References

1. Bendsoe, M.P.; Sigmund, O. *Topology Optimization, Theory, Methods and Applications*; Springer: Berlin, Germany, 2004. [CrossRef]
2. Osher, S.; Fedkiw, R. *Level Set Methods and Dynamic Implicit Surfaces*; Applied Mathematical Sciences; Springer: New York, NY, USA, 2003; Volume 153.
3. Rozvany, G.I.N. *Topology Optimization in Structural Mechanics*; Springer: Vienna, Italy, 1997. [CrossRef]
4. Wang, S.; Wang, M.Y. Radial Basis Functions and Level Set Method for Structural Topology Optimization. *J. Numer. Methods Eng.* **2006**, *65*, 2060–2090. [CrossRef]
5. Sigmund, O. On the usefulness of non-gradient approaches in topology optimization. *Struct. Multidisc. Optim.* **2011**, *43*, 589–596. [CrossRef]
6. Jia, H.; Beom, H.G.; Wang, Y.; Lin, S.; Lui, B. Evolutionary level set method for structural topology optimization. *J. Compstruc.* **2011**, *89*, 445–454. [CrossRef]
7. Eschenauer, H.A.; Olhoff, N. Topology optimization of continuum structures: A review. *Appl. Mech. Rev.* **2001**, *54*, 331–390. [CrossRef]
8. Pourazady, M.; Fu, Z. An Integrated Approach to Structural Shape Optimization. *Comput. Struct.* **1996**, *60*, 279–289. [CrossRef]
9. Cappello, F.; Mancuso, A. A genetic algorithm for combined topology and shape optimizations. *Comput. Aided Des.* **2003**, *35*, 761–769. [CrossRef]
10. Rozvany, G.I.N. A critical review of established methods of structural topology optimization. *Struct. Multidisc. Optim.* **2009**, *37*, 217–237. [CrossRef]
11. Osher, S.; Sethian, J.A. Fronts propagating with curvature dependent speed: Algorithms based on Hamilton-Jacobi formulations. *J. Comput. Phys.* **1998**, *79*, 12–49. [CrossRef]
12. Osher, S.; Fedkiw, R.P. Level Set Methods: An Overview and Some Recent Results. *J. Comput. Phys.* **2001**, *169*, 463–502. [CrossRef]
13. Luo, Z.; Tong, L.; Kang, Z. A level set method for structural shape and topology optimization using radial basic functions. *J. Compstruc.* **2009**, *87*, 425–434. [CrossRef]
14. Xing, X.; Wang, M.Y.; Lui, B.F.Y. Parametric Shape and Topology Optimization with Moving Knots Radial Basis Function and Level Set Method. In Proceedings of the 7th World Congress of Structural and Multidisciplinary Optimization, Seoul, Republic of Korea, 21–25 May 2007; Available online: https://repository.vtc.edu.hk/ive-eng-sp/21 (accessed on 11 May 2025).

15. Xia, Q.; Wang, M.Y. Level Set Based Method for Simultaneous Optimization of Material Property and Topology of Functionally Graded Structures. In Proceedings of the ACM Symposium on Solid and Physical Modeling, Beijing, China, 4–6 July 2007. [CrossRef]
16. Burczyński, T.; Poteralski, A.; Orantek, P. Generalized shape optimization of three-dimensional structures using evolutionary computation. In Proceedings of the 6th World Congresses of Structural and Multidisciplinary Optimization, Rio de Janeiro, Brazil, 30 May–3 June 2005.
17. de Ruiter, M.J.; van Keulen, F. Topology optimization using a topology description function. *Struct. Multidisc. Optim.* **2004**, *26*, 406–416. [CrossRef]
18. Guo, X.; Zhao, K.; Wang, M.Y. A new approach for simultaneous shape and topology optimization based on dynamic implicit surface function. *Control. Cybern.* **2005**, *34*, 255–282.
19. van Dijk, N.P.; Maute, K.; Langelaar, M.; van Keulen, F. Level-set methods for structural topology optimization: A review. *Struct. Multidisc. Optim.* **2013**, *48*, 437–472. [CrossRef]
20. Gandhi, Y.; Minak, G. A Review on Topology Optimization Strategies for Additively Manufactured Continuous Fiber-Reinforced Composite Structures. *Appl. Sci.* **2022**, *12*, 11211. [CrossRef]
21. Huang, J.; Long, K.; Chen, Y.; Geng, R.; Saeed, A.; Zhang, H.; Tao, T. A Framework of the Meshless Method for Topology Optimization Using the Smooth-Edged Material Distribution for Optimizing Topology Method. *Computation* **2025**, *13*, 6. [CrossRef]
22. Kurkin, E.; Barcenas, O.U.E.; Kishov, E. Lukyanov, Topology Optimization and Efficiency Evaluation of Short-Fiber-Reinforced Composite Structures Considering Anisotropy. *Computation* **2024**, *12*, 35. [CrossRef]
23. Dunchenkin, P.V.; Cherekaeva, V.A.; Yakovleva, T.V.; Krysko, A.V. Topological Optimization of Interconnection of Multilayer Composite Structures. *Computation* **2023**, *11*, 87. [CrossRef]
24. Shin, S.; Shin, D.; Kang, N. Topology optimization via machine learning and deep learning: A review. *J. Comput. Des. Eng.* **2023**, *10*, 1736–1766. [CrossRef]
25. Deng, H.; To, A.C. A Parametric Level Set Method for Topology Optimization Based on Deep Neural Network. *J. Mech. Des.* **2021**, *143*, 091702. [CrossRef]
26. Lee, X.Y.; Balu, A.; Stoecklein, D.; Ganapathysubramanian, B.; Sarkar, S. A Case Study of Deep Reinforcement Learning for Engineering Design: Application to Microfluidic Devices for Flow Sculpting. *J. Mech. Des.* **2019**, *141*, 111401. [CrossRef]
27. Faghirnejad, S.; Kontoni, D.P.; Camp, C.V.; Ghasemi, M.R.; Mohammadi Khoramabadi, M. Seismic performance-based design optimization of 2D steel chevron-braced frames using ACO algorithm and nonlinear pushover analysis. *Struct. Multidisc. Optim.* **2025**, *68*, 16. [CrossRef]
28. Faghirnejad, S.; Kontoni, D.P.N.; Ghasemi, M.R. Performance-based optimization of 2D reinforced concrete wall-frames using pushover analysis and ABC optimization algorithm. *Earthq. Struct.* **2024**, *27*, 285–302. [CrossRef]
29. Andreassen, E.; Clausen, A.; Schevenels, M.; Lazarov, B.S.; Sigmund, O. Efficient topology optimization in MATLAB using 88 lines of code. *Struct. Multidisc. Optim.* **2010**, *43*, 1–16. [CrossRef]
30. Sigmund, O. A 99 line topology optimization code written in Matlab. *Struct. Multidisc. Optim.* **2001**, *21*, 120–127. [CrossRef]
31. Christensen, P.W.; Klarbring, A. *An Introduction to Structural Optimization*; Springer: Dordrecht, The Netherlands, 2009. [CrossRef]
32. Wang, M.Y.; Wang, X.; Guo, D. A level set method for structural topology optimization. *Comput. Methods Appl. Mech. Eng.* **2003**, *192*, 227–246. [CrossRef]
33. Allaire, G.; Jouve, F.; Toader, A.-M. Structural optimization using sensitivity analysis and a level-set method. *J. Comput. Phys.* **2004**, *194*, 363–393. [CrossRef]
34. Vučina, D.; Lozina, Ž.; Pehnec, I. Ad-hoc cluster and workflow for parallel implementation of initial-stage evolutionary optimum design. *Struct. Multidisc. Optim.* **2011**, *45*, 197–222. [CrossRef]

computation

MDPI

Review

Optimization of Rock-Cutting Tools: Improvements in Structural Design and Process Efficiency

Yuecao Cao [1], Qiang Zhang [2], Shucheng Zhang [2], Ying Tian [2], Xiangwei Dong [2,*], Xiaojun Song [3] and Dongxiang Wang [2,4]

1 College of Mechanical Engineering, Liaoning Technical University, Fuxin 123000, China
2 College of Mechanical and Electronic Engineering, Shandong University of Science and Technology, Qingdao 266580, China; zhangqiangskd@sdust.edu.cn (Q.Z.)
3 Xi'an Heavy Equipment Tongchuan Coal Mining Machinery Co., Ltd., Loudi 417099, China
4 National Energy Group Coal Coking Co., Ltd., Wuhai 016099, China
* Correspondence: dongxw139@163.com

Abstract: Rock-breaking cutters are critical components in tunneling, mining, and drilling operations, where efficiency, durability, and energy consumption are paramount. Traditional cutter designs and empirical process optimization methods often fail to address the dynamic interaction between heterogeneous rock masses and tool structures, leading to premature wear, high specific energy, and suboptimal performance. Topology optimization, as an advanced computational design method, offers transformative potential for lightweight, high-strength cutter structures and adaptive cutting process control. This review systematically examines recent advancements in topology-optimized cutter design and its integration with rock-cutting mechanics. The structural innovations in cutter geometry and materials are analyzed, emphasizing solutions for stress distribution, wear/fatigue resistance, and dynamic load adaptation. The numerical methods for modeling rock–tool interactions are introduced, including discrete element method (DEM) simulations, smoothed particle hydrodynamics (SPH) methods, and machine learning (ML)-enhanced predictive models. The cutting process optimization strategies that leverage topology optimization to balance objectives such as energy efficiency, chip formation control, and tool lifespan are evaluated.

Keywords: topology optimization; rock-breaking cutter; rock-cutting mechanics; structural design; numerical simulation; energy efficiency

1. Introduction

Rock-breaking cutters are indispensable components in tunneling [1], mining [2], and drilling [3] operations, where their efficiency, durability, and energy consumption directly determine the feasibility and cost-effectiveness of large-scale engineering projects. These tools face extreme mechanical loads and abrasive interactions with heterogeneous rock masses [3], which often lead to premature wear, unpredictable failure, and excessive energy expenditure. Traditional cutter designs, which are largely based on empirical modifications of geometric parameters [4], struggle to address the dynamic interplay between tool structures and complex geological conditions. For instance, conventional methods fail to optimize stress distribution under cyclic loading or adapt to anisotropic rock properties, resulting in suboptimal performance and frequent maintenance [5,6]. The performance of rock-cutting tools is governed by multi-domain influencing parameters, including (1) tool-specific factors—geometry, material properties (hardness and fracture toughness), and

https://doi.org/10.3390/computation13070152

structural configuration; (2) rock mass characteristics—strength heterogeneity, abrasiveness, discontinuities, and geological anomalies; (3) operational parameters—cutting depth, penetration rate, tool spacing, and dynamic loading spectra [7]; and (4) environmental constraints—depth-induced geostress, groundwater ingress, and thermal gradients.

Topology optimization, which is a computational design method, has emerged as a transformative approach to overcome these limitations [8,9]. Unlike conventional trial-and-error methods, topology optimization design enables the systematic generation of lightweight, high-strength structures by redistributing material within a design space while satisfying mechanical constraints [10]. This method is particularly advantageous for rock-breaking cutters, where weight reduction can lower inertial forces during operation [11], and stress homogenization can mitigate crack initiation in high-load regions [12]. Topology optimization achieves performance maximization through intelligent material distribution and has been extensively applied across diverse fields such as aerospace [13], automotive manufacturing [14], biomedical engineering [15], and civil engineering [16]. Current cutting-edge approaches focus on interdisciplinary integration, multi-physics coupling optimization [17], encompassing multi-scale topology optimization [18], and data-driven machine learning optimization [19]. These methodologies, by integrating advanced algorithms and manufacturing technologies, significantly enhance structural functionality, lightweight potential, and manufacturability. Recent advancements in additive manufacturing further enhance the applicability of topology optimization, allowing the fabrication of intricate lattice structures that improve energy absorption and wear resistance [20].

The integration of topology optimization with rock-cutting mechanics requires addressing multi-physics challenges, including thermo-mechanical coupling, dynamic fracture propagation, and real-time adaptive control [21]. Numerical frameworks such as the discrete element method (DEM) [22] and smoothed particle hydrodynamics (SPH) [23] have been instrumental in simulating rock–tool interactions, revealing mechanisms like chip formation and crack propagation under varying load conditions. Meanwhile, machine learning (ML) models are increasingly deployed to predict tool wear and optimize cutting parameters [24], bridging the gap between computational design and operational efficiency. Rock-cutting tools endure extreme conditions, including high-impact loads, abrasive wear, and heterogeneous rock interactions, necessitating robust mechanical properties and fatigue resistance [25,26]. Despite the criticality of such tools, research on topology optimization for diverse cutter types (e.g., disk cutters [27] and conical picks [28]) remains underexplored compared to advancements in aerospace or automotive fields. This gap stems from various inherent challenges, as follows: (1) the complex multi-physics coupling during rock fragmentation complicates accurate modeling [29]; (2) dynamic and stochastic loading induces nonlinear material responses, demanding high-fidelity transient simulations; (3) material heterogeneity imposes constraints on isotropic assumptions in conventional optimization frameworks; and (4) the manufacturing feasibility of intricate optimized geometries under harsh industrial conditions remains a practical barrier [30].

This study aims to review recent advancements in topology-optimized cutter design and its synergy with rock-cutting process optimization. We critically analyze structural innovations, numerical modeling techniques, and adaptive control strategies, emphasizing interdisciplinary contributions from mechanics, materials science, and computational engineering. By addressing key challenges this work provides a roadmap for next-generation smart cutting systems that are capable of operating in extreme geological environments. This study is structured as follows: Section 2 examines structural innovations in rock-breaking cutters, analyzing conventional design limitations and emerging topology optimization strategies. Section 3 evaluates numerical modeling techniques for simulating rock–tool interactions and validating optimized designs. Section 4 explores cutting process optimization strategies, focusing on energy efficiency, chip formation control, and sustainability. Section 5 proposes future directions.

2. Structural Innovations in Rock-Breaking Cutters

2.1. Conventional Cutter Design Limitations

2.1.1. Continuous Rock-Breaking Equipment and Types of Cutters

As shown in Figure 1a, boom-type roadheaders, driven by telescopic booms to operate rotating cutting heads, employ densely distributed conical picks composed of tungsten carbide tips and alloy steel bodies. These tools fracture medium–hard rock formations (uniaxial compressive strength <80 MPa) through high-speed rotation (20–50 rpm), generating combined shear–impact actions, as well as offering flexibility in adapting to complex cross-sections. As in Figure 1b, full-face tunnel boring machines (TBMs) utilize shield-driven propulsion systems, integrating single- or double-disk cutters on cutterheads. Double-disk cutters employ dual-ring designs to improve load distribution and eccentric resistance, promoting controlled radial crack propagation under high thrust forces. The interaction and subsequent fragmentation processes in rock breaking are directly relevant to the design of the TBM cutterhead and the efficiency of TBM excavation. The spacing between adjacent cutters is a key parameter governing this interaction mechanism. As in Figure 1c, disk–saw rock excavators feature oscillating cutting disks adjusted by hydraulic arms for dynamic radial penetration, combining high-speed rotation with sawtooth trajectory-induced tensile–shear interactions to delaminate stratified rock masses. These three equipment types target distinct scenarios—roadway construction, long-tunnel excavation, and precision rock cutting—yet share common technological challenges in tool wear resistance optimization and intelligent rock-breaking control. Notably, remotely controlled roadheaders play a pivotal role in such contexts, offering enhanced safety and operational efficiency in weakly cracked rock masses that are susceptible to collapses. Table 1 [31] presents the principal classification methods for rock-breaking tools used in this study.

Figure 1. Types of tunnel excavation equipment and cutting tools in mining engineering.

Table 1. Classification methods of rock-breaking tools.

Working Mode	Rock–Tool Interaction	Cutting Tool	Adaptability of Rock Strength
Drag/plowing	Continuous rotation	Cutter tooth Scraper Conical pick	<40~60 MPa <60~80 MPa <40~60 MPa
Rotation	Rolling Unreal rolling	Disk cutter Roller cone cutter	<250 MPa <200 MPa
Impact	Impact	Beaker hammer	<100 MPa

2.1.2. Rock-Breaking Mechanism and Mechanical Model

Excavation progress is critically governed by geological constraints (rock properties, structure, and groundwater) and mining operational factors (method selection, equipment efficacy, support needs, and logistics). The interaction of these factors ultimately determines the rate of advance and the overall project timeline. Figure 2 (This figure is adapted from reference [32–34]) illustrates the rock-breaking mechanism of cutting picks, including their interaction with the rotating drum during fragmentation. Figure 3 (This figure is adapted from reference [35]) illustrates the relationship between the disk cutter's normal/rolling forces and rock-breaking mechanisms, particularly highlighting the dual-cutter cooperative fracturing effect. The traditional rock-cutting tool design procedure, which is predominantly based on empirical modifications of geometric parameters such as wedge angles and disk diameters [22], faces significant challenges in addressing the dynamic and heterogeneous nature of rock–tool interactions. Conventional approaches often rely on isotropic material assumptions and static load conditions, which fail to account for the anisotropic mechanical properties of rock masses and cyclic loading. For instance, studies on anchored rock joints under constant normal load and constant normal stiffness boundary conditions reveal that stress softening dominates, while stress hardening occurs under constant normal stiffness due to suppressed shear dilation, highlighting the limitations of static design frameworks in adapting to varying boundary conditions [25].

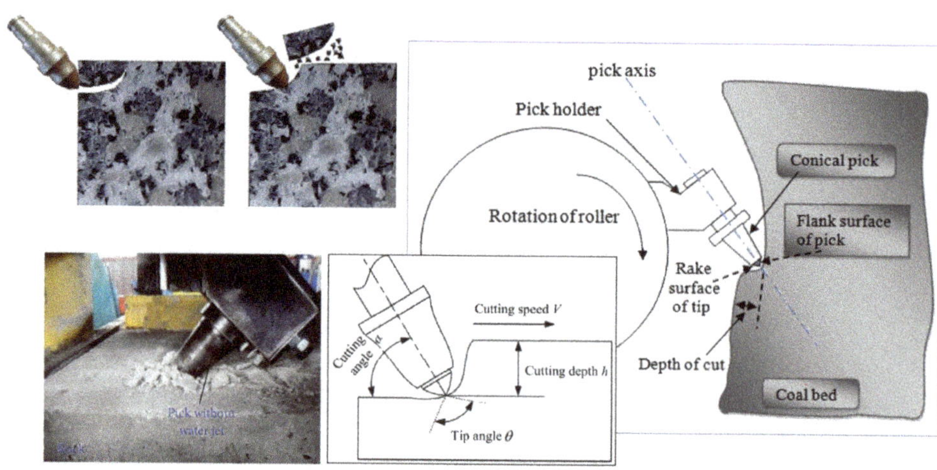

Figure 2. Schematic diagram of the rock-breaking mechanism of cutting picks.

The optimized design of rock-breaking tools requires synergistic advancements in both material properties and structural parameters. At the material level, the wear resistance and impact resistance of the tools are balanced through the integration of gradient-structured cemented carbide substrates with ceramic particles or diamond coatings [36,37]. Surface treatment technologies further enhance surface hardness, while finite element simulations optimize microstructures to inhibit crack propagation [38]. In structural design, tool geometric parameters should be dynamically adjusted according to rock hardness, whereby conical picks with apex angles of 55–100° achieve an optimal balance between economic efficiency and rock-breaking performance [28]. Curved-edge configurations and multi-cutter collaborative layouts effectively reduce ineffective fragmentation while extending service life [39]. The selection of operational parameters (e.g., force and rotational velocity) and tool type involves a fundamental compromise, whereby increasing the force may allow for lower speeds for certain tools, while higher speeds might be viable with specific cutter types under reduced force, all of which are aimed at balancing fragmentation efficiency and tool life. For scaled-up designs, scale effects must be addressed through modified geometric similarity principles, adapted heat treatment and welding processes, and recalibrated dynamic load matching to ensure strength redundancy in large-scale tools and power system stability.

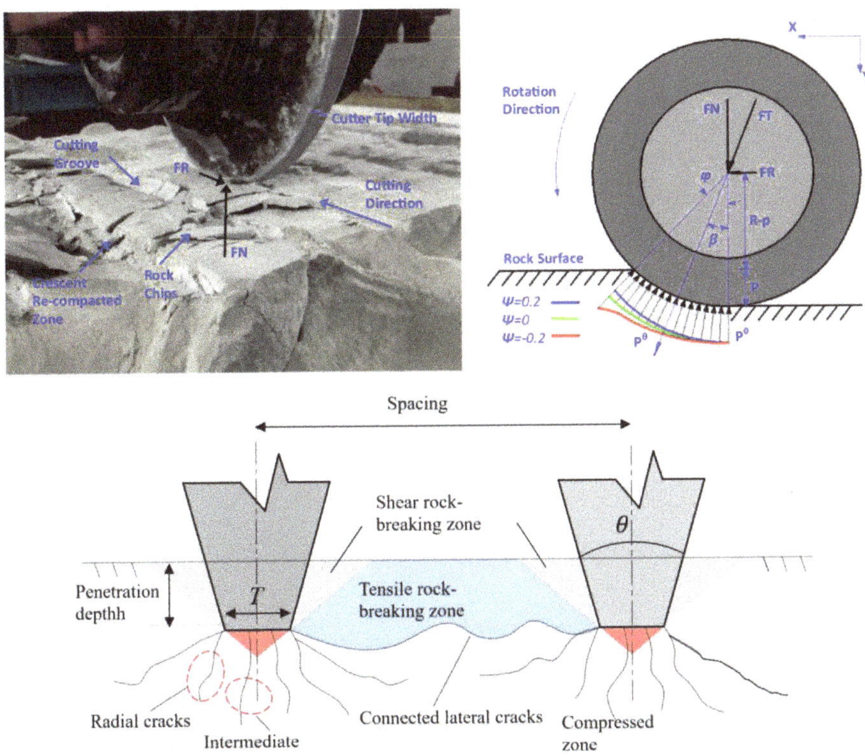

Figure 3. Relation between the disk cutter's normal and rolling forces and rock-breaking mechanisms.

2.1.3. Optimization Objectives and Optimization Methods

Figures 4 and 5 illustrate the influential factors, optimization objectives, and methods for rock-cutting tools aimed at enhancing rock-breaking performance. The optimization focuses on key metrics such as cutting force, specific energy, wear rate, and tool life. By employing topology optimization, finite element analysis, and machine learning, it seeks to improve tool geometry, material distribution, and structural parameters for different rock types and conditions. This enhances cutting efficiency and tool durability, offering a clear guide for subsequent optimization strategies. The optimization process must integrate practical working conditions with intelligent control strategies. For hard rock or highly abrasive formations, diamond composite coatings and chip removal groove designs mitigate wear. Embedded sensors enable real-time tool condition monitoring, while machine learning-based dynamic adjustments of tunneling parameters facilitate adaptive rock-breaking mechanisms [24,40]. Scaled laboratory tests quantify specific energy consumption and wear rates, whereas field pilot tests optimize cutter arrangements through torque and thrust force monitoring [4,22]. Economic analyses demonstrate that although optimized tools incur 20–30% higher initial costs, their extended lifespan of over 50% significantly reduces the overall operational costs.

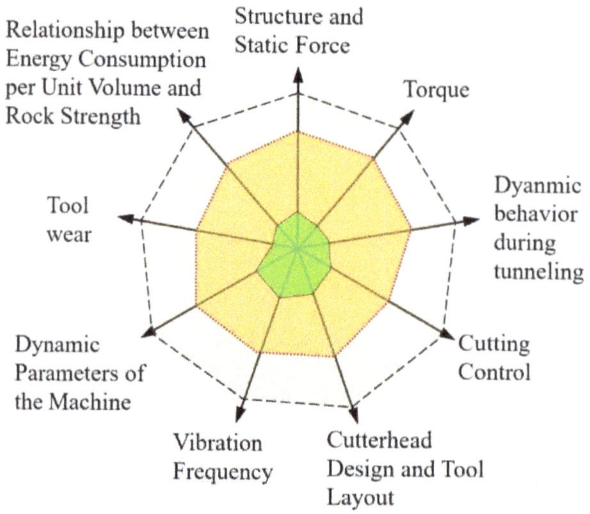

Figure 4. Factors of rock-breaking cutters and rock-cutting process.

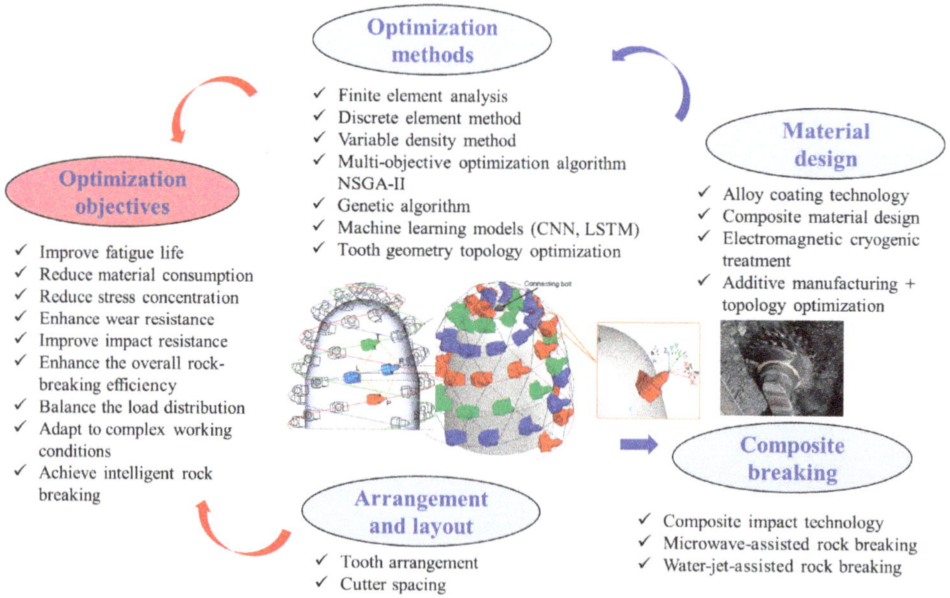

Figure 5. Optimization objectives and methods for improving rock-breaking performances.

Liu et al. [41] proposed an optimization design method for conical pick installation angles based on the coupling of static and kinematic principles. This approach established a geometric relationship model involving impact angle, tilt angle, and skew angle, deriving angular constraints for the resultant force along the pick axis. However, the design process relied solely on rigid-body assumptions and homogeneous rock conditions, limiting its applicability to real-world heterogeneous geological environments. Yasar et al. [32] introduced a semi-theoretical and semi-empirical predictive model for conical pick cutting forces. The model developed a generalized formula incorporating rock uniaxial compressive strength, cutting depth, rake angle, and back-clearance angle. While this model successfully captured the linear relationship between cutting force and depth by addressing limitations in traditional angular functions, it overlooked dynamic interactions between tool geometry and rock brittleness during cutting processes. Consequently, predictions exhibited significant deviations under high-depth cutting or complex operational conditions, highlighting unresolved challenges in balancing theoretical rigor with practical adaptability. Table 2 summarizes the optimization methods and corresponding performance improvements for various rock-cutting tools. A comparative analysis of optimization approaches and their effectiveness is systematically documented in the table.

Table 2. Optimization methods and performance improvements for rock-cutting tools.

Authors and Year	Optimized Component	Optimization Objective(s)	Optimization Method	Performance Improvement
Park et al. (2018), Int. J. Rock Mech. Min. Sci. [5]	Point attack pick cutter and cutter holder assembly	Minimize specific energy; enhance structural stability; extend tool durability	Lab-scale linear cutting tests; finite element analysis; evaluated cut spacing, depth, skew angle, and attack angle	Achieved lower specific energy via optimized skew/attack angles. Positive skew angle linked to slower abrasion rates.
Sun et al. (2018), J. Cent. South Univ. [42]	Cutter layout (assembled radius layout of disk cutters) for TBMs	Optimize cutter layout for balanced forces/moments with coupling and non-interference.	Genetic algorithm; equal life and equal wear principles; comprehensive evaluation model	Assembled radius gap—reduced to 25.8 mm. Unbalanced radial force—decreased by 62.41%.
Palaniappan et al. (2019), Proc. MPES [43]	Conical cemented carbide pick	Reduce the wear rate; analyze cutting forces, cutting efficiency, and specific energy to find the best performance compromise	Coating the pick tip with aluminum titanium nitride; examining wear mechanisms via SEM and X-ray analysis	Hardness improvement: 22.47 GPa; wear rate reduction: 13.9–21.8%.
Kumar et al. (2020), Int. J. Rock Mech. Min. Sci. [44]	Operating parameters of surface miner (depth of cut, cutting speed, and pick temperature)	Minimum pick wear/consumption, higher production, and optimal cutting efficiency	Develop empirical models via Taguchi, MLR, and ANN to study temperature variations in cutting picks	Achieved optimized temperature at 95% confidence level.
Mahmoodzadeh et al. (2021), Autom. Constr. [45]	Prediction of TBM disk cutter life	Develop accurate machine learning models for cutter life prediction	GPR, SVR, DT, and KNN with 200 datasets; five-fold cross-validation	Most accurate model (GPR).

Table 2. *Cont.*

Authors and Year	Optimized Component	Optimization Objective(s)	Optimization Method	Performance Improvement
Fathipour-Azar (2023), Rock Mech. Rock Eng. [46]	Predictive model for mean cutting force (MCF) of conical picks	Establish quantitative correlation between rock strength, tool geometry, cutting data, and MCF	Fine-tune hyperparameters using grid search, random search, GA, PSO, and DE	Best model (DE-XGBoost).
Zhou et al. (2023), Acta Geotech. [24]	Predictive model for specific energy (SE) in roadheader excavation	Develop accurate SE prediction models considering rock properties, pick geometry, and operation parameters	Six ML algorithms (BPNN, Elman, ELM, KELM, RF, and SVR) optimized by sparrow search algorithm (SSA)	SSA-RF—training set: MAE = 0.7938, MAPE = 12.76%, R^2 = 0.9632.
Liu et al. (2024), J. Cent. South Univ. [47]	Prediction model for mean cutting force (MCF) of conical picks	Accurately evaluate MCF for pick design and rock-cutting suitability	Hybrid models (boosting trees + Bayesian optimization (BO))	Best model (BO-CatBoost): outperformed common ML models, especially in handling categorical features (θ with 6 angle types).
Wang et al. (2024), Simul. Model. Pract. Theor. [48]	Disk cutter arrangements and excavation parameters	Reduce cutter wear, minimize specific energy, and balance cutter force during rock-breaking	Enhanced bonding model	Penetration depth $\leq$ 5 mm; tip width > 20 mm; cutter spacing 80–95 mm.
Du et al. (2025), Rock Mech. Rock Eng. [49]	Working parameters of disk cutter	Rock-breaking mechanism of disk cutter to understand how parameters affect rock-breaking behavior	Brazilian tests; coupled FEM–DEM	Revealed shear–tension failure mechanism; quantified parameter–energy relationships.

Empirical designs often lead to uneven stress distribution, causing localized stress concentrations at cutter edges or joints. This accelerates wear and crack initiation, particularly in hard rock, where abrasive interactions dominate. Conventional designs prioritize mechanical robustness over energy efficiency, resulting in a high specific energy consumption. For example, unoptimized cutter spacing and penetration depth in TBMs generate excessive fines and heat, increasing operational costs [50]. Lu et al. [51] demonstrated that conventional conical picks exhibit excessive material usage due to overestimated fatigue life requirements. Through topology optimization driven by dynamic load spectra and finite element analysis, a 23.83% volume reduction was achieved while maintaining structural integrity under cyclic loading, highlighting the necessity of integrating fatigue constraints in topology optimization frameworks.

2.2. Issues for Topology Optimization for Rock-Cutting Tools

Topology optimization technology, through intelligent material distribution design, plays a significant role in achieving lightweight structures, enhanced strength, and improved fatigue resistance. However, the unique working conditions and functional requirements of rock-breaking tools pose distinct challenges for their topology optimization design. Common construction materials for combining knives and disks include tungsten carbide, high-speed steel, and cemented carbides, which are selected for their ultra-high hardness, fracture toughness, and thermal stability.

Structural Adaptability under Complex Dynamic Loads: Rock-breaking tools undergo asymmetric impact loads, high-frequency vibrations, and multi-axial stresses during operation, rendering conventional static optimization models inadequate for accurately representing real-world working conditions. Dynamic response modeling requires the establishment of multi-physics-coupled models. Existing topology optimization methods predominantly rely on static strength constraints, lacking quantitative control over crack initiation and propagation under cyclic loading. To address this, a dynamic load-sensitive objective function should be developed by integrating transient numerical analysis with data-driven prediction algorithms (such as fatigue life prediction).

Material–Structure Synergistic Optimization in Extreme Wear Environments: Rock-breaking tools rely on composite structures combining hard surface materials for wear resistance with tough substrate materials; however, topological optimization often neglects the impact of material gradients on performance. The parametric representation of continuous/discrete material distributions lacks sufficient compatibility with manufacturing processes. The conflict between lightweight requirements and wear-resistant layer thickness creates competing optimization objectives, necessitating multi-objective analysis. There is a need to develop a multi-scale topology optimization framework integrating material microstructure design with macroscopic geometric morphology optimization.

Data Scarcity in Multi-Condition Adaptive Design: Rock-breaking tools need to adapt to varying working conditions, such as different rock hardness levels. However, the limited amount of experimental data restricts the generalization capability of optimization models. Quantifying the geomechanical properties and tool–rock interactions remains challenging. Machine learning models trained on small datasets face high risks of overfitting, making it difficult to explore high-dimensional design spaces effectively. To address this, a digital twin platform for rock–tool interactions should be established, combined with transfer learning to enhance the cross-condition adaptability of optimization models.

Through response surface methodology, Sun et al. [22] demonstrated that cutting depth (h) exerts the most significant influence on disk cutter wear (contribution weight: 42%), followed by spindle speed and swing arm speed. Their optimized parameters reduced specific energy consumption by 41% (from 29.85 to 17.59 MJ/m^3), validating the potential of data-driven parameter tuning in energy efficiency improvement. Lu et al. [51] conducted topology optimization for cantilever roadheader picks driven by fatigue life. A cutting force mathematical model and triaxial load spectrum simulation were used to identify maximum loads for static analysis. Finite element evaluation revealed material redundancy in traditional designs. Volume-minimized topology optimization via the variable density method achieved a 64.42% volume reduction after 43 iterations. Validation demonstrated a maximum stress of 883 MPa (below the permissible 950 MPa), a fatigue life of 1.92×10^4 cycles (meeting the 32-day operational requirements), and a 23.83% material reduction, achieving synergistic improvements in strength, longevity, and lightweight performance.

The topology optimization framework proposed in the reference (Figure 6 [51])—encompassing cutting force simulation, static analysis, and fatigue life prediction—establishes a systematic methodological framework for structural adaptability under complex dynamic loads. The optimized pick achieved a 23.83% reduction in volume while increasing rotational torque by 18% through symmetrical groove design. However, the study did not fully validate the compatibility between the topological configuration and additive manufacturing processes, nor did it investigate the long-term reliability evolution of gradient materials under dynamic service conditions.

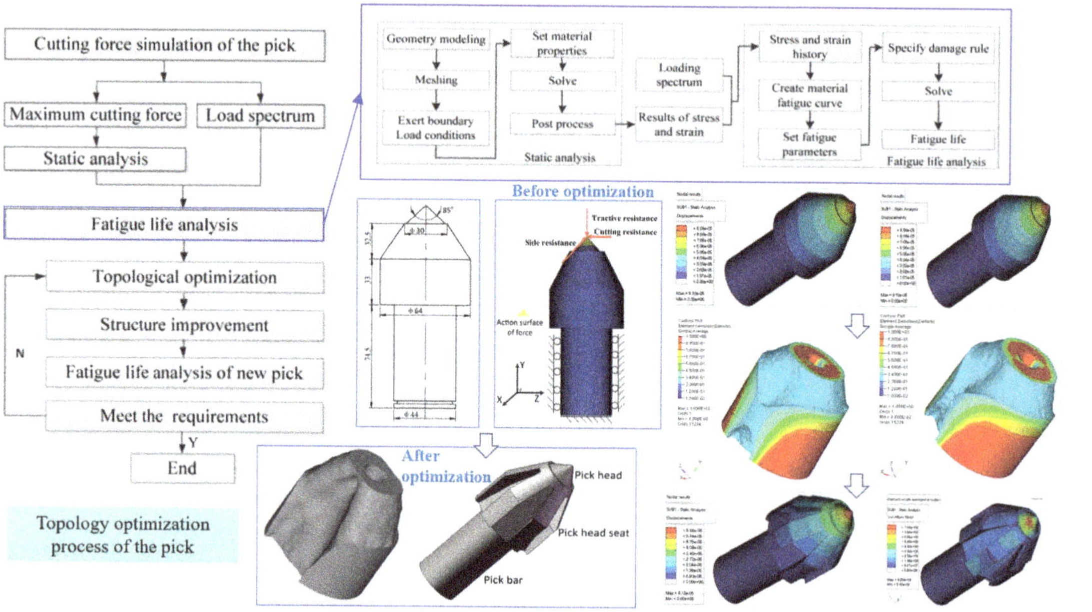

Figure 6. Topology optimization process of the pick cutter.

3. Numerical Modeling of Rock–Tool Interactions

3.1. Numerical Simulation Techniques

Rock fracture evolution represents a quintessential continuum–discontinuum coupling problem. Accurately simulating its complete process requires numerical methods to simultaneously address three critical capabilities—(1) the characterization of continuum mechanical properties, (2) the modeling of discontinuum behaviors, and (3) the resolution of spatiotemporal transition mechanisms between continuum and discontinuum states. However, most existing numerical approaches are confined to specific fracture stages, necessitating hybrid methodologies to achieve full-process simulation [52] (Figure 7 [53]).

Figure 7. Hard alloy disk cutters and the alloy detached after their failure.

Numerical methods for rock fracture simulation are categorized into continuum and discontinuum approaches. Continuum methods (e.g., FEM and XFEM) accurately characterize rock deformation but require mesh refinement or element deletion techniques to model fracture [54]. Discontinuum methods (e.g., DEM) describe discontinuities and large deformations via discrete particle interactions; however, they suffer from computational inefficiency and parameter sensitivity [55] (Figure 8 [56]). Hybrid continuum–discontinuum methods, such as the Continuum–Discontinuum Element Method (CDEM), integrate FEM and DEM to simultaneously simulate continuum deformation and interface fracture. Zhu et al. [57] developed a 3D CDEM hydraulic fracturing model coupling continuum fields with fracture seepage; Yue et al. [58] combined the Material Point Method (MPM) with CDEM to simulate blast-induced fractures; and Gong et al. [59] combined FEM and Discontinuous Deformation Analysis (DDA) to capture progressive rock failure. While these hybrid approaches enable full-cycle fracture evolution modeling, challenges persist in algorithmic complexity and interfacial transition errors, driving research toward unified numerical frameworks.

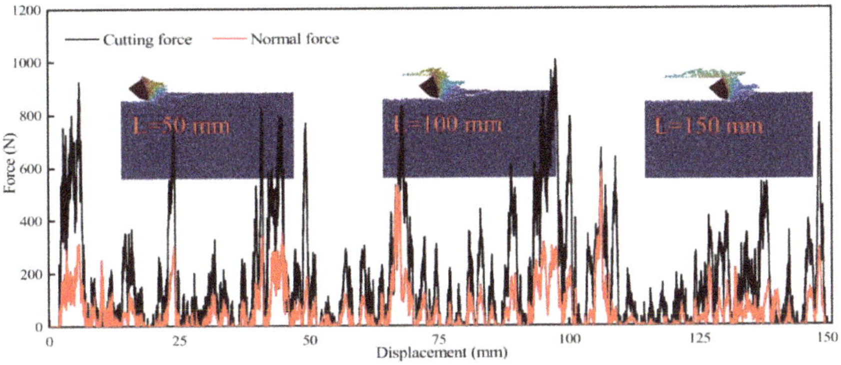

Figure 8. Simulation of the process of a pick cutting rock under confining stress using DEM.

In rock mechanics, numerical methods integrating fracture models and cutter geometries have advanced the understanding of rock-cutting mechanisms. While FEM simulations of disk cutter operations often exhibit over-cutting artifacts in the rock beneath the tip, Geng et al. [60] enhanced cutting force prediction accuracy through optimized element deletion strategies. Li et al. [61] employed PFC3D to analyze lunar rock-cutting loads under shallow depths with varied blade angles. Meshless methods, categorized as continuum approaches (e.g., MPM [62] and SPH [63]), include global weak-form techniques like EFGM [64] (requiring background integration grids) and local weak-form variants such as point interpolation methods and SPM. Leveraging Lagrangian particle properties and mesh-free adaptability, SPM uniquely bridges continuum deformation and discontinuum fracture behaviors, emerging as a robust approach for simulating continuum–discontinuum transitions in rock failure processes (Figure 9).

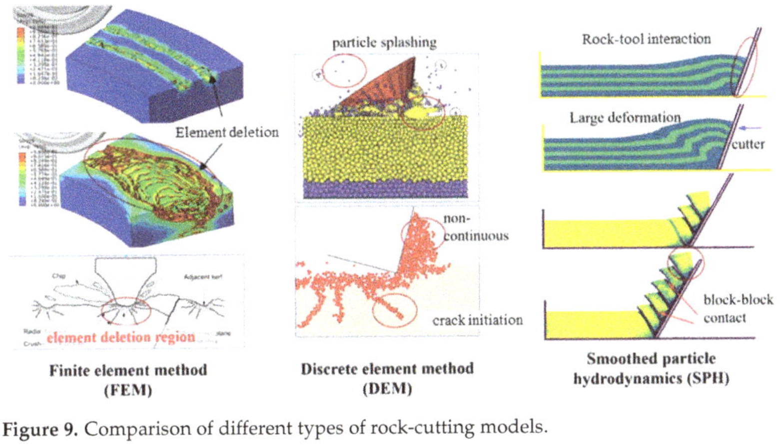

Figure 9. Comparison of different types of rock-cutting models.

3.2. Machine Learning (ML)-Enhanced Predictive Models

Machine learning has revolutionized predictive modeling in rock-cutting optimization by enabling data-driven insights into complex tool–rock interactions. It has been successfully applied to assess excavation efficiency in recent studies. E. Avunduk et al. [65] used the artificial neural network technique to predict the instantaneous cutting rate of the roadheader. Zhang et al. [66] developed a digital twin-driven method for real-time intelligent control for TBM operation. Liu et al. [67] implemented faster R-CNN with a simplified VGG16 backbone to develop an intelligent rock identification system, achieving a high accuracy for single rock types and >80% for complex lithological mixtures, demonstrating strong robustness for underground mine stability assessment.

Hybrid frameworks, such as Light-GBM coupled with Classification and Regression Trees [68], demonstrate superior accuracy in predicting cutting forces and wear rates under multi-condition scenarios, achieving mean absolute errors below 8% when trained on DEM-simulated datasets. Digital twin platforms further leverage real-time sensor data (e.g., strain and temperature) to dynamically adjust cutting parameters, reducing tool wear prediction latency to <2 s in field trials [69]. However, current ML models remain constrained by their dependency on high-quality labeled data, as well as their limited interpretability in capturing multi-physics interactions. Recent advances in physics-informed neural networks (PINNs) show promise in bridging this gap by embedding the governing equations of rock fracture mechanics into loss functions, enhancing both predictive accuracy and physical plausibility [70].

As a representative ML approach, Physics-Informed Neural Networks (PINNs) integrate physical laws with data-driven modeling to overcome these limitations. Table 3 summarizes the key steps for implementing PINN-based tool optimization, from physics-based problem definition to experimental validation.

Table 3. A general procedure for cutting tool optimization with PINN.

Step 1: Problem Definition and Physics-Based Modeling
- **Input Parameters**: Tool geometry (blade angle, edge length), material properties (hardness, elastic modulus), operating conditions (cutting speed, confining pressure).
- **Output Targets**: Stress field, temperature field, crack propagation path, tool wear rate, specific rock-breaking energy.
- **Governing Equations**:
  - **Rock Mechanics**: Elastoplastic constitutive equations, as well as Drucker–Prager or Mohr–Coulomb failure criteria.
  - **Heat Transfer**: Energy conservation equation with thermo-mechanical coupling terms.
  - **Tool–Rock Interaction**: Frictional heating model, wear equations.

Step 2: PINN Architecture Design
- **Network Structure**:
  - **Input Layer**: Tool parameters (e.g., blade angle α, cutting depth d) and spatial coordinates (x, y, t).
  - **Hidden Layers**: Multi-layer perceptron (activation: ReLU/Swish).
  - **Output Layer**: Key physical quantities (stress σ, temperature T, damage factor D).
  - **Loss Function:**
  - $\mathcal{L} = \lambda_{\text{data}}\mathcal{L}_{\text{data}} + \lambda_{\text{phys}}\mathcal{L}_{\text{phys}}$
    - Data Loss $\mathcal{L}_{\text{data}}$: mean square error of experimental or simulation data (such as the cutting tool forces F_x, F_y)
    - Physics Loss $\mathcal{L}_{\text{phys}}$: residual of the governing equation, the boundary condition.

Step 3: Model Validation and Uncertainty Quantification
- **Validation Metrics:**
  - **Error between predictions and independent experimental data.**
  - **Norm of physics equation residuals.**
- **Uncertainty Analysis: Monte Carlo dropout or Bayesian PINN to quantify robustness against input noise.**

Step 4: Tool Optimization
- **Objective: Minimize specific energy or maximize tool life.**
- **Optimization Methods:**
  - **Gradient-Based: Use PINN's automatic differentiation to compute** $\partial E_{specific}/\partial\alpha$ **for gradient descent.**
  - **Global Search: Genetic algorithms for multi-objective Pareto optimization (e.g., trade-off between energy consumption and wear rate).**
- **Experimental Validation: Verify optimized tool designs via experiments or high-fidelity simulations.**

3.3. Experimental Validation

In the research, development, and optimization of rock-breaking tools, experimental techniques play an indispensable role. As a mainstream method for rock-breaking experiments, the linear cutting experiment simulates the rock-cutting process under actual working conditions [35]. The experiment is usually carried out in a controlled pressure environment. The rock sample is fixed on the experimental platform, and the cutting tool cuts the rock at a set speed and load. The cutting force, power consumption, and tool wear are monitored in real time (Figure 10 [35]).

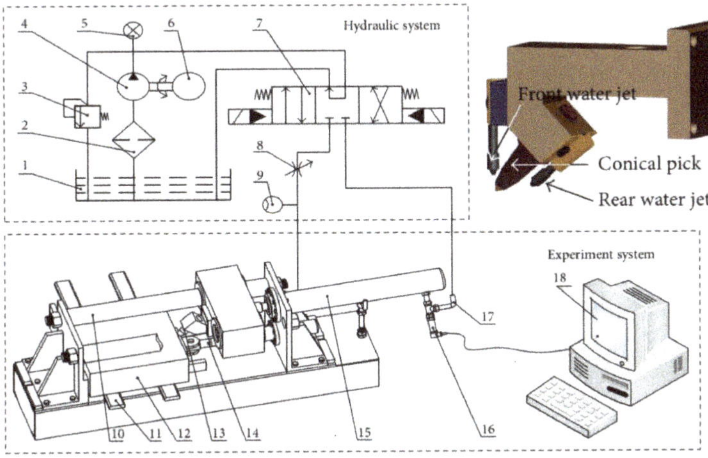

Figure 10. Linear cutting experimental system of water-jet-assisted cutting picks.

Currently, the role of linear cutting experiments is mainly reflected in the following three aspects:

(1) It provides a basis for the selection of tool materials and geometric optimization;
(2) It quantifies the performance of tools under different rock conditions;
(3) It verifies the accuracy of numerical models.

With the evolution of technology, rock-breaking experiments are moving towards automation and digitization. The integration of real-time sensor technology and image recognition systems has significantly improved the accuracy of wear assessment and crack propagation monitoring.

In the future, rock-breaking experiments will be further integrated with artificial intelligence. By leveraging machine learning algorithms, the intelligent analysis and prediction of experimental data can be achieved. At the same time, the improvement in multi-physics field coupling experimental systems will be promoted to more comprehensively simulate the rock fragmentation mechanism under actual working conditions [71]. For example, the development of a thermo-mechanical coupling experimental device will help in understanding the interaction between the cutting tool and the rock in a high-temperature environment, providing crucial support for tool design under extreme working conditions.

4. Cutting Process Optimization

4.1. Energy Efficiency and Specific Energy Reduction

Topology optimization has emerged as a pivotal strategy for enhancing energy efficiency in rock-cutting operations by systematically reducing tool mass while maintaining structural integrity. By redistributing material to minimize stress concentrations and inertial forces, topology-driven designs directly lower the specific energy consumption required for rock fragmentation. For instance, Lu et al. [51] achieved a 64.42% volume reduction in cantilever roadheader picks through variable density methods, while preserving fatigue life. This was accomplished by optimizing load-bearing paths under dynamic cutting forces simulated via MATLAB-based triaxial spectra. The resultant lightweight structures not only decrease power demands but also mitigate heat generation—a critical factor in high-speed tunneling where unoptimized tools can elevate temperatures by 80–120 °C, accelerating wear [20].

Comparative studies highlight topology optimization's superiority over traditional parameter-tuning approaches. While response surface methods, such as Sun et al.'s gray correlation analysis [22], optimize cutting depth and spindle speed to reduce SEC by 41%, these strategies primarily address operational parameters rather than structural inefficiencies. In contrast, topology optimization concurrently optimizes tool geometry and material distribution, where helical groove designs reduced recirculation energy losses through controlled debris ejection [51]. However, current topology optimization frameworks often neglect thermo-mechanical coupling effects, limiting their ability to predict energy dissipation in high-friction scenarios. Future advancements require hybrid models integrating transient thermal analysis with topology-sensitive objective functions to address energy efficiency across mechanical and thermal domains.

4.2. Chip Formation and Debris Management

The control of chip morphology and debris flow is critical to minimizing energy loss and tool clogging during rock-cutting operations. Numerical frameworks combining SPH and DEM or FEM have proven instrumental in simulating dynamic fracture patterns and granular flow dynamics [72]. SPH captures the fragmentation of soft rock layers under tensile–shear coupling, enabling the prediction of chip sizes and ejection trajectories (see Figure 11), while DEM quantifies inter-particle collisions and frictional forces in debris-laden environments. Recent studies by Yu et al. [72] indicate that the use of the SPH-DEM model can establish a refined coupling model of abrasive particles and rock that is capable of addressing a broader range of multiphase and multifield coupling rock-breaking problems (Figure 12 [73]). However, computational costs remain prohibitive for real-time applications, necessitating reduced-order modeling or surrogate-assisted algorithms to balance accuracy and efficiency.

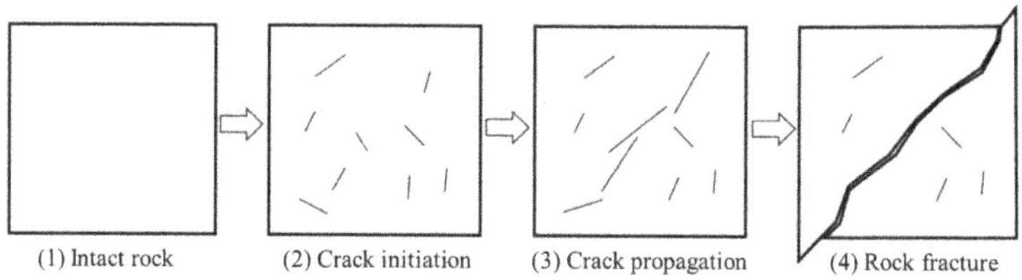

Figure 11. The whole process of rock fracture evolution: a typical continuous–discontinuous problem.

Topology optimization further enhances debris management by tailoring cutter geometries to promote self-cleaning behaviors. Machine learning augments such optimizations, whereby neural networks trained on DEM- or SPH-simulated clogging scenarios identify optimal groove depth-to-width ratios that maximize debris clearance while preserving structural integrity. Nevertheless, field validations under heterogeneous rock conditions remain sparse, highlighting the need for digital twin platforms integrating real-time wear monitoring and adaptive geometry adjustments.

Furthermore, a comprehensive evaluation of TBM performance should also consider the characteristics of the excavated material. Spoil classification provides valuable insights into the fragmentation efficiency, cutter wear, and potential ground conditioning needs, serving as a direct indicator of the excavation process [74]. Similarly, accurate assessment of the final tunnel profile is crucial for verifying design compliance, evaluating overbreak/underbreak, and ensuring structural stability and lining requirements [75].

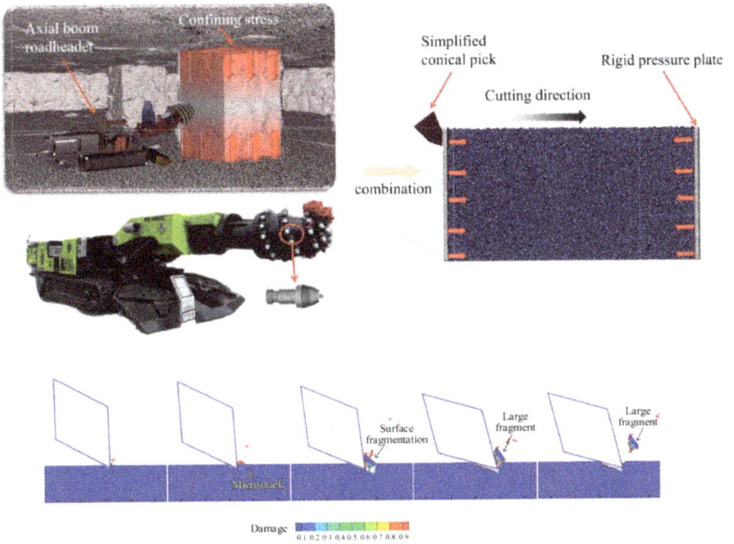

Figure 12. Smoothed particle hydrodynamics (SPH) model for rock-cutting-induced crack propagation and chip separation.

4.3. Sustainability and Scalability

Topology optimization inherently supports sustainability by minimizing material usage while maintaining structural performance. Additive manufacturing further amplifies these benefits by enabling the near-net-shape production of optimized geometries, cutting material waste by up to 45% compared to subtractive methods [76]. Emerging topology optimization algorithms incorporating life-cycle assessment metrics now prioritize designs balancing lightweighting with disassembly feasibility, though industrial adoption remains nascent [77].

Scalability challenges arise when translating lab-scale topology optimization solutions to full-size industrial tools [78]. While small picks (e.g., 50–100 mm in length) achieve 60%+ volume reduction via topology optimization, large disk cutters (>500 mm diameter) face thermo-mechanical instability due to scale effects in heat treatment and residual stress distribution. Multi-scale topology optimization frameworks, which couple macroscopic tool geometry with graded microstructures, mitigate these issues by embedding stress-adaptive lattice patterns in high-stress regions.

4.4. Critical Challenges and Future Directions

Despite significant progress, key challenges persist in topology optimization for rock-cutting applications. Current topology optimization frameworks often simplify dynamic load spectra to mitigate computational burdens in multi-physics coupling, limiting their ability to capture the high-frequency loading effects that are critical for real-time adaptive control. The selection of support systems also directly impacts excavation cycle times. Rigid rock bolt support enables faster installation but requires stable ground conditions, whereas arch-flexible support accommodates deformation at the cost of extended assembly time. Optimizing this trade-off through ground condition prediction can accelerate advance rates while maintaining safety margins. Furthermore, the absence of thermo-mechanical coupling analysis and in situ wear monitoring in existing studies underscores the gaps in predicting tool degradation under extreme thermal and abrasive conditions. To address these limitations, future research must integrate digital twin platforms with edge computing to enable rapid optimization iterations and real-time geometry adjustments. Additionally, synergizing parameter-level optimizations with structural topology optimization solutions could unlock multi-scale optimization strategies, harmonizing process parameters and tool geometries for holistic energy efficiency gains.

5. Conclusions

This review establishes topology optimization as a paradigm-shifting approach for intelligent rock-cutting tool design, systematically overcoming empirical limitations in structural efficiency, durability, and energy consumption. The principal findings are summarized as follows:

(1) The transformative potential of topology optimization in rock-cutting tools enables lightweight, high-strength structures that outperform empirical designs, resolving stress concentration, dynamic load adaptation, and wear resistance challenges.
(2) Integration with advanced methods (DEM/SPH simulations and ML models) achieves the predictive optimization of rock–tool interactions, cutting forces, and tool lifespan.
(3) Key innovations include multi-physics-coupled frameworks for dynamic loading, ML-enhanced predictive models, and sustainable recyclable designs.
(4) Persisting challenges involve thermo-mechanical coupling effects, manufacturing feasibility of complex geometries, and scalability across heterogeneous rock conditions.
(5) Depth-induced difficulties (elevated geostress, rockburst risks, and thermal/water hazards) necessitate intelligent monitoring and adaptive excavation strategies.

Future research directions should focus on multi-scale topology optimization, integrating material microstructures and macro-geometries, digital twin platforms for real-time adaptive control, and AI-driven design frameworks trained on multi-condition datasets. Bridging these gaps will unlock next-generation smart cutting systems that are capable of autonomous adaptation to extreme geological environments, ultimately advancing the sustainability and cost-effectiveness of mining and tunneling operations.

Author Contributions: Conceptualization, Y.C.; methodology, Q.Z. and Y.T.; software, X.D.; validation, Y.C., Q.Z. and S.Z.; formal analysis, Y.T.; investigation, X.S.; resources, X.S., X.D. and D.W.; data curation, X.D.; writing—original draft preparation, X.D. and S.Z.; writing—review and editing, Y.T. and S.Z.; visualization, Y.C.; supervision, D.W.; project administration, Q.Z.; funding acquisition, Q.Z. All authors have read and agreed to the published version of the manuscript.

Funding: This work was supported by the National Natural Science Foundation of China under Grant No. 52234005.

Acknowledgments: All individuals mentioned in this section have given their consent to be acknowledged.

Conflicts of Interest: Author Xiaojun Song was employed by the company Xi'an Heavy Equipment Tongchuan Coal Mining Machinery Co., Ltd. Author Dongxiang Wang was employed by the company National Energy Group Coal Coking Co., Ltd. The remaining authors declare that the research was conducted in the absence of any commercial or financial relationships that could be construed as a potential conflict of interest.

References

1. Li, G.; Wang, W.; Jing, Z.; Zuo, L.; Wang, F.; Wei, Z. Mechanism and numerical analysis of cutting rock and soil by TBM cutting tools. *Tunn. Undergr. Space Technol.* **2018**, *81*, 428–437. [CrossRef]
2. Wang, L.; Zhang, D.; Wang, D.; Feng, C. A review of selected solutions on the evaluation of coal-rock cutting performances of shearer picks under complex geological conditions. *Appl. Sci.* **2022**, *12*, 12371. [CrossRef]

3. Hamzaban, M.T.; Rostami, J.; Dahl, F. Wear of cutting tools in hard rock excavation process: A critical review of rock abrasiveness testing methods. *Rock Mech. Rock Eng.* **2023**, *56*, 1843–1882. [CrossRef]
4. Deng, L.C.; Zhuang, Q.W.; Li, X.Z. Development and application of a full-scale mechanical rock-cutting platform for measuring the cutting performance of TBM cutter. *Measurement* **2022**, *204*, 112036. [CrossRef]
5. Park, J.Y.; Kang, H.; Lee, J.W. A study on rock cutting efficiency and structural stability of a point attack pick cutter by lab-scale linear cutting machine testing and finite element analysis. *Int. J. Rock Mech. Min. Sci.* **2018**, *103*, 215–229. [CrossRef]
6. Kang, H.; Cho, J.W.; Park, J.Y. A new linear cutting machine for assessing the rock-cutting performance of a pick cutter. *Int. J. Rock Mech. Min. Sci.* **2016**, *88*, 129–136. [CrossRef]
7. Innaurato, N.; Oggeri, C.; Oreste, P. Laboratory tests to study the influence of rock stress confinement on the performances of TBM discs in tunnels. *Int. J. Miner. Metall. Mater.* **2011**, *18*, 253–259. [CrossRef]
8. Li, T.; Wu, T.; Ding, X.; Chen, H.; Wang, L. Design of an internally cooled turning tool based on topology optimization and CFD simulation. *Int. J. Adv. Manuf. Technol.* **2017**, *91*, 1327–1337. [CrossRef]
9. Langelaar, M. Topology optimization for multi-axis machining. *Comput. Methods Appl. Mech. Eng.* **2019**, *351*, 226–252. [CrossRef]
10. Chan, T.C.; Reddy, S.V.V.S.; Ullah, A. Effect of spatial moving structure and topology optimization of the CNC turning machine tools. *Int. J. Adv. Manuf. Technol.* **2023**, *129*, 2969–2987. [CrossRef]
11. Prathyusha, A.L.R.; Babu, G.R. A review on additive manufacturing and topology optimization process for weight reduction studies in various industrial applications. *Mater. Today Proc.* **2022**, *62*, 109–117. [CrossRef]
12. Han, Y.; Xu, B.; Duan, Z.; Huang, X. Stress-based multi-material structural topology optimization considering graded interfaces. *Comput. Methods Appl. Mech. Eng.* **2022**, *391*, 114602. [CrossRef]
13. Dong, Y.; Hussain, I.; He, S. Structural topology optimization of aircraft wing leading edge fabricated of multilayer composites. *Aerosp. Sci. Technol.* **2025**, *159*, 109993. [CrossRef]
14. Xiong, F.; Zou, X.; Zhang, Z.; Shi, X. A systematic approach for multi-objective lightweight and stiffness optimization of a car body. *Struct. Multidiscip. Optim.* **2020**, *62*, 3229–3248. [CrossRef]
15. Wu, N.; Li, S.; Zhang, B.; Wang, C.; Chen, B. The advances of topology optimization techniques in orthopedic implants: A review. *Med. Biol. Eng. Comput.* **2021**, *59*, 1673–1689. [CrossRef]
16. Wang, Q.; Yang, W.; Wang, L.; Bai, G.; Ma, G. Reinforcement design and structural performance for the topology optimized 3D printed concrete truss beams. *Eng. Struct.* **2025**, *332*, 120064. [CrossRef]
17. Guibert, A.T.R.; Hyun, J.; Neofytou, A. Facilitating multidisciplinary collaboration through a versatile level-set topology optimization framework via COMSOL multiphysics. *Struct. Multidiscip. Optim.* **2024**, *67*, 159. [CrossRef]
18. Costa, M.R.; Sohouli, A.; Suleman, A. Multi-scale and multi-material topology optimization of gradient lattice structures using surrogate models. *Compos. Struct.* **2022**, *289*, 115402. [CrossRef]
19. Shin, S.; Shin, D.; Kang, N. Topology optimization via machine learning and deep learning: A review. *J. Comput. Des. Eng.* **2023**, *10*, 1736–1766. [CrossRef]
20. Sun, S.; Rankouhi, B.; Thoma, D.J.; Cheadle, M.J.; Maples, G.D. Topology optimization, additive manufacturing and thermohydraulic testing of heat sinks. *Int. J. Heat Mass Transf.* **2024**, *224*, 125281. [CrossRef]
21. Lin, S.Y.; Chang, C.H. Structure design improvement and stiffness reinforcement of a machine Tool through Topology optimization based on machining characteristics. *Appl. Sci.* **2023**, *14*, 61. [CrossRef]
22. Sun, Y.; Guo, C.; Li, Q.; Yue, H.; Zhang, J. Optimization of rock cutting process parameters with disc cutter for wear and cutting energy reduction based on the discrete element method. *J. Clean. Prod.* **2023**, *391*, 136160. [CrossRef]
23. Hu, M.; Gao, T.; Dong, X.; Tan, Q.; Yi, C. Simulation of soil-tool interaction using smoothed particle hydrodynamics (SPH). *Soil Tillage Res.* **2023**, *229*, 105671. [CrossRef]
24. Zhou, J.; Dai, Y.; Huang, S.; Armaghani, D.J.; Qiu, Y. Proposing several hybrid SSA—Machine learning techniques for estimating rock cuttability by conical pick with relieved cutting modes. *Acta Geotech.* **2023**, *18*, 1431–1446. [CrossRef]
25. Kadkhodaei, M.H.; Ghasemi, E.; Hamidi, J.K.; Rostami, J. Evaluation of rock cutting performance of conical cutting tool based on commonly measured rock properties. *Transp. Geotech.* **2024**, *48*, 101318. [CrossRef]
26. Cheluszka, P.; Mikuła, S.; Mikuła, J. Theoretical consideration of fatigue strengthening of conical picks for rock cutting. *Tunn. Undergr. Space Technol.* **2022**, *125*, 104481. [CrossRef]
27. Li, J.; Gong, Y.; Zhao, S.; Sun, W.; Xu, Y. Material and processing optimization on disc cutter of tunnel boring machine for failure prevention. *Eng. Fail. Anal.* **2022**, *138*, 106363. [CrossRef]
28. Cai, X.; Yuan, J.; Zhou, Z.; Zhang, S.; Wang, S. Numerical investigation on the influence of cutting parameters on rock breakage using a conical pick. *Eng. Fract. Mech.* **2024**, *312*, 110607. [CrossRef]
29. Rui, F.; Zhao, G.F.; Zheng, Y.; Gong, Q.; Zhao, X. Electromagnetic-thermo-mechanical coupled modelling of microwave-assisted TBM disc cutting. *Tunn. Undergr. Space Technol.* **2023**, *138*, 105171. [CrossRef]
30. Krauze, K.; Mucha, K.; Wydro, T.; Pawlik, J.; Wróblewska, P. Mass and Volumetric Abrasive Wear Measurements of the Mining Conical Picks. *Sustainability* **2023**, *15*, 850. [CrossRef]

31. Copur, H.; Balci, C.; Bilgin, N.; Tumac, D.; Avunduk, E. Predicting Cutting Performance of Chisel Tools By Using Physical And Mechanical Properties of Natural Stones. In Proceedings of the ISRM International Symposium—EUROCK 2012, Stockholm, Sweden, 28–31 May 2012.
32. Yasar, S. A general semi-theoretical model for conical picks. *Rock Mech. Rock Eng.* **2020**, *53*, 2557–2579. [CrossRef]
33. Liu, X.; Liu, S.; Li, L.; Cui, X. Experiment on conical pick cutting rock material assisted with front and rear water jet. *Adv. Mater. Sci. Eng.* **2015**, *2015*, 506579. [CrossRef]
34. Wang, Z.; Zeng, Q.; Wan, L.; Lu, Z.; Wang, H. Investigation of the influence of cutting parameters on conical pick cutting performance and rock damage. *Machines* **2022**, *10*, 1034. [CrossRef]
35. Pan, Y.; Liu, Q.; Liu, Q.; Liu, J.; Peng, X. Full-scale linear cutting tests to check and modify a widely used semi-theoretical model for disc cutter cutting force prediction. *Acta Geotech.* **2020**, *15*, 1481–1500. [CrossRef]
36. Chinnasamy, M.; Rathanasamy, R.; Samanta, B.; Pal, S.; Palaniappan, S. Microstructure evolution, phase formation, mechanical and tribological response of deep cryogenically treated hard WC-6% Co cutting bits. *J. Mater. Res. Technol.* **2023**, *27*, 1293–1306. [CrossRef]
37. Li, F.; Liu, W.; Gao, D.; Li, Y. Study on super impact resistant polycrystalline diamond compacts with homogeneous PCD/WC-Co interlayer. *Int. J. Refract. Met. Hard Mater.* **2024**, *119*, 106558. [CrossRef]
38. Meng, Q.; Zhang, B.; Wang, B.; Wang, Y.; Cao, H. Application of Laser Cladding Technology on TBM Cutter Repairment and Enhancement. *Indian Geotech. J.* **2024**, *55*, 1374–1382. [CrossRef]
39. Song, K.; Yang, H.; Xie, J.; Karekal, S. An optimization methodology of cutter-spacing for efficient mechanical breaking of jointed rock mass. *Rock Mech. Rock Eng.* **2022**, *55*, 3301–3316. [CrossRef]
40. Huang, X.; Liu, Q.; Liu, B.; Wang, D.; Wang, X. Development and in-situ application of a real-time cutting tool forces monitoring system in TBM tunnelling. *Tunn. Undergr. Space Technol.* **2022**, *124*, 104453. [CrossRef]
41. Liu, S.; Cui, X.; Du, C.; Fu, L. Method to determine installing angle of conical point attack pick. *J. Cent. South Univ. Technol.* **2011**, *18*, 1994–2000. [CrossRef]
42. Sun, H.; Guo, W.; Liu, J.; Song, L.; Liu, X. Layout design for disc cutters based on analysis of TBM cutter-head structure. *J. Cent. South Univ.* **2018**, *25*, 812–830. [CrossRef]
43. Palaniappan, S.K.; Pal, S.K.; Chinnasamy, M. Efficiency of rock cutting and wear behavior of coated bits via lab-scale linear rock-cutting machine: Experimental approach. *Int. J. Geomech.* **2023**, *23*, 06022041. [CrossRef]
44. Kumar, C.; Kumaraswamidhas, L.A.; Murthy, V.; Prakash, A. Experimental investigations on thermal behavior during pick-rock interaction and optimization of operating parameters of surface miner. *Int. J. Rock Mech. Min. Sci.* **2020**, *133*, 104360. [CrossRef]
45. Arsalan, M.; Mokhtar, M.; Hawkar, H.; Sazan, N.; Hunar, F.; Ahmed, M.; Mohammad, K.; Hoger, M. Machine learning forecasting models of disc cutters life of tunnel boring machine. *Autom. Constr.* **2021**, *128*, 103779.
46. Fathipour-Azar, H. Mean cutting force prediction of conical picks using ensemble learning paradigm. *Rock Mech. Rock Eng.* **2023**, *56*, 221–236. [CrossRef]
47. Liu, Z.; Liu, Y.; Sun, J.; Yang, J.; Yang, B.; Li, D. Intelligent evaluation of mean cutting force of conical pick by boosting trees and Bayesian optimization. *J. Cent. South Univ.* **2024**, *31*, 3948–3964. [CrossRef]
48. Wang, X.; Li, S.; Li, Z.; Chao, Y.; Zhao, S.; Peng, K. Optimizing cutter wear in TBM operations through numerical analysis of enhanced rock-cutting interaction. *Simul. Model. Pract. Theory* **2024**, *135*, 102976. [CrossRef]
49. Du, W.; Gao, J.; Zhang, C.; Ma, Q.; Zhang, J.; Cheng, A. A Numerical Study on the Rock Breakage Mechanism with TBM Disk Cutter in Calcareous Cemented Sand Pebble Stratum Using a Coupled FEM-DEM Method. *Rock Mech. Rock Eng.* **2025**, *58*, 2319–2347. [CrossRef]
50. Fu, J.; Yin, X.; Liu, F.; Liu, H.; Cui, J. Investigation on thermal behavior of TBM disc cutter under different cooling conditions. *Case Stud. Therm. Eng.* **2023**, *49*, 103392. [CrossRef]
51. Lu, Z.; Wan, L.; Zeng, Q.; Zhang, X.; Gao, K. The structural optimization of roadheader conical picks based on fatigue life. *Int. J. Model. Simul. Sci. Comput.* **2018**, *9*, 1850013. [CrossRef]
52. Marji, M.; Hosseini Nasab, H.; Hossein Morshedi, A. Numerical modeling of crack propagation in rocks under TBM disc cutters. *J. Mech. Mater. Struct.* **2009**, *4*, 605–627. [CrossRef]
53. Fang, Y.; Li, X.; Cao, Y.; Liu, H.; Guo, Y. Wear Characteristics and Optimization Measures of Disc Cutters During Large-Diameter Slurry Tunnel Boring Machine Advancing in Soil-Rock Composite Strata: A Case Study. *Lubricants* **2025**, *13*, 170. [CrossRef]
54. Song, Y.; Yang, S.Q.; Li, K.S.; Yin, P.; Pan, P. Mechanical behavior and fracture evolution mechanism of composite rock under triaxial compression: Insights from three-dimensional DEM modeling. *Rock Mech. Rock Eng.* **2023**, *56*, 7673–7699. [CrossRef]
55. Li, Y.-M.; Zhao, G.-F.; Jiao, Y.; Yan, C.; Wang, X. A benchmark study of different numerical methods for predicting rock failure. *Int. J. Rock Mech. Min. Sci.* **2023**, *166*, 105381. [CrossRef]
56. Wang, S.; Shi, X.; Wu, Y. DEM-based 2D numerical simulation of the rock cutting process using a conical pick under confining stress. *Comput. Geotech.* **2024**, *165*, 105885. [CrossRef]

57. Zhu, X.; Feng, C.; Cheng, P.; Wang, X.; Li, S. A novel three-dimensional hydraulic fracturing model based on continuum-discontinuum element method. *Comput. Methods Appl. Mech. Eng.* **2021**, *383*, 113887. [CrossRef]
58. Yue, Z.; Zhou, J.; Feng, C.; Wang, X.; Peng, L. Coupling of material point and continuum discontinuum element methods for simulating blast-induced fractures in rock. *Comput. Geotech.* **2022**, *144*, 104629. [CrossRef]
59. Gong, B.; Wang, S.; Sloan, S.W.; Sheng, D.; Tang, C. Modelling rock failure with a novel continuous to discontinuous method. *Rock Mech. Rock Eng.* **2019**, *52*, 3183–3195. [CrossRef]
60. Geng, Q.; Wei, Z.; Ren, J. New rock material definition strategy for FEM simulation of the rock cutting process by TBM disc cutters. *Tunn. Undergr. Space Technol.* **2017**, *65*, 179–186. [CrossRef]
61. Li, P.; Jiang, S.; Tang, D.; Xu, O. A PFC3D-based numerical simulation of cutting load for lunar rock simulant and experimental validation. *Adv. Space Res.* **2017**, *59*, 2583–2599. [CrossRef]
62. Raymond, S.J.; Jones, B.D.; Williams, J.R. Modeling damage and plasticity in aggregates with the material point method (MPM). *Comput. Part. Mech.* **2019**, *6*, 371–382. [CrossRef]
63. Wang, Y.; Bui, H.H.; Nguyen, G.D.; Ranjith, P.G. A new SPH-based continuum framework with an embedded fracture process zone for modelling rock fracture. *Int. J. Solids Struct.* **2019**, *159*, 40–57. [CrossRef]
64. Tunsakul, J.; Jongpradist, P.; Kim, H.M.; Nanakorn, P. Evaluation of rock fracture patterns based on the element-free Galerkin method for stability assessment of a highly pressurized gas storage cavern. *Acta Geotech.* **2018**, *13*, 817–832. [CrossRef]
65. Avunduk, E.; Tumaç, D.; Atalay, A.K. Prediction of roadheader performance by artificial neural network. *Tunn. Undergr. Space Technol.* **2014**, *44*, 3–9. [CrossRef]
66. Zhang, L.; Guo, J.; Fu, X.; Tiong, R.; Zhang, P. Digital twin enabled real-time advanced control of TBM operation using deep learning methods. *Autom. Constr.* **2024**, *158*, 105240. [CrossRef]
67. Liu, X.; Wang, H.; Jing, H. Research on intelligent identification of rock types based on faster R-CNN method. *IEEE Access* **2020**, *8*, 21804–21812. [CrossRef]
68. Mahmood, J.; Mustafa, G.; Ali, M. Accurate estimation of tool wear levels during milling, drilling and turning operations by designing novel hyperparameter tuned models based on LightGBM and stacking. *Measurement* **2022**, *190*, 110722. [CrossRef]
69. Xie, Y.; Lian, K.; Liu, Q.; Zhang, C.; Liu, H. Digital twin for cutting tool: Modeling, application and service strategy. *J. Manuf. Syst.* **2021**, *58*, 305–312. [CrossRef]
70. Niaki, S.A.; Haghighat, E.; Campbell, T.; Poursartip, A.; Vaziri, R. Physics-informed neural network for modelling the thermo-chemical curing process of composite-tool systems during manufacture. *Comput. Methods Appl. Mech. Eng.* **2021**, *384*, 113959. [CrossRef]
71. Zhao, Y.; Sun, C.; Gao, Y.; Gao, S.; Guo, J. Microwave-Assisted Linear Cutting of Sandstone with a Conical Pick: Experimental Study. *Rock Mech. Rock Eng.* **2025**, *58*, 1021–1038. [CrossRef]
72. Yu, R.; Dong, X.; Li, Z.; Fan, M. A coupled SPH–DEM model for erosion process of solid surface by abrasive water-jet impact. *Comput. Part Mech.* **2023**, *10*, 1093–1112. [CrossRef]
73. Yu, R.; Dong, X.; Jing, Z.; Fan, M.; Li, Z. Meshfree modeling of brittle surface erosion by sharp-angled particle impact with Johnson–Holmquist-II (JH-2) model. *Tribol. Int.* **2023**, *187*, 108710. [CrossRef]
74. Oggeri, C.; Fenoglio, T.M.; Vinai, R. Tunnel spoil classification and applicability of lime addition in weak formations for muck reuse. *Tunn. Undergr. Space Technol.* **2014**, *44*, 97–107. [CrossRef]
75. Costamagna, E.; Oggeri, C.; Segarra, P.; Castedo, R.; Navarro, J. Assessment of contour profile quality in D&B tunnelling. *Tunn. Undergr. Space Technol.* **2018**, *75*, 67–80.
76. Jihong, Z.H.U.; Han, Z.; Chuang, W.; Lu, Z.; Yuan, S. A review of topology optimization for additive manufacturing: Status and challenges. *Chin. J. Aeronaut.* **2021**, *34*, 91–110.
77. Borda, F.; La Rosa, A.D.; Filice, L.; Gagliardi, F. Environmental impact of process constrained topology optimization design on automotive component' life. *Int. J. Mater. Form.* **2023**, *16*, 48. [CrossRef]
78. Li, H.; Yamada, T.; Jolivet, P.; Furuta, K.; Kondoh, T. Full-scale 3D structural topology optimization using adaptive mesh refinement based on the level-set method. *Finite Elem. Anal. Des.* **2021**, *194*, 103561. [CrossRef]

computation

MDPI

Article

A Framework of the Meshless Method for Topology Optimization Using the Smooth-Edged Material Distribution for Optimizing Topology Method

Jingbo Huang [1], Kai Long [1,*], Yutang Chen [1], Rongrong Geng [1], Ayesha Saeed [1], Hui Zhang [1] and Tao Tao [2]

[1] School of New Energy, North China Electric Power University, Beijing 102206, China; jingbohuang2002@163.com (J.H.); cyt5237@163.com (Y.C.); gengrr3642@163.com (R.G.); ayeshasaeededu@gmail.com (A.S.); zhanghui82@ncepu.edu.cn (H.Z.)
[2] China Southern Power Grid Technology Co., Ltd., Guangzhou 510080, China; taot0804@163.com
* Correspondence: longkai1978@163.com; Tel.: +86-15116910571

Abstract: Density variables based on nodal or Gaussian points are naturally incorporated in meshless topology optimization approaches, pursuing distinct topological layouts with solid and void solutions. However, engineering applications have been hampered by the fact that the authentic structure boundary cannot be identified without manual intervention. To alleviate this issue, the Smooth-Edged Material Distribution for Optimizing Topology (SEMDOT) method is developed within the context of meshless approximation. In meshless analysis, the non-overlap cell variables instead of nodal or Gaussian-based variables are adopted to characterize the existence or absence of sub-regions. This work proposes a non-penalized SEMDOT where an interpolation-based heuristic sensitivity expression is utilized. The 2D and 3D compliance minimization problems serve to validate the efficiency and applicability of the proposed non-penalized SEMDOT approach based on the framework of the meshless method. The numerical results demonstrated that the proposed approach is capable of generating final designs with continuous and smooth edges or surfaces.

Keywords: topology optimization; meshless method; element-free Galerkin; SEMDOT; non-penalization scheme

1. Introduction

Structural topology optimization refers to the ideal material layout with the most exceptional structural performance within a specified design area. Early approaches relied on conventional finite element (FE) methods for structural analysis. Bulks of approaches have arisen since Bendsøe and Kikuchi's pioneering work [1]. Among them, the Solid Isotropic Material with Penalization (SIMP) artificial model has been extensively accepted, in which the elemental Young's modulus is treated as the power function of the relative density [2,3]. However, the SIMP approach is susceptible to checkerboard patterns and mesh dependence without a restriction or relaxation scheme. Patches of checkerboard patterns are visible in the final designs due to the direct application of the material distribution derived from the FE analysis. Numerous choices and tactics, including the application of higher order FEs, the constraint on a global or local gradient, slope constraint or perimeter control, and various filters, have been suggested to mitigate these issues [4,5].

Nodal variables are adopted as an alternative approach for suppressing the checkerboard patterns. The checkerboard patterns can be viewed as the discontinuous material distribution that occurred from numerical instabilities. Therefore, by constructing the continuous material distribution, the checkerboard patterns are suppressed without the need for additional restrictions. The typical constructions will be achieved by the bilinear shape function interpolation [6,7], moving least square approximation [8], non-local Shepard interpolation [9,10], and B-spline function fitting [11]. This concept is also extended to the topology optimization utilizing isogeometric analysis and fiber angle optimization of composite systems with continuous spatial variation [12–14]. For instance, Wang et al. suggested a displacement-independent adaptive point refinement technique for topology optimization using a material density field [15].

Encouraged by the success of the node-based variables, some scholars have proposed a combination of various topology optimization methods and meshless or mesh-free approximation, including the element-free Galerkin (EFG) method [16–18], reproducing kernel particle method [19], smooth particle hydrodynamics method [20], and generalized finite difference method [21]. In addition to the classic stiffness maximization issues [22], the topology optimization merged with the mesh-free approaches has benefits in large deformation problems owing to the avoidance of elemental distortion [23–26]. These approaches have been successfully used in the design of compliant mechanisms [18,24], multi-material structures [27], thermal structures [28,29], and periodic structures [30].

Despite the significant progress made on the topology optimization implemented with mesh-free approaches, there are still difficulties. First of all, the influence domain of nodes might overlap with each other in the meshless method. As the nodal variables describe the existence or absence of the nodes and their surroundings, it is challenging to precisely define the structural boundary. Figure 1 depicts a typical topology optimization result acquired from Ref. [21]. Visually, the distribution of nodes or Gauss points makes it difficult to determine the resulting boundary, which forms a barrier in widespread engineering applications. Recently, Fu et al. [31,32] proposed a new topology optimization algorithm named the Smooth-Edged Material Distribution for Optimizing Topology (SEMDOT), capable of directly generating smooth boundaries without the need for post-processing methods. The SEMDOT algorithm assigns extra grid points to elements and pursues the solid and void design of grid points rather than elements in traditional methods such as SIMP and BESO. As the number of grid points is much higher than that of elements, a smooth boundary can be formed during optimization. Also, the SEMDOT approach has been extended into the additive manufacturing technique [33–35], natural convection heat transfer optimization problems [36], and sheet metal forming process problems [37]. To address the mentioned difficulties, the current work develops SEMDOT in the framework of a meshless analysis approach, aiming to optimize the continuum structure without further graphics post-processing techniques. Furthermore, in typical element variables topology optimization methods, boundary zig-zag phenomena are often observed [38,39]. In contrast to the existing meshless-based topology optimization, the theoretical contribution of the present paper is to emphasize the application of regional variables instead of nodal or Gaussian point variables. Furthermore, a non-penalization version of the SEMDOT approach is developed in the meshless framework, enabling 0/1 discrete solutions as opposed to the penalization scheme. The proposed method ensures the preservation of smooth boundaries, also overcoming the zig-zag boundary phenomenon typical of several optimization approaches.

Figure 1. The typical topology optimization [21].

The remainder of the paper is organized as follows. In Section 2, the element-free Galerkin (EFG) formulation and treatment for boundary conditions are introduced briefly. Section 3 formulates the optimization issue using the SEMDOT approach. A heuristic sensitivity expression is provided, and the optimizer employs a method of moving asymptotes. Section 4 provides several numerical examples to validate the effectiveness of the proposed optimization method. The conclusions are summarized in the final section.

2. EFG Formulation and Treatment for Boundary Conditions

The EFG method represents the problem design Ω as a collection of nodes dispersed throughout the problem domain and its boundaries. In current investigations, the moving least square (MLS) approximation is employed to estimate the displacement field at a point of interest within the problem domain, utilizing the nodal parameter u_I. It yields the displacement function, which has the form

$$u(z) = \sum_{I=1}^{n} \varphi_I(z)u_I \tag{1}$$

where n is the number of nodes in the support domain of the point at z for the MLS shape function $\varphi_I(z)$. The MLS shape function can be expressed by

$$\boldsymbol{\varphi}_I(z) = \sum_{j=0}^{m} p_j(z)\left(\boldsymbol{A}^{-1}(z)\boldsymbol{B}(z)\right)_{jI} = \boldsymbol{P}^{\mathrm{T}}\boldsymbol{A}^{-1}\boldsymbol{B}_I \tag{2}$$

where m is the number of terms of polynomial basis and is usually much smaller than n. For a linear basis in two dimensions, the basis function of the spatial coordinates $\boldsymbol{P}$ vector is given by

$$\boldsymbol{P}^{\mathrm{T}} = \begin{bmatrix} 1 & s & t \end{bmatrix} = \boldsymbol{p}^{\mathrm{T}}(z) \tag{3}$$

where $[s, t]$ is used for a two-dimensional problem.

In Equation (2), the weighted moment matrices $\boldsymbol{A}$ and $\boldsymbol{B}$ are given by

$$A(z) = \sum_{I=1}^{n} \omega_I(z - z_I)(\boldsymbol{p}, z_I)\boldsymbol{p}^{\mathrm{T}}(z_I) \tag{4}$$

$$\boldsymbol{B}(z) = (\boldsymbol{B}_1, \boldsymbol{B}_2, \cdots, \boldsymbol{B}_n) \tag{5}$$

$$\boldsymbol{B}_I = \omega_I(\boldsymbol{z})\boldsymbol{p}(\boldsymbol{z}_I) \tag{6}$$

where ω_I is a weighting function. The following Equations are the collection of frequently used one-dimensional weight functions. The cubic spline weight function has the following form:

$$\omega_I(\boldsymbol{z}-\boldsymbol{z}_I) \equiv \omega_I(r) = \begin{cases} \frac{2}{3} - 4r^2 + 4r^3, & r \leq \frac{1}{2}, \\ \frac{4}{3} - 4r + 4r^2 - \frac{4}{3}r^3, & \frac{1}{2} < r \leq 1, \\ 0, & 0. \end{cases} \tag{7}$$

The quadratic spline weight function can be formulated as follows:

$$\omega_I(\boldsymbol{z}-\boldsymbol{z}_I) \equiv \omega_I(r) = \begin{cases} 1 - 6r^2 + 8r^3 - 3r^4, & r \leq 1, \\ 0, & r > 1. \end{cases} \tag{8}$$

In two dimensions, a nodal domain of influence encompasses a region within the domain, and square domains are utilized here. The expression denotes the tensor product weight function at any point:

$$\omega(\boldsymbol{z}-\boldsymbol{z}_I) = \omega(r_s)\omega(r_t) = \omega_s\omega_t \tag{9}$$

where

$$r_s = \frac{\|s - s_I\|}{d_{ms}}, r_t = \frac{\|t - t_I\|}{d_{mt}} \tag{10}$$

$$d_{ms} = d_{\max} c_{sI}, d_{mt} = d_{\max} c_{tI} \tag{11}$$

In Equation (11), c_{sI} and c_{tI} are determined at a specific node by searching for sufficient neighboring nodes that satisfy the basis in both directions. Typically, the scaling parameter $d_{\max}$ falls between 2 and 4.

Notably, the usage of MLS approximation results in the shape function that lacks the Kronecker delta property. Utilizing Lagrange multipliers, penalty function methods, modified variational principles, and coupling with FEs [40,41], a variety of techniques have been proposed to impose the essential boundary conditions. In this work, the interpolating properties of the shape function will be guaranteed using the singular weight function [40,41]. Equation (7) or Equation (8) can thus be reformulated as

$$\widetilde{\omega}_I(\boldsymbol{z}) = \frac{\omega_I(\boldsymbol{z})}{\|\boldsymbol{z} - \boldsymbol{z}_I\|^2 + \varepsilon} \ (\varepsilon > 0) \tag{12}$$

where the constant parameter ε is set to 10^{-5}.

The discrete equilibrium equation has the following expression:

$$\boldsymbol{K}\boldsymbol{u} = \boldsymbol{F} \tag{13}$$

It is observed that Equation (13) has the identical form as that in the FE equilibrium equation, which simplifies the derivative of sensitivity analysis within the context of the mesh-free approach. The symbols $\boldsymbol{u}$ and $\boldsymbol{F}$ are the nodal displacement vector and external force vector, respectively. The global stiffness matrix $\boldsymbol{K}$ is constructed using the nodal stiffness matrix, which is defined by

$$\boldsymbol{K}_{IJ} = \int_{\Omega} \boldsymbol{B}^{\mathrm{T}}\boldsymbol{D}\boldsymbol{B}\mathrm{d}\Omega \tag{14}$$

Note that K_{IJ} disappears when nodes I and J are not within the same support domain of the same quadrature point of integration.

All integrations in the preceding discussion are calculated across the global domain and traction boundary. In order to evaluate these integrals, as illustrated in Figure 2, the problem domain is discretized into a sequence of non-overlapping background cells [42].

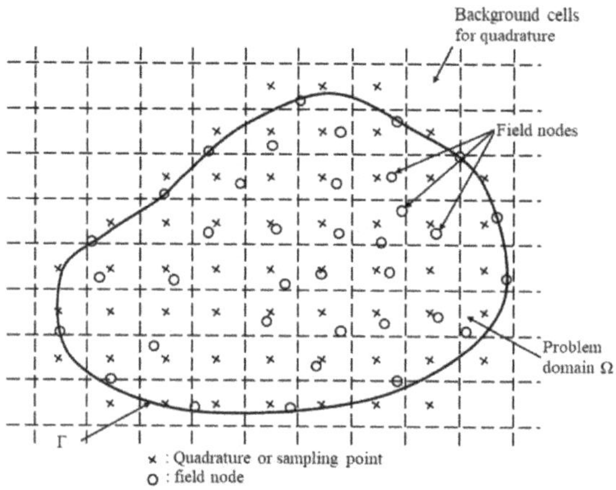

Figure 2. Illustration of background cells in the meshless method.

3. Topology Optimization Problem Solved by SEMDOT

3.1. Interpolation Scheme in SEMDOT Method

The structural design domain is assumed to be partitioned into total N_c integration cells. Each integration cell has a unique design variable x_c ($c = 1, 2, \cdots, N_c$) ranging between 0 and 1. The variables $\tilde{x}$ are filtered using the subsequent filter [43,44]:

$$\tilde{x}_c = \frac{\sum_{i \in N_c} (R - \Delta(i,e)) v_i x_i}{\sum_{i \in N_c} (R - \Delta(i,e)) v_i} \tag{15}$$

where N_c is the set of the ith cell for whose spatial distance to the centroid of the cth cell $\Delta(i, c)$ falls within the provided radius R, and v_i is the ith cell's volume.

Interpolating the Young's modulus using the following function of the physical density variable [43,44] yields

$$E_c = \left[\tilde{x}_c^p + \left(1 - \tilde{x}_c^p\right)\varepsilon\right] E_0 \tag{16}$$

where E_0 denotes Young's modulus of the base material, and a tiny positive number ε (=10^{-6}) is chosen to prevent singularity while solving the static equilibrium equation. For the interpolation of Young's modulus, the penalty factor p is utilized. In the conventional SIMP approach, the typical value for p is 3 to push the elemental densities towards 0 and 1. When p equals 1, Equation (16) can be rewritten as follows:

$$E_c = \left[\tilde{x}_c + \left(1 - \tilde{x}_c\right)\varepsilon\right] E_0 \tag{17}$$

Equation (17) can also be interpreted that Young's modulus can be calculated by interpolating the solid and void phases linearly.

The topology optimization problem of continua aiming for the maximum system stiffness can be formulated as follows:

$$\begin{aligned} &\text{find}: \boldsymbol{x} \\ &\text{minimize}: c \\ &\text{subject to}: V/V_0 \le f \\ &\qquad\qquad\quad 0 \le x_i \le 1 \end{aligned} \tag{18}$$

where c represents the structural compliance; V and V_0 are the entire volume of the final design and initial design, respectively; and f is the prescribed volume fraction.

3.2. Smooth Boundary

The symbol $\tilde{x}_n$ denotes the filtered variable for the nodes. Consequently, it is possible to interpolate and project the projected variables at the grid points $\overline{x}_g$ based on the nodal value. The smooth boundary can therefore be implicitly represented by the level-set function $\kappa(x,y)$:

$$\kappa(s,t) = \begin{cases} \overline{x}_g - \Lambda > 0 \text{ for solid region} \\ \overline{x}_g - \Lambda = 0 \text{ for boundary} \\ \overline{x}_g - \Lambda < 0 \text{ for void region} \end{cases} \tag{19}$$

where $\kappa(s, t)$ is the level-set function at the grid point. The "floating" value Λ is determined by the volume constraint being met.

The cell's filtered variables can be reassigned to the nodes, yielding the nodal filter variables $\tilde{x}_n$. The physical density at an arbitrary point can be expressed as follows:

$$\tilde{x}_g = \sum \varpi^c(\zeta,\eta)\tilde{x}_c \tag{20}$$

where (ζ, η) are the local grid point coordinates. The shape function $\varpi^c(\zeta,\eta)$ is always positive.

Applying the relaxed Heaviside function provides the projected variables as [43,44]

$$\overline{x}_g = \frac{\tanh(\beta/2) + \tanh(\beta\tilde{x}_g - \beta/2)}{2\tanh(\beta/2)} \tag{21}$$

where β is the Heaviside parameter that determines the level of sharpness. This projection, as opposed to the penalization in the standard SIMP approach, is the key to obtaining the 0/1 discrete solution. The illustration for the smooth boundary is shown in Figure 3.

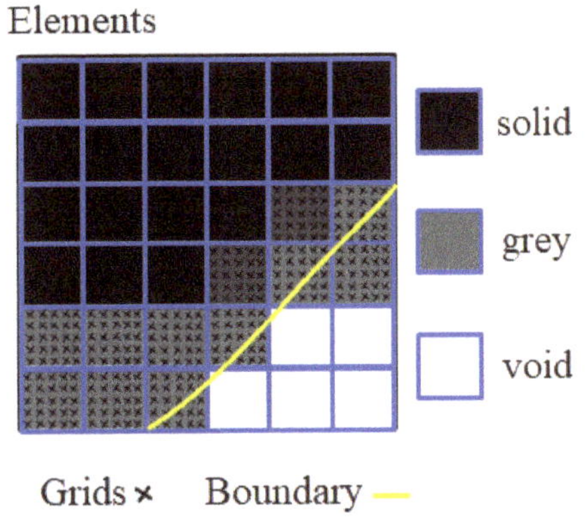

Figure 3. Illustration of topological boundary formed in SEMDOT.

By assembling grid points in their appropriate cells, the filtered variables are updated by

$$\widetilde{x}_c^{new} = \sum \overline{x}_c / M_c \tag{22}$$

where $\widetilde{x}_c^{new}$ is the updated filtered variable for the subsequent round of optimization, and M_c is the total number of grid points in the cell.

3.3. Sensitivity Analysis

Regarding the conventional SIMP approach, the sensitivity of the compliance c with respect to $\widetilde{x}_c$ can be expressed by

$$\frac{\partial c}{\partial \widetilde{x}_c} = \boldsymbol{u}^{\mathrm{T}} \frac{\partial \boldsymbol{K}}{\partial \widetilde{x}_c} \boldsymbol{u} \tag{23}$$

When calculating the term $\frac{\partial K}{\partial \widetilde{x}_c}$, the following equation is required.

$$\frac{\partial E_c}{\partial \widetilde{x}_c} = (1-\varepsilon) p \widetilde{x}_c^{p-1} E_0 \tag{24}$$

More recently, the discrete variable sensitivities in a non-penalization way proposed by Liang et al. [45] are given as

$$\frac{\partial c}{\partial \widetilde{x}_e} = \begin{cases} \boldsymbol{u}_e^{\mathrm{T}} \boldsymbol{k}_e \boldsymbol{u}_e \big|_{\widetilde{x}_e=1} & \widetilde{x}_e = 1 \\ \varepsilon \boldsymbol{u}_e^{\mathrm{T}} \boldsymbol{k}_e \boldsymbol{u}_e \big|_{\widetilde{x}_e=1}, & \widetilde{x}_e = 0 \end{cases} \tag{25}$$

where $\widetilde{x}_e$ represents the physical density of the eth element, which is comparable to the $\widetilde{x}_c$ in this work. The symbols $\boldsymbol{u}_e$ and $\boldsymbol{k}_e$ are the elemental displacement vector and stiffness matrix in the FE analysis, respectively.

Here, a heuristic sensitivity is derived from the linear combination of the discrete sensitivity in two conditions, labeled as follows [46]:

$$\frac{\partial c}{\partial \widetilde{x}_c} \to [\widetilde{x}_c + (1-\widetilde{x}_c)\varepsilon] \boldsymbol{u}^{\mathrm{T}} \frac{\partial \boldsymbol{K}}{\partial \widetilde{x}_c} \boldsymbol{u} \bigg|_{\widetilde{x}_c=1} \tag{26}$$

The heuristic sensitivity in Equation (26) will replace Equation (23) as an input parameter for the optimizer when the non-penalization SEMDOT approach is employed.

3.4. Optimizer

The 0 and 1 discrete solutions is realized by projection rather than penalization. In this regard, the SEMODT approach is similar to the Floating Projection Topology Optimization (FPTO) method [47,48], excluding the variables updating scheme. A benefit of the SEMDOT approach is that the optimization solver, such as Optimality Criterion (OC), and mathematical programming are optional. As the default optimizer, the Method of Moving Asymptotes (MMA) [49], which is recognized as one of the most dependable and efficient optimizers in the topology optimization community, will be utilized. To facilitate comprehension, the complete SEMDOT technique procedure in the framework of the meshless method is illustrated in Figure 4.

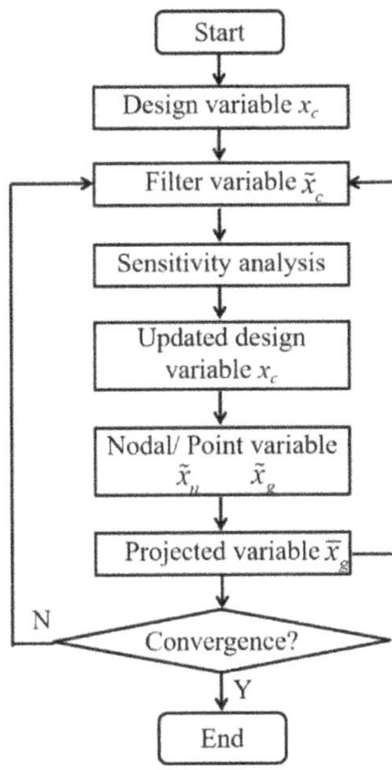

Figure 4. Flowchart of SEMDOT in the framework of meshless method.

4. Numerical Examples

This section will present representative 2D and 3D numerical examples to illustrate the applicability of the proposed SEMDOT approach in the framework of the meshless method. In all examples, the geometric parameters, material properties, and loads are dimensionless. In each integration cell, a 4 × 4 Gauss quadrature is utilized to determine the stiffness of EFG. The solutions are achieved using a linear basis function with the cubic spline weight function. In the MMA optimizer, a move limit of 0.05 is adopted. In Equation (20), the parameter β starts at 1 and is increased by 0.5 for each iteration while the maximum iteration is set to 100 to maintain a proper balance between the accuracy and computational cost. All numerical examples are conducted by means of the software MATLAB^{TM}.

4.1. Example 1

To investigate the effect of the penalty factor on the optimized results, the benchmark Messerschmitt–Bölkow–Blohm (MBB) beam with a design domain dimension of 120 × 40 is considered here, as shown in Figure 5. A total of 121 × 41 uniformly dispersed nodes are adopted for the discretization. The left side is fastened horizontally, and the right bottom corner is supported vertically. The vertical force $F = 1$ is applied at the top left corner. The static compliance is minimized while the target volume fraction is set to 50%. The radius is set to $R = 6$. A total of 5 × 5 grid points are used in each cell. As depicted in Figure 6, two optimized structures are achieved by the use of the penalty factor of $p = 3$ and the non-penalization scheme. Convergence processes with the 10th, 30th, 50th, 70th, and 90th topologies are depicted in Figure 7 from left to right.

Figure 5. Design domain of MBB beam.

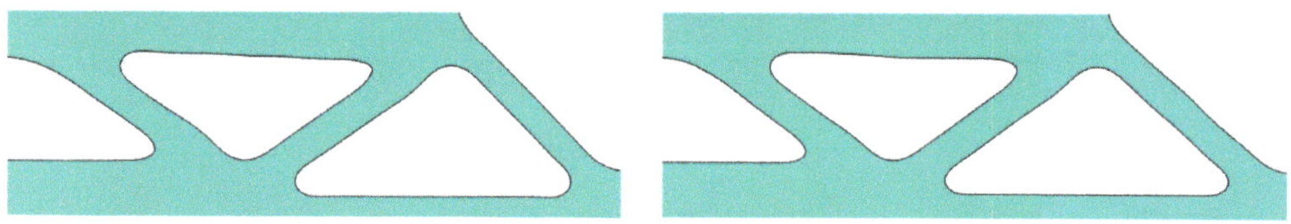

(**a**) (**b**)

Figure 6. Optimized structures were obtained by (**a**) non-penalization SEMDOT with $c = 200.963$ and (**b**) original SEMDOT with $c = 193.284$ using a penalty factor of $p = 3$.

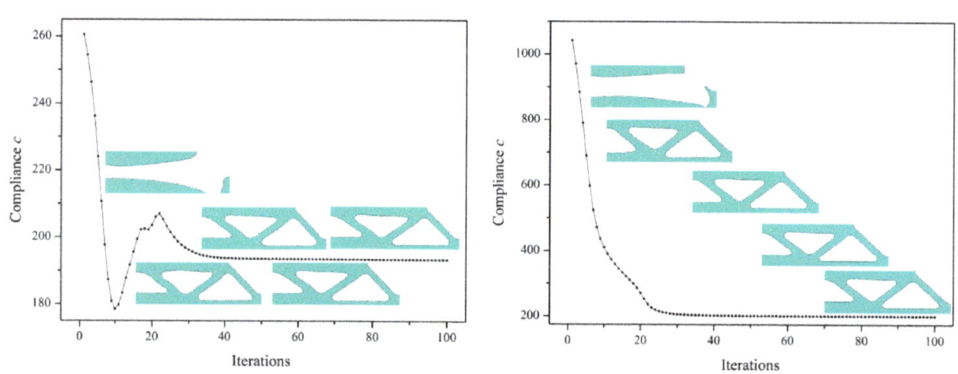

(**a**) (**b**)

Figure 7. Comparison of convergence processes with (**a**) non-penalization scheme and (**b**) penalization scheme having $p = 3$.

As shown in Figure 6, it can be seen that the optimized structures resemble each other. It is possible to obtain a smooth and identifiable boundary in both circumstances. In the two cases, convergence processes of the objective function exhibit distinct properties. When p equals 3, the initial compliance starts with a relatively high value, as shown in Figure 7b. The compliance rapidly falls in a reasonably low number of iterations and converges to a nearly constant value. When the non-penalization scheme is employed, the compliance value is relatively lower. With a sharp decline, the curve appears to encounter a bump. The curve quickly goes up and then reaches a plateau until convergence.

To validate the non-penalization version of the SEMDOT method, the aforementioned problem with three different discretizations with 241 × 81, 361 × 121, and 481 × 161 evenly distributed nodes is investigated. Figure 8 shows the optimized topologies where all discretizations converge to similar designs. These occurrences demonstrated conclusively that the discretization's independence may be accomplished using the suggested SEMDOT approach.

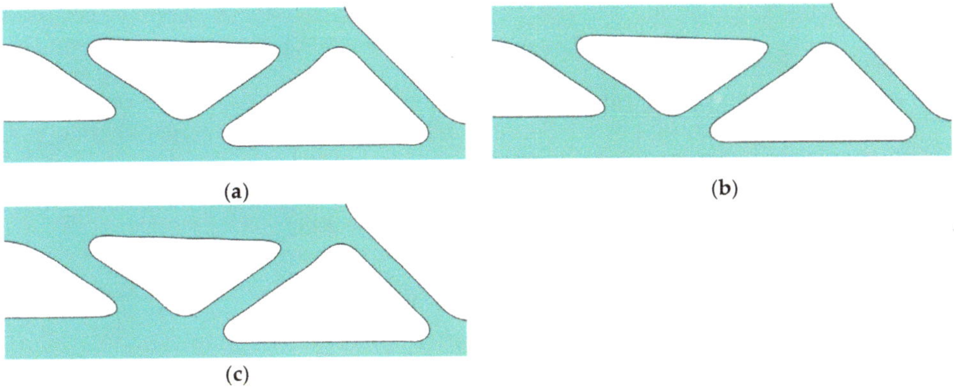

Figure 8. The optimized topologies use three different discretizations: (**a**) 241 × 81 with $c = 195.845$, (**b**) 361 × 121 with $c = 197.322$, and (**c**) 481 × 161 with $c = 198.598$.

4.2. Example 2

In this example, both the common FE and meshless techniques are used to solve the same problem. For the purposes of comparison, the standard elemental and nodal variables are used. In the FE discretization, the design domain is meshed into 120 × 40 bilinear elements, and the relative density variable is allocated to each element. We adopt a three-field SIMP method coupled with FE analysis [40]. In addition, the mesh-free approach leveraging independent density variables is implemented [8]. The design domain contains a total of 121 × 41 nodes that are evenly distributed. For visual post-processing, the threshold value of 0.5 is applied, which reserves elements whose relative density exceeds 0.5. The optimized topologies obtained by the above two methodologies are shown in Figure 9.

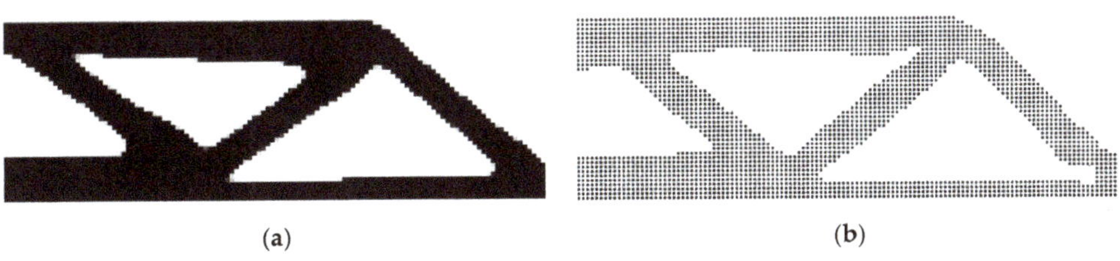

Figure 9. The optimized topologies obtained by (**a**) the finite element method with the elemental density variables (c = 190.706) and (**b**) the mesh-free method with the nodal density variables (c = 230.361).

FE boundary demonstrates the zigzag phenomenon, as depicted in Figure 9a. In contrast, the final design comprises the discrete points derived from the mesh-free approximation with nodal variables in Figure 9b. Although its boundaries can be directly observed, there is no guarantee for the complicated and engineering structures. The continuous material field is constructed for the nodal variables, implying that immediate variables exist in the design domain even if every nodal variable is 0 or 1. Under this circumstance, the final design may overestimate the compliance and further explain why the nodal variables are not appropriate in meshless topology optimization. Compared to Figure 8, it can be concluded that the proposed method is capable of generating results with smooth boundaries within the framework of the meshless approach.

4.3. Example 3

This example aims to illustrate the applicability of the proposed method in large-scale structures. Here, a 3D cantilever beam is taken as an example. Figure 10 shows the admissible design domain with a length of 48, a width of 4, and a height of 30, which is discretized by a uniformly distributed node size of 49 × 31 × 5. The left face is entirely clamped, while a vertically concentrated force $F = 1$ is applied to the midpoint on the right face. Here, a 30% volume fraction is imposed, and a radius of $R = 3$ is utilized. A total of 5 × 5 × 5 grid points are assigned to each cell. Figures 11 and 12 display the optimized topology of the 3D cantilever beam and the corresponding convergence process.

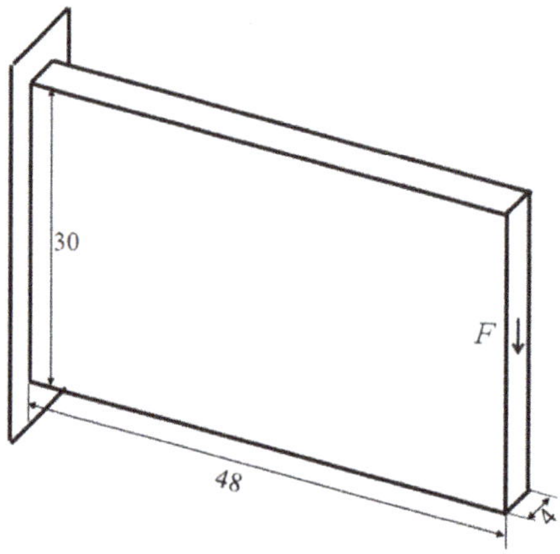

Figure 10. Design domain of 3D cantilever beam.

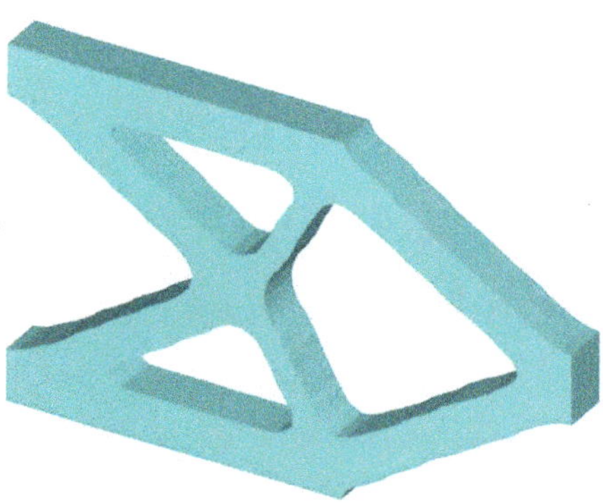

Figure 11. Resulting 3D topology obtained by the proposed method.

As expected, the convergence process in Figure 12 has a similar trend to that depicted in Figure 7a. The rough topology has basically emerged at the early stage, which implies that the proposed method can deal with large-scale problems in a low number of iterations. We find that the surface of the optimized structure is sufficiently smooth and continuous without requiring any manual post-processing methods. In summary, the proposed method is capable of generating the optimized structure with a smooth surface.

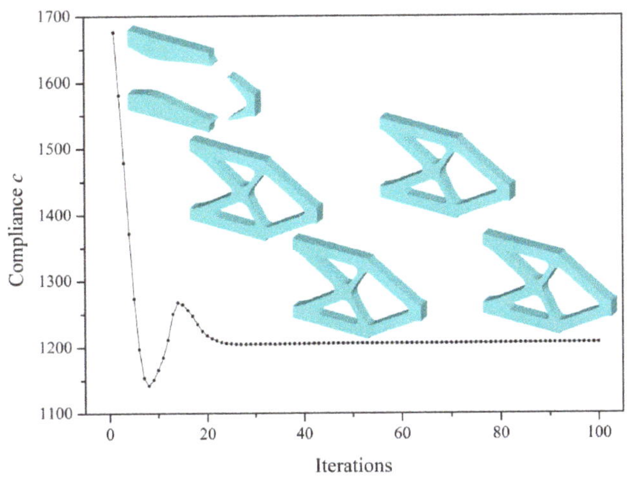

Figure 12. Convergence process of a 3D cantilever beam.

5. Conclusions

In this paper, a non-penalization SEMDOT method for topology optimization is proposed within the framework of the meshless approach. In contrast to existing meshless approximation topology optimization methods, the cell variables instead of the nodal or Gauss variables are employed to represent the presence or absence of structure. The 0/1 discrete solution is implemented using the projection rather than the penalization scheme. Furthermore, a heuristic sensitivity is conducted for the MMA optimizer. The proposed method is validated via several 2D and 3D numerical examples. Comparisons between penalized and non-penalized SEMDOT are investigated. The numerical results demonstrate that the final designs can be featured with continuous and smooth boundaries. Therefore, it can be concluded that the proposed methodology can mitigate the defects of previous meshless topology optimization methods.

In terms of static optimization problems, the minimum compliance formulation with non-penalization has achieved significant success in both academic research and engineering applications. It would be intriguing to extend the SEMDOT method to more intricate dynamic problems and thermal-solid interaction problems in our future work. To improve the accuracy of sensitivity analysis, it should also include the effects of dynamic responses. The optimization objectives may focus on minimizing the amplitudes of dynamic displacement and stress. This requires the development of precise models that account for temperature-dependent material properties. Moreover, efficient algorithms will be designed to handle both thermal and mechanical constraints and objectives concurrently.

Author Contributions: J.H.: Validation, software, and methodology; K.L.: conceptualization, methodology, and writing—original draft preparation and revision; Y.C.: validation, software, methodology, and revision; R.G.: writing and editing; A.S.: writing and editing; H.Z.: writing—reviewing and editing; T.T.: writing—reviewing and editing. All authors have read and agreed to the published version of the manuscript.

Funding: This work was financially supported by the National Key R&D Program (grant No. 2024YFE0208600), the New Energy Joint Laboratory of China Southern Power Grid Corporation (grant No. GDXNY2024KF03), and the National Natural Science Foundation of China (grant No. U24B2090). The order of listing does not reflect the relative importance of each contribution as all have been vital to the completion of this study.

Data Availability Statement: The data presented in this study are available upon request from the corresponding author.

Conflicts of Interest: Author Tao Tao is employed by the company China Southern Power Grid Technology Co, Ltd. The remaining authors declare that the research was conducted in the absence of any commercial or financial relationships that could be construed as a potential conflict of interest.

References

1. Bendsøe, M.P.; Kikuchi, N. Generating optimal topologies in structural design using a homogenization method. *Comput. Methods Appl. Mech. Eng.* **1988**, *71*, 197–224. [CrossRef]
2. Bendsøe, M.P.; Sigmund, O. Material interpolation schemes in topology optimization. *Arch. Appl. Mech.* **1999**, *69*, 635–654. [CrossRef]
3. Zhou, M.; Rozvany, G.I.N. The COC algorithm, part II: Topological, geometrical and generalized shape optimization. *Comput. Methods Appl. Mech. Eng.* **1991**, *89*, 309–336. [CrossRef]
4. Sigmund, O. Numerical instabilities in topology optimization: A survey on procedures dealing with checkerboards, mesh-depdendencies and local minima. *Struct. Optim.* **1998**, *16*, 68–75. [CrossRef]
5. Sigmund, O. Morthology-based black and white filters for topology optimization. *Struct. Multidisc Optim.* **2007**, *33*, 401–424. [CrossRef]
6. Rahmatalla, S.F.; Swan, C.C. A Q4/Q4 continuum structural topology optimization implementation. *Struct. Multidisc Optim.* **2004**, *27*, 130–135. [CrossRef]
7. Matsui, K.; Terada, K. Continuous approximation of material distribution for topology optimization. *Int. J. Numer. Mech. Engng.* **2004**, *59*, 1925–1944. [CrossRef]
8. Long, K.; Zuo, Z.; Zuberi, R.H. Study on parameters for topological variables field interpolated by moving least square approximation. *Acta Mechanica Solida Sinica* **2009**, *22*, 180–188. [CrossRef]
9. Kang, Z.; Wang, Y. Structural topology optimization based on non-local Shepard interpolation of density field. *Comput. Methods Appl. Mech. Eng.* **2011**, *200*, 3515–3525. [CrossRef]
10. Kang, Z.; Wang, Y. A nodal variable method of structural topology optimization based on Shepard interpolant. *Int. J. Numer. Mech. Engng.* **2012**, *90*, 329–342. [CrossRef]
11. Qian, X. Topology optimization in B-spline space. *Comput. Methods Appl. Mech. Eng.* **2013**, *265*, 15–65. [CrossRef]
12. Wang, Y.; Xu, H.; Pasini, D. Multiscale isogeometric topology optimization for lattice materials. *Comput. Methods Appl. Mech. Eng.* **2017**, *316*, 568–585. [CrossRef]
13. Wang, Y.; Xiao, M.; Xia, Z.; Li, P.; Gao, L. From computer-aided design (CAD) toward human-aided design (HAD): An isogeometric topology optimization approach. *Engineering* **2023**, *22*, 94–105. [CrossRef]
14. Xia, Q.; Shi, T. Optimization of composite structures with continuous spatial variation of fiber angle through Shepard interpolation. *Compos. Struct.* **2017**, *182*, 273–282. [CrossRef]
15. Wang, Y.; Kang, Z.; He, Q. An adaptive refinement approach for topology optimization based on separated density field description. *Comput. Struct.* **2013**, *117*, 10–22. [CrossRef]
16. Zheng, J.; Long, S.; Li, G. The topology optimization design for continuum structures based on the element free Galerkin method. *Eng. Anal. Bound. Elem.* **2010**, *34*, 666–672.
17. Zheng, J.; Long, S.; Li, G. Topology optimization of free vibrating continuum structures based on the element free Galerkin method. *Struct. Multidiscip. Optim.* **2012**, *45*, 119–127. [CrossRef]
18. Wang, Y.; Luo, Z.; Wu, J.; Zhang, N. Topology optimization of compliant mechanisms using element-free Galerkin method. *Adv. Eng. Softw.* **2015**, *85*, 61–72. [CrossRef]
19. Zhou, J.X.; Zhou, W. Meshless approximation combined with implicit topology description for optimization of continuum. *Struct. Multidiscip. Optim.* **2007**, *36*, 347–353. [CrossRef]
20. Lin, L.; Guan, Y.J.; Zhao, G.Q.; Naceur, H.; Lu, P. Topology optimization of plane structures using smooth particle hydrodynamics method. *Int. J. Numer. Meth Engng.* **2017**, *110*, 726–744. [CrossRef]
21. Zhao, Q.; Fan, C.M.; Wang, F.; Qu, W. Topology optimization of steady-state heat conduction structures using meshless generalized finite difference method. *Eng. Anal. Bound. Elem.* **2020**, *119*, 13–24. [CrossRef]
22. Zhao, F. A meshless Pareto-optimal method for topology optimization. *Eng. Anal. Bound. Elem.* **2013**, *37*, 1625–1631. [CrossRef]
23. Seonho, C.; Juho, K. Topology design optimization of geometrically non-linear structures using mesh-free method. *Comput. Methods Appl. Mech. Eng.* **2006**, *195*, 5909–5925.
24. Du, Y.; Chen, L.; Tian, Q.; Wu, Z.J. Topology synthesis of thermomechanical compliant mechanisms with geometrical nonlinearities using meshless method. *Adv. Eng. Softw.* **2008**, *40*, 315–322. [CrossRef]

25. Luo, Z.; Zhang, N.; Wang, Y.; Gao, W. Topology optimization of structures using meshless density variable approximants. *Int. J. Numer. Mech. Engng.* **2013**, *93*, 443–464. [CrossRef]
26. He, Q.; Kang, Z.; Wang, Y. A topology optimization method for geometrically nonlinear structures with meshless analysis and independent density field interpolation. *Comput. Mech.* **2014**, *54*, 629–644. [CrossRef]
27. Cui, M.T.; Chen, H.F.; Zhou, J.L.; Wang, F. A meshless method for multi-material topology optimization based on the alternating active-phase algorithm. *Eng. Comput.* **2017**, *33*, 871–884. [CrossRef]
28. Zhang, J.; Wang, S.; Zhou, G.; Gong, S.; Yin, S. Topology optimization of thermal structure for isotropic and anisotropic materials using the element-free Galerkin method. *Eng. Optimiz.* **2020**, *52*, 1097–1118. [CrossRef]
29. Zhang, J.; Liu, T.; Wang, S.; Gong, S.; Peng, J.; Zuo, Q. Thermomechanical coupling multi-objective topology optimization of anisotropic structures based on element-free Galerkin method. *Eng. Optimiz.* **2022**, *54*, 428–449. [CrossRef]
30. Zhang, J.; Zhang, H.; Chen, J.; Liu, T.; Peng, J.; Zhang, D. Topology optimization of periodic mechanical structure with orthotropic materials based on the element-free Galerkin method. *Eng. Anal. Bound. Elem.* **2022**, *143*, 383–396. [CrossRef]
31. Fu, Y.F.; Rolfe, B.; Chiu, L.N.S.; Wang, Y.; Huang, X.; Ghabraie, K. SEMDOT: Smooth-edged material distribution for optimizing topology algorithm. *Adv. Eng. Softw.* **2020**, *150*, 102921. [CrossRef]
32. Fu, Y.F.; Rolfe, B.; Chiu, L.N.S.; Wang, Y.; Huang, X.; Ghabraie, K. Smooth topological design of 3D continuum structures using elemental volume fractions. *Comput. Struct.* **2020**, *231*, 106213. [CrossRef]
33. Fu, Y.F.; Rolfe, B.; Chiu, L.N.S.; Wang, Y.; Huang, X.; Ghabraie, K. Design and experimental validation of self-supporting topologies for additive manufacturing. *Virtual Phys. Prototy.* **2019**, *14*, 382–394. [CrossRef]
34. Fu, Y.F.; Rolfe, B.; Chiu, L.N.S.; Wang, Y.; Huang, X.; Ghabraie, K. Parametric studies and manufacturability experiments on smooth self-supporting topologies. *Virtual Phys. Prototy.* **2020**, *15*, 22–34. [CrossRef]
35. Fu, Y.F.; Ghabraie, K.; Rolfe, B.; Wang, Y.; Chiu, L.N.S. Smooth design of 3D self-supporting topologies using additive manufacturing filter and SEMDOT. *Appl. Sci.* **2021**, *11*, 238. [CrossRef]
36. Zhang, K.; Li, B.; Du, F.; Liu, H.; Hong, J. Topology optimization of natural convection heat transfer using SEMDOT algorithm based on the reduced-order model. *Int. Commun. Heat. Mass.* **2021**, *129*, 105676. [CrossRef]
37. Goncalves, M.; Andrade-Campos, A.; Barroqueiro, B. On the design of mechanical heterogeneous specimens using multilevel topology optimization. *Adv. Eng. Softw.* **2023**, *175*, 103314. [CrossRef]
38. Liu, S.; Li, Q.; Liu, J.; Chen, W.; Zhang, Y. A realization method for transforming a topology optimization design into additive manufacturing structures. *Engineering* **2018**, *4*, 277–285. [CrossRef]
39. Yang, Y.; Zheng, Y.; Gao, L.; Wang, Y. Automatic construction method for editable CAD models of isogeometric topology optimization results. *Struct. Multidiscip. Optim.* **2023**, *66*, 208. [CrossRef]
40. Chen, J.S.; Wang, H.P. New boundary condition treatments in meshfree computation of contact problems. *Comput. Methods Appl. Mech. Eng.* **2000**, *187*, 441–468. [CrossRef]
41. Netuzhylov, H. Enforcement of boundary conditions in meshfree methods using interpolating moving least squares. *Eng. Anal. Bound. Elem.* **2008**, *32*, 512–516. [CrossRef]
42. Hilber, H.M.; Hughes, T.J.; Taylor, R.L. Improved numerical dissipation for time integration algorithms in structural dynamics. *Earthq. Eng. Struct. Dyn.* **1977**, *5*, 283–292. [CrossRef]
43. Wang, F.; Lazarov, B.S.; Sigmund, O. On projection methods, convergence and robust formulations in topology optimization. *Struct. Multidisc. Optim.* **2011**, *43*, 767–784. [CrossRef]
44. Li, Q.; Liang, G.; Luo, Y.; Zhang, F.; Liu, S. An explicit formulation for minimum length scale control in density-based topology optimization. *Comput. Methods Appl. Mech. Eng.* **2023**, *404*, 115761. [CrossRef]
45. Liang, Y.; Cheng, G. Further elaborations on topology optimization via sequential integer programming and Canonical relaxation algorithm and 128-line MATLAB code. *Struct. Multidisc. Optim.* **2020**, *61*, 411–431. [CrossRef]
46. Fu, Y.F.; Long, K.; Rolfe, B. On non-penalization SEMDOT using discrete variable sensitivities. *J. Optimiz. Theory App.* **2023**, *198*, 644–677. [CrossRef]
47. Huang, X. On smooth or 0/1 designs of the fixed-mesh element-based topology optimization. *Adv. Eng. Softw.* **2021**, *151*, 102942. [CrossRef]
48. Huang, X. Smooth topological design of structures using the floating projection. *Eng. Struct.* **2020**, *208*, 110330. [CrossRef]
49. Svanberg, K. The method of moving asymptotes: A new method for structural optimization. *Int. J. Numer. Methods Eng.* **1987**, *24*, 359–373. [CrossRef]

MDPI AG
Grosspeteranlage 5
4052 Basel
Switzerland
Tel.: +41 61 683 77 34

Computation Editorial Office
E-mail: computation@mdpi.com
www.mdpi.com/journal/computation

www.ingramcontent.com/pod-product-compliance
Lightning Source LLC
Chambersburg PA
CBHW040805250926
51850CB00007BA/1085
* 9 7 8 3 7 2 5 8 7 1 0 4 9 *